LUDWIG BEMELMANS
A BIBLIOGRAPHY

Ludwig Bemelmans

A BIBLIOGRAPHY

With 77 reverently drawn irrelevant drawings by Ludwig Bemelmans

EDITED AND COMPILED BY

Murray Pomerance

H

James H. Heineman, Inc.

New York

1993

James H. Heineman, Inc.
475 Park Ave.
New York, NY 10022

to Ariel

I don't like to write—it's hard work. I would rather lead my life walking around reading what others have written. I write only for money—and only when the water rises to my throat.

LUDWIG BEMELMANS
Splendide Apartment, 1942

CONTENTS

Nellie Perret, my wife and friend, has hunted this with me; and much more.

———

Madeleine Bemelmans has been a spring of information and sympathetic encouragement.

———

Long-suffering and exhaustive research assistance has been generously given by James Daley in New York; Jay Glickman, Philip Ower and Steven Woodward in Toronto; Brad Spurgeon in Paris; Linda Wasylyk Perlis and Harry Perlis in Milano; Lynn Shakinovsky in Johannesburg.

———

I am also especially grateful to the many individuals and organizations without whose assistance this project could never have been brought to this stage:

The staff of the Reference Department of the William Robarts Library at the University of Toronto; and in particular Susan Johnson, Mary McTavish, and Mary Jo Stevenson, who must have wondered when I, too, would say, "There isn't any more."

Frans Donker of Book City, Toronto. Bettina Herre of Carlsen Verlag, Hamburg. Elsa Naudé of Human & Rousseau, Cape Town. Lydia Snyman of Anansi-Uitgewers, Cape Town. Petra Verleger of Bertelsmann Club, Gütersloh.

Winston Atkins of the Harry Ransom Humanities Research Center, University of Texas at Austin. The Berg Collection of the New York Public Library. Mary Bogan of the William Allan White Library, Emporia State University. Dott. Carla Guiducci Bonanni of Biblioteca Nazionale Centrale, Firenze. The Reading Room of The British Library. Joan L. Clark of the Cleveland Public Library. Pat Coulter of the Toronto Public Library. Lori N. Curtis of the McFarlin Library, University of Tulsa. Connie Dosch of the Los Angeles Public Library. H. J. Duijzer of Stadsbibliotheek Haarlem, The Netherlands. Cathy Grant of the Metropolitan Toronto Reference Library. Donna Greenberg of the Theater Department, Toronto Public Library. Lori Leirdahl of the University of Minnesota Library's Kerlan Collection. Karen Lightner of The Free Library of Philadelphia. J. L. Logan of Princeton University Library. Margaret Maloney of the Osborne Collection, Toronto. Greg McKinney, Joyce Dewsbury and Rita Smith of the Baldwin

Library, University of Florida at Gainesville. Brian Nettlefold of the College Education Center Library, North Bay. Eliane Perez of Biblioteca Nacional, Rio de Janeiro. Sarah Phillips of Harvard College Library, Cambridge. Nora J. Quinlan of the Special Collections, Rare Books Room, University of Colorado Library at Boulder. M. Rincker of Deutsche Bibliothek, Frankfurt am Main. Petra Seidel of Staats- und Universitätsbibliothek Hamburg. Jill Shefrin of the Osborne Collection, Toronto. Lois Spencer of Scott Library, York University, Toronto. Winston Taod of the Library of Congress. Dana Tenney of the Osborne Collection, Toronto. Steve Vallillo of the Billy Rose Theater Collection, New York Public Library at Lincoln Center. Astrid Vrehen of the Koninklijke Bibliotheek, 's-Gravenhage, The Netherlands. Dorothy Welles of the Los Angeles Public Library. Janet Whitson of the Detroit Public Library. Norleen Young of the Indiana State Library Newspaper Collection. Young Yun of Butler Library, Columbia University. The staff of the Inter-Library Loan Department of the Library of Ryerson Polytechnical Institute. The Reference Section of the Library of the University of Illinois at Urbana-Champaign.

———

Ingrid Abeln of Diogenes Verlag AG, Zürich. Eve Adam of Random House, New York. Ian Ainsworth, Toronto. Skip Alsdorf, Port Chester, New York. Audrey Arellanes, Alhambra California. Alexandra Arrowsmith of Callaway Editions, New York. Suzanne Baboneau of Hamish Hamilton Ltd, London. Frank Balazs of Guild America. Lisa Bankoff of ICM New

York. Carolyn Bauer of Columbia Pictures, Los Angeles. Frank Beacham, New York. Diane Benjamin of Victor Gollancz Ltd, London. Nancy Berg of Penguin USA. Jill Black of The Bodley Head, London. Helene Blanc of Columbia Pictures, Los Angeles. Barbara Boote of The Macdonald Group, London. The British Publishers Association. Art Buchwald, Washington. Dale Carlin of Funstuff NY. Kathleen Carlin of *McCall's*. Cynthia Cathcart of Condé Nast Publications, New York. Micheline Charest of CINAR Films, Montreal. Carol Christiansen of Doubleday, Inc. Cynthia Comsky, Beverly Hills. Dave Connell of Children's Television Workshop, New York. Saul Cooper, Los Angeles. Mrs P. Cornwall of Tiptree Book Services Ltd, Colchester. Margaret Cracroft of William Heinemann Ltd, London. Hume Cronyn, New York. Linda Davis of Collins Publishers, London. Sandra Davis of Gale Research Company, Detroit. Dawn De Zago of Random House, New York. André Deutsch CBE, London. Hikmet Dogu of the Museum of Modern Art Library, New York. Prof. Eric Domville of the University of Toronto. Willem A. Donker of Ad. Donker, Rotterdam. Nicky Drumbolis, Toronto. Diana Dunn of Eden Toys. Jacqueline Eastman, Birmingham. L'École des loisirs, Paris. Diana Edkins of Condé Nast Publications, New York. Eden Edwards of *The Horn Book Magazine*. Dan Einstein of UCLA Film and Television Archive, Los Angeles. Lucy Evankow of Scholastic Books, New York. Karen Fedorock of CBS, New York. Ricardo Feltre of Editora Moderna Ltda, São Paulo. Nora Fennell of *Woman's Day*. Stephen Fieser, Harrisburg, Pennsylvania. Agnes Fisher of Macmillan Publishing

Company. David Fisher of *Life* Magazine. Sam Frank, Los Angeles. Andrew Franklin of Hamish Hamilton Ltd, London. Anthony Freund of *Esquire*. Ursula Futschik of Scherz Verlag, Bern. Anne Garwood of William Heinemann Ltd, London. Eugenio Gallego of Mondadori España, Madrid. András Geröly of Artisjus, Budapest. Morton Glickman, Toronto. Eva-Maria Glüsenkamp of Deutscher Bücherbund, Stuttgart. Livia Gollancz, London. Armin Gontermann of Gustav Lübbe Verlag, Bergisch Gladbach. Ariane Goodman of Collins Publishers, London. Robert Gottlieb of *The New Yorker*. Elaine Greene, London. Ellen Grout of Pan Books, London. Ian Halford of Trade Winds Press, Durban. Barbara Hammond, Port Chester, New York. Julia Hanna of David R. Godine Publisher, Boston. Janne Friis Hansen of Thaning & Appels Publishers, Frederiksberg, Denmark. Isabel Harbridge of Oficina Comercial de España, Toronto. Sloan Harris of ICM New York. Helen Hawyard of Peters, Fraser & Dunlop, London. Regina Hayes of Penguin USA. Hans Georg Heepe of Rowohlt Verlag, Reinbek. Catharine Heinz of the Broadcast Pioneers' Library, National Association of Broadcasters, Washington. Lee-Ellen Herlihy of Houghton Mifflin Co., Boston. Jay Hickerson, Hamden, Connecticut. Jim Hirschfeld of Robert Keeshan Associates, New York. Ellen Hoch of Hallmark Cards. Heidi Hodson of André Deutsch Ltd, London. Marcena Hopkins of *Town & Country*. Peter Howard, Berkeley, California. Barbara Huff of the Junior Literary Guild. Olivia Hurd of Peaceable Kingdom Press, Berkeley. Yoshitaka Iritani of Iwanami Shoten, Tokyo. Mary Janaky of Western Publishing Co.,

Racine. Traudel Jansen of Kiepenheuer & Witsch, Köln. Susan Jensen of Condé Nast Publications, New York. Sue Jeremiah of Hutchinson Publishing Group, London. Gunilla Jonsson of the Kungliga Biblioteket, Stockholm. Jessamyn Kahn, Toronto. Hans Kaiser of Neuer Kaiser Verlag — Buch und Welt, Klagenfurt. Theodor Katz, Stockholm. Carleton Kelsey, Amagansett. Kay Kiyonaga, Toronto. Ikuko Kobayashi of Fukuinkan Shoten, Tokyo. Al Kochko, Muskegon Museum of Art, Muskegon, Michigan. Nancy Kosenka, Berkeley, California. Jan Kristensen of Thaning & Appels Publishers, Frederiksberg Denmark. Maria Kristoferson of Wahlström & Widstrand, Stockholm. Conny Kröll of Wolfgang Krüger Verlag, Frankfurt am Main. Jean-Luc Labrecque of Polidiffusion, Montréal. Laurent Laffont of Éditions Robert Laffont, Paris. James Lawson, Vancouver. Leo Lerman of Condé Nast Publications. Bob Levitino of Random House, New York. Cathy Lim of NBC. Judith Lowry, New York. Lawrence A. Lupkin of The Putnam Berkley Group, Inc., New York. Jette Madsen of Carlsen/if, København. Nadia Mannarino, Ridgewood, New Jersey. Sheila Marbain, New York. Silvia Marchesi of Longanesi & C., Editori in Milano. Catherine Marquard of the New York Public Library. Rick Marshall, Philadelphia. Nicole Martin of CINAR Films, Montreal. Terry McDonell of *Esquire*. McGraw-Hill Publishers, New York. Inez Metzl, New York. Larry Miller of Random House, New York. Marjorie Miller of the Library of the Fashion Institute of Technology, New York. Linda Mitchell, Hollis, New York. The late William C. Mitchell, Hammer Galleries, New York. Joe Montez of the Learning

Corporation of America, Los Angeles. Mina Mulvey of *Good Housekeeping*. Koji Ogawa of Dainippon Kaiga, Tokyo. Tomoko Okuda of Yugaku-sha Ltd., Tokyo. Lise-Lott Olofsson of Norstedts Förlag, Stockholm. Jette Pagh of Wangels Forlag a/s, Valby Sweden. Paragon House, New York. The late George Albert and Claironel Foster Perret, New York. Steve Pettinger of *Saturday Evening Post*. Gail Phillips of Western Publishing Co., Racine. Lisa Poehlmann of the Emmy Gifford Children's Theater, Omaha. Allan Press of Columbia Pictures, New York. Brian Quinn of The Museum of Television and Radio, New York. Pat Raemer of Intervisual Communications, Los Angeles. Martine Redman of International Playthings. Walt Reed of Illustration House, New York. Ornella Robbiati of Arnoldo Mondadori Editore, Milano. Jean Rose of Octopus Publishing Group, Rushden Northants. Doris Rother of the Kunstverein für die Rheinlande und Westfalen, Düsseldorf. Robert Roy, Montreal. Pamela Royds of André Deutsch Ltd, London. John Ryder of The Bodley Head, London. John Sargent of Simon & Schuster, New York. Tessa Sayle, London. George Schaefer, Beverly Hills. Cassandra Schafhausen of CINAR Films, Montreal. Stuart Scheftel, New York. Morton Schindel, Weston, Connecticut. Dianne Schmiesing of the Children's Theater Company of Minneapolis. Scholastic Publishers, New York. W. Schultz of Bording Grafik and Jacob Thomsen of Det Kongelige Bibliotek, København. Judy Scott of Hallmark Cards. Raymond-Josué Seckel of the Département des livres imprimés de la Bibliothèque nationale, Paris. Susan Sedman of Condé Nast Publications, New York. Ursula Selzer, Toronto. David Shatzky of the Children's Broadcast Institute, Toronto. Howard Shaw of Hammer Galleries, New York. Jody Shields, New York. Shannon Shupack of Book-of-the-Month Club. Joel Silver of the Book Department of Indiana University's Lilly Library. Donna Slawsky of Harper Collins, New York. Michele Smotony of Intervisual Communications, Los Angeles. Ron Staley of the North American Radio Archive, Los Angeles. Hermann Staub of the Börsenverein des Deutschen Buchhandels, Frankfurt am Main. Eric Stein of DIC Enterprises, Burbank. Christian Stottele of Ravensburger Buchverlag Otto Maier GmbH, Ravensburg. William Stringfellow of *House Beautiful*. Stacie Strong of Intervisual Communications, Los Angeles. Sandy Tanski of *McCall's*. Brenda Taylor of Little, Brown Publishers, Boston. Kathy Thomas of Hammer Galleries, New York. Melba Todd of Neiman-Marcus, Fort Worth. François du Toit, Pretoria. Ingeboerg M. Trahms-Radloff of Interbooks, Zürich. John Twomey, Toronto. Universitats Bibliothek Wien. William B. Walker of The Metropolitan Museum of Art, New York. Lee J. Walp, Marietta, Ohio. Robin Warner of Western Publishing Co., New York. Frank Wend of Buchverlage Ullstein Langen Müller, Berlin. M. K. Wong of *Town & Country*. Franzesca Zoller, Toronto.

LUDWIG BEMELMANS
A BIBLIOGRAPHY

Bookman's Folly

Bookman's Folly

A THOROUGHGOING NAIF, I began in the late 1970s to collect information about the published works of Ludwig Bemelmans with the easy and ridiculous conviction that published books, like foxes, leave unmistakable trails behind them. More than a dozen years later, I am happy merely to have survived the investigations, which led me to more than eighty publishers in sixteen countries to get answers to questions most of my respondents were certainly not used to being asked. If I learned much about Ludwig Bemelmans and his times, and even more about publishing, it is also true that with many of my queries I found no satisfaction at all.

The beginning of this was innocent enough. I picked up *The World of Bemelmans* on a summer's afternoon at the Amagansett Free Library, in 1973. I was a fish with nothing to read, and the jacket was a hooked worm. I read on the beach, I read before bed, I read everywhere, totally ignorant of who Ludwig Bemelmans was. (I had not been a child brought up with Madeline.) The writing was straightforward, tasty, even beguiling, and soon enough I had *The Street Where the Heart Lies*. That book touched in me some indefinite longing to be in Paris, a city I had mused little about, strangely enough; and I addressed my new appetite by reading the text again; and then again. It was one of those books that having read you want to possess. Conveniently, of course, the thing was out of print.

I think the frustration of not being able to get my hands on a copy of that book led me to start a hunt for Ludwig Bemelmans editions. I began in little shops here and there, as all collectors must; and at what seemed a geological pace the collection grew, but that is another story. The relevance for the moment is that once I had acquired four or five titles I began to see, quite literally, that there was an *oeuvre* out there. It would be conceivable to make a kind of *picture* of that thing.

I think that there would have been no attempt at the present volume, however, had I not come upon Donald Gallup's astounding bibliography of the works of Ezra Pound, printed so handsomely in the Cambridge Bibliography series. In all my excursions through bookshops in many countries I have met no one who does not esteem this elegant work. It re-awakened all my earliest compulsions to make precious pattern out of happenstance chaos, and I thought to myself that one day, purely as a hobby, I would jot out a bibliography of someone, too. Later, of course, I wondered, "Why not Bemelmans?"

All of this is by way of explaining how simply and how casually it was that the seduction of this enterprise began. I merely started on one page, and the pages merely piled up. And as the pages piled up, they were riddled with openings, with problems, with textural inconsistencies. A number of bibliographic problems can now be set out, which might interest the general reader even as they madden the bibliographer.

First, there is the scope of the material at hand. Ludwig Bemelmans, who was born in Meran in the Austrian Tyrol (currently Merano, Italy), on April 27, 1898, and who died in New York City on October 1, 1962, produced an astounding volume of work. There are over 200 main titles under his name, including editions in Afrikaans, Swedish, Dutch, Japanese, Hungarian, Spanish, Zulu and many other languages. He published hundreds of times in periodicals, was anthologized profusely, made illustrations for his own work and others' that are virtually countless. His manuscripts reproduced like snails: there is but a handful of titles in one edition only; most ran to at least three editions; twelve titles appear in more than five editions and of *Madeline* there are no less than thirty-one.

Nor were the works of his hand restricted to books of words or pictures. He designed the private bar in the residence of Jascha Heifetz; realized wall paintings for the old Hapsburg House Restaurant at 313 East 55 Street in New York; and made Madeline drawings for the children's dining room of the Onassis yacht. He richly decorated at least three apartments on Gramercy Park: an apartment in the Hotel Irving where he put a map of Paris on the bedroom ceiling so that, insomniac, he could by flashlight take walks along the Seine; his studio in what is now the Sonnenberg House on Gramercy Park South; and another in the National Arts Club, of which he made a kind of forest, and in which he died. He made wall drawings in his apartment at 10 East 78 Street. For a time he had a studio on 8th Street where he painted Tyrolean scenes on the window shades which enchanted May Massee, an editor at Viking Press who visited him there, sufficiently to urge that he produce what turned out to be *Hansi*, his first published book. He painted his office at Metro-Goldwyn-Mayer in Hollywood; and then Metro-Goldwyn-Mayer painted it back again. The so-called "Bemelmans bar" in the Carlyle Hotel, laid over with his murals, remains one of the attractions of New York. Later, mostly after his death, his material was adapted in many media by numerous other creative people.

As some of his writing attests, Bemelmans was a gourmand and innkeeper as much as a writer or artist. His affiliation with the old Luchow's Restaurant on East 14th Street, New York, is documented in much of his prose. He was co-owner of the Hapsburg House; and a kind of *éminence grise* of the White Turkey Inn near Danbury, Connecticut. For some time he warmed a hotel in the Tyrol, the Postgasthof at Lech am Arlberg, Austria, owned by very dear friends; and he was the proprietor, later on, of La Colombe at 4, rue de la Colombe, Paris. One of his letterheads gives as locations of residence East 73 Street, New York; Danbury, Connecticut; Paris; Lech am Arlberg; and aboard the Dolphin, Porto d'Ischia, Golfo di Napoli, Italy. Of much of this he was certainly unceasingly a raconteur and some of his talk was aired by the Columbia Broadcasting System: on its show, "Of Men and Books," in the 1940s and on Edward R. Murrow's "Person to Person" December 7, 1956, 10:30 - 11:00 p.m.

Like the protagonist of a series of stories he published in *Town & Country*, Ludwig Bemelmans was a "man of the world." He had done a tour in Buffalo as part of the United States Army; worked and lived all over New York; travelled Europe intimately and spent much time in Latin America; taken up residence on the Rue Gît-le-Coeur in Paris more or less at the same time the French New Wave Cinéma was exploding on the same street. Even metaphorically the world was his oyster: his overture in publishing was in 1926 in *The World Magazine* (see G61). The last material published during his life, *The Street Where the Heart Lies*, came in 1963 from The World Publishing Company of Cleveland and New York (see A40). Like the author, both publishers exist today in the space of archive and memory.

If Bemelmans' sources were widely dispersed geographically, they were also situated in what has come to be a kind of time warp. A considerable part of the publishing came during the Second World War. Many of the records of this material have therefore been lost or destroyed; and many of the companies and individuals who were involved have disappeared without leaving trace.

But even if it had been possible neatly to encapsulate Ludwig Bemelmans as a writer there would have remained the problem of focus. In delineating arbitrarily—that is the only way to do it—the scope of what one will set out to do in a book like this, one has to have in mind some sort of reader, either very sophisticated in bibliographic study or relatively raw. As I was raw I wanted the book to be simple, but to contain more information than would be found in a mere listing of titles. The more information I wanted the more, in years, I found; and every time I found something it came with its own holes: missing pieces of "information" I presumed to exist but of which I had no present clue, and of whose reality I had, in fact, no hard proof. Kenneth Burke it was who said we all have a way of cutting the cheese of the world; and this particular cheese is authentic Emmenthal, with at least sixteen holes to the slice.

There is a great deal of latitude about what to include in, and exclude from, a bibliography. One can list, for example, *editions* of books. Or one can list *printings*. And these are quite far from being the same. *Madeline*, for instance, Bemelmans' most widely known work, is now reprinted almost every year and has been, regularly, through almost thirty printings, since Viking Press took it over in 1958. But through all this there have not been so many different Viking *editions*. Further, many bibliographers make the assumption that *local* editions are the ones of particular interest since readers will find them easiest to come by. Certainly, in the United States and Canada, it is American editions one will run into in antiquarian shops for the most part. But it intrigued me about Bemelmans that there were foreign editions in so many different languages. And that these foreign books were indeed quite beautiful to see, and to read, and to contemplate.

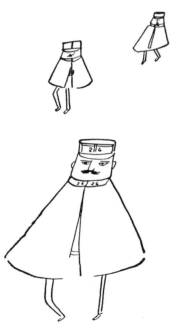

I decided, therefore, at the start, to list *every edition, in any language, of every book of which Ludwig Bemelmans was the author.*

This meant a very great search indeed, past the limits of the catalogue of the Library of Congress and into the national bibliographies of other countries; as well as to the catalogues of holdings of The British Library in London and La Bibliothèque Nationale in Paris and the Kungliga Biblioteket in Stockholm, to name but three great storehouses. That search, too, was only the beginning because over the years it became clear that all of these searches had to be re-checked and re-checked again; and substantiated with secondary checks in such sources as the *Cumulative Book Index*, *Books in Print*, *Publisher's Weekly*, and the shelf list of the Library of Congress—not one of which, as I came in pain to learn, can seriously be relied upon. From an unprepossessing bookshelf in a place like Ludlow, England or southern New Jersey I would find in the palm of my hand a book that should have been listed in one of these references, and that was not!

Formal referencing systems, indeed, are also made of cheese. I have not only discovered books that are not listed where they ought to be but listings of ghost editions that do not, and never did, exist. *Books in Print* carried for almost ten years leading up to 1990 a listing for a book that was planned but never actually published. On the other hand, I have discovered periodical publications not listed in the *Reader's Guide to Periodical Literature*, even though they appear in magazines that *are* indexed in that book, such as *The New Yorker*. I have discovered, indeed, publications in *The New Yorker* not even indexed in the specialized *Index to The New Yorker*.

It hardly needs to be said that there are a great many maga-

zines that have been scanned for the period 1930-1964 —
virtually every page of every issue: *Holiday, Esquire, Harper's
Bazaar, Town & Country*, to name but four. In general, the number of alphabetical listings in which I have hunted between BEL
and BEN for the name BEMELMANS must run to the thousands.
BELTRAMI — BEMBO — BENAIDES — BENCHLEY. And on countless
shelves: in bookstores new and antiquarian, in libraries here and
there, at church jumbles, at garage sales on how many
streets. . . .

Foreign materials are indexed with varying accuracy — and
the indexes, indeed, give information in a way that is inter-
nally systematic for them but not necessarily helpful for the
bibliographer. Page sizes are a simple example. Figures are
typically given in publisher's catalogues, national bibliographies, Library of Congress indexes, for page height; but not
for page width. And the page height is sometimes the height
of the paper page; but just as often the height of the book in
its coverings, measured along the outside of the cover, which
is usually somewhat larger; and sometimes neither of the
above. The year but not the month or day of publication is
sometimes given; sometimes nothing is given. And so on. I
came in the end to assume that nothing would suffice but to
query the publishers; and to believe, in a preposterous simple-
mindedness, that publishers confronted with clear questions
would provide clear answers.

Publishers would know, I told myself, exactly how many
copies of a book they printed; exactly on what date they put it
out; and what they charged for it at that time. And they would

have a library copy I could actually look at, if none appeared to exist anywhere else.

Here there were problems that might not confront someone trying to compile a bibliography of a more recent author, or even, in some sense, an earlier one. Bemelmans published much of his material with publishers who were not always in a position to be strict about their record-keeping at the time of publication; and who often, soon afterward, simply disappeared. Mr. Lovat Dickson, for instance, published Bemelmans in London in 1935; sold his business; and eventually moved, as I learned in 1991, to Toronto where he died in 1987; his publication records are, as far as I can determine, completely lost. Had I known earlier that he could have been one of the gentlemen sitting next to me at the Robarts Library in Toronto, I would have been in a position to speak with him about the *Hansi* I can in no other way now trace. So it goes. Blüchert Verlag of Hamburg published Bemelmans from 1954 onward; their records of Bemelmans at some point came to his agent for German books, Dr. Felix Guggenheim of Los Angeles, who died without leaving documents in anyone's care. Editorial Sudamericana of Buenos Aires disappeared in the wind. So did Editora Moderna of Quito. So has MacFadden-Bartell. And Bibliotheca in Budapest. And *Collier's* magazine. And much more.

Further, publishers do not have unchanging attitudes toward their own records even when the records do exist. For example, while it was possible when I contacted them in person in 1984 to get very precise publication-date information from the still

existing house of Hamish Hamilton in London (which has subsequently come under new ownership) they had nothing to say
about print runs at all. And when I wrote back in 1990, all of
their records had been locked and sent to deep storage and they
had absolutely nothing to say about anything. I tried to contact
some of the printers who had done the work for them but these
had officially gone out of business or simply vanished without
leaving prints.

   As an example of how it is sometimes difficult even to locate
the current stronghold of a publisher's records (let alone to find
out what they contain) it is worth citing the case of the Deux
Coqs d'Or edition of *Madeline*—a book that came to my atten-
tion in the first place entirely through serendipity. I had to
engage in extensive communication with people in Sacramento
and Los Angeles, California; Paris; New York; Montréal; Toronto; and Racine, Wisconsin merely to learn how Éditions
Cocorico of 1954 became Éditions des Deux Coqs d'Or of 1971
and where I might currently apply to search the archive. When
I applied, of course, I learned that the archive was non-existent.
Virtually the same scenario was repeated with many other publishers on five continents. On the other hand there are numerous publishers who maintain to this day complete and perfectly
clear files about books published more than thirty years ago,
and some who are even willing to share the contents.

   Publishers are not consistently informed about their own
books. It fell to me to give a leading executive at Simon and
Schuster word that his company had published *Madeline* in
1939. He knew all about the book; he had probably grown up

on it; but it was news that he was helping run the company that had given it life.

Even with the most devoted of publishers, who may well wish to open their books, there can be hopeless problems. Mr. André Deutsch CBE was kind enough to let me see his personal copies of a number of books published by him, and some published by other people, when I was in London in 1984. Subsequently André Deutsch Ltd sent their entire children's collection, barring nothing, as a donation to the Department of Special Collections of the McFarlin Library of the University of Tulsa. When I needed more information and contacted that department it turned out they had only one Deutsch book by Bemelmans, and no paperwork, and no information, and nothing else. Neither André Deutsch Ltd nor the McFarlin Library have been able to determine what became of the missing material except that it left the United Kingdom and is not recorded as having arrived in the United States.

Perhaps the most devious turnings in the labyrinth of bibliography look straightforward enough at first. A particularly revealing problem was presented when in August 1990 I came across a British paperback edition of *Madeline* about which I'd never heard (see A24o). Published by Sphere Books in London in 1968, this book contained publisher's text that referred directly to the Sphere editions of the other four Madeline titles available at the time: *Madeline's Rescue*, *Madeline and the Bad Hat*, *Madeline and the Gypsies*, and *Madeline in London*. I wondered whether these other books also existed; and, if they did, whether they looked just like *Madeline* in format. I began by

very thoroughly searching all the British book catalogues available, including the British Library holdings, the *Cumulative Book Index*, *Whitaker's*, and the *British National Bibliography*. There were no references to the four books I sought, of course. *But there was also no reference to the one book I had held in my hands.*

The fact that catalogues gave no listing, therefore, did *not* mean the books did not exist. I had to press on to the publisher and on September 7 I wrote asking for copies of the four unseen books and publication information about all five. My letter went unanswered. Sphere was held by Hamish Hamilton Ltd at the time and on February 15, 1991 I wrote to the publication director of that firm repeating all of my earlier questions. At the beginning of March I received a response from the Publishing Director of Sphere itself, a division of Macdonald & Co and not at all connected with Hamish Hamilton. "I'm sorry you never received my letter of a month or so ago," it began, pressing upon the Canadian postal system, one of the sore spots of this entire project. "André Deutsch Ltd, (105/106 Great Russell St, London, WC1B 3LJ) published the hardback of the Ludwig Bemelmans books according to our records. It's unclear as to whether Sphere ever published them as there is no record in *Books in Print* from 1971 onwards. In our contracts files there is a mention of them, but no actual contract and I wonder if perhaps the paperbacks were never published." Well. I knew very well that Deutsch had printed *some* of the hardbacks, and I was not at all surprised to learn there was no reference in the *British Books in Print*. But why would there be a mention in the contracts files? And, to be sure, I shared my correspondant's suspicion that the books may have been licensed but never actually published.

I went onto a limb. I wrote back March 11 that I had in fact held *Madeline* and asked if I could know when it had been published, how many had come out, and at what exact price. I also asked whether the Publication Director of Sphere *would, in my place, assume* the other books had appeared, given the following blurb in *Madeline*: "If you liked this you will also like the Sphere editions of *Madeline's Rescue, Madeline and the Bad Hat, Madeline and the Gypsies* and *Madeline in London.*" On 15 April she answered that she could find nothing on *Madeline* at all; that Sphere began in 1967 and that no one there kept decent records until 1973. No SBN card. Nothing.

During this time I had also been pursuing other lines. In the middle of April I sent out a number of more or less identical letters to Bemelmans' various British agents, asking whether they might have specific information about 43 British titles that still posed problems for me. Most said they knew nothing; but Elaine Greene most kindly replied in some detail about publishers. Included with her letter was a photocopy of a memorandum of agreement between André Deutsch Ltd and Sphere books according to which the latter was given the right to reprint all five of my mystery titles in a paper edition between 1967 and 1972 within the British Commonwealth, excluding Canada, at 6 shillings or less. Sphere had typed into the agreement that it would publish the said books in February 1968. This tallied precisely with the details of the book I had seen, which had come out at 5 shillings in 1968 and was in paper covers. There was therefore good reason to suppose the other titles followed. I wrote to Tessa Sayle, whose predecessor Hope Leresche was the agent involved with the sale of *Madeline's Rescue*. She answered 8 May, 1991: "I regret to have to tell you that I am unable to answer your questions. We have a contract with Deutsch for this title but that's all."

April 30 I wrote again to the Publications Director of Sphere, this time mentioning the memorandum of agreement that had come into my hands. I wrote in sufficient detail that if records were available at Sphere she would be equipped to find them.

By April I had also been in contact for almost a year with the Managing Director of André Deutsch Children's Books, who had been exceptionally helpful in a number of matters involving Deutsch titles. It occurred to me to hope that if Deutsch had licensed out the *Madeline* titles to Sphere they might have their own records. I wrote May 22, 1991 about the four phantom Sphere titles and mentioned the memorandum of agreement. On 13 June she replied offering to search further in the records which had passed to Scholastic Publications of which Deutsch was now a member. But she said, as well, that she clearly remembered *Madeline* to have been distinctly unsuccessful for Sphere when first it came out. It was her personal guess that they had cancelled plans to publish the other four books on these grounds.

Her theory sounded eminently whole. It accounted for why there would have been an original memorandum; for why *Madeline*, and *Madeline* only, would have appeared; for why nothing else would have been referred to anywhere.

The Publishing Director of Sphere books, however, wrote a letter that I received June 24 with her own personal surmise. She thinks Sphere must, in fact, have published the other four books, most likely at 6 shillings, and in editions of 20,000 copies each.

It is a fascinating and difficult situation. Two different people in British publishing, both high-ranking, both with much experience and a great desire to be helpful to me, sift through the very limited information available to them and come out with directly contradictory conclusions: that *only Madeline was published*; and that *all five Madeline titles appeared*. I can report only that I have seen *Madeline* but none of the others; I have seen no direct evidence to suggest the others exist; nor have I seen evidence to suggest they do not. In this bibliography I have listed the first and withheld listings of the others. I am still looking.

On and on. There are curiosities regarding almost all the publishers involved in the business of this book. Though some kept flawless records some kept none. Some who did keep records refuse as a matter of policy to release the information, even though the books appeared more than thirty years ago. Some do not answer their mail, or the telephone, or the fax.

One can, of course, attempt to examine the horse's mouth. The author himself kept very bad records. One of his habits was to discard royalty notices. It has therefore been nothing short of miraculous that his widow, after so many years, has been able to piece together fragments of so many mysteries for me. The family never did have the information about print runs and publication dates that so many other people should have had; but in her memory for dates, for locations, for titles, indeed for precise references in her husband's text, Madeleine Bemelmans has a flawless and witty memory.

Ludwig Bemelmans rarely wrote about the details of his publishing in what I have seen of his personal correspondence, much of which has been lost. He would say that he was working on such-and-such, that things were going well, and he would tell his publishers, who were also his friends, when he would be leaving Paris or any other of a dozen haunts and arriving in New York. I kept wishing I could have found him writing, "I'm glad to hear you're publishing 5,000 copies of *Madeline's Rescue*," or something to that effect, but he didn't write things like that for me to see in the few snippets I have caught. In general terms he told his wife he didn't want his correspondence circulated after he died and she has been faithful to him.

L.B. had several literary agents for works in English, whose records of contracts are homogeneously spotty. Madeleine Bemelmans has been more than generous in letting me examine all of the published books she has in her collection, but she does not have everything; and, indeed, had not heard of many of the editions I mentioned. There are publishers I could identify who apparently did not think it prudent, polite or wise to let the author or his widow have a single copy of books they published under Ludwig Bemelmans' name.

Even in the most tantalizing chase there is a time to rein in. The present volume represents the best I feel I can do at this moment, after a very long spell of both reward and vexation in

confounding terrain. Some readers will no doubt discover er-
rors or omissions and if they wish to communicate these to me
I shall be delighted to receive them and, having researched the
material, to incorporate it into a future edition of this book if
there is to be one. There is a renaissance of Bemelmans today,
and I feel certain more material is just beyond the horizon.

I am grateful to Mr. James H. Heineman for his faith and
vision, and to a great many other people who are named on the
preceding pages. I hope here to introduce the work of Ludwig
Bemelmans to some readers who have not known it before; and
to make Bemelmans more accessible and more enjoyable to
readers who already cherish him.

If a thousand times in my work I have wished to believe I had
drawn a tight line around everything Ludwig Bemelmans published, I admit I have also secretly known it is only in dreams
that we can say with the author of *Madeline*, "That's all there is."
All the rest, in truth, is Bookman's Folly.

Murray Pomerance
Toronto
January, 1993

Books Authored by Ludwig Bemelmans

Books Authored by Ludwig Bemelmans

LISTED HERE are all editions of all titles authored by Ludwig Bemelmans and actually published anywhere in the world. Titles are given whether in the original English or in a foreign translation; and in the case of translations, translators are credited wherever it was possible to learn their names.

The word "edition" has no single clear meaning in bibliography; I take it here to refer to any aggregate of books printed from new plates. In the case of Bemelmans, where the new plate is only for the title page and includes an alteration only in the year of publication the book in question is probably from a reprint, not a new edition; and similarly, plate changes are routinely made for title versos in reprinting, so those do not count to make new editions either. Reprints within the same publishing house are not generally included here under their own number unless there is something especially interesting about them from the point of view of the author's career or bibliographic curiosity.

I have assigned the A-numbers alphabetically *by title*, not chronologically; but then, under each A-number, the books are listed chronologically. (Perhaps it is interesting to note how many of the editions appeared after the author's death. Readers will find a full chronological listing of titles at the end of the book.) Perhaps an explanation is in order. One can arrange a bibliography in a number of ways and the arrangement will both reflect and guide the usage. I have designed this book for the reader who, holding a volume containing Ludwig Bemelmans' work, wishes to either authenticate it or to determine where it should be placed in a general listing. Therefore, the book descriptions will not so much infallibly describe an absent volume to a reader as help him verify, if he is studying it, a book that is in his hands.

The following comments and guidelines will help readers with Section A.

TITLE PAGE: I have tried to the best of my ability to give a full representation of the title page as printed. The "|" symbol indicates a line break. I have not indicated fancy type fonts. The word "colophon" in title descriptions and in descriptions of spines refers to the publisher's printed trademark or device; though many current students of bookmaking speak in this case of "printers devices" the word "colophon" is technically correct and was in usage when most of Bemelmans' books appeared. It should be noted immediately that virtually all Bemelmans title pages—and, indeed, many Bemelmans books—are illustrated, often, though not invariably, by the author himself. Therefore description of the picturing is part of the affair; and I can say at this point that I have tried to be thorough about describing pictures when they appear in key positions in all of the books (that is to say title pages, covers, frontispieces, dedication pages, back covers, endpapers). I give rather plain descriptions of colors, intended to be useful to someone who is comparing this text with the actual book held in hand. Given that printing fades over time, and that many of these books are old, the colors may not now be visible as originally printed.

PAGINATION: I attempt as well to give a full description of the collation, or pagination, of the book. All page numbers that are *printed* in the book appear directly; all page numbers that are *not printed* appear here in square brackets, as in [1]. The method I used for counting the pages was to work backward from the first printed page number in the book if there were printed page numbers; and if there were papers before the ultimate first page, whether 1 or [1] or i or [i], to give the number of leaves, whether printed or not. Blank leaves are called "blank leaves" and printed leaves are called "leaves," whether they are printed on one or both sides. Many of the books have endpapers, of which one side is glued to the inside of the boards and the other floats free: these are the "lining paper" and "free endpaper" respectively and the two are typically continuous; often illustrated. I do not count the free endpaper as one of the leaves. At the end of the book I refer as "leaves" or "blank leaves" to any sheets after the last sheet containing a number on either side. So, for instance, if the book has endpapers at front and back, begins with two blank leaves, has no numbers until page 3, ends on a page with no number on the back of p. 244, with, then, two blank leaves; I would indicate: "2 blank leaves, [1]-[245] pp., 2 blank leaves; endpapers." And so on. It should be noted that this particular way of paginating does *not* give an indication that the page numbering of this hypothetical book begins on page 3; it merely indicates that the first and last pages are not numbered. As a device it does not exhaustively describe the volume, or pretend to; but it allows a reader who is holding the book in hand to know which edition he is holding.

Many of the children's books have no page numbering, so I have followed the above procedure for endpapers and simply counted the number of leaves. I have not attempted to describe every single illustration, in order, in these books. The illustrations are profuse; and a verbal description does not do them justice.

COVERINGS: I give also a description of the covering and of the dust jacket, if there was one and I was able to learn of it. Publishers will sometimes switch cover stock from one impression of a book to another; and sometimes even within one impression if resources are suddenly limited. As the impression number is not infallibly recorded on the title page verso, it can be difficult to know which of two or more differing coverings contains the first impression of the first edition. I have made indication of multiple coverings whenever such a procedure has come to my attention; but the color or stamping of the cover is clearly not unimpeachable evidence for labelling an edition. The spine information is printed here exactly as it appears, with the "|" symbol referring to a line break if words appear vertically beneath one another. Where there is no reference made with | marks, the text appears horizontally on the spine. In some instances, book spines have been destroyed or bound over for libraries.

PUBLICATION INFORMATION: The publication information is given insofar as I have been able to obtain it and obtaining it has been a vexing problem in many instances. (a) When the publication year alone is given it is very often from a catalogue or index, but sometimes from a publisher who at this stage has no clearer idea of when the book came out. (b) Prices quoted are in local currencies, at the time of publication of the book. (c) The phrase "sets of sheets printed" refers typically to the number of books; except where the publisher's convention was to bind only some of the available sheets into books and I have indicated this, if possible. Many publishers, of course, either do not know or will not say how many copies of a book they originally put out; and there is really no other reliable source of information.

In regard to the above paragraph I should mention that there is often ambiguous or incompatible information printed in catalogues and indexes. For instance publishers very often delay publication of a book for one reason or another, *after arranging to have an originally intended publication date printed in an index sold to*

libraries. I have been as accurate as was permitted under the circumstances and have gone to some trouble to acquire the information, as reliable as it is, that can be found here. Wherever in compiling publication information I came across a disagreement between a publisher's statement and a printed reference, I made it a practice to trust the publisher unless the publisher directly stated, verbally or in writing, that their own information was not likely to be trustworthy. I would very much have liked to give number of copies, exact date, and price for every single edition reported here; and I spent a number of years specifically in trying to ascertain these; but there is much in the garden of verse not precisely recorded. Much depends, too, on the country of publication. While the French keep rather accurate records of the date of publication they keep bad ones about the size of editions; the Germans are often exactly the reverse. Americans keep records, but tend to squirrel them away. The British tend to know what they happen to know on any given day, and if one is not lucky one discovers nothing.

PAGE DESCRIPTIONS: The title verso of the books and other preliminary pages are described in some detail. I do not make a fetish of printing out *every word* on the title verso, but include what seems important, interesting, or telltale; sufficiently, I believe, to make identification of a volume possible. It is not, for instance, always revealing to give the copyright. Typically the copyrights for the books were held by Ludwig Bemelmans until his death in 1962, and were dated for the year of the publication of the first edition. Subsequently the copyrights went to the estate of Bemelmans, or to Madeleine Bemelmans, or to Madeleine Bemelmans and Barbara Bemelmans (Ludwig and Madeleine Bemelmans' daughter). Madeleine Bemelmans is sometimes spelled Madeline Bemelmans on copyright listings and Barbara Bemelmans is sometimes referred to as Barbara Bemelmans Marciano.

CONTENTS: The contents are given for the first editions in any language, where there were contents listed. I have tried my best to give the connections between chapters of books and periodical publications but it has not invariably been possible for me to see the periodical publications in full, in order to check the text. Some of the magazines are no longer around; some magazine offices do not keep records. However, many of the magazines have been extraordinarily helpful to me in this project. In the contents section a semicolon separates chapters one from another and the chapter numbers, titles, and pages are given as in the text.

ILLUSTRATIONS: The illustrations, if there are any, are counted. Sometimes editions appeared which seemed the same as earlier editions but which contained fewer or more illustrations.

COPY: In the "Copy examined" section, the reference "MP" is to my own collection, and other collections are credited. Those wishing to secure copies here located in libraries should be cautioned that at least some of the source libraries have lost their copies since I consulted them.

SPECIAL INFORMATION: Special information about editions is given under "Notes." There has been no systematic attempt here to catalogue subsidiary distributions but they are mentioned if they are interesting in some way. Typically, the American editions of adult books were distributed on the same publication date in Canada by one or another of about four publishers located in Toronto: most frequently Macmillan of Canada, Blue Ribbon Books, or McClelland and Stewart; at a price commensurate with the Canadian dollar value of the initial American publication price. I have not fastidiously listed these distributions. In a similar way, some of the French publications were distributed simultaneously in Belgium.

———

A NOTE ABOUT *I Love You I Love You I Love You:* A word should be added about A21, *I Love You I Love You I Love You*. The formal title of the book is printed exactly as above, with no commas. In virtually all cases the primary phrase is repeated thrice on vertically arranged lines. However, some of the editions place punctuation upon the spine: I Love | You, | I Love | You, | I Love | You! (see A21a and A21c). The back of the dust jacket for A21a, also, says "Author: Bemelmans. Title: *I Love You, I Love You, I Love You!*" Then, in all editions, the second (and title) chapter is printed with commas, *I Love You, I Love You, I Love You*, but it originated in *Vogue* with dashes. As many reviewers will have assumed the title should have been written with commas, I have preserved them in references to reviews of the book in section J; but elsewhere I have printed the title with exactly the punctuation that appears on the title pages of the editions. Without punctuation the title may seem a little ungrammatical, but it is visually stunning. Bemelmans had a stamp made with the title on three lines, and used it to sign amicable letters such as this one to a secretary at The Viking Press, arranging for a captive audience:

Will you have a compleat collection of me, from *My War*, to *Splendide*, sent to:

Warden A. F. Dowd,
The Indiana State Prison,
Michigan City, Box 41
Indiana.

With a note requesting him to place them into the prison library, and charge same to me.

[stamp:]
I LOVE YOU
I LOVE YOU
I LOVE YOU

Chronological List of Bemelmans Titles

1934 HANSI

1936 THE GOLDEN BASKET

1937 THE CASTLE NUMBER NINE

1937 MY WAR WITH THE UNITED STATES

1938 LIFE CLASS

1938 QUITO EXPRESS

1939 MADELINE

1939 SMALL BEER

1940 FIFI

1941 HOTEL SPLENDIDE

1941 THE DONKEY INSIDE

1941 AT YOUR SERVICE

1942 ROSEBUD

1942 I LOVE YOU I LOVE YOU I LOVE YOU

1943 NOW I LAY ME DOWN TO SLEEP

1945 THE BLUE DANUBE

1946 HOTEL BEMELMANS

1947 DIRTY EDDIE

1947 A TALE OF TWO GLIMPS

1948 THE BEST OF TIMES

1949 THE EYE OF GOD

1950 SUNSHINE: A STORY ABOUT THE CITY
OF NEW YORK

1952 THE HAPPY PLACE

1952 HOW TO TRAVEL INCOGNITO

1953 MADELINE'S RESCUE

1953 FATHER, DEAR FATHER

1953 THE BORROWED CHRISTMAS

1954 THE HIGH WORLD

1955 MADELINE'S CHRISTMAS IN TEXAS

1955 PARSLEY

1955 TO THE ONE I LOVE THE BEST

1955 THE WORLD OF BEMELMANS

1956 MADELINE'S CHRISTMAS

1956/57 MADELINE AND THE BAD HAT

1957 THE WOMAN OF MY LIFE

1958 MADELINE AND THE GYPSIES

1958 MY LIFE IN ART

1960 WELCOME HOME!

1960 ARE YOU HUNGRY ARE YOU COLD

1960 HOW TO HAVE EUROPE ALL TO YOURSELF

1961 MADELINE IN LONDON

1961 (BEMELMAN'S) ITALIAN HOLIDAY

1962 ON BOARD NOAH'S ARK

1962 MARINA

1963 THE STREET WHERE THE HEART LIES

1966 THE ELEPHANT CUTLET

A1. Are You Hungry Are You Cold

[1960]

a. First edition:

TITLE PAGE: In black, on the left of the page, a drawing of a young woman's head; in black, to the right: Are You Hungry | Are You Cold | by Ludwig Bemelmans | The World Publishing Company | Cleveland and New York

PAGINATION: 1 blank leaf, 245 pp., 1 leaf, 3 blank leaves; endpapers. 20.4 x 13.7 cm.

COVERINGS: Yellow cloth-covered boards stamped on front in black with author's signature over a red flourish; and on spine in black a young woman's head | in red: Are | You | Hungry | Are | You | Cold | black asterisk | in red: Bemelmans | in black, at base: World. Top edges stained red, others untrimmed. Red dust jacket printed in yellow, black and white.

PUBLISHED: September 12, 1960 at $3.95. Number of sets of sheets printed cannot be determined; the publisher no longer exists and the records cannot be found.

On *verso of title leaf*: Published by The World Publishing Company 2231 West 110th Street, Cleveland 2, Ohio Published simultaneously in Canada . . . First Edition. *Author's disclaimer* on page [5]: With the exception of Hitler, who really was a dog, it must be stated that the persons and places in this story are other than here put down. *Half-title* on page [1]. *Printer's colophon* on leaf following page 245: This book was set in Baskerville and Masterman Types, Printed, and Bound by The Haddon Craftsmen. Design is by Larry Kamp. Endpapers plain.

CONTENTS on page [7]: Part One: 1. Light Cavalry, 11; 2. The Evening Bells, 17; 3. Papa and the Great Society of Tin Soldiers, 23; 4. Bal Militaire, 32; 5. The Riding Lesson, 37; 6. Pêche Melba, 42; 7. The Wild Asparagus, 51; 8. The Spanish Confession, 62; 9. The Bullfight, 66; 10. The Chandelier, 76; 11. The Fire, 92; 12. Mademoiselle Durant, 100; 13. Le Père Framboise, 107; 14. Gladys in Color, 120. Part Two: 1. Hohenlinden, 127; 2. Frau Lampe, 133; 3. Guten Appetit, 138; 4. Reinhild and Hitler, 145; 5. The Tower, 152; 6. Play With Soldiers, 158; 7. Dialogue A. The Hunter Wasp, 162: B. On Being on The Right Side, 164; 8. The Silvery Pike, 169; 9. Papa's Promotion, 176; 10. The Death of Veronique, 185; 11. The German Lesson, 193; 12. The Inquisition, 197; 13. Are You Hungry Are You Cold, 207; 14. The Assassins, 217; 15. The Proposal, 226; 16. The Return of Alain, 235; 17. Farewell to Youth, 240.

COPY EXAMINED: MP.

b. American paperback edition ([1961]):

TITLE PAGE: The title page is divided horizontally by a wavy vertical rule.

At left, in black: Are You Hungry | Are You Cold | A Signet Book | colophon

At right, in black: By | Ludwig | Bemelmans

Beneath, in black: Published by The New American Library

PAGINATION: [1] - [192] pp. 18 x 10.7 cm.

COVERINGS: Paper covers printed on front with a sepia photograph and with author in black and title in red, and on spine, at top, in black: P | 2008 | in red: Are You Hungry Are You Cold | in black: Ludwig Bemelmans. All edges stained red.

PUBLISHED: October, 1961 at $0.60. Number of sets of sheets printed cannot be determined, as the publisher's records are lost.

On *verso of title leaf*, page [4]: Author's disclaimer, as in A1a. First Printing, October, 1961. Printed in the United States of America.

CONTENTS: on pages [5] - [6]: Part One: 1. Light Cavalry, 7; 2. The Evening Bells, 12; 3. Papa and the Great Society of Tin Soldiers, 17; 4. Bal Militaire, 24; 5. The Riding Lesson, 28; 6. Pêche Melba, 32; 7. The Wild Asparagus, 39; 8. The Spanish Confession, 48; 9. The Bullfight, 51; 10. The Chandelier, 59; 11. The Fire, 71; 12. Mademoiselle Durant, *77*; 13. Le Père Framboise, 82; 14. Gladys in Color, 92. Part Two: 1. Hohenlinden, 96; 2. Frau Lampe, 101; 3. Guten Appetit, 105; 4. Reinhild and Hitler, 111; 5. The Tower, 116; 6. Play With Soldiers, 121; 7. Dialogue A. The Hunter Wasp, 124; B. On Being on The Right Side, 125; 8. The Silvery Pike, 130; 9. Papa's Promotion, 136; 10. The Death of Veronique, 143; 11. The German Lesson, 149; 12. The Inquisition, 152; 13. Are You Hungry Are You Cold, 160; 14. The Assassins, 168; 15. The Proposal, 176; 16. The Return of Alain, 183; 17. Farewell to Youth, 187.

COPY EXAMINED: Mrs. Madeleine Bemelmans.

c. British edition ([1961]):

TITLE PAGE: In black: Are You Hungry | Are You Cold | Ludwig Bemelmans | colophon André Deutsch

PAGINATION: [1] - 221 pp., 1 blank leaf; endpapers. 19.6 x 13 cm.

COVERINGS: Black cloth-covered boards plain on front and stamped on spine, in gold, Are You | Hungry | Are You | Cold | a rule | Ludwig | Bemelmans | at base: colophon | André Deutsch. Edges trimmed. Olive drab, red, and turquoise dust jacket with a black drawing of a girl's head, printed in white and black.

PUBLISHED: April 7, 1961 at 15s. Number of sets of sheets printed cannot be determined as the publisher's records have disappeared in passage to the United States. On *verso of title leaf,* page [4]: First Published 1961 by André Deutsch Limited 105 Great Russell Street London WC1 Printed in Great Britain by Ebenezer Baylis and Son LTD Worcester and London. *Publisher's synopsis* on page [1]. *Frontispiece* on page [2]: a black drawing of the head of a girl. *Author's disclaimer* on page [5]: as in A1a. Endpapers plain.

Note: Are You Hungry Are You Cold was licensed by André Deutsch Limited March 20, 1961 to The Harborough Publishing Company, 35 Great Russell Street, London for publication in paperback under the Ace Books imprint. Ace Books were distributed in Australia by the Grenville Publishing Company, Sydney, N.S.W. However, there is no evidence that Ace Books ever actually published this book.

CONTENTS on page [7]: Part One: 1. Light Cavalry, 11; 2. The Evening Bells, 17; 3. Papa and the Great Society of Tin Soldiers, 22; 4. Bal Militaire, 30; 5. The Riding Lesson, 35; 6. Pêche Melba, 39; 7. The Wild Asparagus, 47; 8. The Spanish Confession, 57; 9. The Bullfight, 60; 10. The Chandelier, 69; 11. The Fire, 83; 12. Mademoiselle Durant, 91; 13. Le Père Framboise, 97; 14. Gladys in Colour, 108. Part Two: 1. Hohenlinden, 115; 2. Frau Lampe, 121; 3. Guten Appetit, 126; 4. Reinhild and Hitler, 133; 5. The Tower, 139; 6. Play With Soldiers, 144; 7. Dialogue. A. The Hunter Wasp, 147. B. On Being on the Right Side, 149; 8. The Silvery Pike, 154; 9. Papa's Promotion, 160; 10. The Death of Veronique, 168; 11. The German Lesson, 175; 12.

The Inquisition, 178; 13. Are You Hungry Are You Cold, 187; 14. The Assassins, 196; 15. The Proposal, 205; 16. The Return of Alain, 213; 17. Farewell to Youth, 217.

COPY EXAMINED: MP.

d. German edition ([1961]):

TILE PAGE: In black: Ludwig Bemelmans | *Allons enfants . . .* | Roman | Kiepenheuer & Witsch | Köln • Berlin

PAGINATION: [1] - [312] pp.; endpapers. 20.1 x 12 cm.

COVERINGS: Dark burgundy linen-weave cloth-covered boards plain on front and stamped on spine, in gold, Ludwig | Bemelmans | Allons | enfants . . . Edges trimmed. Royal blue dust jacket printed in white, black and red.

PUBLISHED: 1961 at DM 16,80. 4,000 sets of sheets printed. On *verso of title leaf*: Titel der amerikanischen Originalausgabe | Are You Hungry Are You Cold | Einzig autorisierte Ubertragung von Nino Erne. *Half-title* on page [1]: Ludwig Bemelmans • Allons enfants . . . | black drawing of a basket. *Author's disclaimer* on page [5]: Mit Ausnahme des Hundes Hitler, den es wirklich gegeben hat, entsprechen die Personen und Orte dieses Buches nicht der Wirklichkeit. Endpapers of plain, heavy-weave paper.

CONTENTS (INHALT) on page 7: Erster Teil. Leichter Kavallerie, 11; Abendglocken, 19; Papas Zinnsoldaten, 26; Bal Militaire, 38; Die

Reitstunde, 45; Pêche Melba, 51; Wilder Spargel, 62; Die spanische Beichte, 76; Stierkampf, 80; Der Kronleuchter, 92; Feuer, 111; Mademoiselle Durant, 121; Père Sylvan und Père Framboise, 129; Gladys in Farben, 145. Zweiter Teil. Hohenlinden, 155; Frau Lampe, 163; Guten Appetit, 169; Reinhild und Hitler, 178; Der Turm, 186; Soldatenspiel, 194; Zum silbernen Hecht, 207; Papas Beförderung, 217; Veronique, 228; Deutschstunde, 239; Inquisition, 244; Bist du hungrig? Ist dir kalt?, 263; Les Assassins, 276; Trauerpferd, 288; Alains Rückkehr, 299; Abkehr von der Jugend, 305.

COPY EXAMINED: MP.

e. Italian edition ([1962]):

TITLE PAGE: In black: La Guerra | in Casa | Romanzo | di Ludwig | Bemelmans | Traduzione di | Adriana Pellegrini | colophon | Longanesi & C. | Milano

PAGINATION: [1] - [410] pp.; endpapers. 18.2 x 11.7 cm.

COVERINGS: Paper-covered boards of light beige, plain on front and stamped on spine, in gold within a black rectangle, Ludwig | Bemelmans | >– – –< | La | Guerra | in | Casa, and outside the rectangle, in gold, Longanesi & C. Top edges stained gray. Full color dust jacket printed in white. The inside of the dust jacket contains a list of Longanesi titles.

This is *La Gaja Scienza* volume 199.

PUBLISHED: May, 1962 at L1800. 3,000 sets of sheets printed. On *verso of title leaf*, page [6]: Proprietà Letteraria Riservata. Traduzione dall'-originale inglese Are You Hungry Are You Cold di Adriana Pellegrini. *Author's disclaimer* on page [9]. *Half-title* on page [7]. *Series half-title* on page [3]: << La Gaja Scienza >> volume 199. On page [319]: Finito di Stampare Nell'Aprile 1962 Nella Cromotipia E. Sormani - Milano. Printed in Italy. Endpapers plain.

CONTENTS (INDICE DEI CAPITOLI) on pages: [305] - [306]: In blue: Parte Prima—In black: 1. Cavalleria leggera, 13; 2. Le campane della sera, 21; 3. Papà e la grande società dei soldatini di piombo, 28; 4. Bal militaire, 40; 5. Lezione di equitazione, 46; 6. Pêche Melba, 52; 7. Gli asparagi selvatici, 63; 8. La confessione spagnola, 77; 9. La corrida, 81; 10. Il lampadario, 94; 11. L'incendio, 113; 12. Mademoiselle Durant, 122; 13. Padre Framboise, 130; 14. Gladys a colori, 146. In blue: Parte Seconda—in black: 1. Hohenlinden, 155; 2. Frau Lampe, 163; 3. Guten Appetit, 170; 4. Reinhild e Hitler, 179; 5. La torre, 187; 6. Giocare coi soldati, 195; 7. Dialogo, 199; 8. Il luccio d'argento, 208; 9. La promozione di papà, 217; 10. La morte di Veronique, 228; 11. La lezione di tedesco, 238; 12. l'inquisizione, 242; 13. Hai fame . . . hai freddo, 255; 14. Gli assassini, 268; 15. La proposta, 280; 16. Il ritorno di Alain, 291; 17. Addio alla giovinezza, 297.

COPY EXAMINED: Mrs. Madeleine Bemelmans.

f. British cheap edition ([1963]):

TITLE PAGE: In black: Are You Hungry | Are You Cold | Ludwig Bemelmans | in white, within a black rectangle: C | in black, within a black-hatched rectangle: F | in black: Contemporary Fiction | André Deutsch | London 1963

PAGINATION: [3] - 221 pp., 1 blank leaf; front endpapers. 18.5 x 12.2 cm.

COVERINGS: Royal blue cloth-covered boards plain on front and stamped on spine, in silver, Are You Hungry Are You Cold Ludwig Bemelmans; at base a silver rectangle leaving a blue C open | in silver on a silver-hatched rectangle: F. Top edges stained maroon and others trimmed. Maroon, black and white dust jacket printed in black.

PUBLISHED: January 1963 at 6s. Number of sets of sheets printed cannot be determined, as the publisher's records disappeared in passage to the United States. *Verso of title leaf* contains *Author's disclaimer*, as in A1a, and the statement, "This Contemporary Fiction edition was produced in 1963 for sale to its members only by the proprietors, Readers Union Ltd, at Aldine House, 10-13 Bedford Street, London W.C.2 and at Letchworth Garden City, Herts." *Frontispiece* on page [4]: as in A1c. *Half-title* on page [3]. Front endpapers plain.

CONTENTS on page [7]: As in A1c.

COPY EXAMINED: MP.

g. British paperback edition ([1965]):

TITLE PAGE: In black: Are You Hungry | Are You Cold | a rule in black | Ludwig Bemelmans | colophon | A Mayflower-Dell Paperback

PAGINATION: [1] - [176] pp. 18 x 11 cm.

COVERINGS: Full-color paper cover showing a young woman's head, printed in green with title and author on front (and in red with an advertising excerpt), and on spine, upon a green strip, in yellow: Are You Hungry Are You Cold Ludwig Bemelmans; at base, in white upon a green patch: colophon. No dust jacket.

This is Mayflower-Dell Paperback No. 0295.

PUBLISHED: August 1965 at 3s 6d. Number of sets of sheets printed cannot be determined, as the publisher's records are unavailable and the publisher no longer exists. On *verso of title leaf:* Are You Hungry Are You Cold Ludwig Bemelmans Originally published in Great Britain by André Deutsch Ltd. Published as a Mayflower-Dell Paperback, August 1965. Made and printed in Great Britain by C. Nicholls & Company Ltd., The Philips Park Press, Manchester. *Author's disclaimer* on verso of title leaf: as in A1a.

CONTENTS on page [5]: Part One: 1. Light Cavalry, 9; 2. The Evening Bells, 13; 3. Papa and the Great Society of Tin Soldiers, 17; 4. Bal Militaire, 24; 5. The Riding Lesson, 27; 6. Pêche Melba, 31; 7. The Wild Asparagus, 37; 8. The Spanish Confession, 45; 9. The Bullfight, 47; 10.

The Chandelier, 54; 11. The Fire, 66; 12. Mademoiselle Durant, 72; 13. Le Père Framboise, 77; 14. Gladys in Colour, 86. Part Two: 1. Hohenlinden, 93; 2. Frau Lampe, 97; 3. Guten Appetit, 101; 4. Reinhild and Hitler, 106; 5. The Tower, 110; 6. Play With Soldiers, 115; 7. Dialogue. A. The Hunter Wasp, 117. B. On Being on the Right Side, 118; 8. The Silvery Pike, 122; 9. Papa's Promotion, 127; 10. The Death of Veronique, 133; 11. The German Lesson, 139; 12. The Inquisition, 141; 13. Are You Hungry Are You Cold, 148; 14. The Assassins, 156; 15. The Proposal, 163; 16. The Return of Alain, 169; 17. Farewell to Youth, 172.

COPY EXAMINED: MP.

A2. At Your Service [1941]

TITLE PAGE: Upon a white rectangle held by a bellboy in a double-paged black and white photograph of a hotel lobby, in black: At Your Service | The Way of Life in a Hotel | By Ludwig Bemelmans

PAGINATION: [1] - 64 pp.; endpapers. 23 x 15.2 cm.

COVERINGS: Cloth-covered boards of buff color, stamped on front, in blue, with title above, and author below, a red rule, and with a blue and red figure of a waiter, and on spine, in blue, At

Your Servece • The Way of Life in A Hotel • Row, Peterson. No dust jacket.

This is part of The Way of Life Series.

PUBLISHED: The week of March 22, 1941 at 96¢. Number of sets of sheets printed cannot be determined, as the publisher's records are unavailable. On *verso of title leaf*, page [4]: Copyright, 1941, by Row, Peterson and Co., Evanston, Ill. Manufactured in the United States. 1509 [a colophon for Row-Peterson Unitext]. *A note about the author on page* [4], with a black and white photograph by Richard L. Simon of Simon and Schuster. *Half-title* on page [1]: upon a black and white photograph of a bellboy: The | Way of Life | Series | Editorial Director, | Walter Prescott Webb | Professor of History, | The University of Texas. *Frontispiece* on page [2]: a black and white photograph of a hotel lobby spreads across to the title page. Endpapers plain.

ILLUSTRATIONS: Although the book is profusely illustrated with drawings and photographs, there are no illustrations by the author.

COPY EXAMINED: Cornell University Library, Ithaca, New York.

A3. The Best of Times [1948]

a. First edition:

TITLE PAGE: In a pale blue square matching the frontispiece in size, in black: Ludwig Bemelmans | in white: the best | of times | in black: An Account of Europe Revisited, With 50 Color | and 110 Black Illustrations by The Author | Simon and Schuster - New York

PAGINATION: [1] - [192] pp. Pages [1] and [192] are pasted down upon the insides of the boards; pages [2]-[3], and again pages [190]-[191] are printed as endpapers with a black drawing of an artist busy at work in a hotel room. 32.3 x 25.2 cm.

COVERINGS: Burgundy cloth-covered boards stamped on front with a black drawing of a gendarme and a gentleman and with the author's signature, and on spine, in black, The | Best | of | Times | signature: Ludwig Bemelmans | at base: Simon | and | Schuster. Pages trimmed. Full-color dust jacket printed with a watercolor of the Place Vendôme, Paris and with title in yellow.

PUBLISHED: The week of November 6, 1948 at $3.95. The number of sets of sheets printed cannot be determined, as the publisher does not maintain old records. *Verso of title leaf,* page [10], contains a note from the author, as follows: "I wish to say 'thank you' to the editors of *Holiday Magazine,* without whose generosity of mind and pocket this book would not have been possible. After the most casual arrangements and without writing anything down on a contract form or even the back of a menu, I left, virtually from the table of the restaurant at which Ted Patrick suggested the voyage. I traveled wherever I would have gone had I been on my own holiday. I stayed everywhere as long as I liked. I wrote of and made pictures of what I thought would interest the people back home, who found travel just now impossible or inconvenient. The co-operation of the magazine with the publishers of this book has helped to make these surely the very best of times. All in all, no one could have asked for greater considerations. I have endeavored to hand the freedom given me over to the pages that follow." There is also a black drawing of a dog and cat sleeping and a printer's note: "Designed and produced by the Sandpiper Press and Artists and Writers Guild, Inc." *Frontispiece* on page [8]: a full-color watercolor of the Place Vendôme, Paris, with a caption, "It was the best of times, it was the worst of times, it was . . . the winter of despair, we had everything before us, we had nothing before us, . . ." *Note about the Author* on page [189] including this statement: As has his friend, the playwright Ferenc Molnar, so Bemelmans has an apartment of six rooms, one of which is in New York, the second in Paris, others in London, Rome and Capri, and the last in a mountain village in Tyrol. *Author's Foreword* on page

[11]. White endpapers printed in black with a picture of a writer busy at his table in his studio, with a dozing dog; as in A39a.

CONTENTS on page [13]: 1. Come Fly with Me, 18; 2. Number 13 Rue St. Augustin, 32; 3. Back Again in Paris, 42; 4. Switzerland, 60; 5. Under A Tyrolean Hat, 76; 6. Return to Munich, 90; 7. Story of A Bavarian, 106; 8. Gypsy Music, 126; 9. Les Saucissons d'Arles, 140; 10. Venice, 150; 11. Promenade Sur Mer, 164; 12. Bon Voyage, 178; 13. Postscript, 187.

"Come Fly With Me" is here reprinted from *Holiday*, January, 1947, where it appeared as "Come, Fly With Me to Paris;" see E100. "Number 13 Rue St. Augustin" is here reprinted from *Town and Country*, May, 1947; see E105. Part of "Back Again In Paris" is here reprinted from *Holiday*, February, 1947; see E101; part is from *Holiday*, May, 1948, where it appeared as "Folie de Grandeur;" see E112. "Switzerland" is here reprinted from *Holiday*, March, 1947; see E102. "Under A Tyrolean Hat" is here reprinted from *Holiday*, April, 1947; see E103. "Return To Munich" is here reprinted from *Holiday*, May, 1947; see E104. "Story of A Bavarian" is here reprinted from *Holiday*, June, 1947; see E107, E108, E109 and E110. "Gypsy Music" is here reprinted from *Holiday*, April, 1948; see E111. "Les Saucissons d'Arles" is here reprinted from *Holiday*, October, 1948 where it appeared as "Mademoiselle Regrets;" see E115. "Venice" is here reprinted from *Holiday*, August, 1948; see E113. "Promenade sur

Mer" is here reprinted from *Holiday*, September, 1948; see E114; although a portion originated as "The Isle of God" in *The New Yorker*, August 5, 1939; see E26. Many of the illustrations appeared in *Holiday* and *Town and Country*; the black drawings on pages 165, 166, 168, 169, 171, 173, and 176 are from *Small Beer*, see A39. The jacket and frontispiece drawing, "Place Vendôme, Paris" was published in the June 1, 1940 issue of *Vogue*; see E38 and G64.

ILLUSTRATIONS: A list of the color illustrations begins on page [14]. There are some 105 black drawings by the author including the endpapers and a drawing on each of the two jacket flaps. A full-color photographic collage appears on page 56. There are some 46 full-color illustrations by the author. Black and white photographs appear on pages [119], 147, and [148].

COPY EXAMINED: MP.

b. British issue ([1949]):

TITLE PAGE: In a pale blue square matching the frontispiece in size, in black: Ludwig Bemelmans | in white: the best | of times | in black: An Account of Europe Revisited, with 50 Color | and 110 Black Illustrations by The Author | upon a white sticker, 1.7 x 19.7 cm., pasted across the imprint: The Cresset Press - London.

Pagination, measurements, covering and dust jacket as in A3a.

PUBLISHED: Issued by The Cresset Press,

London, the week of September 17, 1949 at 18s. The number of sets of sheets issued cannot be determined. All contents, text and illustrations as in A3a.

COPY EXAMINED: The British Library, Great Russell Street, London.

A4. The Blue Danube [1945]

a. First edition:

TITLE PAGE: On glossy paper, in black: Ludwig Bemelmans | in blue: The Blue Danube | in black: Illustrated | by | The Author | in brown, green, and black: a drawing of a dinner plate, a piece of bread, and a beer stein | in black: New York | The Viking Press 1945

PAGINATION: 3 leaves, [1] - 153 pp., 1 blank leaf; endpapers. Unnumbered glossy leaves carrying full-color illustrations are inserted after pages 4, 10, 16, 24, 44, 60, 68, 76, 84, 92, 108, 124, 128, and [136]. 21.2 x 14.3 cm.

COVERINGS: Royal blue cloth-covered boards stamped on front, in red, with an illustration of a boating party at Regensburg; on spine, in navy: The Blue Danube; in red: Bemelmans; in navy: The Viking Press. Top edges stained red. Full-color dust jacket printed in red and white.

PUBLISHED: April 6, 1945 at $3.00. 37,000 sets of sheets printed, 37,000 copies bound. On

verso of title leaf: This edition is produced in full compliance with all war production board conservation orders. Published by the Viking Press in April 1945. *Half-title* on recto of first leaf. *Other books by the author* on verso of first leaf, listing seven titles. Pale green endpapers with a dark green drawing of a bandstand beside a river.

Some of this material appeared in *Town & Country*, March and April, 1945. See E86 and E87.

LIST OF ILLUSTRATIONS on recto of third leaf: (Note: Pages given face illustrations.) The Burgomaster kneeled down on the stone quay, held out his umbrella, and tried to hook the raft, 4; The Island was a thorn in the flesh of the Bureau of Taxation, particularly in the hide of Oberassessor Nebenzahl, 10; Old Anton sat with his back toward his sisters to keep the smoke of his pipe away from them, 16; "The gentleman wishes a handkerchief, a gift, perhaps?" said Herr Stolz, smiling, 24; The Gauleiter decided to move his chair. He looked across to where the people of the Island sat, 44; He stood absolutely still, his provocative and obscene face uplifted, 60; "Forgive the disorder, Bishop," said the old sisters. "Since old Anton is gone, it's hard to keep things straight," 68; The prisoner turned around. He wanted time only as an excuse to save some face, 76; They sat up in bed and worried about the prisoner, 84; The pump stopped yammering. Saint Martha was a little higher than Saint Anna; Saint Anna looked up the river, 92; "Shh," said the accompanist, "it's only me." Old Anton's face looked up at them, 108; Old Anton sang: "So that no one could say with lack of respect that she died of neglect," 124; "But it's impossible. It cannot be," said the poet, 128; Saint Martha and Saint Anna kneeled in prayer, 136.

COPY EXAMINED: MP

b. British edition ([1946]):

TITLE PAGE: On glossy paper, in black: Ludwig Bemelmans | in blue: The Blue Danube | in black: Illustrated | by | The Author | in brown, green, and black: a drawing of a dinner plate, a piece of bread, and a beer stein | in black: London | Hamish Hamilton Ltd. 1946

PAGINATION: 1 leaf, [1] - [144] pp.; endpapers. Unnumbered glossy leaves carrying full-color illustrations are inserted after pages 8, 12, 18, 24, 42, 50, 62, 68, 72, 76, 90, 104, 118, and 128. 18.5 x 12.3 cm.

COVERINGS: Royal blue linen-weave cloth-covered boards stamped on front, in gold: between two rules, The Blue Danube; on spine, in gold: Ludwig Bemelmans The Blue Danube; at base: colophon | Hamish | Hamilton. Full-color dust jacket printed in red and white.

PUBLISHED: September 20, 1946 at 8s 6d. Number of sets of sheets printed cannot be determined, as the publisher cannot withdraw old records from storage. On *verso of title leaf*, page [2]: First Published 1946 Printed in Great Brit-

ain by Morrison and Gibb Ltd., London and Edinburgh. *Half-title* on recto of first leaf. *Other books by the author* on verso of first leaf, listing six titles. Pale green endpapers with a dark green drawing of a bandstand beside a river.

LIST OF ILLUSTRATIONS on page 3: (Note: For full titles, see A4a. Pages given face illustrations.) Burgomaster, 8; Island, 12; Anton, 18; Gentleman, 24; Gauleiter, 42; He stood, 50; Forgive, 62; Prisoner, 68; They sat up, 72; Pump, 76; "Shh," 90; Old Anton sang, 104; "But . . .," 118; Saint Martha and Saint Anna, 128.

COPY EXAMINED: MP.

c. Cheap edition ([1946]):

TITLE PAGE: On glossy paper, in black: Ludwig Belmelmans | in blue: The Blue Danube | in black: Illustrated | by | The Author | in brown, green, and black: a drawing of a dinner plate, a piece of bread, and a beer stein | in black: The Sun Dial Press | Garden City New York

PAGINATION: As in A4a. 21.2 x 14.3 cm.

COVERINGS: Covered as in A4a except that all spine stamping is in red. Edges unstained. Dust jacket not examined.

PUBLISHED October 7, 1946 at $1.49. 20,000 sets of sheets printed. On *verso of title leaf:* Sun Dial Press Reprint Edition 1946, by special arrangement with The Viking Press Printed in The U.S.A. *Half-title,* other books by the author and *List of illustrations* as in A4a. Pale green endpapers with a dark green drawing of a bandstand beside a river.

COPY EXAMINED: MP.

d. British reprint ([1947]):

TITLE PAGE: On glossy paper, in black: Ludwig Bemelmans | in blue: The Blue Danube | in black: Illustrated | by | The Author | in brown, green, and black: a drawing of a dinner plate, a piece of bread, and a beer stein | in black: London | Hamish Hamilton Ltd. 1947

PAGINATION: As in A4c. Unnumbered glossy leaves carrying full-color illustrations are inserted after pages 8, 12, 21, 28, 36, 45, 53, 60, 69, 76, 101, 108, 117, and 124. 18.3 x 12.3 cm.

COVERINGS: As in A4c. Full-color dust jacket printed in red and white.

PUBLISHED: July 1947 at 8s 6d. Number of sets of sheets printed cannot be determined, as the publisher cannot withdraw old records from storage. On *verso of title leaf*, page [2]: First published September 1946 Reprinted July 1947 Printed by Morrison and Gibb Ltd., London and Edinburgh. *Half-title* on recto of first leaf. *Other books by the author* on verso of first leaf, listing seven titles. Pale green endpapers with a dark green drawing of a bandstand beside a river.

Note: British Books in Print for 1951 lists a Hamish Hamilton 1950 reprint for 3s 6d, in hard covers. No such edition has been discovered elsewhere, so it is likely that it was planned but never brought to completion.

LIST OF ILLUSTRATIONS on page [3]: (Note: For full titles, see A4a. Pages given face illustrations.) Burgomaster, 8; Island, 12; Anton, 21; Gentleman, 28; Gauleiter, 36; He stood, 45; Forgive, 55; Prisoner, 60; They sat up, 69; Pump, 76; "Shh," 101; Old Anton sang, 108; "But . . .," 117; Saint Martha and Saint Anna, 124.

COPY EXAMINED: MP.

e. Australian edition ([1948]):

TITLE PAGE: On glossy paper, in black: Ludwig Bemelmans | in blue: The Blue Danube | in black: Illustrated | by | The Author | in brown, green, and black: a drawing of a dinner plate, a piece of bread, and a beer stein | in black: Hamish Hamilton | London and Melbourne 1948

PAGINATION: 1 leaf, [1] - [144] pp.; endpapers. Unnumbered glossy leaves carrying full-color illustrations are inserted after pages 6, 10, 16, 32, 38, 42, 48, 64, 68, 76, 80, 96, 112, and 128. 18.4 x 12.3 cm.

COVERINGS: Royal blue linen-weave cloth-covered boards stamped on front, in red, between two rules: The Blue Danube; on spine, in red, Ludwig | Bemelmans The Blue Danube; at base: colophon | Hamish | Hamilton. Full-color dust jacket printed in red and white.

PUBLISHED: 1948 at 10s 6d. Number of sets of sheets printed cannot be determined, as the publisher cannot withdraw old records from storage. On *verso of title leaf,* page [2]: First Published September 1946 Reprinted July 1947 Australian edition, 1948 Registered at the G.P.O., Melbourne, for transmission by post as a book. Wholly set up, Printed and bound in Australia for E. C. Harris, 431 Bourke Street, Melbourne, Australasian Representative of Hamish Hamilton Ltd., London, by The Specialty Press Pty. Ltd., Melbourne. At the bottom, British printing information is blocked out by black dots. *Half-title* on recto of first leaf. *Other books by the author* on verso of first leaf, listing six titles. At bottom of page [144], Beneath a black rule: The Specialty Press Pty. Ltd. Plain white endpapers.

LIST OF ILLUSTRATIONS on page 3: (Note: For full titles, see A4a. Pages given face illustrations.) Burgomaster, 7; Island, 10; Anton, 17; Gentleman, 32; Gauleiter, 38; He stood, 43; Forgive, 49; Prisoner, 64; They sat up, 69; Pump, 76; "Shh," 81; Old Anton sang, 96; "But . . .," 113; Saint Martha and Saint Anna, 128.

COPY EXAMINED: MP.

A5. The Borrowed Christmas [1953]

TITLE PAGE: Within a drawn black cloud, between two angels bearing candles, in black script: the Borrowed | Christmas | by | Ludwig Bemelmans | in black print: beginning of text | Copyright MCMLIII, by Ludwig Bemelmans

PAGINATION: Unpaged. 8 leaves. 19.5 x 15.5 cm.

COVERINGS: Paper covers. Front cover printed in red, brown and black with a drawing of a black rectangle upon a brick wall, a Santa Claus playing a cornet, and a second Santa Claus playing tympani drums, and the text, Merry Christmas | and Best Wishes for A Happy New Year. Back cover is printed with a drawing of an angel carrying a bass drum with crossed drumsticks over the head, and the text, American Artists Group, N.Y. | No. 40 Printed in U.S.A. The black rectangle of the front cover recto carries through to the front cover verso.

PUBLISHED: 1953 for limited private distribution. Number of sets of sheets printed is not known and cannot be determined, as the Group is no longer in existence and the available records make no mention of print runs. The American Artists Group included more than eighty artists around the United States. *Author's acknowledgment* on verso of last leaf: The author wishes to thank Ted Patrick, editor of *Holiday* Magazine where this story first appeared.

The contents are here reprinted from *Holiday* Magazine, December, 1952, see E143; reprinted as "A Christmas Story" in *Father, Dear Father*, A11.

ILLUSTRATIONS: Excluding drawings on either side of the covers, there are 8 black drawings by the author.

COPY EXAMINED: The Lilly Library, Indiana University, Bloomington, Indiana.

A6. The Castle Number Nine [1937]

TITLE PAGE: Within a vertical yellow rectangle, in red: The Castle Number Nine | in black: Story and Pictures by | Ludwig Bemelmans | The Viking Press • New York | 1937

PAGINATION: Unpaged. 24 leaves; endpapers. 24.9 x 19 cm.

COVERINGS: Green linen-weave cloth-covered boards stamped on front in gold: a figure of a castle within grillwork; on spine, in gold: Bemelmans [star] The Castle Number Nine [star] Viking. Full-color dust jacket printed in red.

PUBLISHED: November 1, 1937 at $2.00. 12,500 sets of sheets printed; 500 copies bound. On *recto of first leaf:* a black and yellow drawing of a castle within grillwork, and the text in black: "Give them honor. | Give them fame! | A health to hands | That fight the flame!" On *verso of first leaf:* First published November 1937 Printed in The United States of America Lithographed by William C. D. Glaser, New York. Endpapers are printed in green, white and yellow with an illustration by the author of a castle, ducks, swans, and frolicking bunnies.

6,000 copies from the print run were selected November, 1937 for distribution in a special binding, and with slight alterations to the spine, by the Junior Literary Guild.

ILLUSTRATIONS: Exclusive of the endpapers and the drawing on the recto of the first leaf, there are 29 black and yellow, 2 black and red, and 14 full-color illustrations by the author.

COPY EXAMINED: MP.

A7. Dirty Eddie [1947]

a. First edition:

TITLE PAGE: In black: Ludwig Bemelmans | Dirty | Eddie | New York • The Viking Press • 1947

PAGINATION: [i] - xii pp., [1] - 240 pp., 2 blank leaves; endpapers. 20.2 x 13.8 cm.

COVERINGS: Yellow-striped royal blue cloth-covered boards printed on spine in yellow: Bemelmans Dirty Eddie Viking. Top edges stained yellow. Gray-blue dust jacket printed in white.

PUBLISHED: August 18, 1947 at $2.75. 30,000 sets of sheets printed; 30,000 copies bound. On *verso of title leaf*, page [vi]: Published by The Viking Press in August 1947 Parts of this book appeared serially in *Town & Country* Printed in U.S.A., by The Haddon Craftsmen. *Half-title* on page [i]. *Other books by the author* on page [iii], listing nine titles. *Epigraph* on page [vii]: Ad usum Delphini. *Author's disclaimer* on page [ix]: The characters in this book, including Dirty Eddie, are fictional, and any resemblance to living persons or pigs is pure coincidence. Endpapers plain.

CONTENTS on page [xi]: First Part: A Star Is Born. 1. Talent Scout, 3; 2. Through the Eye of the Needle, 10; 3. Belinda's Wedding, 26. Second Part: Lust for Gold. 4. Fat Canary, 35; 5. Message Out of a Bottle, 48; 6. The Sun Bath, 57. Third Part: Life with Moses Fable. 7. Folk Music, 69; 8. Fresh Paint, 81; 9. Shop Talk, 88. Fourth Part: Shoulder to the Wheel. 10. Belinda in Mourning, 97; 11. Will You Marry Me?, 106; 12. Story Conference, 122; 13. At the Gare Saint-Lazare, 126; 14. Nightwine, 133; 15. The Rich Uncle, 142. Fifth Part: In the Beautiful San Fernando Valley. 16. Dirty Eddie, 153; 17. And Then, and Then, and Then, and Then, 164; 18. Trouble with an Actor, 170; 19. Research, 180; 20. Time and Money, 197. Sixth Part: Your Sins Are Forgiven. 21. Snowy Night in Malibu, 205; 22. X'Isle, 221; 23. It's Fishing Time Again, 229; 24. Come Rain, Come Shine, 237.

Note: This book was reprinted at least twice before publication.

"Belinda's Wedding" appeared originally in somewhat different form in *Town & Country*, June 1946, as "Servant Trouble"; see E91; there were 2 color illustrations and 1 line drawing, all by the author, that do not appear in the book. "Fat Canary," "Message Out of A Bottle," and "The Sun Bath," all in slightly different form, appeared originally in *Town & Country*, July 1946, as "The Fat Canary"; see E92; there were 7 black illustrations that do not appear in the book. "Folk Music," "Fresh Paint," and "Shop Talk," all in slightly different form, appeared originally in *Town & Country*, August 1946, as "The Fat Canary"; see E95; there were 4 black illustrations that do not appear in the book. "Belinda in Mourning," part of "Will You Marry Me?," "Story Conference," and "At The Gare Saint-Lazare," all in slightly different form, appeared originally in *Town & Country*, September 1946, as "The Fat Canary"; see E96; there were 2 illustrations that do not appear in the book. "Dirty Eddie;" "And Then, and Then, and Then, and Then;" "Trouble with an Actor" and part of "Time and Money," all in slightly different form, appeared originally in *Town & Country*, October 1946, as "The Fat Canary"; see E97; there was 1 illustration, captioned "The twelfth pig was black, and because of that his mother called him Dirty Eddy" that does not appear in the book. "X'Isle, It's Fishing Time Again" and "Come Rain, Come Shine," all in slightly different form, appeared originally in *Town & Country*, November 1946, as "The Fat Canary"; see E98; there were 3 black illustrations that do not appear in the text.

COPY EXAMINED: MP.

b. British edition ([1948]):

TITLE PAGE: In black: Ludwig Bemelmans | a rule | Dirty Eddie | colophon | Hamish Hamilton | London

PAGINATION: [1] - 260 pp.; endpapers. 18.5 x 12 cm.

COVERINGS: Blue cloth-covered boards plain on front, stamped in gold on spine, sideways, Dirty Eddie Ludwig | Bemelmans | at base: colophon | Hamish | Hamilton. Dust jacket not examined.

PUBLISHED: June 11, 1948 at 8s 6d. Number of sets of sheets printed cannot be determined, as the publisher cannot withdraw old records from storage. On *verso of title leaf:* First published in Great Britain, 1948. *Ad usum Delphini*. Printed in Great Britain by Western Printing Services Ltd., Bristol. *Author's disclaimer* on verso of title leaf, as in A7a. *Half-title* on page [3]. Endpapers plain.

CONTENTS on page 7: 1. Talent Scout, 11; 2. Through the Eye of the Needle, 19; 3. Belinda's Wedding, 36; 4. Fat Canary, 45; 5. Message Out of a Bottle, 59; 6. The Sun Bath, 69; 7. Folk Music, 81; 8. Fresh Paint, 94; 9. Shop Talk, 101; 10. Belinda in Mourning, 109; 11. Will You Marry Me?, 120; 12. Story Conference, 136; 13. At the Gare Saint-Lazare, 141; 14. Nightwine, 148; 15. The Rich Uncle, 158; 16. Dirty Eddie, 169; 17. And Then, and Then, and Then, and Then, 181; 18. Trouble with an Actor, 188; 19. Research, 198; 20. Time and Money, 216; 21. Snowy Night in Malibu, 223; 22. X'Isle, 240; 23. It's Fishing Time Again, 249; 24. Come Rain, Come Shine, 257.

COPY EXAMINED: The British Library, Great Russell Street, London.

c. Swedish edition ([1948]):

TITLE PAGE: In black: Ludwig Bemelmans | Den | Dramatiska | Grisen | Översättning av | Bengt Janzon och Kar de Mumma | Stockholm | Wahlström & Widstrand

PAGINATION: [1] - [244] pp. 22.2 x 14.5 cm.

COVERINGS: Full-color paper covers printed in black with author and title. The cover illustration is not by Bemelmans. No dust jacket.

PUBLISHED: 1948 at 10 kr. Number of sets of sheets printed cannot be determined, as the publisher's records have lapsed. On *verso of title leaf*, page [4]: Originalets titel: Dirty Eddie. Ronzo

Boktryckeri AB, Stockholm 1948. *Note about the author,* beginning on page 5. *Half-title* on page [1]. *Publisher's blurb* on back cover.

Note: Kar de Mumma is the pen name of Erik Zetterström.

COPY EXAMINED: The Royal Library, Stockholm.

d. French edition ([1950]):

TITLE PAGE: In black: Ludwig Bemelmans | Cochon | d'Eddie! | (Dirty Eddie) | Roman traduit de l'Anglais | par Désirée Manfred | colophon | Robert Laffont | 30, rue de l'Université, 30 | Paris

PAGINATION: [1] - [304] pp., 1 blank leaf, 1 leaf. 18.4 x 11.6 cm.

COVERINGS: Teal and white paper cover printed on front with title, author, translator and publisher all in black and with imprint Pavillons in teal, and on spine in black, between two double white rules, Cochon | d'Eddie! | par | Ludwig | Bemelmans | at base: Robert | Laffont | Pavillons.

PUBLISHED: August 17, 1950 at 450 F. Number of sets of sheets printed cannot be determined, as the publisher's records have lapsed. On *verso of title leaf,* page [6]: Imprimé en France. *Half-title* on page [3]. *Epigraph* on page [7]: Ad usum delphini. *Author's disclaimer* on page [8]: Les personnages de ce livre, y compris Dirty Eddie, sont entièrement fictifs, et toute ressemblance qui

serait découverte entre eux et des personnes ou des cochons réels, doit être attribuée à la seule coïncidence. *Printer's colophon* on recto of concluding leaf: Achève d'imprimer sur les presses de l'Imprimerie Wallon À Vichy pour Robert Laffont, Éditeur à Paris, — Le 17 Août 1950; —.

A number of copies of this edition were taken in September 1950 by the Club Français du Livre and distributed to membership in cloth covers with a cover illustration by Alexic Keunen. The Club du Livre du Mois distributed soft-covered copies, and some copies were distributed in Belgium by the Club Belge du Livre, Bruxelles. The book club editions were printed at S.I.L.I.C. in Lille.

CONTENTS on page [303]: Première Partie: I. La chasse au talent, 9; II. Par le trou d'une aiguille, 20; III. Belinda se marie, 40. Deuxième Partie: La Soif de L'Or. IV. Coq en pâte, 49; V. Prophétie trouvée dans une bouteille, 66; VI. Le Bain de Soleil, 78. Troisième Partie: Avec Moses Fable. VII. Chansons du pays, 89; VIII. Peinture fraîche, 106; IX. Propos de boutique, 114. Quatrième Partie: Un Coup d'Épaule. X. Belinda en deuil, 123; XI. Voulez-vous m'épouser?, 136; XII. Conférences, 155; XIII. A la gare Saint-Lazare, 161; XIV. Nightwine, 169; XV. L'oncle riche, 182. Cinquième Partie: San Fernando, Charmante Vallée. XVI. Dirty Eddie, 193; XVII. Et alors, et alors, et alors, et alors, 207; XVIII. Discussion avec un acteur, 215; XIX. Recherches, 227; XX. Le Temps, l'Argent, 248. Sixième

Partie: Vos Peches Seront Pardonnées. XXI. Nuit de neige, 255; XXII. X'Ile, 276; XXIII. Prends ta ligne, et partons, 287; XXIV. Après la pluie, le beau temps, 297.

COPY EXAMINED: MP.

e. First American paperback edition ([1951]):

TITLE PAGE: In black: Ludwig Bemelmans | Dirty | Eddie | colophon | A Signet Book | Published by The New American Library

PAGINATION: [1] - [192] pp. 18.1 x 10.5 cm.

COVERINGS: Orange and yellow paper cover with a full-color illustration of a man helping a woman out of a fur stole, on front. Printed in white with author and title and at top, in black, "A Racy Peek into Hollywood's Private Lives." The back cover has a photograph of the author. Printed on spine in black, 858 Dirty Eddie Ludwig Bemelmans. No dust jacket.

This is Signet Books No. 858.

PUBLISHED: March 28, 1951 at 25¢. The number of sets of sheets printed cannot be determined, as the publisher's records are lost. On *verso of title leaf:* Copyright, 1944, 1945, 1946, 1947, by Ludwig Bemelmans. Published as a Signet Book By Arrangement with The Viking Press First Printing, March, 1951 Parts of this book appeared serially in *Town & Country. Epigraph* on page [6]: Ad usum Delphini. *Author's disclaimer* on verso of title leaf, as in A7a. *Publisher's adver-*

tisements on first leaf and last page of book. *Contents* on page [5].

COPY EXAMINED: MP.

f. British paperback edition ([1952]):

TITLE PAGE: In black: Dirty Eddie | Ludwig Bemelmans | colophon | Pan Books Ltd : London

PAGINATION: [1] - [222] pp., 1 leaf. 17.6 x 11.1 cm.

COVERINGS: Orange and yellow paper cover with a full-color illustration of a black pig, a red-headed woman, a man in a turquoise shirt and multicolored tie, and a movie camera, on front. Printed in black and mauve with author and title. Spine is printed, in black, Dirty Eddie Bemelmans; in white: Pan; then in blue and black: colophon; and at base, in white: 197. No dust jacket.

This is Pan Book No. 197.

PUBLISHED: February 15, 1952 at 2s. 40,000 sets of sheets printed. On *verso of title leaf:* First published in Great Britain 1948 by Hamish Hamilton Ltd. This edition published 1952 by Pan Books Ltd., 8 Headfort Place, London, S.W.I. Printed and bound in England by Hazell Watson and Viney Ltd Aylesbury and London. *Epigraph* on verso of title leaf: Ad usum Delphini. *Author's disclaimer* on verso of title leaf, as in A7a. *Publisher's advertisements* on last leaf in book.

COPY EXAMINED: The British Library, Great Russell Street, London.

g. Italian edition ([1953]):

TITLE PAGE: Within a black border, in black: Silenzio, | Non Si Gira! | di | Ludwig Bemelmans | Arnoldo Mondadori Editore

PAGINATION: [1] - [160] pp. 20 x 14 cm.

COVERINGS: Full-color paper covers printed in white. Printed on spine, in black upon white: Ludwig Bemelmans - Silenzio, Non Si Gira!; and at base, upon teal blue: bl 41. No dust jacket.

PUBLISHED: March 4, 1953 at 150 Lire. Number of sets of sheets printed is unknown and cannot be determined, as the publisher's records have lapsed. On *verso of title leaf*, page [2]: I Romanzi della Palma - Nuova Serie - Numero 41. 4 Marzo 1953 prima edizione. Titolo dell'opera originale: Dirty Eddie. Traduzione di Carlo Rossi Fantonetti. Stampato in Italia - Printed in Italy.

This is I Romanzi della Palma No. 41.

COPY EXAMINED: Mrs. Madeleine Bemelmans.

h. Second American paperback edition ([c.1960]):

Dirty Eddie was published by Grosset and Dunlap in the late 1950s or early 1960s, with a 1949 copyright, at $1.00. The precise date of publication and the number of sets of sheets printed cannot be determined, as the publisher's records have been lost. A copy of this edition has not been found for examination.

A8. The Donkey Inside [1941]

a. First edition:

TITLE PAGE: In black: The Donkey Inside | by | Ludwig Bemelmans | Illustrated by The Author | a drawing of a figure in sombrero and serape with two bags | 1941 | New York | The Viking Press

PAGINATION: [1] - 224 pp.; endpapers. 21.3 x 14.3 cm.

COVERINGS: Yellow buckram-covered boards stamped on front in red with the title page drawing; on spine, in red: The | Donkey | Inside | sideways: Bemelmans | at base: The | Viking | Press. Top, front, and bottom edges stained red. Full-color dust jacket printed in white upon turquoise bands.

PUBLISHED: January 17, 1941 at $3.00. 7,900 sets of sheets printed; 7,725 copies bound. On *verso of title leaf*, page [4]: Printed in U.S.A. by the Vail-Ballou Press Bound by H. Wolff Book Manufacturing Co. Published in January 1941. *Acknowledgment* on verso of title leaf: Material appearing in a few chapters of this book has already been used by the author in articles in *Town & Country, Vogue, Globe*, and *The New Yorker*. Special acknowledgment is made to Harry Bull, editor of *Town & Country. Half-title* on page [1], including *other books by the author*, listing three titles. *Second half-title* on page [9]. *Author's note,* beginning on page 223, signed at Club Pichincha, Quito, Ecuador. Brown endpapers printed with a black drawing of a woman at a table with a bottle, a lamp, and insects flying into a sugar container.

The book was reprinted April 1945 at $3.00. The publication year was printed on the title page. The endpapers were white printed in brown. The board coverings were rose and the spine stamping, in red, was: The | Donkey | Inside | sideways: Bemelmans | at base: The | Viking | Press.

CONTENTS on page [5]: l. The S. S. *Mesias,* 11; 2. On a Bench in a Park, 23; The Guayaquil and Quito Railway, 37; Quito, 43; 5. About the Inhabitants of Quito, 49; 6. The Morale of the Natives, 59; 7. The Boots of General Altamir Pereira, 69; 8. Benitin and Eneas, 79; 9. The Ride with Rain, 91; 10. The Ride with the Long Night, 101; 11. The Day with Hunger, 109; 12. This Is Romance, 117; 13. Dream in Brooklyn, 129; 14. The Headhunters of the Amazon, 137; 15. Adolf in Quito, 151; 16. Prison Visit, 161; 17. Poor Animal, 169; 18. The Promised Land, 175; 19. Buenos Días, Gran Hotel, 185; 20. The Painted Grapes, 193; 21. The Friends of Ecuador, 203; 22. To a White Rose, 211; 23. The S. S. *Santa Lucía,* 219.

"The S. S. *Mesias*" is here reprinted from *Town & Country,* June, 1940; see E37. Some of the material in "Quito" first appeared in "Back to Quito," *House Beautiful,* February, 1939; see E20.

"The Morale of The Natives" is here reprinted from *Town & Country,* November, 1940; see E45. Portions of "The Boots of General Altamir Pereira" are here reprinted from *Vogue,* April 1, 1938, where they appeared in slightly different form as "Chile con amore: a sentimental journey from Valparaiso to Quito"; see E13. "Adolf in Quito" is here reprinted from *The New Yorker,* September 28, 1940, where it was titled, "Our Footloose Correspondents: Adolf in Ecuador"; see E44. "Prison Visit" is here reprinted from *Globe,* November 1937, where it appeared in slightly different form as "Prison? It's Wonderful"; see E11. "Poor Animal" is here reprinted from *Globe,* December 1937-January 1938, where it appeared in slightly different form as "Poor Animal!"; see E12. "The Promised Land" appeared originally, in somewhat different form, as "The Donkey Inside: Escape and Farewell," in *Town & Country,* May 1940; see E34. "Buenas Días, Gran Hotel" is here reprinted from *Town & Country,* March, 1940; see E32. "The Painted Grapes" is here reprinted form *Town & Country,* September, 1940; see E42. *The Donkey Inside* was condensed in *Reader's Digest,* April 1941; see E53.

ILLUSTRATIONS: Exclusive of the endpapers and the title leaf drawing, there are 4 full-color illustrations by the author, listed on page [7]: The Plaza Independencia, Quito, after page 44; Luchow's Restaurant on a Sunday Evening, after page 112; The House and Garden of André Roosevelt in Quito, after page 180; Indians in the

Patio of the Hotel Sucre in Otavalo, after page 194. The Luchow's illustration is a portion of an illustration that appeared earlier in "Busboy's Holidays: Dinner at Luchow's and a Trip to the Sea," *Town & Country*, July 1938; see E16. The House and Garden of André Roosevelt appeared over the caption, "In Quito: Cirilio paints the blinds while André Roosevelt inspects his melon patch" as part of "The Donkey Inside: Escape and Farewell," in *Town & Country*, May 1940; see E34.

COPY EXAMINED: MP.

a (bis). Deluxe limited edition ([1941]):

PAGINATION: [1] - [2] pp., 1 leaf, 1 signed leaf, [3] - 224 pp.; endpapers. 21.3 x 14.3 cm.

COVERINGS: Three quarter brick red and one quarter sunflower yellow leatherette-covered boards stamped on front, within a gold rectangle, in gold: Bemelmans | The Donkey Inside; on spine, in gold over yellow: The | Donkey | Inside; and over red: Bemel- | Mans; and at bottom: Viking. Pages untrimmed and uncut. No dust jacket. Book is preserved in a black slipcase.

PUBLISHED: January 17, 1941 at $5.50. 175 sets of sheets bound from a printing of 7,900 sets. *Verso of title leaf, acknowledgment, contents* and *illustrations* as in A8a. The recto of the first leaf following page [2] bears the text: One hundred and seventy-five | copies of the first edition | have

been specially bound | with an original illustration | in color | this copy is number. The recto of the following leaf contains the author's signature in black and, between two hand-made sunflower yellow rules, a black ink drawing hand-colored by the author.

COPY EXAMINED: Mrs. Madeleine Bemelmans.

b. South American edition ([1941]):

TITLE PAGE: In black, Over a rule: Ludwig Bemelmans | a diamond | El Burro por Dentro | (The Donkey Inside) | a diamond | Primera Edicion | Traducida del Ingles | Quito - Ecuador

PAGINATION: [1] - 202 pp., 1 leaf, 1 blank leaf, 1 leaf. No endpapers. 19.5 x 14.2 cm.

COVERINGS: Off-white (pale gray) paper covers printed in black and red with a drawing of a peasant and a burro (not by the author) on front and a red colophon bearing the words "Ediciones Patria" on the back. Spine plain. No dust jacket.

PUBLISHED: July 30, 1941 at 6 sucres. The number of sets of sheets printed cannot be determined, as the publisher has disappeared and the records cannot be found. On page [2]: In a black rectangle, between two rules: 1941 | under a toothed rule: Editora Moderna. - Carrera Sucre 22 - Telefono 21-60 | Plaza de San Francisco. *Half-title* on page [1]. *Introduction*, "Entra 'El Burro' Como Llevando al Lector de la Mano. . . ." by Don Che, pages 5-7. *Author's note*

(Nota del Autor) on page [201]. *Printer's note* on recto of final leaf: Este libro acabose de imprimir en San Francisco de Quito, a los treinta dias del mes de Julio de mil novecientos cuarenta y uno, en los Talleres Graficos de Editora Moderna Plaza de San Francisco Sucre 22 - Telefono 21-60 - Casilla 61 - Quito Ecuador.

CONTENTS following page 202: 1, En el vapor "Mesias," 10; 2, En una banca del parque, 19; 3, El Ferrocarril Guayaquil & Quito, 31; 4, Quito, 37; 5, Los habitantes, 43; 6, La Moral de los Nativos, 53; 7, Las botas del General Atamir Pereira, 61; 8, Benitin y Eneas, 69; 9, Cabalgata con la lluvia, 79; 10, Cabalgata con la noche large, 87; 11, Un día de hambre, 93; 12, Esto es Tomance, 99; 13, Ensueno en Brooklyn, 109; 14, Los Cazadores de cabezas del Amazonas, 117; 15, Adolfo en Quito, 131; 16, Visita al Panoptico, 139; 17, Pobre animal, 147; 18, Tierra de promision, 153; 19, Buenos días, Gran Hotel, 103 [sic.: actually 163]—20, Las uvas pintadas, 171; 21, Los amigos del Ecuador, 181; 22, A una rosa blanca, 189; 23, A bordo del "Santa Lucía," 197.

COPY EXAMINED: Yale University Library.

c. British edition ([1947]):

TITLE PAGE: Within a vertical pink rectangle bordered with a black flourished line, in black: Ludwig Bemelmans | a rule | The | Donkey | Inside | Illustrated by the Author | colophon | Hamish Hamilton | London

PAGINATION: [1] - [155] pp.; endpapers. 21.6 x 14 cm.

COVERINGS: Red linen-weave cloth-covered boards plain on front and stamped on spine, in silver, The Donkey Inside Bemelmans; at base: Hamish | Hamilton. Full-color dust jacket printed in white on turquoise bands.

PUBLISHED: November 21, 1947 at 9s 6d. Number of sets of sheets printed cannot be determined, as the publisher cannot withdraw old records from storage. On *verso of title leaf*, page [4]: First published 1947 Made and printed in Great Britain by The Stanhope Press Limited Rochester Kent. *Half-title* on page [1], including a pink drawing of a figure in sombrero and serape carrying two bags. *Other books by the author* on page [2], listing seven titles. *Author's note* on page [155]. Endpapers plain.

CONTENTS on page [5]: l. The S. S. *Mesias*, 9; 2. On a Bench in a Park, 17; 3. The Guayaquil and Quito Railway, 27; 4. Quito, 31; 5. About the Inhabitants of Quito, 35; 6.The Morale of the Natives, 42; 7. The Boots of General Altamir Pereira, 49; 8. Benitin and Eneas, 55; 9. The Ride with Rain, 63; 10. The Ride with the Long Night, 70; 11. The Day with Hunger, 75; 12. This Is Romance, 80; 13. Dream in Brooklyn, 88; 14. The Headhunters of the Amazon, 94; 15. Adolf in Quito, 104; 16. Prison Visit, 110; 17. Poor Animal, 116; 18. The Promised Land, 120; 19. Buenos Días, Gran Hotel, 128; 20. The Painted Grapes, 134; 21. The Friends of Ecuador, 141;

22. To a White Rose, 146; 23. The S. S. *Santa Lucía*, 152.

ILLUSTRATIONS: Excluding the half-title drawing, there are 4 full-color illustrations by the author, listed on page [7]: The Plaza Independencia, Quito, after page 40; Luchow's Restaurant on a Sunday Evening, after page 72; The House and Garden of André Roosevelt in Quito, after page 120; Indians in the Patio of the Hotel Sucre in Otavalo, after page 136.

COPY EXAMINED: MP.

d. British cheap edition ([1949]):

TITLE PAGE: In black: Ludwig Bemelmans | The | Illustrated | Donkey | By The Author | Inside | Readers Union | with Hamish Hamilton • London 1949

PAGINATION: As in A8d. 20.3 x 13 cm.

COVERINGS: Chartreuse linen-weave cloth-covered boards stamped on front in magenta with facsimile signature of author and Readers Union colophon, and on spine with a magenta swatch through which the title shows in chartreuse. White dust jacket printed in magenta, with author and title in white.

PUBLISHED: 1949 at an unknown price. Price, exact publication date and number of sets of sheets printed cannot be determined, as the publisher cannot withdraw old records from storage. On *verso of title leaf,* page [4]: Readers Union colophon in black. This volume was produced in 1948 in complete conformity with the authorised economy standard. First published in England by Hamish Hamilton Ltd. in 1947, it has been set in Monotype Bembo, 12 point, and reprinted at Rochester by The Stanhope Press Ltd. It is one of the books produced for sale to its members only by Readers Union Ltd., of 38 William IV Street, Charing Cross, London, and of Letchworth, Hertfordshire. *Half-title* on page [1], with a black drawing of a figure in sombrero and serape carrying two bags. *Other books by the author* on page [2], listing seven titles. *Author's note* on page [155]. Endpapers plain.

CONTENTS on page [5]: As in A8d.

ILLUSTRATIONS: As in A8d.

COPY EXAMINED: MP.

e. First paperback edition ([1964]):

TITLE PAGE: In black: The | Donkey Inside | by | Ludwig Bemelmans | Illustrated by the author | A Dutton | colophon | Paperback | New York | E. P. Dutton & Co., Inc. | 1964

PAGINATION [1] - 224 pp. 18.5 x 11 cm.

COVERINGS: Full-color paper covers printed on front with author and title in black and on spine, in blue: The Donkey Inside; in black: Ludwig Bemelmans; at base, in red and white: | colophon | in black: D142.

This is Dutton Paperback No. D142.

PUBLISHED: The week of May 18, 1964 at $1.35. The number of sets of sheets printed cannot be determined, as the publisher's records have been lost in transition to new ownership. On *verso of title leaf*, page [6]: This paperback edition of "The Donkey Inside" First published 1964 by E. P. Dutton & Co., Inc. Printed in the U.S.A. Reprinted by special arrangement with The Viking Press, Inc. *Half-title* on page [1]. *Frontispiece* on pages [2]-[3]: a black reproduction of the drawing on the endpapers of A8a. *Author's note* begins on page 223.

CONTENTS on page [7]: As in A8a.

ILLUSTRATIONS: Besides the frontispiece, there is a single black drawing of a figure in sombrero and serape carrying two bags on page [10], and 4 illustrations, originally in color, here reprinted in black and white, listed on page [9] as in A8a.

COPY EXAMINED: MP.

f. Second paperback edition ([1990]):

TITLE PAGE: In black: The | Donkey Inside | by | Ludwig Bemelmans | Illustrated by the author | colophon | Paragon House | New York

PAGINATION: [1] - 224 pp. 21 x 13.8 cm.

COVERINGS: Full-color laminated paper covers printed on front with a full-color illustration of a donkey in an Ecuadorian village (by Roberta Ludlow), title in brown and purple, and author in green and purple; on spine, in black: Athena colophon | in brown — — —Ludwig— — — | Bemel-

mans | in purple: — — —The— — — | Donkey Inside; at base, in black: colophon | Paragon | House. Edges trimmed. No dust jacket.

This book is part of *The Armchair Traveller Series*.

PUBLISHED: September, 1990 at $10.95. Number of sets of sheets printed cannot be determined, as the publisher refuses to release the information. On *verso of title leaf*, page [6]: First Paragon House edition, 1990. Copyright © 1968 by Madeline Bemelmans and Barbara Bemelmans. This book is printed on acid-free paper. On page [1]: A listing of books in *The Armchair Traveller Series*, including 17 titles. *Frontispiece* on pages [2] - [3]: a black drawing of a woman at a table with a bottle, a lamp, and insects flying into a sugar container, used for the endpapers of the original edition, see A8a. *Author's Note* on pages 223 - 224: as in A8a. On *back cover*: The Armchair Traveller Series. Athena Books. Paragon House 90 Fifth Avenue, New York, N.Y. 10011.

CONTENTS on pages [7] - [8]: As in A8a.

ILLUSTRATIONS: On page [10] there is a black drawing of a figure in sombrero and serape with two bags, used for the title page of the original edition, see A8a. Exclusive of this and the frontispiece, there are 4 black and white reproductions of the full-color illustrations used in the original edition, listed on page [9]: The Plaza Independencia, Quito, after page 44 (originally published in *Vogue*); Luchow's Restaurant on a Sunday Evening, after page 112; The House and

Garden of André Roosevelt in Quito, after page 180; Indians in the Patio of the Hotel Sucre in Otavalo, after page 194 (all three of which appeared originally in *Town & Country*).

COPY EXAMINED: MP.

A9. The Elephant Cutlet [1966]

(No title page.)

PAGINATION: 4°. [4] pp. 17.9 x 13 cm.

COVERINGS: Grey cardboard covers with a cream paper plate printed in red and black on front. In red: The Elephant Cutlet | in black: design of an elephant | in red: by Ludwig Bemelmans. Tied with red yarn. No endpapers. Top edges uncut.

PUBLICATION: Exact date of publication unknown. All copies were for private distribution only. 100 sets of sheets printed. *Printer's colophon* on page [4]: Printed from handset 16 point Narrow Bembo Italic by Audrey Arellanes, Alhambra, California, 1966. Design of Elephant repeated from title plate in black with copy number hand-inked in red upon the riding blanket. "The Elephant Cutlet" from *My War With The United States* by Ludwig Bemelmans. Copyright 1937 by Ludwig Bemelmans. Reprinted by permission of The Viking Press, Inc., 100 copies

The booklet is printed in black, with the ex-ception of a single line in the center of page [2]: "Cutlets from Every Animal in the World".

The text is here reprinted from *My War With the United States*, A33. See as well E9. The pamphlet is one of a group printed by Audrey Arellanes at The Bookworm Press; these were generally selected from texts the printer had been fond of. Also included in the catalog was *Selections from Fireflies* by Rabindranath Tagore; and Excerpts from the Letters of Thomas Bird Mosher to Washington Irving Way at the Huntington Library, San Marino.

COPY EXAMINED: Audrey Arellanes, copy No. "A". The printer wrote in a personal communication, ". . . it is a lettered copy; in a similar manner the numbered copies were marked on the elephant on the colophon page."

A10. The Eye of God [1949]

a. First edition:

TITLE PAGE: In black: Ludwig Bemelmans | The Eye | of God | a novel | New York • 1949 • The Viking Press

PAGINATION: [i] - vi pp., [1] - 312 pp., 1 blank leaf; endpapers. 20.3 x 13.5 cm.

COVERINGS: Tan linen-weave cloth-covered boards stamped on front in brown with a moose

head and printed on spine, in green: Bemel- |
mans | The | in brown: Eye | in green: of | in
brown: God | in green, at base: Viking. Mauve
dust jacket with a full-color picture, printed in
white.

PUBLISHED: October 28, 1949 at $3.00.
20,000 sets of sheets printed; 20,000 copies
bound. On *verso of title leaf,* page [iv]: Published
by The Viking Press in October 1949 Printed in
U.S.A. by The Colonial Press Inc., Clinton,
Mass. *Acknowledgment* on page [iv]: Acknowledgment is made to *Town & Country,* which published
several sections of this novel serially, and to *The
New Yorker,* in which a story, "The Antlers of the
Alpenrose," used in part here, appeared. *Other
books by the author* on page [ii], listing eleven titles.
Half-title on page [i]. Four-color glossy endpapers by the author.

CONTENTS on page [v]: Part One: 1. Village
Chronicle, 3; 2. The Alpenrose, 25; 3. Look at
Him, 31; 4. The High World, 42. Part Two: 5.
The Enzian, 53; 6. Under New Management,
64; 7. Gemütlichkeit, 71; 8. While the Soup
Gets Cold, 79; 9. Big and Little Hedwig, 90;
10. The Sisters of Compassion, 100; 11. Good
Man and Bad Doctor, 111; 12. The Knife
Thrower, 116; 13. Fraulein Berta's Day Off,
123. Part Three: 14. The Pole and Marusja,
137; 15. Entertainment, 151; 16. The Lucky
Ones, 160; 17. The Rescue of Mussolini, 168;
18. Some of My Best Friends, 179; 19. On
Monte Grotto, 193. Part Four: 20. The Inven-
tory, 209; 21. Poor Papa, 221; 22. Keep House,
Keep House, 229; 23. The Pilgrimage, 240; 24.
Remember the Zoo in Vienna?, 248; 25. The
General's Hunt, 252; 26. Patron of the Arts,
263; 27. The Privileged Prisoners, 274; 28. The
True Princess, 283; 29. Oh, Promise Me, 296;
30. Chronicle II, 306.

"Village Chronicle," "The Alpenrose," "Look
at Him," and "The High World" appeared originally in somewhat different form as "The Master
of the Alpenrose," *Town & Country,* June 1949;
see E118. "The Enzian," "Under New Management," "Gemütlichkeit," "While The Soup Gets
Cold" and "Big and Little Hedwig" appeared
originally in somewhat different form as "Serpents in Aspen," *Town & Country,* July 1949; see
E119. "Entertainment," "The Lucky Ones," "The
Rescue of Mussolini" and parts of "Some of My
Best Friends" appeared originally in somewhat
different form as "Holiday for Heroes," *Town &
Country,* August 1949; see E121. "On Monte
Grotto," "The Inventory," "Poor Papa," parts of
"Keep House, Keep House," and parts of "The
General's Hunt" appeared originally as "The
Turn of the Tide," *Town & Country,* September
1949; see E123. A part of "The Alpenrose," part
of "The Enzian," and part of "While The Soup
Gets Cold" appeared in somewhat different form
in *The New Yorker,* May 24, 1947 as "The Antlers
of the Alpenrose"; see E106.

Note: An Italian edition of this book was in
preparation by Arnoldo Mondadori Editore of

Verona, in a translation by Amina Pandolfi, but was never published.

COPY EXAMINED: MP.

b. British edition ([1950]):

TITLE PAGE: In black: The Snow Mountain | Ludwig Bemelmans | Hamish Hamilton | London

PAGINATION: [1] - 288 pp.; endpapers. 19.8 x 12.9 cm.

COVERINGS: Turquoise cloth-covered boards plain on front, stamped on spine in gold: Ludwig | Bemelmans | a rule | The | Snow | Mountain | at base: Hamish | Hamilton. Yellow dust jacket printed in red, white and dark turquoise.

PUBLISHED: May 26, 1950 at 10s 6d. Number of sets of sheets printed cannot be determined, as the publisher cannot retrieve old records from storage. On *verso of title leaf*, page [4]: First published in Great Britain, 1950 by Hamish Hamilton Ltd. Printed in Great Britain by The Stanhope Press Ltd., Rochester, Kent. *Other books by the author* on page [2], listing six titles. *Half-title* on page [1]. Four-color glossy endpapers by the author, as in A10a.

CONTENTS on page [5]: Part One: 1. Village Chronicle, 7; 2. The Alpenrose, 27; 3. 'Look at Him', 33; 4. The High World, 43. Part Two: 5. The Enzian, 50; 6. Under New Management, 60; 7. Gemütlichkeit, 67; 8. While The Soup Gets Cold, 74; 9. Big and Little Hedwig, 84; 10. The Sisters of Compassion, 93; 11. Good Man and Bad Doctor, 103; 12. The Knife Thrower, 108; 13. Fraulein Berta's Day Off, 115. Part Three: 14. The Pole and Marusja, 127; 15. Entertainment, 141; 16. The Lucky Ones, 150; 17. The Rescue of Mussolini, 157; 18. 'Some of My Best Friends', 167; 19. On Monte Grotto, 180. Part Four: 20. The Inventory, 192; 21. Poor Papa, 203; 22. Keep House, Keep House, 210; 23. The Pilgrimage, 221; 24. Remember The Zoo in Vienna?, 229; 25. The General's Hunt, 233; 26. Patron of The Arts, 243; 27. The Privileged Prisoners, 254; 28. The True Princess, 262; 29. Oh Promise Me, 274; 30. Chronicle II, 283; Author's Note, facing page 288.

The "Author's Note" does not appear in the first edition. It reads in part, "The reader will wonder how it was possible for the Author, who was in America during the war, to record the intimate detail of the scene at Aspen. . . . [signed], Postgesthof, Lech am Arlberg, Austria."

COPY EXAMINED: MP.

c. British paperback edition ([1950]):

TITLE PAGE: In black: The Snow Mountain | Ludwig Bemelmans | Hamish Hamilton | London

PAGINATION: [1] - 288 pp.; endpapers. 19.7 x 13 cm.

COVERINGS: White cardboard covers printed on front with author and title and, beneath a rule, in red: "Star Editions to be sold on the continent of Europe only", and on spine, in red: Ludwig | Bemelmans a diamond The Snow | Mountain a diamond, at base: Star | a red star | Editions. No dust jacket.

PUBLISHED: 1950 at an unknown price. Number of sets of sheets printed cannot be determined, as the publisher cannot withdraw old records from storage. *Verso of title leaf, half-title, list of other titles by the author, endpapers, author's note and contents* as in A10b.

COPY EXAMINED: MP.

d. Danish edition ([1951]):

TITLE PAGE: In black: Ludwig Bemelmans | Guds Øje | På dansk ved | Georgjedde | Eiler Wangels Forlag ^A/_S | København - MCMLI

PAGINATION: [1] - 240 pp. 21 x 15.3 cm.

COVERINGS: Blue and gray paper covers printed in yellow on front and on spine, in yellow upon black: Bemel- | Mans | G | U | D | S | Ø | J | E. No dust jacket.

PUBLISHED: 1951 at KR 9:75. Number of sets of sheets printed cannot be determined, as the publisher's records have lapsed. On *verso of title leaf*, page [3]: Copyright 1950. Oversat fra Amerikansk efter "The Snow Mountain".

CONTENTS (INDHOLD) on page [5]: 1. del

side 7-41; 2. del side 43-104; 3. del side 105-157; 4. del side 159-239; Efterskrift, 240.

COPY EXAMINED: Mrs. Madeleine Bemelmans.

A11. Father, Dear Father [1953]

a. First edition:

TITLE PAGE: With a black drawing of a little girl and poodle on a sofa in black: Father, | Dear | Father | by Ludwig Bemelmans | 1953 | New York | The Viking Press

PAGINATION: 1 blank leaf, [i] - [vi] pp., [1] - 247 pp.; endpapers. 21.3 x 14.3 cm.

COVERINGS: Aqua linen-weave cloth-covered boards stamped on front in magenta with a drawing of a poodle and the author's signature; on spine: Father, Dear Father | By Ludwig Bemelmans. Full-color dust jacket printed in black, red and white.

PUBLISHED: August 24, 1953 at $3.50. 15,000 sets of sheets printed; 14,849 copies bound. On *verso of title leaf*, page [iv]: Published by the Viking Press in August 1953 Printed in the U.S.A. by The Vail-Ballou Press, Inc. *Acknowledgment* on page [iv]: The author wishes to express his thanks to the editors of *Holiday, Town & Country,*

Vogue, Collier's, and *Woman's Day,* in which portions of this book appeared in somewhat different form. *Other books by the author* on page [ii], listing thirteen titles. *Half-title* on page [i]. *Second half-title* on page [1]. Endpapers plain.

CONTENTS on page v: 1. Little Bit and the *America,* 3; 2. My French Mattress, 28; 3. Visit to Versailles, 37; 4. Of Cows' Milk and Laval's Dog, 48; 5. Gramercy Nocturne, 61; 6. The Unknowns in Vienna, 75; 7. Rome Express, 86; 8. The Spaghetti Train, 95; 9. The Isle of Capri, 110; 10. Cinderella Island, 131; 11. Science and Man, 152; 12. "Proletariat of the World, Unite", 164; 13. Vesuviana, 194; 14. I Always Travel on Holidays — A Christmas Story, 211; 15. The Bowery, 242. (There is a black drawing of a poodle with butterfly at the head of the contents.)

"Little Bit and The *America*" is here reprinted from *Collier's,* January 10, 1953, where it appeared as "The Dog That Travelled Incognito"; see E145. "The Isle of Capri" is here reprinted from *Holiday,* November 1949, where it appeared as "Isle of Capri"; see E124. "Cinderella Island" is here reprinted from *Holiday,* December 1949, where it appeared as "Cinderella Isle"; see E126. "Vesuviana" is here reprinted from *Holiday,* January 1952, where it appeared as "Mighty Vesuvius!"; see E139. "The Christmas Story" from chapter 14 is here reprinted from *Holiday,* December 1952, where it appeared as "The Borrowed Christmas;" see E143 and as well A5 and H1.

ILLUSTRATIONS: Excluding the title and contents drawings, there are 90 black drawings by the author and one black illustration, on page 216, reproduced from elsewhere.

COPY EXAMINED: MP.

a (bis). Deluxe limited edition ([1953]):

TITLE PAGE: With a black drawing of a little girl and poodle on a sofa, in black: Father, | Dear | Father | By Ludwig Bemelmans | 1953 | New York | The Viking Press

PAGINATION: 1 leaf, 1 signed leaf, [i] - [vi] pp., [1] - 247 pp.; endpapers. 22 x 14.6 cm.

COVERINGS: Red buckram blind-stamped on front with poodle and author's signature; and stamped on spine, in gold: Bemel- | mans | Fa- ther, | Dear | Father | at base: Viking. Pages untrimmed and uncut. No dust jacket. Book is covered in cellophane and preserved in a gray vellum-covered sleeve.

PUBLISHED: August 24, 1953 at $15.00. 151 copies bound from a printing of 15,000 sets of sheets; 100 of the copies were for sale. *Verso of title leaf, acknowledgment, contents* and *illustrations* as in A11a. The recto of the first leaf bears the text: This First Edition of | Father, Dear Father | is limited to | one hundred and fifty-one copies, | of which one hundred are for sale, | each one containing | an original drawing in color | signed by the author | [hand-numbered in magenta]. The recto of the following leaf contains the author's signature in black and a black ink drawing hand-colored by the author. Endpapers in gray vellum.

COPY EXAMINED: MP.

b. British edition ([1953]):

TITLE PAGE: With a black drawing of a little girl and poodle on a sofa, in black: Father, | Dear | Father | By Ludwig Bemelmans | Hamish Hamilton London

PAGINATION: [1] - 254 pp., 1 blank leaf; endpapers. 21.6 x 13.9 cm.

COVERING: Blue cloth-covered boards stamped on front in silver with the drawing from the title page; on spine, in silver: Father, | Dear | Father | a flourish | Ludwig | Bemelmans | at base: Hamish | Hamilton. Full-color dust jacket printed in black and white.

PUBLISHED: October 22, 1953 at 12s 6d. Number of sets of sheets printed cannot be determined, as the publisher cannot withdraw old records from storage. On *verso of title leaf*, page [4]: First published in Great Britain, 1953 by Hamish Hamilton Ltd. 90 Great Russell St. London, W.C.I Made and printed in Great Britain by Morrison and Gibb Limited, London and Edinburgh. *Other books by the author* on page [2], listing eight titles. *Half-title* on page [1]. *Second half-title* on page [7]. Endpapers plain.

This edition was reprinted February 28, 1957.

CONTENTS on page [5] with a black drawing of a poodle and a butterfly: l. Little Bit and the *America*, 9; 2. My French Mattress, 34; 3. Visit to Versailles, 43; 4. Of Cows' Milk and Laval's Dog, 54; 5. Gramercy Nocturne, 67; 6. The Unknowns in Vienna, 81; 7. Rome Express, 92; 8. The Spaghetti Train, 101; 9. The Isle of Capri, 116; 10. Cinderella Island, 138; 11. Science and Man, 159; 12. 'Proletariat of the World, Unite', 171; 13. Vesuviana, 201; 14. I always Travel on Holidays —A Christmas Story, 218; 15. The Bowery, 249.

ILLUSTRATIONS: As in A11a. The excerpted black illustration is on page 223.

COPY EXAMINED: MP.

c. German edition ([1953]):

TITLE PAGE: In black: Ludwig Bemelmans | Mit Kind und Krümel | Nach Europa | Kiepenheuer & Witsch | Köln • Berlin

PAGINATION: [1] - [264] pp.; endpapers. 20.2 x 12.7 cm.

COVERINGS: Mint green cloth-covered boards stamped on front with author's signature and a poodle in yellow; and on spine, in yellow: Ludwig Bemelmans - Mit Kind und Krümel Nach Europa. Top edges stained yellow. Dust jacket printed in magenta, yellow, and green with black line drawings, author in yellow and title in yellow and white.

PUBLISHED: 1953 at an unknown price. The exact publication date, price and number of sets of sheets printed cannot be determined, as the publisher cannot release the information. On *verso of title leaf,* page [6]: Titel der im Verlag Viking Press erschienenen Amerikanischen Ausgabe: Father, dear Father. Deutsch von Hildegard Blomeyer. 1. - 4. Tausend 1953. *Colophon* on page [1]. *Half-title* on page [3]. Endpapers plain.

COPY EXAMINED: Mrs. Madeleine Bemelmans.

d. French edition ([1954]):

TITLE PAGE: In black: Ludwig Bemelmans | Père, cher | Père . . . | (traduit de l'américain | par | Simone Le chevrel) | Editions Domat | 160, rue St-Jacques, Paris

PAGINATION: [1] - [318] pp., 1 blank leaf. 18.5 x 11.6 cm.

COVERINGS: White paper covers with an angel flying and a girl with many suitcases printed in black; in red: author, title and publisher on front; on spine, in black: Ludwig | Bemelmans | in red: Pere, | cher | Pere | at base, in black: Domat. Glassine jacket.

PUBLISHED: September 10, 1954 at FF570. The number of sets of sheets printed cannot be determined as neither the publisher nor the publisher's records can be located. On *verso of title leaf,* page [6]: En accord avec Viking Press. *Printer's note (Achevé d'imprimer)* on page [318]: Achevé d'Imprimer [colophon] sur Les Presses d'Aubin Liguge (Vienne) Le 10 Sept. 1954. *Half-title* on page [3]. No table of contents.

ILLUSTRATIONS: There are 12 black drawings by the author.

COPY EXAMINED: MP.

e. New American edition (1992):

TITLE PAGE: Spread upon a double-page, in black: Father, | Dear | [Signature] Father | between two rules: Volume I in A New Bemelmans Series | a black line drawing of a butler and maid lifting a mattress upstairs | Written and | Illustrated by | Ludwig Bemelmans [at left:] H James H. Heineman New York 1992

PAGINATION: 5 leaves, [1] - 300 pp., 4 leaves, 1 blank leaf; endpapers. 21.4 x 14 cm.

COVERINGS: One-third gray linen-weave cloth-covered, and two-thirds royal blue paper-covered boards; blind-stamped on the front with a drawing of a girl seated with a poodle and the author's signature, and stamped on spine, in gold, between two rules: Volume | I [over a rule:] Father, Dear Father [under the rule:] Ludwig Bemelmans [at base:] H [between two rules:] 1992. Front edges not trimmed. Grey and royal blue dust jacket printed in blue, black and white.

PUBLISHED: September 15, 1992 at about $22.95. 3,000 sets of sheets printed. On *verso of title* [fourth] *leaf:* © 1953 by Ludwig Bemelmans. Renewed © 1985 by Madeleine Bemelmans and Barbara Bemelmans Marciano All rights reserved This book was first published in 1953 and reflects the writing of the time. First published in this edition in the United States of America in 1992 H James H. Heineman, Inc., 475 Park Avenue, New York, NY 10022. *Half-title* on recto of second leaf. *Second half-title* on page [1]. *Frontispiece* on recto of first leaf: an illustration of a girl seated with a poodle. *Other titles in this series* on recto of third leaf: Volume II *I Love You. I Love You. I Love You* Volume iii *How to Travel Incognito, Other books by the author* on recto of third leaf, including eleven titles. On *recto of first end leaf* (with an illustration of a poodle): Books Forming a Series By and About Ludwig Bemelmans, listing, with ISBN numbers, three novels, *Father, Dear Father, I Love You. I Love You. I Love You* and *How to Travel Incognito*, and as well the present bibliography. Also the text: Other Titles in Preparation. *Author's signature* and *publisher's blurb* on recto of second end leaf. *Printer's colophon* on recto of third end leaf: This book was composed in Cochin and Nicolas Cochin Black by The Sarabande Press, New York. It was printed and bound by Arcata Graphics Company, New York on 60# Sebago cream white antique paper. The typography and binding were designed by Beth Tondreau Design, New York. On *recto of fourth end leaf:* an illustration of a taxi (from p. 44). Endpapers plain.

CONTENTS on recto of fifth leaf (with an illustration of a poodle with butterfly): 1. Little Bit and the *America*, 3; 2. My French Mattress, 33; 3. Visit to Versailles, 44; 4. Of Cows' Milk and Laval's Dog, 58; 5. Gramercy Nocturne, 73; 6. The Unknowns in Vienna, 90; 7. Rome Express, 104; 8. The Spaghetti Train, 115; 9. The Isle of Capri, 133; 10. Cinderella Island, 159; 11. Science and Man, 185; 12. "Proletariat of the World Unite", 200; 13. Vesuviana, 237; 14. I Always Travel on Holidays—A Christmas Story, 257; 15. The Bowery, 294.

ILLUSTRATIONS: Aside from the title page drawing, the frontispiece, the contents drawing, and the end-leaf drawing, there are 90 black illustrations by the author.

COPY EXAMINED: MP.

A12. Fifi [1940]

TITLE PAGE: Within a vertically rectangular border of stretching rose-colored cats, in black: fifi | a black and rose drawing of a poodle with a bow in its hair | in black: by | Ludwig Bemelmans | Simon and Schuster | New York

PAGINATION: Unpaged. 27 leaves. 30.6 x 22.6 cm.

COVERINGS: Full-color paper-covered boards printed with title in white and turquoise and author in black on front. Spine not seen. Full-color dust jacket printed in black, white and turquoise. Back cover of the book is in turquoise with a white and pink illustration of a poodle.

PUBLISHED: November 12, 1940 at $2.00. Number of sets of sheets printed cannot be determined, as the publisher has not maintained records from 1940. On *verso of title leaf:* Manufactured in the United States of America by The Reehl Litho Co., New York. The recto of the first leaf and verso of the last leaf are pasted down onto the insides of the boards. The verso of the first leaf and recto of the second, and again the verso of the second last leaf and recto of the last, are printed as endpapers in rose pink with stretching black cats and stretching white poodles.

The text originally appeared in *Town & Country*, August 1940; see E41.

ILLUSTRATIONS: Excluding the endpapers and title-leaf drawing, there are 6 full-color, and 1 yellow and red, illustrations; and 35 illustrations in various combinations of rose pink, brown, and green; all by the author.

COPY EXAMINED: MP.

A13. The Golden Basket [1936]

TITLE PAGE: In black: The | Golden | Basket | by Ludwig Bemelmans | The Viking Press • New York | 1936

PAGINATION: [1] - [96] pp.; endpapers. 24.7 x 18.3 cm.

COVERINGS: Red linen-weave cloth-covered boards blind-stamped with a swan on front, and stamped on spine in blue, Bemelmans [star] The Golden Basket. Full-color dust jacket printed in yellow.

PUBLISHED: September 11, 1936 at $2.00. 10,000 sets of sheets printed; 9,000 copies bound. On *verso of title leaf,* page [4]: First Published September 1936 . . . Lithographed by William C. D. Glaser, New York. *Half-title* on page [1], including a small brown, black and yellow drawing of the Hotel du Panier d'Or. The endpapers are yellow printed in red with an aerial view of Bruges.

6,000 copies of this edition were selected by the Junior Literary Guild and distributed to membership at an unknown price with slight alterations to binding and the book spine.

This book is the recipient of the Newbery Award.

ILLUSTRATIONS: Excluding the endpapers and the half-title drawing, there are 23 full-color and 35 black illustrations by the author.

COPY EXAMINED: MP.

A14. Hansi
[1934]

a. First edition:

TITLE PAGE: In black: Hansi | Story and Pictures | by | Ludwig Bemelmans | The Viking Press New York | 1934

PAGINATION: Unpaged. 32 leaves; endpapers. 30.4 x 22.6 cm.

COVERINGS: One-sixteenth blue cloth-covered, and fifteen-sixteenths full-color paper-covered, boards printed on front with a boy's face, and author and title in black. Spine plain. Full-color dust jacket printed in black.

PUBLISHED: October 11, 1934 at $2.00. 7,500 sets of sheets printed; 5,000 copies bound. On *verso of title leaf*; First Published, October 1934 Printed in the United States of America. Full-color endpapers show a cross-section of "Uncle Herman's House."

2,500 copies of this edition were selected in October, 1934 by the Junior Literary Guild and distributed to membership at an unknown price with slight alterations to binding and the book spine.

The book was reprinted several times, and in 1962 with the following on the title verso: Seventh Printing (from new plates) 1962.

ILLUSTRATIONS: Excluding the endpapers there are 24 black and 21 full-color illustrations by the author. The 4-color separations for this book were done by Kurt Wiese.

COPY EXAMINED: MP.

b. Second edition ([1934]):

Hansi was published in the Fall of 1934 by E. M. Hale and Co., Eau Claire, Wisconsin, at $3.00. Because neither the publisher nor the publisher's records can be located the precise publication date and number of sets of sheets printed cannot be determined. A copy of this edition has not been found for examination.

c. British edition ([1935]):

Hansi was published in March 1935 by Lovat Dickson Ltd, London, at 7s 6d. As neither the publisher nor the publisher's records can be found, the number of sets of sheets printed cannot be stated. It has not been possible to find a copy of this edition for examination.

d. Special edition ([1940]):

TITLE PAGE: In black: Hansi | Story and Pictures | by | Ludwig Bemelmans | E. M. Hale and Company | This special edition is published by arrangement with | the publisher of the regular edition, The Viking Press

PAGINATION: Unpaged. 32 leaves; endpapers. 24.1 x 19 cm.

COVERINGS: Dark gray cloth-covered boards printed in black and red. There is a boy's face, and author and title are in black. Printed on spine, in black: Hansi Bemelmans; at base: Cadmus | Books. No dust jacket.

PUBLISHED: 1940 at $1.32. Number of sets of sheets printed cannot be determined, as neither the publisher nor the publisher's records could be located. On *verso of title leaf:* [colophon] Published by The Viking Press. A note about the book appears on the verso of the front free-endpaper. Yellow endpapers printed in turquoise with a Cadmus Books colophon.

ILLUSTRATIONS: As in A14a.

COPY EXAMINED: MP.

e. Japanese edition ([1953]):

TITLE PAGE: In black: Yamano Kurismas | bun • e • Ludwig • Bemelmans | a drawing of the sun shining through the mountains | Iwanami Shoten Goraku

PAGINATION: 2 leaves, [1] - [88] pp., 2 leaves. 20.1 x 15.8 cm.

COVERINGS: Paper-covered boards printed cerulean blue with publisher in black, title in black and yellow, a black, red and yellow picture of Hansi, and a black and yellow colophon on front; and on spine, in black: Katakana and Hirakana, Yamano Kurismas; and at base, in black on a yellow bar continuing from the [colophon] on front: 3. The cerulean blue back cover has a red, black and yellow picture of an angel. Top edges stained gray. Dust jacket reproduces covers of

boards. The front flyleaf gives book care instructions for children; the back flyleaf gives a synopsis of the story.

PUBLISHED: December 10, 1953 at ¥150. 148,300 sets of sheets printed. *Other books for children from the same publisher* on recto of second-last leaf. Also: First Japanese edition. Tokyo-to Chiyoda-ku Kanda Hitotsubashi 23 Co. Ltd. Printed by Dainihon Insatzu Kaisha. Designed by Tanaka. Hansi by Ludwig Bemelmans authorized by The Viking Press, New York. The recto of the first leaf and the verso of the final leaf are glued to the boards. The verso of the first leaf and recto of the second, and again the verso of the second-last leaf and recto of the last, are printed as endpapers with the same illustration as in A14a, except that the elephant colophon of the publisher appears in both lower corners holding a book in its trunk.

ILLUSTRATIONS: Aside from the title page illustration and endpapers, there are 18 color and 24 black illustrations by the author.

COPY EXAMINED: Mrs. Madeleine Bemelmans.

A15. The Happy Place [1952]

TITLE PAGE: In black: by Ludwig Bemelmans | The | Happy Place | Illustrated by | the Author | Little, Brown and Company • Boston

PAGINATION: 2 leaves, [1] - 58 pp., 1 leaf; endpapers. 20.5 x 13.5 cm.

COVERINGS: Chartreuse cloth-covered boards stamped in brown on front with drawings of rabbit, frog and elephant and author and title; on spine: The Happy Place • Ludwig Bemelmans • Little, Brown. Full-color dust jacket printed in brown and black.

PUBLISHED: September 18, 1952 at $2.50. 10,050 sets of sheets printed, 9,640 copies bound. On *verso of title leaf:* First Edition printed in the United States of America. *Acknowledgment* on verso of title leaf: The author wishes to thank Mr. William A. H. Birnie, Editor of *Woman's Home Companion*, in whose pages this story first appeared. *Half-title* on recto of first leaf; *second half-title* on page [1] with black drawing of a bunny in a basket. *Frontispiece* on verso of first leaf: a full-color illustration of an elephant sitting in a snowy kiosk. Endpapers plain.

The text appeared first in *Woman's Home Companion*, April 1951; see E133.

ILLUSTRATIONS: Excluding frontispiece and half-title drawing there are 4 full-color illustrations by the author and 18 black drawings as well, including one or two dancing elephants on the recto of the concluding leaf.

COPY EXAMINED: MP.

A16. The High World [1954]

a. First edition:

TITLE PAGE: In black: The | High | World | Story and pictures by | Ludwig Bemelmans | Harper & Brothers : New York

PAGINATION: 6 leaves, 1 - 38 pp., 2 leaves, 39 - [78] pp., 2 leaves, 79 - [108] pp., 1 leaf, 109 - [114] pp., 1 leaf, 1 blank leaf; endpapers. 23.3 x 16.3 cm.

COVERINGS: Cloth-covered boards of red stamped on front with a drawing of an old man carrying a child in blue; on spine, in white: Bemelmans The High World Harper. Full-color dust jacket printed in black.

PUBLISHED: October 6, 1954 at $2.75. 15,000 sets of sheets printed. On *verso of title leaf:* Copyright, 1954, by Ludwig Bemelmans Copyright, 1950, by the Curtis Publishing Company Printed in the United States of America Parts of this story have appeared in *Holiday* magazine. *Author's acknowledgment* on recto of third leaf [beside a black drawing of a gun]: The author wishes to thank Ted Patrick, Editor of *Holiday* magazine, in whose pages part of this story has appeared. *Half-title* on recto of first leaf, with black drawing of chamois. *Second half-title* on recto of fifth leaf, with black drawing of dandelion at lower right. *Frontispiece* on verso of first leaf: a black drawing of an old man with skis and a child in a snowfall. *Printer's note* on recto of leaf following page [114]: Set in Linotype Janson Format by Ervine Metzl and John Rynerson Lithographed by the Murray Printing Company Published by Harper & Brothers, New York. Dark blue endpapers with white drawings: a mountain storm at the front, a crane operation at back.

CONTENTS on recto of fourth leaf: The Freedom of the Chamois, 1; The Cave, 7; The First Christmas, 15; The Cure, 35; The High World, 49; The Second Christmas, 58; The Long Shadow, 71; The Third Christmas, 109. A black drawing of a child calling is beneath the chapter titles.

Some of this material appeared originally in *Holiday*, December, 1950 as "Christmas in Tyrol;" see E130.

ILLUSTRATIONS: Excluding the endpapers, the half-title drawings, the frontispiece, the contents drawing, and the acknowledgment drawing, there are 40 black and 4 full-color illustrations by the author.

COPY EXAMINED: MP.

b. First British edition ([1958]):

TITLE PAGE: In black: The | High | World | Story and pictures by | Ludwig Bemelmans | Hamish Hamilton : London

PAGINATION: 6 leaves, 1 - [114] pp., 2 blank leaves; endpapers. 21.9 x 15.4 cm.

COVERINGS: Cloth-covered boards of bright green, plain on front. The spine is stamped in silver: The High World Ludwig Bemelmans with colophon at base. Full-color dust jacket printed in black.

PUBLISHED: July 24, 1958 at 15s. Number of sets of sheets printed cannot be determined, as the publisher cannot withdraw old records from storage. On *verso of title leaf:* The High World First published in Great Britain, 1958 Printed in Great Britain by Knightly Vernon & Son London, E.15. *Acknowledgment* on third leaf [with a drawing of a gun]: The author wishes to thank Ted Patrick, Editor of *Holiday* magazine, in whose pages part of this story has appeared. *Half-title* on recto of first leaf with full-page drawing of a chamois. *Second half-title* on recto of fifth leaf, with a black drawing of a dandelion at the lower right. *Frontispiece* on verso of first leaf: an old man with skis and baby in a snowfall, in black. Dark blue endpapers with white drawings: a mountain storm at the front, a crane operation at back.

CONTENTS on recto of fourth leaf: As in A16a.

ILLUSTRATIONS: Exclusive of endpapers, frontispiece, and drawings with acknowledgment and half-titles, there are 40 black and 4 full-color illustrations by the author.

COPY EXAMINED: The British Library, Great Russell Street, London.

c. First German edition ([1960]):

TITLE PAGE: In black: Ludwig Bemelmans | Alle Jahre wieder | Kiepenheuer & Witsch | Köln • Berlin

PAGINATION: [1] - 32 pp., 1 leaf, 33 - 48 pp., 2 leaves, 49 - 88 pp., 2 leaves, 89 - [120] pp., 1 leaf, 121 - [126] pp., 1 blank leaf; endpapers. 23.1 x 16.3 cm.

COVERINGS: Cloth-covered boards of red stamped in black on front with a drawing of an old man carrying a child, and on spine, in black: Bemelmans Alle Jahre Wieder. Top edges stained gray. Yellow dust jacket with a full-color illustration, printed in black.

PUBLISHED: 1960 at DM 7,80. Number of sets of sheets printed cannot be determined, as the publisher cannot release the information. On *verso of title leaf*, page [4]: Titel der Originalausgabe The High World aus dem Amerikanischer von Peter Crivelli. Printed in Germany 1960. On page [5]: a black drawing of a gun. *Half-title* on page [1], with black drawing of chamois. *Second half-title*, plain, on page [9]. On *page* [8]: a black drawing of dandelion. *Frontispiece* on page [2]: a black drawing of an old man with skis and a child in a snowfall. Plain white endpapers.

CONTENTS (INHALTSVERZEICHNIS) on page [7]: Die Gamsfreiheit, 11; Die Höhle, 19; Das erste Weihnachtsfest, 27; Die Kur, 47; Die hohe Welt, 61; Das zweite Weihnachtsfest, 71; Der lange Schatten, 85; Das dritte Weihnachtsfest, 121. A black drawing of a child calling in the mountains faces the chapter titles on page [6].

ILLUSTRATIONS: Excluding the drawings listed above, there are 40 black and 4 full-color illustrations by the author.

COPY EXAMINED: Mrs. Madeleine Bemelmans.

d. Second British edition ([1961]):

TITLE PAGE: In black: The | High World | by | Ludwig Bemelmans | Illustrated by | The Author | colophon | Hamish Hamilton | London

PAGINATION: [1] - 104 pp.; loose endpapers. 19.8 x 12.5 cm.

COVERINGS: Bright green cloth-covered boards stamped in brown on front with author's name, title, and a picture of a hunter; and on spine: The High World Ludwig Bemelmans; at base: colophon. Dust jacket not examined.

PUBLISHED: March 16, 1961 at 5s 6d. Number of sets of sheets printed cannot be determined, as the publisher cannot withdraw old records from storage. On *verso of title leaf:* First published in Great Britain, 1958 First published in The Heron Series, 1960. *Publisher's listing* on page [2]: The Heron Series [containing four titles]. *Acknowledgment* on page [5]: As in A16b. *Half-title* on page [1]. *Second half-title* on page [9] with a drawing of a dandelion in the center.

CONTENTS on page [7]: The Freedom of the Chamois, 11; The Cave, 17; The First Christmas, 25; The Cure, 45; The High World, 58; The Second Christmas, 67; The Long Shadow, 78; The Third Christmas, 99.

ILLUSTRATIONS: Exclusive of the half-title, there are 15 black illustrations by the author.

COPY EXAMINED: The British Library, Great Russell Street, London.

e. Second German edition ([1961]):

TITLE PAGE: In black: Ludwig Bemelmans | Alle Jahre wieder | Im Bertelsmann Lesering

PAGINATION: [1] - 32 pp., 1 leaf, 33 - 48 pp., 2 leaves, 49 - 88 pp., 2 leaves, 89 - [120] pp., 1 leaf, 121 - [126] pp., 1 blank leaf; endpapers. 23.1 x 16.3 cm.

COVERINGS: Tangerine cloth-covered boards stamped in black on front with a drawing of an old man carrying a child, and on spine, in black: Bemelmans Alle Jahre Wieder. Top edges stained gray. Yellow dust jacket with a full-color illustration, printed in black.

PUBLISHED: 1961 at an unknown price. Number of sets of sheets printed cannot be determined, as the publisher's records have lapsed. On *verso of title leaf*, page [4]: The High World, Copyright 1954 by Ludwig Bemelmans Copyright

1950 by the Curtis Publishing Company Alle deutschen Rechte im Verlag Kiepenheuer & Witsch, Köln Lizenzausgabe für den Bertelsmann Lesering mit Genehmigung des Verlages Kiepenheuer & Witsch, Köln Ausstattung: Ludwig Bemelmans Gesamtherstellung Mohn & Co GmbH, Gütersloh Printed in Germany • Buch Nr. 2809. On page [5]: a black drawing of a gun. *Half-title* on page [1], with black drawing of chamois. *Second half-title*, plain, on page [9]. On page [8]: a black drawing of dandelion. *Frontispiece* on page [2]: a black drawing of an old man with skis and a child in a snowfall. Plain white endpapers.

CONTENTS (INHALTSVERZEICHNIS) on page [7]: Die Gamsfreiheit, 11; Die Höhle, 19; Das erste Weihnachtsfest, 27; Die Kur, 47; Die hohe Welt, 61; Das zweite Weihnachtsfest, 71; Der lange Schatten, 85; Das dritte Weihnachtsfest, 121. A black drawing of a child calling in the mountains faces the chapter titles on page [6].

ILLUSTRATIONS: Excluding the drawings listed above, there are 40 black and 4 full-color illustrations by the author.

COPY EXAMINED: Bertelsmann Club GmbH, Gütersloh, West Germany.

A₁₇. Hotel Bemelmans [1946]

a. First edition:

TITLE PAGE: Across the top of the page, in black: Hotel • vertically, down the right side of the page: Bemelmans | within the rectangular space framed by the two words of the title: a black drawing of a busboy with a mammoth bouquet and a small dog | by Ludwig Bemelmans | 1946 | New York : The Viking Press

PAGINATION: 1 blank leaf, [1] - 380 pp., 1 blank leaf; endpapers. 21.3 x 14.4 cm.

COVERINGS: Cadmium yellow linen-weave cloth-covered boards stamped on front with a turquoise horizontal bar bordered by two straight turquoise, and two wavy scarlet, rules through which the title shows in yellow, and with a drawing of a waiter and a sculpture in scarlet; on spine, with the same rule and bar structure as on front, but larger, through which the title shows in yellow, and at base: Viking. Full color dust jacket printed in yellow.

PUBLISHED: September 6, 1946 at $3.00. 25,000 sets of sheets printed; 25,000 copies bound. On *verso of title leaf,* page [4]: Published by The Viking Press in September 1946 Printed in U.S.A. by The Haddon Craftsmen *Acknowledgment* on page [4]: Portions of this book are from the author's earlier volumes: Life Class, Hotel Splendide, Small Beer, and I Love You. I Love You. I Love You. "The Splendide Animals," "Mespoulet's Promotion," and "Otto Kahn's Top Hat" are new stories. Acknowledgment is made to *The New Yorker, Town and Country, Vogue, Harper's Bazaar,* and *This Week,* in which some of these stories were originally published. The illustration on the jacket originated as a black-and-white drawing in Small Beer, which was later redrawn in color by the artist as a cover for *The New Yorker,* and is reproduced here by courtesy of that magazine. *Half-title* on page [1]. *Other books by the author* on page [2], listing eight titles. *Second half-title* on page [7]. White endpapers are printed with a turquoise drawing, by the author, of a huge head waiter overseeing a large crowd dancing and dining.

CONTENTS on page [5], with a black drawing of a chef at work: 1. I Was Born in a Hotel, 9; 2. Monsieur Victor of the Splendide, 29; 3. The Animal Waiter, 37; 4. Grapes for Monsieur Cape, 44; 5. Herr Otto Brauhaus, 56; 6. Art at the Splendide, 63; 7. The Lost Mandolin, 72; 8. Mr. Sigsag Goes to Sea, 85; 9. Life Class, 101; 10. The Brave Commis, 111; 11. The Splendide Animals, 117; 12. No Trouble at All, 121; 13. Easy Money, 133; 14. If You're Not a Fool, 142; 15. Affair, 154; 16. Coming Out, 166; 17. Cinderella and Santa Claus, 180; 18. Dinner Out, 189; 19. Seven Hundred Brides, 204; 20. Improved Jewish Wedding, 226; 21. The Postmaster from Przemysl, 233; 22. Japanese Evening, 239; 23. The

Ballet Visits the Magician, 245; 24. Kalakobé, 253; 25. Cotillion, 260; 26. The Hispano, 267; 27. The Magician Does a New Trick, 274; 28. The Homesick Bus Boy, 281; 29. My Valet Lustgarten, 290; 30. The New Suit, 301; 31. Teddy, 314; 32. Mespoulet's Promotion, 326; 33. The Dreams of the Magician, 340; 34. Otto Kahn's Top Hat, 349; 35. A Night in Granada, 360; 36. The Murderer of the Splendide, 366.

"Monsieur Victor of The Splendide" is here reprinted from *Town & Country*, September 1941, where it appeared as "The Splendide: The Perfect Behavior of a Crazy Fool;" see E60; it was published earlier in *Hotel Splendide*, see A18. "The Animal Waiter" is here reprinted from *The New Yorker*, May 11, 1940, where it appeared as "Mespoulets of the Splendide;" see E35; it was published earlier in *Hotel Splendide*; see A18. "Grapes for Monsieur Cape" is here reprinted from *Town & Country*, September 1940, where it appeared as "The Painted Grapes;" see E42; it was published earlier in *Life Class*; see A23. "Herr Otto Brauhaus" appeared in *Life Class*; see A23. "Art at The Splendide" is here reprinted from *The New Yorker*, June 1, 1940, where it appeared as "Art at the Hotel Splendide;" see E36; it was published earlier in *Hotel Splendide*; see A18. "Mr. Sigsag Goes to Sea" is here reprinted from *Town & Country*, July 1938, where it appeared as "Busboy's Holidays: Dinner at Luchow's and a Trip to the Sea;" see E16. It was published earlier in *Life Class*; see A23. "Life Class" is here reprinted from *Life Class*; see A23. "The Brave Commis" is here reprinted from *Life Class*; see A23. "The Splendide Animals" appears here for the first time. "No Trouble at All" is here reprinted from *Vogue*, March 1, 1937; see E5; it was reprinted in *Town & Country*, June 1957; see E176; and it appeared as "'No Trouble at All'" in *Small Beer*; see A39. "Easy Money" is here reprinted from *Hotel Splendide*; see A18. "If You're Not a Fool," "Affair," "Coming Out," "Cinderella and Santa Claus," "Dinner Out," "Seven Hundred Brides," "Improved Jewish Wedding," "The Postmaster from Przemysl" and "Japanese Evening" are all reprinted from *Life Class*; see A23. "The Ballet Visits the Magician" is here reprinted from *The New Yorker*, July 6, 1940, where it was published as "The Ballet Visits the Splendide's Magician;" see E39. "Kalakobé" is here reprinted from *Life Class*; see A23. "The Hispano" is here reprinted from *The New Yorker*, March 22, 1941, where it was published as "The Splendide's Hispano;" see E52; it was published earlier in *Hotel Splendide*; see A18. "The Magician Does a New Trick" is here reprinted from *The New Yorker*, July 27, 1940, where it was published as "The Splendide's Magician Does a New Trick;" see E40; it was published earlier in *Hotel Splendide*; see A18. "The Homesick Bus Boy" is here reprinted from *The New Yorker*, November 9, 1940, where it was published as "The Homesick Bus Boy of the Splendide;" see E46; it was published earlier in *Hotel Splendide*; see A18. "My Valet Lustgarten" is here reprinted from *The New Yorker*, October 11, 1941, where it was published as "The Valet of the Splendide;" see E62; it was published earlier in *Hotel Splendide*; see A18. "The New Suit" was published earlier in *Hotel Splendide*; see A18. "Teddy" appeared in *I Love You, I Love You, I Love You* as "Sweet Death in the Electric Chair;" see A21 and E67. "Mespoulet's Promotion" appears here for the first time. "The Dreams of The Magician" is here reprinted from *Hotel Splendide*; see A18. "Otto Kahn's Top Hat" appears here for the first time. "A Night in Granada" is here reprinted from *The New Yorker*, December 21, 1940, where it was published as "The Splendide's Night in Granada;" see E48; it was published earlier in *Hotel Splendide*; see A18. "The Murderer of the Splendide" is here reprinted from *The New Yorker*, November 29, 1941; see E64; it was published earlier in *Hotel Splendide*; see A18.

Note: The second printing measures 21.1 x 14.1 cm. and is bound in lime green cloth-covered boards stamped in dark green. *The verso of title leaf reads*: Second Printing November 1946.

ILLUSTRATIONS: Excluding the endpapers and the contents and title-leaf drawings, there are 100 black drawings by the author.

COPY EXAMINED: MP.

b. Swiss edition ([1947]):

TITLE PAGE: In black: Ludwig Bemelmans | Hotel Splendid | a black drawing of a waiter burdened with flowers, and a little dog | Alfred Scherz Verlag Bern

PAGINATION: [1] - 288 pp., 1 blank leaf; endpapers. 21 x 13.9 cm.

COVERINGS: Gold linen-weave cloth-covered boards stamped in front with author and title in gold and with eight golden stars, and on spine, in gold: Ludwig | Bemel- | mans | - | Hotel | Splendid and at base, P. S. White. Dust jacket printed in red, black and yellow.

PUBLISHED: Fall 1947 at Swiss Fr 13,50. The number of sets of sheets printed cannot be determined, as the publisher's records are lost. On *verso of title leaf*, page [4]: Aus dem Englischen übertragen von Viktoria Vonderau. 1. Auflage 1947. Copyright 1947 by Alfred Scherz Verlag Bern. Printed in Switzerland by Rösch, Vogt & Co., Bern. *Half-title* on page [1].

Note: Though the title leaf suggests this is an edition in German of A18, *Hotel Splendide*, the actual contents show instead that it is an edition of A17, *Hotel Bemelmans*; see as well A17c. This book is not the same as *Hotel Splendide*, A18f, published in English by Alfred Scherz in 1945.

CONTENTS (INHALTSVERZEICHNIS) on page [5]: Ich bin in einem Hotel geboren, 7; Monsieur Victor vom Hotel Splendid, 28; Der Kellner der Tiere, 37; Trauben für Monsieur Cape, 45; Kunst im Splendid, 58; Die verlorene Mandoline, 67; Herr Sigsag sticht in See, 82; Aktklasse, 99; Der tapfere Commis, 110; Tiere im Splendid, 116; Keinerlei Mühe, 120; Wenn Sie kein Narr sind, 132; Die Affäre, 146; Debut, 159; Aschenbrödel und St. Nikolaus, 175; Der Postmeister von Przemysl, 185; Kalakobé, 191; Kotillon, 199; Der Hispano, 206; Der Zauberer erfindet einen neuen Trick, 213; Der Heimwehkranke Chasseur, 221; Mein Kammerdiener Lustgarten, 231; Mespoulets Beförderung, 243; Otto Kahns Zylinder, 258; Eine Nacht in Granada, 268; Der Mörder des Splendid, 274.

ILLUSTRATIONS: As in A17a.

COPY EXAMINED: Mrs. Madeleine Bemelmans.

c. German edition ([1955]):

TITLE PAGE: In black: Ludwig Bemelmans | Hotel Splendid | Roman | Kiepenheuer & Witsch | Koln • Berlin

PAGINATION: [1] - [294] pp., 1 blank leaf; endpapers. 20.6 x 12.4 cm.

COVERINGS: Red linen-weave cloth-covered boards stamped on front with a black figure of a waiter balancing a steaming dish upon a tray and with signature of author in yellow. Spine is stamped with a yellow sticker printed in red: Ludwig | Bemelmans | a rule | Hotel | Splendid. Top edges stained yellow. Red, black and yellow dust jacket printed in yellow.

PUBLISHED: 1955 at DM 14,80. 4,000 sets of sheets printed. On *verso of title leaf*, page [6]: Titel der englischen Originalausgabe: Hotel Splendid * Deutsch von Viktoria Vonderau Illustrationen: Ludwig Bemelmans Schutzumschlag: Werner Labbe Gesamtherstellung: Raiffeisendruckerei G. m.b.H. Neuwied am Rhein Printed in Germany. *Colophon* on page [1]: a basket of vines. *Half-title* on page [3]. Endpapers plain.

* There is no table of contents in the book. Though the verso of the title leaf suggests this is a German edition of A18, *Hotel Splendide*, the actual contents would suggest instead that it is a German edition of A17, *Hotel Bemelmans*; however, "Herr Otto Brauhaus," "Easy Money," "Dinner Out," "Seven Hundred Brides," "Improved Jewish Wedding," "Japanese Evening," "The Ballet Visits the Magician," "The New Suit," "Teddy," "The Dreams of the Magician," and "A Night in Granada," all from the first edition, A17a, are here omitted.

ILLUSTRATIONS: There are 57 black drawings by the author.

COPY EXAMINED: MP.

d. British edition ([1956]):

TITLE PAGE: In black: Hotel | Bemelmans | By | Ludwig | Bemelmans | a black drawing of a busboy with a mammoth bouquet and a small dog | Hamish Hamilton | London

PAGINATION: 2 blank leaves, [1] - [262] pp., 2 blank leaves; endpapers. 21.7 x 13.8 cm.

COVERINGS: Aqua cloth-covered boards plain on front and stamped on spine, in red: Hotel Bemelmans [three stars] Ludwig | Bemelmans; at base: colophon. Red and turquoise dust jacket printed with a black illustration of a chef decorating a cake and with author and title in white.

PUBLISHED: May 24, 1956 at l6s. Number of sets of sheets printed cannot be determined, as the publisher cannot retrieve old records from storage. On *verso of title leaf*, page [4]: First published in Great Britain 1956 by Hamish Hamilton Ltd 90 Great Russell Street London WCI Portions of this book are from the author's earlier volumes: *Life Class, Hotel Splendide, Small Beer,* and *I Love You, I Love You, I Love You.* Printed in Great Britain by Western Printing Services Limited, Bristol *Half-title* on page [1]. *Second half-title* on page [7]. *Other books by the author* on page [2], listing twelve titles. Endpapers plain.

CONTENTS on page 5, with a black drawing of a chef at work: 1. I Was Born in a Hotel, 9; 2. Monsieur Victor of the Splendide, 29; 3. The Animal Waiter, 37; 4. Grapes for Monsieur Cape, 44; 5. Herr Otto Brauhaus, 56; 6. Mr. Sigsag Goes to Sea, 63; 7. Life Class, 79; 8. The Brave Commis, 89; 9. No Trouble at All, 95; 10. Easy Money, 107; 11. If You're Not a Fool, 116; 12. Coming Out, 128; 13. Cinderella and Santa Claus, 142; 14. The Ballet Visits the Magician, 151; 15. Kalakobé, 159; 16. The Hispano, 161; 17. The Magician Does a New Trick, 174; 18. My Valet Lustgarten, 181; 19. The New Suit, 192; 20. Teddy, 205; 21. Mespoulet's Promotion, 217; 22. Otto Kahn's Top Hat, 231; 23. A Night in Granada, 242; 24. The Murderer of the Splendide, 248.

ILLUSTRATIONS: Excluding the title-leaf and contents drawings, there are 71 black drawings by the author.

COPY EXAMINED: MP.

e. Paperback edition ([c.1960]):

A paper edition of *Hotel Bemelmans* was published at $1.49 in the late 1950s or early 1960s, with a 1948 copyright, by Grosset & Dunlap, New York. It has not been possible to find a copy for examination, or to learn anything about the exact publication date or number of sets of sheets printed, since the publisher's records have been lost.

A18. Hotel Splendide [1941]

a. First edition:

TITLE PAGE: In black: Hotel | in cross-hatched black: Splendide | on a swatch of pink, a black drawing of a bowing waiter | in black: Ludwig Bemelmans | 1941 | The Viking Press • New York

PAGINATION: [1] - 192 pp.; endpapers. 21.3 x 14.4 cm.

COVERINGS: Gray cloth-covered boards stamped on front in blue with a figure of a bowing waiter and printed on spine, in blue, Hotel | Splendide | Bemelmans | at base: The | Viking | Press. Top, front and bottom edges stained pink. Teal dust jacket with gold fleurs-de-lys and a pink boar's head, printed in white.

PUBLISHED: December 1, 1941 at $2.50. 17,000 sets of sheets printed; 16,695 copies bound. On *verso of title leaf,* page [4]: Published December 1, 1941 Printed in the United States of America. *Acknowledgment* on page [4]: Some of this material first appeared in *The New Yorker,* to which grateful acknowledgment is made. *Half-title* on page [1] with the text, "By the author of The Donkey Inside, Small Beer, Life Class, My War with The United States". *Second half-title* on page [7] with pink crown. Pink endpapers printed with scrubwomen in white and blue, drawn by the author.

CONTENTS on page [5]: 1. The Animal Waiter, 9; 2. Art at The Hotel Splendide, 19; 3. The Lost Mandolin, 31; 4. Easy Money, 47; 5. Kalakobé, 57; 6. A Night in Granada, 67; 7. The Hispano, 75; 8. The Homesick Bus Boy, 83; 9. The New Suit, 95; 10. The Ballet Visits The Magician, 111; 11. The Magician Does A New Trick, 121; 12.

The Dreams of The Magician, 131; 13. My Valet Lustgarten, 143; 14. The Banquet, 157; 15. The Murderer of The Splendide, 175.

"The Animal Waiter" is here reprinted from *The New Yorker,* May 11, 1940, where it was published as "Mespoulets of the Splendide;" see E35. "Art at The Hotel Splendide" is here reprinted from *The New Yorker,* June 1, 1940; see E36. "The Lost Mandolin" is here reprinted from *The New Yorker,* July 12, 1941, where it was published as "The Lost Mandolin of the Splendide;" see E59. "Easy Money" is here reprinted from *The New Yorker,* September 14, 1940, where it was published as "Easy Money at the Splendide;" see E43. "A Night in Granada" is here reprinted from *The New Yorker,* December 21, 1940, where it was published as "The Splendide's Night in Granada;" see E48. "The Hispano" is here reprinted from *The New Yorker,* March 22, 1941, where it was published as "The Splendide's Hispano;" see E52. "The Homesick Bus Boy" is here reprinted from *The New Yorker,* November 9, 1940, where it was published as "The Homesick Bus Boy of the Splendide;" see E46. "The Ballet Visits The Magician" is here reprinted from *The New Yorker,* July 6, 1940, where it was published as "The Ballet Visits the Splendide's Magician;" see E39. "The Magician Does A New Trick" is here reprinted from *The New Yorker,* July 27, 1940, where it was published as "The Splendide's Magician Does a New Trick;" see E40. "My Valet Lustgarten" is here reprinted from *The New*

Yorker, October 11, 1941, where it was published as "The Valet of the Splendide;" see E62. "The Banquet" is here reprinted from *The New Yorker,* January 24, 1942, where it was published as "The Splendide's Meringue Glacée;" see E66. "The Murderer of The Splendide" is here reprinted from *The New Yorker,* November 29, 1941; see E64.

ILLUSTRATIONS: Exclusive of the endpapers, the title-page drawing, and the figure upon the second half-title, there are 15 black and pink drawings by the author at the heads of the chapters.

COPY EXAMINED: MP.

a (bis). Limited deluxe edition ([1941]):

TITLE PAGE: In black: Hotel | in cross-hatched black: Splendide | on a swatch of pink, a black drawing of a bowing waiter | in black: Ludwig Bemelmans | 1941 | The Viking Press • New York

PAGINATION: 1 leaf, [1] - 192 pp.; endpapers. 21.2 x 14.4 cm.

COVERINGS: Gold, green and rose colored drapery-covered boards with a black sticker on spine printed in gold, between two rules: Bemelmans | Hotel | Splendide | Viking. Top, front and bottom edges stained pink. No dust jacket.

PUBLISHED: December 1, 1941 at $6.50. 305 copies specially bound from a printing of 17,000

sets of sheets. *Verso of title leaf, contents, acknowledgment, half-titles* and *illustrations* as in A18a, with first half-title on the recto of the first leaf. Page [1] is specially printed, as follows: [In pink:] Of the First Edition | There have been bound | in the draperies of a famous New York hotel | and signed by the author | two hundred and forty-five | numbered copies for sale and | sixty copies for private distribution | this copy is | [number] | [signature]. Endpapers as in A18a.

COPY EXAMINED: MP.

b. British edition ([1942]):

TITLE PAGE: In black: Hotel | Splendide | on a swatch of pink, a black drawing of a bowing waiter | in black: Ludwig Bemelmans | 1942 | Hamish Hamilton • London

PAGINATION: [1] - 192 pp.; endpapers. 18.5 x 12.3 cm.

COVERINGS: Royal blue cloth-covered boards stamped on front in gold with a figure of a waiter bowing; on spine: Hotel | Splendide | Ludwig | Bemelmans | at base: colophon | Hamish | Hamilton. Teal dust jacket with gold fleurs-de-lys and pink boar's head, printed in white.

PUBLISHED: November, 1942 at 7s 6d. Number of sets of sheets printed cannot be determined, as the publisher cannot withdraw old records from storage. On *verso of title leaf:* First published—November 1942 Bishop and Sons Ltd., Printers, Edinburgh. *Half-title* on page [1], with a pink crown. *Acknowledgment* on page [5]: Some of this material first appeared in *The New Yorker*, to which grateful acknowledgment is made. Pink endpapers with drawings of scrub-women in white and blue by the author.

CONTENTS on page [7]: As in A18a.

ILLUSTRATIONS: Excluding the endpapers, title drawing and half-title drawing, there are 15 black and pink illustrations by the author on the chapter heads.

COPY EXAMINED: December, 1942 reprint examined. The British Library, Great Russell Street, London.

c. Swedish edition ([1943]):

TITLE PAGE: In black: Hotell Splendide | Av Ludwig Bemelmans | Till svenska av Hilda Holmberg | a drawing of a bowing waiter | Hugo Gebers Förlag, Stockholm

PAGINATION: [1] - [238] pp.; endpapers. 19.3 x 12.5 cm.

COVERINGS: White paper covers printed in black and orange with a drawing of a bowing waiter on front; on spine: seven black rules | three orange stars | seven black rules | Ludwig | Bemelmans | Hotell | Splendide | seven black rules | three orange stars | seven black rules. No dust jacket.

PUBLISHED: 1943 at 6 kr 75 öre. Number of sets of sheets printed cannot be determined, as the publisher does not communicate. On *verso of*

title leaf, page [4]: Originals titel Hotel Splendide. Almqvist & Wiksells Boktryckeri Aktiebolag Uppsala 1943. *Half-title* on page [1], with colophon. Endpapers plain.

CONTENTS (INNEHÅLL) on page [238]: Den djurränlige kyparen, 5; Konst på hotell Splendide, 17; Den förlorade mandolinen, 32; Lättförtjänta pengar, 52; Kalakobé, 65; En natt i Granada, 78; Hispanon, 87; Smörgånissens hemlängtan, 97; Den nya kostymen, 111; Baletten på visit hos illusionisten, 130; Illusionistens nya trick, 142; Illusionistens drömmar, 153; Min betjänt Lustgarten, 168; Kalaset, 186; Mördaren på Splendide, 214.

ILLUSTRATIONS: One black drawing by the author appears at the head of each chapter.

COPY EXAMINED: Mrs. Madeleine Bemelmans.

d. Reprint of cheap edition ([1944]):

TITLE PAGE: In black: Hotel | in cross-hatched black: Splendide | a black drawing of a bowing waiter | in black: Ludwig Bemelmans | The Sun Dial Press • Garden City, N.Y.

PAGINATION: [1] - 192 pp.; endpapers. 20 x 14 cm.

COVERINGS: Gray linen-weave cloth-covered boards stamped on front in navy with a figure of a bowing waiter and printed on spine, in navy, Hotel | Splen- | dide | Bemelmans | at base: Sun

Dial | Press. Top edges stained black. Teal dust jacket with gold fleurs-de-lys and a pink boar's head, printed in white. (*Note:* There is a variant binding with gray vinyl-covered boards.)

PUBLISHED: February 21, 1944 at $1.00. 7,000 sets of sheets printed. On *verso of title leaf,* page [4]: 1944 The Sun Dial Press. *Acknowledgment, contents, first half-title* as in A18a. *Second half-title* on page [7] without crown. Endpapers as in A18a.

ILLUSTRATIONS: Aside from the endpapers and the title drawing, there are 15 black illustrations by the author on the chapter heads.

COPY EXAMINED: MP.

e. Military edition ([1945]):

TITLE PAGE: Within a black rectangle divided horizontally: at left: Published by Arrangement with | The Viking Press, Inc., New York | Some of this material first appeared | in *The New Yorker* | Copyright, 1940, 1941, by | Ludwig Bemelmans; at right: Hotel | Splendide | by | Ludwig Bemelmans | Editions for the Armed Services, Inc. | A non-profit organization established by | The Council on Books in Wartime, New York

PAGINATION: [1] - [192] pp. 9.7 x 13.8 cm.

COVERINGS: Teal blue paper covers printed in black, yellow, and red.

PUBLISHED, most likely in February, 1945. Distributed free abroad to members of the Armed Services and also within the United States to servicemen. Probably between 50,000 and 155,000 sets of sheets printed. On *verso of title leaf,* page [2]: Manufactured in the United States of America.

This is Editions for the Armed Services Book No. P-4.

CONTENTS on page [3]: 1. The Animal Waiter, 5; 2. Art at The Hotel Splendide, 14; 3. The Lost Mandolin, 26; 4. Easy Money, 42; 5. Kalakobé, 53; 6. A Night in Granada, 63; 7. The Hispano, 70; 8. The Homesick Bus Boy, 78; 9. The New Suit, 90; 10. The Ballet Visits The Magician, 106; 11. The Magician Does A New Trick, 116; 12. The Dreams of The Magician, 125; 13. My Valet Lustgarten, 137; 14. The Banquet, 153; 15. The Murderer of The Splendide, 171.

There are no illustrations.

COPY EXAMINED: Mrs. Madeleine Bemelmans.

f. Swiss edition ([1945]):

TITLE PAGE: In black: Ludwig Bemelmans | Hotel Splendide | colophon: a black bird in profile with the word "Phoenix" beneath | The Scherz Phoenix Books | Alfred Scherz Publishers | Berne Switzerland

PAGINATION: [1] - 206 pp., 1 blank leaf. 17.5 x 10.5 cm.

COVERINGS: Stiff teal blue paper covers printed on front with a black 35 in a white oval;

within an open white book, author and title in black; the publisher at top and bottom in white upon a black ribbon. Spine not seen. No dust jacket.

This is Phoenix Books No. 35.

PUBLISHED: 1945 at an unknown price. The exact publication date, price and number of sets of sheets printed is not likely to be determinable. The publisher has no records of this book. On *verso of title leaf*, page [4]: First Edition Copyright 1945 by Alfred Scherz Publishers, Berne (Switzerland) Printed in Switzerland (Effingerhof, Brugg). *Half-title* on page [1]: Scherz Phoenix Books | Volume 35 | Ludwig Bemelmans | Hotel Splendide.

Note: This book is not the same as A17b, *Hotel Splendid*, published in 1947 by Alfred Scherz.

CONTENTS on page [5]: 1. The Animal Waiter, 7; 2. Art at the Hotel Splendide, 17; 3. The Lost Mandolin, 31; 4. Easy Money, 49; 5. Kalakobé, 61; 6. A Night in Granada, 73; 7. The Hispano, 81; 8. The Homesick Bus Boy, 89; 9. The New Suit, 101; 10. The Ballet Visits the Magician, 117; 11. The Magician Does a New Trick, 127; 12. The Dreams of the Magician, 137; 13. My Valet Lustgarten, 149; 14. The Banquet, 165; 15. The Murderer of the Splendide, 187.

ILLUSTRATIONS: As in A18a, but the illustrations are all black.

COPY EXAMINED: Università Degli Studi di Venezia.

g. Second American paperback edition ([1947]):

TITLE PAGE: In black: Hotel Splendide | By Ludwig Bemelmans | a black drawing of a waiter bowing | Penguin Books, Inc • New York

PAGINATION: 3 leaves, 1 - 136 pp., 1 leaf. 18 x 10.8 cm.

COVERINGS: Full-color paper cover showing mustachioed waiter serving boar's head in a crown. Top, front and bottom edges stained pink. No dust jacket.

This is Penguin No. 637.

PUBLISHED: August 1947 at $0.25. Number of sets of sheets printed cannot be determined, as the publisher's records have been lost. On *verso of title leaf:* Published by Penguin Books, Inc., and Reprinted by Arrangement with The Viking Press First Penguin Books Edition, August, 1947. A *note about the book* on recto of first leaf. *List of Penguin books* on concluding leaf.

CONTENTS on third leaf: 1. The Animal Waiter, 1; 2. Art At the Hotel Splendide, 8; 3. The Lost Mandolin, 17; 4. Easy Money, 29; 5. Kalakobé, 37; 6. A Night in Granada, 45; 7. The Hispano, 50; 8. The Homesick Bus Boy, 56; 9. The New Suit, 64; 10. The Ballet Visits the Magician, 75; 11. The Magician Does a New Trick, 82; 12. The Dreams of the Magician, 89; 13. My Valet Lustgarten, 98; 14. The Banquet, 109; 15. The Murderer of the Splendide, 123.

ILLUSTRATIONS: Aside from the title drawing, there are 15 black drawings by the author at the chapter heads.

COPY EXAMINED: MP.

h. Danish edition ([1947]):

TITLE PAGE: In black: Ludwig Bemelmans | Hotel Splendide | Illustreret af Forfatteren | København 1947 | beneath a black rule: Thaning & Appels Forlag

PAGINATION: [1] - [200] pp. 17.7 x 11.8 cm.

COVERINGS: Yellow cardboard covers printed on front in blue with a drawing (from page [7]); in red: title, author and publisher; on back in blue: publisher's blurb. Printed in red on spine: Ludwig | Bemelmans | Hotel | Splendide and at base Thaning | & Appel. Edges trimmed and unstained. Publisher's address is given at the bottom of the back cover: Bogtrykkeriet Antikva A/S - København V.

PUBLISHED: 1947 at Dkr 7,75. Precise publication date and number of sets of sheets printed cannot be determined, as the publisher's records have been lost. On *verso of title leaf:* Oversat fra Amerikansk efter "Hotel Splendide" af Povl Frejlev. *Half-title* on page [1].

CONTENTS (INDHOLD) on page [5]: 1. Den dyrevenlige Tjener, 7; 2. Kunsten paa Hotel Splendide, 17; 3. Den forsvundne Mandolin, 29; 4. Finanslivet paa Hotel Splendide, 45; 5. Kalakobe, 55; 6. En Nat i Granada, 65; 7. Hispano'en, 73; 8. Hjemve, 81; 9. Det nye Tøj, 91; 10. Balletbesøg hos Troldmanden, 105; 11. Troldmandens nye Hundekunster, 115; 12. Troldmandens Drømme, 125; 13. Min Kammertjener Lustgarten, 137; 14. Døden i den elektriske Stol, 151; 15. Banketten, 165; 16. Morderen paa Hotel Splendide, 183.

"Døden I den Elektriske Stol" is here reprinted from *I Love You. I Love You. I Love You.* A21, where it appears as "Sweet Death in the Electric Chair."

ILLUSTRATIONS: There are 16 black illustrations by the author, on the chapter heads.

COPY EXAMINED: Library of Congress, Washngton, D.C.

i. British paperback edition ([1948]):

TITLE PAGE: In black: Hotel | Splendide | by Ludwig Bemelmans | a black drawing of a bowing waiter | Penguin Books | in Association with | Hamish Hamilton

PAGINATION: [1] - 142 pp., 1 leaf. 18 x 11 cm.

COVERINGS: Sky blue and white paper covers printed in black and blue. Printed on spine in black upon white: Hotel Splendide; in black upon blue: Ludwig Bemelmans; at base: colophon | 670. No dust jacket.

PUBLISHED: December 1948 at 1s 6d. The average British Penguin print run for the period was 50,000. On *verso of title leaf:* First published 1942 Published in Penguin Books 1948 Made and printed in Great Britain for Penguin Books Ltd, Harmondsworth, Middlesex by Richard Clay and Company, Ltd., Bungay, Suffolk. *Acknowledgment* on verso of title leaf: Some of this material first appeared in *The New Yorker*, to which grateful acknowledgement is made. *Half-title* on page [1]: Penguin Books | 670 | Hotel Splendide | by Ludwig Bemelmans | colophon. A *note about the book* appears on the inside of the front cover. The pages of the last leaf are printed with publisher's advertisements.

CONTENTS on page [5]: 1. The Animal Waiter, 7; 2. Art at the Hotel Splendide, 14; 3. The Lost Mandolin, 23; 4. Easy Money, 35; 5. Kalakobé, 43; 6. A Night in Granada, 51; 7. The Hispano, 56; 8. The Homesick Bus Boy, 62; 9. The New Suit, 70; 10. The Ballet Visits the Magician, 82; 11. The Magician Does a New Trick, 89; 12. The Dreams of the Magician, 96; 13. My Valet Lustgarten, 105; 14. The Banquet, 116; 15. The Murderer of the Splendide, 129.

ILLUSTRATIONS: Exclusive of the title drawing, there are 15 black illustrations by the author at the chapter heads.

COPY EXAMINED: MP.

j. Argentinian edition ([1948]):

Hotel Splendide was published in 1948 by Editorial Sudamericana of Buenos Aires, at R 5,50. The book had 233 pages and was in a Spanish translation by León Mirlas. As the publisher and the publisher's records have vanished, it is not possible to determine the exact publication date and the number of sets of sheets printed. A copy of this edition has not been found for examination.

k. First Italian edition ([1956]):

Hotel Splendide was published as *Clienti in Marsina* by Arnoldo Mondadori Editore of Verona in January 1956 at 200 Lire. On *verso of title page:* Unica traduzione autorizzata dall'americano di Letizia Fuchs Vidotto. The book was No. 42 of the Girasole Biblioteca Economica Mondadori series. The publisher's records are incomplete, and so the number of sets of sheets printed cannot be determined. A copy of this edition has unfortunately not been found for examination.

l. German edition ([1957]):

TITLE PAGE: In black: Ludwig Bemelmans | Hotel Splendid | Roman | a rule | Ullstein Bücher
PAGINATION: [1] - [200] pp. 17.7 x 11.6 cm.
COVERINGS: Green and purple paper covers printed with author and title in green and black within a yellow rectangle on front; in black upon green: 147 | in white and black: colophon | Ludwig Bemelmans • Hotel Splendid. No dust jacket.
This is Ullstein Buch Nr. 147.
PUBLISHED: 1957 at DM 1,90. Number of sets of sheets printed cannot be determined, as the publisher's records have been lost. On *verso of*

title leaf, page [4]: Ullstein Buch Nr. 147. Übersetzt von Viktoria Vonderau. Printed in Germany, West-Berlin 1957. *Colophon* on page [1].

There are no illustrations.

COPY EXAMINED: Mrs. Ludwig Bemelmans.

m. Second Italian edition ([1962]):

TITLE PAGE: In black: Ludwig Bemelmans | Clienti | in Marsina | Traduzione di Letizia Fuchs Vidotto | Arnoldo Mondadori Editore.

PAGINATION: [1] - [208] pp., 1 blank leaf. 18.5 x 10.5 cm.

COVERINGS: Glossy paper cover printed on front with a full-color illustration by the author of a waiter holding a silver dish and at top: fra sguatteri e maggiordorni; under picture: Ludwig Bemelmans | Clienti | in Marsina | edizione integrale | a thick sky blue rule broken with a solid orange circle in which Lire | 300 appears in black | Mondadori. Spine not seen. No dust jacket.

This book is I Libri del pavone n. 316.

PUBLISHED: December 1962 at 300 Lire. The number of sets of sheets printed cannot be determined, as the publisher's records are lost. On *verso of title leaf,* page [4]: Tutti i diritti riservati © Arnoldo Mondadori Editore 1956 Titolo Dell'Opera originale Hotel Splendide i edizione B.E.M. Gennaio 1956 I Edizione i Libri Del Pavone Dicembre 1962. *Half-title* on page [1]: I Libri Del Pavone volume 316. With publisher's colophon at bottom. On *verso of cover*: a printed description of the book and a brief note about the author, all in Italian. On page [208]: Questo volume è stato impresso nel mese di Dicembre dell'anno MCMLXII nelle Officine Grafiche Veronesi dell'Editore Arnaldo Mondadori. Stampato in Italia.

ILLUSTRATIONS: There are no illustrations in this book.

COPY EXAMINED: Biblioteca Communale di Milano Palazzo Sormani.

n. Third American paperback edition ([1963]):

TITLE PAGE: In black: Hotel | Splendide | a black drawing of a waiter bowing | Ludwig Bemelmans | The Viking Press • New York

PAGINATION: [1] - 192 pp. 19.8 x 12.7 cm.

COVERINGS: Purple paper covers with gold fleurs-de-lys and a pink boar's head, printed in white. No dust jacket.

This is Compass Books No. C129.

PUBLISHED: The week of May 27, 1963 at $1.35. Number of sets of sheets printed cannot be determined, as the publisher's records have been lost. On *verso of title leaf,* page [4]: Compass Books Edition Issued in 1963 by The Viking Press, Inc. Several of the stories in this book appeared originally in *The New Yorker* Printed in the U.S.A. by The Murray Printing Co. *Half-title* on page [7]. *Other books by the author* on page [1], listing twenty-four titles published by The Viking Press.

CONTENTS on page [5]: As in A18a.

ILLUSTRATIONS: As in A18a.

COPY EXAMINED: MP.

A19. How to Have Europe All to Yourself [1960]

TITLE PAGE: In black: How to have | Europe | all to (in gray:) Your | in black and gray: a drawing of a bus boy saluting | in black: Self | European Travel Commission | 1960

PAGINATION: Unpaged. 16 leaves. 25.5 x 20 cm.

COVERINGS: Full-color paper covers printed on front with title in red and author in purple and an illustration showing the staff of a palm-studded hotel; and on back with a list of European Travel Commission Representatives in the U.S.

PUBLISHED: 1960 at an unknown price. Number of sets of sheets printed cannot be determined, as the publisher and the publisher's records cannot be found. *Introduction* by the author, signed with his initials; and the text, "In Europe, | January 23, 1960" on the verso of title leaf and facing page.

ILLUSTRATIONS: Excluding the title-leaf drawing, there are 22 black drawings by the author.

COPY EXAMINED: MP.

A20. How to Travel Incognito [1952]

a. First edition:

TITLE PAGE: In black: Ludwig Bemelmans | How to | Travel Incognito | Illustrated by The Author | a black drawing of three bags | Little, Brown and Company • Boston

PAGINATION: 4 leaves, [1] - 244 pp., 1 leaf, 1 blank leaf; endpapers. 19.8 x 13.3 cm.

COVERINGS: Turquoise cloth-covered boards stamped on front in navy with a drawing of three bags (by the author), and on spine, in navy: How | to Travel | Incognito | Bemelmans | at base: Little, Brown. Full-color dust jacket printed in red and turquoise.

PUBLISHED: April 29, 1952 at $3.00. 15,000 sets of sheets printed, 14,985 copies bound. On *verso of title leaf:* First Edition printed in The United States of America. *Acknowledgment* on verso of title leaf: The author wishes to thank Ted Patrick, editor of *Holiday*, in whose pages part of this story was printed. *Half-title* on recto of first leaf. *Second half-title* on page [1]. *Dedication* on recto of third leaf set within a black drawing of a table set for two with wine and wine glasses, the Eiffel Tower and a dog, beneath two trees: *To | Armand de la Rochefoucault | Who said to me one evening | as we sat in a small tavern | which is called the*

| *Little Nest of St. Cucuface,* | *and which is located in the* | *Forest of St. Cloud,* | *outside of Paris:* | *"Why don't you write* | *something amusing, to cheer up* | *the sorry world."* White endpapers printed with a turquoise drawing of the Seine at the Pont Alexandre III.

CONTENTS on recto of fourth leaf: 1. In a First-Class Compartment, 3; 2. How to Be a Prince, 30; 3. Madame l'Ambassadrice, 52; 4. The Perfect Marriage, 82; 5. The Curé de St. Cucugnan, 108; 6. The Château de Plaisir, 121; 7. The Postponed Wedding, 136; 8. Consuelo, 149; 9. Escapade, 161; 10. Masquerade, 172; 11. The Calendar Man, 193; 12. A Good Morning, a Quiet Evening, 210.

"How to Be a Prince" is here reprinted from *Holiday*, April 1951; see E132. "Madame l'Ambassadrice" is here reprinted from *Holiday*, May 1951, where it was published as "Madame Takes the Count;" see E134. "The Perfect Marriage" is here reprinted from *Holiday*, June 1951; see E135. "Masquerade" is here reprinted from *Holiday*, July 1951, where it appeared as "Mad Masquerade;" see E136.

ILLUSTRATIONS: Excluding the endpapers, the title leaf drawing and the drawing with the dedication, there are 48 black drawings by the author.

COPY EXAMINED: MP.

b. British edition ([1952]):

TITLE PAGE: In black: Ludwig Bemelmans | How to | Travel Incognito | Illustrated by The Author | a black drawing of three bags | Hamish Hamilton

PAGINATION: 3 leaves, [1] - 245 pp., 2 blank leaves; endpapers. 19.8 x 13.5 cm.

COVERINGS: Green linen-weave cloth-covered boards plain on front, stamped on spine, in silver: How to | Travel | Incognito | Ludwig | Bemelmans | at base: colophon. Full-color dust jacket printed in red and turquoise.

PUBLISHED: May 20, 1952 at 12s 6d. Number of sets of sheets printed cannot be determined, as the publisher cannot retrieve old records from storage. On *verso of title leaf:* First published in Great Britain 1952 by Hamish Hamilton Ltd. 90 Great Russell Street, London, W.C.I Printed in Great Britain by Lowe and Brydone (Printers) Limited, London, N.W.10. *Half-title* on recto of first leaf. *Dedication* on recto of third leaf: as in A20a. Endpapers plain.

CONTENTS on page [1]: As in A20a.

ILLUSTRATIONS: As in A20a.

COPY EXAMINED: MP.

c. First German edition ([1953]):

TITLE PAGE: In black: Ludwig Bemelmans | a long rule | « Incognito » | durch Frankreich und Paris | a shortened rule | Eine vergnügte Geschichte | mit 52 Zeichnungen | des Autors | a black drawing of three bags | Bei Wolfgang Krüger | Hamburg

PAGINATION: [1] - [248] pp., 1 leaf, 1 blank leaf; endpapers. 19.1 x 11.9 cm.

COVERINGS: Cream-colored linen-weave cloth-covered boards stamped on front with title in red, and on spine in blue: Bemelmans / in red: »Incognito«; at base, in red and blue: colophon. Top edges stained blue. Full-color dust-jacket printed in red and black.

PUBLISHED: 1953 at DM 9,80. Number of sets of sheets printed cannot be determined, as the publisher's records cannot be located. On *verso of title leaf*, page [4]: Titel der englischen Original-Ausgabe How to travel incognito Berechtigte Ubertragung von Richard Moering und Wolfgang Krüger Printed in Germany 1953. *Half-title* on page [1]. *Dedication* on page [5], set within a black drawing of a table set for two with wine and wine glasses, the Eiffel Tower and a dog, beneath two trees: Für Àrmand de la Rochefoucault mit dem ich eines Abends | in der kleinen Taverne im | Walde von St. Cloud sass, die | sich «Schlupfwinkel von | St. Cucuface» nennt, und der | plötzlich zu mir sagte: | «Schreiben Sie doch mal was | Amüsantes und Erfrischendes | um unsere triste Welt heute | zu erheitern!» *Printer's colophon* on verso of second last leaf: Satz und Druck: Poeschel & Schulz-Schomburgk, Eschwege/Werra Einbände: Klemme & Bleimund, Bielefeld Ent-

würfe für Umschlag und Einband: Hans Hermann Hagedorn. Endpapers plain.

CONTENTS (INHALTSVERZEICHNIS) on page [7]: 1. In einem Abtail I. Klasse, 9; 2. Wie man Prinz wird, 37; 3. Madame l'Ambassadrice, 59; 4. Die vollkommene Ehe, 88; 5. Der Pfarrer von St. Cucugnan, 114; 6. Das Château de Plaisir, 125; 7. Die verschobene Hochzeit, 140; 8. Consuelo, 154; 9. Entführung, 166; 10. Maskerade, 177; 11. Der Kalendermann, 197; 12. Ein schöner Morgen und ein ruhiger Abend, 214.

ILLUSTRATIONS: Aside from the title-leaf and dedication drawings, there are 48 black drawings by the author.

COPY EXAMINED: MP.

d. German paperback edition ([1957]):

TITLE PAGE: In black: Ludwig Bemelmans | << Incognito >> | durch Frankreich | und Paris | Eine vergnügte Geschichte | mit 50 Zeichnungen | des Autors | a black drawing of luggage | colophon |

PAGINATION: [1] - [58] pp. 19 x 11.4 cm.

COVERINGS: Yellow paper covers printed in red, brown and black with an illustration of a man sleeping on a train and the author and title in black. The spine is yellow and printed in white: Ludwig Bemelmans • Incognito 235 and at base ro | ro | ro. No dust jacket.

This is rororo Taschenbuch Nr. 235.

PUBLISHED: October, 1957 at DM 1,50. 50,000 sets of sheets printed, under licence from Wolfgang Krüger Verlag. On *verso of title leaf*, page [4]: Titel der englischen Originalausgabe << How to Travel Incognito >>. Berechtigte Übertragung von Richard Moering und Wolfgang Krüger. rororo Taschenbuch Ausgabe veröffentlicht im Oktober 1957. Ungekürzte Ausgabe. Printed in Germany. *Colophon* on page [1]. *Note about the author* on page [2]. *Dedication* on page [5]. There is a yellow, black and brown illustration of a bowing waiter on the back cover.

ILLUSTRATIONS: As in A20a.

COPY EXAMINED: Mrs. Madeleine Bemelmans.

e. French edition ([1957]):

TITLE PAGE: In purple: incognito | c. 1957; Upon a blue strip, in black: Ludwig Bemelmans; Upon a yellow strip, in black: traduction | de | Jean Rosenthal

PAGINATION: [i] - [xiv], [1] - [302] pp.; endpapers. 20.5 x 13.2 cm.

COVERINGS: Yellow linen-weave cloth-covered boards stamped on the front with a drawing of a black chair and a suitcase and a white homburg; on the spine, in black: Ludwig Bemelmans; in white: Incognito. No dust jacket.

PUBLISHED: 1957 at FF 9,55. Number of sets of sheets printed cannot be determined, as the publisher will not enter into communication. On page [iv]: © 1957 by le club français du livre. *Half-title* on page [iii]. *Second half-title* on page [v], in purple. The title appears on page [vii]. On page [ii]: vol 216 | romans | colophon. *Third half-title* on page [1], with a blue slip bearing in black the dedication as in A20a. *Préface* on pages [ix] - [xiii] par Marcel Achard. Endpapers are white printed with a magenta drawing of a bed with wallpaper.

COPY EXAMINED: Mrs. Madeleine Bemelmans.

f. Dutch edition ([1959]):

TITLE PAGE: In black: Incognito | of | De Verfijnde Kunst Der | Zelfverheffing | door | Ludwig Bemelmans | a black drawing of suitcases | Met tekeningen van de schrijver | 1959 | Ad. Donker • Rotterdam

PAGINATION: [1] - [234] pp., 1 blank leaf; endpapers. 21.5 x 13.5 cm.

COVERINGS: Sunflower yellow linen-weave cloth-covered boards stamped on front in red with suitcases; on spine, in red: Incognito, of de verfijnde kunst der zelfverheffing; and at base: Ad. Donker. Full-color dust jacket, predominantly yellow, printed in red.

PUBLISHED: Fall, 1959 at 8,90 Fl. 3,000 sets of sheets printed. On *verso of title leaf*, page [4]: Oorspronkelijke titel: How to Travel Incognito. Nederlandse vertaling: J. de Boer-van Strien. © Uitgeversmaatschappij Ad. Donker n.v. 1959. *Half-title* on page [1]. *Dedication* on page [5], within a drawing of a table in the woods, as in A20a: Voor Armand de la Rochefoucault die op een avond in het Bois de Boulogne, even buiten Parijs toen wij in een eethuisje zaten, genaamd ,Het nestje van St. Cucuface', tot mij zei: ,,Waarom schrijf je niet iets leuks, om deze miserabele wereld wat op te fleuren?" Endpapers printed with a yellow drawing of a quai beside the Pont des Arts.

CONTENTS (INHOUD) on page [7]: 1. In een eersteklas coupé, 9; 2. Een cocktail party, 17; 3. Over dienstpersoneel en hoe men in Frankrijk goedkoop kan dineren, 24; 4. Hoe men leeft als een vorst, 35; 5. Mevrouw de Ambassadrice, 55; 6. Het volmaakte huwelijk, 82; 7. De pastoor van St. Cucugnan, 106; 8. Het kasteel Plaisir, 118; 9. Het uitgestelde huwelijk, 132; 10. Consuelo, 145; 11. Escapade, 156; 12. Maskerade, 166; 13. De Kalender-man, 185; 14. Een goede morgen en een rustige avond, 200.

ILLUSTRATIONS: Aside from the title page drawing, the dedication drawing, and the endpapers, there are 48 black drawings by the author.

COPY EXAMINED: Mrs. Madeleine Bemelmans.

g. New American edition (1992):

TITLE PAGE: Spread upon a double-page, in black, at left: Signature, H James H. Heineman New York 1992; at right: How to | Travel | Incognito | between two rules: Volume III in a New Bemelmans Series | a black line drawing of a casbah | Written and | Illustrated by | Ludwig Bemelmans

PAGINATION: 5 leaves, [1] - [196] pp., 1 leaf; endpapers. 21.4 x 14 cm.

COVERINGS: One-third gray linen-weave cloth-covered, and two-thirds flannel gray paper-covered boards; blind-stamped on the front with a drawing of three valises and the author's signature; and stamped on spine, in gold between two rules: Volume | III; above a rule: How to Travel

Incognito; below the rule: Ludwig Bemelmans; at base: H; between two rules: 1992. Front edges not trimmed. Gray and teal green dust jacket printed in teal green, black and white.

PUBLISHED: September 15, 1992 at $23.95. 3,000 sets of sheets printed. On *verso of title* [fourth] *leaf:* © 1952 by Ludwig Bemelmans. Renewed © 1980 by Madeleine Bemelmans and Barbara Bemelmans Marciano All rights reserved This book was first published in 1952 and reflects the writing of the time. First published in this edition in the United States of America in 1992 H James H. Heineman, Inc., 475 Park Avenue, New York, NY 10022. *Half-title* on recto of first leaf, with an illustration of three valises. *Second half-title* on page [1]. *Other titles in this series* on recto of second leaf: Volume I *Father, Dear Father* Volume II *I Love You I Love You I Love You; other books by the author* on recto of second leaf, including eleven titles. On page [196]: Books Forming a Series By and About Ludwig Bemelmans, listing, with ISBN numbers, three novels, *Father, Dear Father, I Love You. I Love You. I Love You* and *How to Travel Incognito*, as well as the present bibliography. Also the text: Other Titles in Preparation. Author's signature and *publisher's blurb* on recto of end leaf. *Printer's colophon* on verso of end leaf (with an illustration of a bowing waiter): "This book was composed in Cochin and Nicolas Cochin Black by The Sarabande Press, New York. It was printed and bound by Arcata Graphics Company, New York on 60# Sebago cream white antique paper. The typography and binding were designed by Beth Tondreau Design, New York." *Dedication* on recto of fourth leaf, as in A20a. Endpapers plain.

CONTENTS on recto of fifth leaf (with an illustration of an ocean liner): 1. In a First-Class Compartment, 3; 2. How to Be a Prince, 25; 3. Madame L'Ambassadrice, 43; 4. The Perfect Marriage, 67; 5. The Curé de St. Cucugnan, 88; 6. The Château de Plaisir, 98; 7. The Postponed Wedding, 110; 8. Consuelo, 120; 9. Escapade, 129; 10. Masquerade, 138; 11. The Calendar Man, 155; 12. A Good Morning, a Quiet Evening, 168.

ILLUSTRATIONS: Aside from the title page drawing, the contents drawing, the half-title drawing, the end-leaf drawing, and the dedication drawing there are 47 black illustrations by the author.

COPY EXAMINED: MP.

A21. I Love You I Love You I Love You [1942]

a. First edition:

TITLE PAGE: In black: I Love You | I Love You | I Love You | Ludwig Bemelmans | New York : The Viking Press : 1942

PAGINATION: [1] - 207 pp.; endpapers. 21.3 x 14.3 cm.

COVERINGS: Yellow linen-weave cloth-covered boards stamped on front in pink with a drawing of a man with a cigarette holding a little girl holding a poodle; on spine, a pink drawing of a little girl | Bemelmans | in yellow, showing through a vertical pink rectangle: I Love | You, | I Love | You, | I LOVE | YOU! | a pink drawing of a butler | at base: The Viking Press. Top edges stained pink. Pink dust jacket printed in black and white.

PUBLISHED: September 4, 1942 at $2.50. 7,500 sets of sheets printed; 7,500 copies bound. On *verso of title leaf*, page [4]: Published in September 1942 Printed in U.S.A. by American Book-Stratford Press. *Acknowledgment* on page [4]: Acknowledgment is made to *Harper's Bazaar*, *The New Yorker*, *Town and Country*, and *Vogue*, in which some of these stories first appeared. *Other books by the author* on page [2], listing five titles, with a black drawing of an angel. Plain endpapers printed with a pink drawing of the West Side Highway.

CONTENTS on page [5], with a black drawing of a gendarme: 1. Souvenir, 9; 2. I Love You, I Love You, I Love You, 27; 3. Star of Hope, 39; 4. Pale Hands, 51; 5. Watch The Birdie, 75; 6. Bride of Berchtesgaden, 97; 7. Chagrin d'Amour, 113; 8. Head-Hunters of the Quito Hills, 125; 9. Vacation, 145; 10. Cher Ami, 161; 11. Camp Nomopo, 175; 12. Sweet Death in the Electric Chair, 191.

"Souvenir" is here reprinted from *Vogue*, June 1, 1942, where it appeared as "Souvenir: Memory of the Normandie, the 'Femme Fatale' of Ships;" see E70. "Head-Hunters of the Quito Hills" is here reprinted from *The New Yorker*, April 12, 1941, where it was published in somewhat different form as "A Reporter at Large: The Head-Hunters of the Quito Hills;" see E55. "Pale Hands" is here reprinted from *The New Yorker*, September 6, 1941, where it appeared as "Pale Hands Beside the Circular Bar;" see E61. "Watch The Birdie" is here reprinted from *The New Yorker*, June 6, 1942; see E71. "I Love You, I Love You, I Love You" is here reprinted from *Vogue*, June 1, 1940; see E38. "Vacation" is here reprinted from *Town & Country*, April 1941; see E54. "Cher Ami" is here reprinted from *Vogue*, October 15, 1941, where it appeared as "Cher Ami: The Servant Problem of Ludwig Bemelmans;" see E63. "Chagrin d'Amour" is here reprinted from *Town & Country*, December 1941, where it appeared as "Le Chagrin d'Amour Est Formidable;" see E65. "Camp Nomopo" is here reprinted from *Town & Country*, July 1942, where it appeared as "Little Girl with a Headache (Camp No Mo Pie);" see E72. "Sweet Death in The Electric Chair" is here reprinted from *Harper's Bazaar*, March 1, 1942; see E67.

ILLUSTRATIONS: In addition to the endpapers, the drawing with the author's list, and the contents drawing, there are 69 black drawings by the author.

COPY EXAMINED: MP.

b. British edition ([1943]):

TITLE PAGE: In black: I Love You | I Love You | I Love You | Ludwig Bemelmans | Hamish Hamilton • London

PAGINATION: [1] - 207 pp.; endpapers. 18.4 x 12.2 cm.

COVERINGS: Royal blue linen-weave cloth-covered boards plain on front, stamped on spine, in gold, within a gold arch: I Love | You | I Love | You | I Love | You | a double rule | Ludwig | Bemel- | mans | at base, within an oval: colophon | Hamish | Hamilton. Blue dust jacket printed in black and white.

PUBLISHED: December 1943 at 7s 6d. Number of sets of sheets printed cannot be determined, as the publisher cannot withdraw old records from storage. On *verso of title leaf*, page [4]: First Published 1943 Printed by Bishop & Sons, Ltd., Nicolson Square, Edinburgh. *Half-title* on page [1]. *Other books by the author* on page [2], with a black drawing of an angel, listing one title. Endpapers as in A21a.

CONTENTS on page [5], with a black drawing of a gendarme: As in A21a.

ILLUSTRATIONS: As in A21a.

COPY EXAMINED: MP.

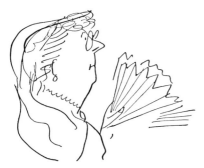

c. Cheap edition ([1945]):

TITLE PAGE: In black: I Love You | I Love You | I Love You | Ludwig Bemelmans | The Sun Dial Press, Garden City, N.Y.

PAGINATION: As in A21a. 19.1 x 13.6 cm.

COVERINGS: Gray vinyl - covered boards stamped on front in magenta as in A21a; and on spine, in magenta, as in A21a with, at base: Sun Dial | Press. Top edges stained pink; front edges untrimmed. Pink dust jacket printed in black and white.

PUBLISHED: February 13, 1945 at $1.00. 10,000 sets of sheets printed. On *verso of title leaf*, page [4]: 1945 The Sun Dial Press. *Other books by the author, contents,* and *illustrations* as in A21a.

COPY EXAMINED: MP.

d. Military edition ([1945]):

TITLE PACE: The title page, within a black rectangle, is divided horizontally. At left: Published by Arrangement with | The Viking Press, Inc., New York | Copyright 1939, 1940, 1941, 1942 | By Ludwig Bemelmans | Manufactured in the United States of America; at right: I Love You | I Love You | I Love You | by | Ludwig Bemelmans | Editions for the Armed Services, Inc. | A non-profit organization established by | The Council on Books in Wartime, New York

PAGINATION: [1] - [128] pp. 9.7 x 14 cm.

COVERINGS: Black paper cover printed in white, yellow, red and blue.

PUBLISHED: Most likely in May, 1945. Distributed free abroad to members of the Armed Services and also within the United States to servicemen. Probably between 50,000 and 155,000 sets of sheets printed. *Title verso* and *acknowledgments* are on page [2].

This is Editions for the Armed Services Book No. S-3.

CONTENTS on page [3]: 1. Souvenir, 5; 2. I Love You, I Love You, I Love You, 17; 3. Star of Hope, 22; 4. Pale Hands, 30; 5. Watch The Birdie, 45; 6. Bride of Berchtesgaden, 58; 7. Chagrin d'Amour, 69; 8. Head-Hunters of The Quito Hills, 75; 9. Vacation, 89; 10. Cher Ami, 98; 11. Camp Nomopo, 105; 12. Sweet Death in The Electric Chair, 115.

ILLUSTRATIONS: There are 9 black illustrations by the author.

COPY EXAMINED: Mrs. Madeleine Bemelmans.

e. *Swiss edition* ([1946]):

TITLE PAGE: Ludwig Bemelmans | Ich Liebe Dich | Ich Liebe Dich | Ich Liebe Dich | Mit Zeichnungen vom Verfasser | colophon | Alfred Scherz Verlag Bern

PAGINATION: [1] - [200] pp.; endpapers. 18.4 x 11 cm.

COVERINGS: Pink paper-covered boards printed in maroon with a scene of the Place de la Madeleine on front. Spine plain. In a pink slipcase, printed on front in maroon with a scene of the Place de la Madeleine and the author, title and publisher and on spine: Ludwig | Bemel- | mans | in pink, upon a maroon ground: Ich | Liebe | Dich and at bottom, in maroon: colophon | Scherz.

PUBLISHED: Spring, 1946 at Swiss Fr 7,80. Number of sets of sheets printed cannot be determined, as the publisher's records have been lost. On *verso of title leaf*, page [4]: Einzig autorisierte Übersetzung aus dem Amerikanischen von Viktoria Vonderau. Titel des Originals << I Love You, I Love You, I Love You >>. Erste Auflage 1946. Printed in Switzerland by Buchdruckerei Karl Augustin, Thayngen. *Half-title* on page [1]. Endpapers plain.

CONTENTS (INHALTSVERZEICHNIS) on page [5]: 1. Souvenir, 7; 2. Ich Liebe Dich, Ich Liebe Dich, Ich Liebe Dich, 25; 3. Stern der Hoffnung, 35; 4. Bleiche Hände, 47; 5. Gib Acht Aufs Vögelchen, 69; 6. Braut in Berchtesgaden, 91; 7. Chagrin d'Amour, 107; 8. Kopfjäger aus den Bergen von Quito, 119; 9. Ferien, 139; 10. Cher Ami, 153; 11. Ferienlager Nomopo, 167; 12. Sanfter Tod auf Dem Elektrischen Stuhl, 181.

ILLUSTRATIONS: As in A21a.

COPY EXAMINED: Mrs. Madeleine Bemelmans.

f. Danish edition ([1946]):

TITLE PAGE: In black: Ludwig Bemelmans | Ih, Hvor Jeg | Elsker Dig | oversat af | Povl Frejlev | Illustreret af Forfatteren | København 1946 | a rule | Thaning & Appels Forlag

PAGINATION: [1] - 128 pp. 19.5 x 12.5 cm.

COVERINGS: The hardcover issue was not seen. Softcover issue: Purple paper covers printed in black and white with an illustration of the Place Vendôme; on spine, in black upon a white rectangle: Ludwig | Bemel- | mans | Ih, | hvor | jeg | elsker | dig; and at base, in black, between two rules: Thaning | & | Appel. No dust jacket.

PUBLISHED: 1946 in hardcover at KR 5,30 and in paperback at KR 3,45. Precise publication dates and number of sets of sheets printed cannot be determined, as the publisher's records are unavailable. On *verso of title leaf*, page [4]: Originalens Titel: "I Love You, I Love You, I Love You." Nordlundes Bogtrykkeri, København. *Half-title* on page [1].

CONTENTS (INDHOLD) on page [5]: Souvenir, 7; Ih, hvor jeg elsker dig, 19; Haabets Stjerne, 27; Hvide Haender, 35; Pas paa Pipfuglen, 51; Brud fra Berchtesgaden, 67; Chagrin d'Amour, 78; Hovedjaegerne fra Quito, 86; Vinterferie, 100; Cher Ami, 109; Nomopo-Lejren, 118. Note that "Sweet Death in the Electric Chair," the final chapter in A21a, is here omitted.

ILLUSTRATIONS: Illustrations by the author.

COPY EXAMINED: Mrs. Madeleine Bemelmans.

g. French edition ([1947]):

TITLE PAGE: In black: Je T'Aime | Je T'Aime | Je T'Aime | Ludwig Bemelmans | Texte français de Mad. E A. Blanchet | et Robert Fazy | colophon: a book with a hand writing Au Blé qui lève | at the left: Paris | 12, rue Cornuschi | in the center: Lausanne | 45a, Galeries du Commerce | at right: Montreal P.Q. | 750, rue Saint-Gabriel

PAGINATION: [1] - [7], 1-180 pp., 1 leaf. 18.7 x 12.5 cm.

COVERINGS: Grayish paper covers, with title and a heart in red; author, translators, publisher and colophon in black. The spine could not be examined.

PUBLISHED: April 12, 1947 at FF 140. Number of sets of sheets printed cannot be determined, as neither the publisher nor the publisher's records can be located. On *verso of title leaf*, page [6]: Copyright by Editions du Ble Qui Leve. Tous droits de traduction, reproduction et adaptation réservés pour tous pays, y compris l'U.R.S.S. *Half-title* on page [3], reading Je T'Aime | Je T'Aime | Je T'Aime. On page [4]: a black drawing of an angel with harp by Bemelmans and, Ouvrages parus: Tout Peut Arriver, de Georges et Helen Poposchvily Texte français de Madame Blanchet. On page [181]: Achevé d'imprimer le 12 avril 1947 sur les presses de l'Imprimerie Bader & CIE à Mulhouse.

CONTENTS (TABLE DES MATIERES) on page [7], with a black drawing of a gendarme: 1. Au Bon Vieux Temps, 11; 2. Je T'Aime, Je T'Aime, Je T'Aime, 29; 3. Confidences, 43; 4. Les Mains Blèmes, 55; 5. Intermède, 73; 6. Lèse Majesté, 91; 7. Couleur Locale, 105; 8. Une Tête, Monsieur?, 115; 9. Vacances, 131; 10. Cher Ami, 143; 11. Camp Nomopo, 155; 12. La Chaise Électrique, 169.

ILLUSTRATIONS: The book contains 68 black illustrations by the author.

COPY EXAMINED: La Bibliothèque nationale.

h. Paperback edition ([1948]):

I Love You I Love You I Love You was published in paperback at 25¢ in the week of November 27, 1948 by New American Library, as part of the New American Library of World Literature. The exact date of publication and number of sets of sheets printed cannot be determined, as the publisher's records have been lost. It has not been possible to examine a copy of this edition.

This is Signet Books No. 693.

i. New American edition (1992):

TITLE PAGE: Spread upon a double-page, on left: author's signature and H James H. Heineman New York 1992; on right, in black: I Love You | I Love You | I Love You | between two rules: Volume II In A New Bemelmans Series | A black line drawing of two people kissing | at right: Written and | Illustrated by Ludwig Bemelmans

PAGINATION: 5 leaves, [1] - 153 pp., 4 leaves, 2 blank leaves; endpapers. 21.4 x 14 cm.

COVERINGS: One-third gray linen-weave cloth-covered, and two-thirds cherry red paper-covered boards; blind-stamped on the front with a drawing of a cigar-smoking man in an armchair and a little girl, and the author's signature; stamped on spine, in gold, between two rules: Volume | II over a rule: I Love You I Love You I Love You under the rule: Ludwig Bemelmans; at base: H; between two rules: 1992. Front edges not trimmed. Gray and red dust jacket printed in red, black and white.

PUBLISHED: September 15, 1992 at $23.95. 3,000 sets of sheets printed. On *verso of title* [fourth] *leaf:* © 1942 by Ludwig Bemelmans. Renewed © 1970 by Madeleine Bemelmans and Barbara Bemelmans Marciano All rights reserved This book was first published in 1942 and reflects the writing of the time. First published in this edition in the United States of America in 1992 H James H. Heineman, Inc., 475 Park Avenue, New York, NY 10022. *Half-title* on recto of second leaf. *Second half-title* on page [1]. *Frontispiece* on recto of first leaf: a drawing of a violinist. *Other titles in this series* on recto of third leaf: Volume I Father, Dear Father Volume III How to Travel Incognito. *Other books by the author* on recto of third leaf, including eleven titles. On the first printed end leaf: Books Forming a Series By and About

Ludwig Bemelmans, listing, with ISBN numbers, three novels, *Father, Dear Father, I Love You, I Love You, I Love You* and *How to Travel Incognito*, as well as the present bibliography. Also the text: Other Titles in Preparation. *Author's signature* and *publisher's blurb* on recto of second end leaf. *Printer's colophon* on recto of third end leaf: This book was composed in Cochin and Nicolas Cochin Black by The Sarabande Press, New York. It was printed and bound by Arcata Graphics Company, New York on 60# Sebago cream white antique paper. The typography and binding were designed by Beth Tondreau Design, New York. Recto of fourth end leaf contains an illustration of a reclining cigarette-smoker in a t-shirt (from p. 25). Endpapers plain. The back flyleaf of the dust jacket contains a photograph of the author.

CONTENTS on recto of fifth leaf, with a black drawing of a monkey pointing at a rabbit: 1. Souvenir, 3; 2. I Love You, I Love You, I Love You, 16; 3. Star of Hope, 25; 4. Pale Hands, 34; 5. Watch the Birdie, 52; 6. Bride of Berchtesgaden, 69; 7. Chagrin d'Amour, 82; 8. Head Hunters of the Quito Hills, 91; 9. Vacation, 106; 10. Cher Ami, 107; 11. Camp Nomopo, 127; 12. Sweet Death in the Electric Chair, 139. [Chapter 10 in fact appears on page 117.]

ILLUSTRATIONS: Aside from the title page drawing, the frontispiece, the end page drawing, and the contents drawing there are 69 black illustrations by the author.

COPY EXAMINED: MP.

A22. [Bemelmans'] Italian Holiday [1961]

TITLE PAGE: In black, facsimile signature: Bemelmans' | in black: Italian Holiday | Written and illustrated by Ludwig Bemelmans | with a Foreword by Ted Patrick | Houghton Mifflin Company Boston | The Riverside Press Cambridge | 1961

PAGINATION: [i] - [x] pp., [1] - 102 pp.; endpapers. 28.1 x 21.9 cm.

COVERINGS: One-quarter sienna cloth-covered, and three-quarter ochre paper-covered, boards, stamped on front paper in sienna with a cactus in a flowerpot; on spine, in ochre: facsimile signature; Bemelmans Italian Holiday; at base: HMCO. Full-color dust jacket printed in white and black.

PUBLISHED: October 17, 1961 at $5.00. 7,200 sets of sheets printed. On *verso of title leaf*, page [iv]: The contents of this book have appeared, in different form, in *Holiday* magazine. Design by Ervine Metzl First Printing Printed in the U.S.A. *Frontispiece* on page [ii]: a black drawing of Gatto Bianco Capri. *Half-title* on page [i]: facsimile signature: Bemelmans' | plain print: Italian | Holiday. The endpapers are ochre printed in sienna with an Italian urban scene.

Note: An undetermined number of copies of

this edition were distributed by the Book-of-the-Month Club to its membership in December 1961 at an unknown price. The book was accompanied by a copy of the *Book-of-the-Month Club News* for December 1961, which contained a synopsis.

CONTENTS on page [v]: Foreword by Ted Patrick, vii; Magic Rome, 1; Midas Tour of Italy, 7; Diary with a Blank Page, 21; Isle of Capri, 41; Cinderella Isle, Ischia, 59; The Road to Salerno, 77; Mighty Vesuvio, 93.

"Midas Tour of Italy" is here reprinted from *Holiday*, January 1956, where it appeared as "Midas' Tour of Italy;" see E170. "Diary with a Blank Page" is here reprinted from *Holiday*, September 1949; see E122. "Isle of Capri" is here reprinted from *Holiday*, November 1949; see E124. "Cinderella Isle, Ischia" is here reprinted from *Holiday*, December 1949, where it appeared as "Cinderella Isle;" see E126. "The Road to Salerno" is here reprinted from *Holiday*, October 1950, where it appeared as "Road to Salerno;" see E128. "Mighty Vesuvio" is here reprinted from *Holiday*, January 1952, where it appeared as "Mighty Vesuvius!;" see E139.

ILLUSTRATIONS: In addition to the endpapers and frontispiece, there are 30 black illustrations by the author.

COPY EXAMINED: MP.

A23. Life Class [1938]

a. First edition:

TITLE PAGE: In black: Life Class | Illustrated by The Author | Ludwig Bemelmans | New York • MCMXXXVIII | The Viking Press

PAGINATION: 1 blank leaf, [i] - vi pp., [1] - 260 pp., 1 leaf, 1 blank leaf; endpapers. 20.7 x 13.6 cm.

COVERINGS: Scarlet linen-weave cloth covered boards. On front a full-color vertical sticker carries an illustration of a torso upon a plinth. On the spine a yellow sticker is printed in turquoise: Bemelmans Life Class Viking. Top edges stained yellow. Full-color dust jacket printed in turquoise and white.

PUBLISHED: November 14, 1938 at $2.50. 6,000 sets of sheets printed; 4,000 copies bound. The book was reprinted October 1939 and again in 1942. On *verso of title leaf*, page [iv]: Printed in U.S.A. by the Vail-Ballou Press Published in November 1938. *Half-title* on page [i]. *Second half-title* on page [1]. *Other books by the author* on page [ii], listing one title. Endpapers plain.

CONTENTS on page v: Prologue: Lausbub, 3. Part One: I. My First Actress, 27; II. Monsieur Victor, 36; III. Grapes for Monsieur Cape, 45; IV. Herr Otto Brauhaus, 59; V. Mr. Sigsag Goes to Sea, 70; VI. Life Class, 89; VII. The Brave Commis, 101. Part Two: I. If You're Not a Fool, 111;

II. Affair, 124; III. Coming Out, 138; IV. Cinder-ella and Santa Claus, 154; V. Kalakobé, 163; VI. S. S. Zuider Zee, 174; VII. Seven Hundred Brides, 187. Part Three: I. Improved Jewish Wedding, 211; II. The Postmaster from Przemysl, 219; III. Japanese Evening, 226; IV. Dinner Out, 232; V. The Good Son, 239. Epilogue: Sawmill in Tirol, 252.

"My First Actress" is here reprinted from *Stage*, May 1938; see E14 and E117. "Grapes for Monsieur Cape" is here reprinted from *Town & Country*, September 1940, where it appeared as "The Painted Grapes;" see E42. "Mr. Sigsag Goes to Sea" is here reprinted from *Town & Country*, July 1938, where it appeared as "Busboy's Holidays: Dinner at Luchow's and a Trip to the Sea;" see E16. "Coming Out" appeared, in somewhat different form, in *Town & Country*, September 1938, as "The Coming Out Party;" see E17.

ILLUSTRATIONS: There are 31 black drawings by the author.

COPY EXAMINED: MP.

b. British edition ([1939]):

TITLE PAGE: In black: Life Class | Illustrated by The Author | Ludwig Bemelmans | London | John Lane The Bodley Head

PAGINATION: 1 blank leaf, [i] - vi pp., [1] - 260 pp., 1 leaf, 1 blank leaf; endpapers. 22 x 14 cm.

COVERINGS: Taupe linen-weave cloth-covered boards plain on front, stamped on spine:

over a vertical maroon rectangle within a doubled aqua border, in aqua: Life | Class | an abbreviated flourish | Ludwig | Bemelmans | at base, in maroon: The Bodley Head. Top edges stained maroon. Bottom edges untrimmed. Maroon dust jacket printed in black and blue.

PUBLISHED: September 1939 at 8s 6d. Number of sets of sheets printed cannot be determined, as the publisher's records were lost during the Second World War. On *verso of title leaf*, page [iv]: First published in England in 1939 Made and Printed in Great Britain by Butler & Tanner Ltd., Frome and London. *Half-title* on page [i]. *Second half-title* on page [1]. Endpapers plain.

This edition was reprinted November 28, 1947 at 8s 6d; and again, smaller but in all other respects the same, as a cheap edition September 3, 1951 at 5s.

CONTENTS on page v: As in A23a.

ILLUSTRATIONS: As in A23a.

COPY EXAMINED: MP.

c. Paperback edition ([1948]):

TITLE PAGE: In black: Life Class | Illustrated | by | The Author | Ludwig Bemelmans | colophon | Penguin Books | West Drayton • Middlesex

PAGINATION: [i] - vi pp., 7 - [249] pp., 3 leaves. 18 x 11 cm.

COVERINGS: Royal blue and white paper cover printed on front in black with author and title; "Biography" in blue; on spine, in black upon white: Life Class; in black upon blue: Ludwig Bemelmans; at base in black: colophon, 615. No dust jacket.

This is Penguin No. 615.

PUBLISHED: The week of May 8, 1948 at 1s 6d. Number of sets of sheets printed cannot be determined, as the publisher does not respond to inquiry. On *verso of title leaf*, page [iv]: First published in England in 1939 Published in Penguin Books 1948 Made and Printed in Great Britain for Penguin Books Limited by R. & R. Clark, Ltd. Edinburgh. *Half-title* on page [i]: Penguin Books | 615 | Life Class | by Ludwig Bemelmans. A *note about the book* appears on the inside of the front cover. The three concluding leaves contain publisher's advertisements.

CONTENTS on page v: Prologue: Lausbub, 7. Part One: I. My First Actress, 27; II. Monsieur Victor, 36; III. Grapes for Monsieur Cape, 45; IV. Herr Otto Brauhaus, 59; V. Mr. Sigsag Goes to Sea, 69; VI. Life Class, 87; VII. The Brave Commis, 98. Part Two: I. If You're Not a Fool, 104; II. Affair, 117; III. Coming Out, 131; IV. Cinderella and Santa Claus, 147; V. Kalakobé, 156; VI. S. S. Zuider Zee, 167; VII. Seven Hundred Brides, 180. Part Three: I. Improved Jewish Wedding, 201; II. The Postmaster from Przemysl, 209; III. Japanese Evening, 216; IV. Dinner Out, 222; V. The Good Son, 228. Epilogue: Sawmill in Tirol, 240.

ILLUSTRATIONS: As in A23a.

COPY EXAMINED: MP.

A24. Madeline [1939]

a. First edition:

TITLE PAGE: Within a vertical yellow rectangle, in black: Madeline | a black and yellow drawing of a little girl | in black: story & pictures by | Ludwig Bemelmans | Simon and Schuster • New York | 1939

PAGINATION: Unpaged. 24 leaves; endpapers. 30.5 x 23 cm.

COVERINGS: Paper-covered boards printed on front with a full-color illustration of a nun, twelve little girls in yellow, and the Eiffel Tower; author and title in white; on back with a black drawing of a little girl on a yellow ground; and on a full-color spine, upon a yellow strip, in black: Madeline by Ludwig Bemelmans. The full-color dust jacket is printed in white on front; on the back there is a black drawing of the Tuileries Gardens facing the Louvre and the text, "The little girls and the man feeding the pigeons are in the Tuileries Gardens facing the Louvre. Ludwig Bemelmans has used this and many other scenes in his pictures for this book." The flyleaves contain a publisher's introduction and a list of illustrations "for those who may wish to identify the Paris scenes Ludwig Bemelmans has pictured in this book."

PUBLISHED: September 15, 1939 at $2.00. Number of sets of sheets printed cannot be determined, as the publisher keeps no records for more than ten years. The edition was reprinted in 1950. On *verso of title leaf:* All rights reserved including the right of reproduction in whole or in part in any form Copyright, 1939, by Ludwig Bemelmans Published by Simon and Schuster, Inc. 386 Fourth Avenue, New York Manufactured in The United States of America. *Half-title* in red on recto of second leaf. Endpapers printed with a full-color illustration of the Place de la Concorde.

A pre-publication excerpt appeared as part of a biographical article about the author, mentioning the circumstances that inspired him to write it; see J72. On the origins of Madeline see also J456.

This is a Caldecott Honor book.

ILLUSTRATIONS: In addition to the endpapers and the title-drawing, there are 39 black and yellow and 8 full-color illustrations by the author.

Note: This book represents an early example of photo-offset lithography, a process which makes possible the mass reproduction of dense and beautiful color in illustration.

COPY EXAMINED: MP.

b. Danish edition ([1947]):

TITLE PAGE: A black and yellow drawing of a little girl | In black: Madeline | Tegnet og fortalt af Ludwig Bemelmans | Oversat af Piet Hein | Illustrationsforlaget

PAGINATION: Unpaged. 28 leaves. 30 x 20.8 cm.

COVERINGS: Full-color laminated paper-covered boards printed on front with an illustration of a nun, twelve little girls and the Eiffel Tower and title and author in white; upon a yellow spine, in black: Madeline af Ludwig Bemelmans. The back cover is pale blue and contains a black illustration of the Tuileries and a list of the color illustrations inside. No dust jacket.

PUBLISHED: 1947 at Dkr 8,50. Number of sets of sheets printed cannot be determined, as the publisher's records have been lost. Second, third, fourth and fifth impressions were issued respectively in 1959, 1963, 1971 and 1979. (Descriptions of the third and fifth impressions follow below.) On *verso of title leaf:* a blurb about the book, and: Titlen på den Amerikanske Udgave (Originaludgaven) er Madeline Udgivet af Simon and Schuster . New York. *Half-title* on recto of fourth leaf. On verso of fourth leaf: 3. oplag [third impression]. A. C. Schmidt A/S København. The recto of the first and verso of the last leaves are glued to the boards; and the verso of the first leaf and recto of the second, and verso of the second-last and recto of the last leaves, are printed as endpapers with a full-color illustration of the Place de la Concorde.

ILLUSTRATIONS: As in A24a.

COPY EXAMINED: Mrs. Madeleine Bemelmans.

c. First Swiss edition ([1947]):

TITLE PAGE: Within a yellow rectangle in black: Madeline | a black and yellow drawing of a little girl | Bilder und Verse | Von | Ludwig Bemelmans | Alfred Scherz Verkag Bern

PAGINATION: Unpaged. 24 leaves. 29.7 x 21 cm.

COVERINGS: Yellow paper-covered boards printed on front with title, author, and publisher in black, with a full-color illustration of a nun and twelve little girls at the Eiffel Tower set in a white border. Spine plain. No dust jacket.

PUBLISHED: In Fall, 1947 at Swiss Fr. 8,50. The number of sets of sheets printed cannot be determined, as the publisher's records have been lost. On *verso of title leaf:* Titel Des Amerikanischen Originals: ,,Madeline" Erschienen bei Simon und Schuster, New York. 1. Auflage 1947. Alle Rechte Vorbehalten. *Half-title* on recto of second leaf.

ILLUSTRATIONS: As in A24a.

COPY EXAMINED: Scherz Verlag, Bern.

d. First Swedish edition ([1948-1949]):

FIRST ISSUE (1948)

TITLE PAGE: Within a pale yellow rectangle, in black: Madeline | a black and yellow picture of a little girl | Ritad och Berättad av | Ludwig Bemelmans | Oversatt av | Nils Ludwig | Beyronds Förlag—Malmö

PAGINATION: Unpaged. 24 leaves. No endpapers. 30.2 x 21.3 cm.

COVERINGS: Pale yellow paper covers printed with author, title and publisher in black. A list of the color illustrations appears on the back cover.

PUBLISHED: 1948 at SKR 5:25. Number of sets of sheets printed unknown at both publisher and printer. On *verso of title leaf:* Titeln på den Amerikanska Upplagan (originalupplagan) Är Madeline Utgiven av Simon and Schuster, New York. Also on title verso: publisher's blurb about the book. *Half-title* on recto of second leaf.

ILLUSTRATIONS: There are 39 black and yellow and 8 full-color illustrations by the author.

A second issue (1949) shows the following variations from the 1948 *first issue* described above: Plain white endpapers. 29.7 x 21.6 cm. Yellow paper-covered boards with a full-color illustration, bordered in white, of a nun with twelve little girls at the Eiffel Tower; on the back cover, a black and yellow drawing of a nun and twelve little girls in the Tuileries Gardens facing the Louvre, plus the list of the color plates and: Beyronds, Malmö and F. E. Bording A/S. Kbhvn. (F. E. Bording was the printer). Price SKR 7:50; number of sets of sheets printed unknown.

COPIES EXAMINED: The Royal Library, Stockholm.

e. First British edition ([1952]):

TITLE PAGE: Within a vertical yellow rectangle, in black: Madeline | a black and yellow drawing of a little girl | in black: story & pictures by | Ludwig Bemelmans | colophon | Derek Verschoyle

PAGINATION: Unpaged. 24 leaves; endpapers. 30 x 21.8 cm.

COVERINGS: Full-color paper-covered boards printed in white with author and title on front; on spine in black upon a yellow strip: Madeline by Ludwig Bemelmans; in white upon a black strip: André Deutsch. Full-color dust jacket printed in white.

PUBLISHED: November 21, 1952 at 12s 6d. Approximately 10,000 sets of sheets printed. *Half-title* on recto of second leaf. Endpapers white.

Note: The illustrated endpapers were inadvertently left off the first printing of this edition and added subsequently. This book was on Derek Verschoyle's first list, published in *The Bookseller* July 5, 1952.

ILLUSTRATIONS: In addition to the title page drawing there are 39 black and yellow and 8 full-color illustrations by the author.

COPY EXAMINED: Mr. André Deutsch

f. First German edition ([1954]):

TITLE PAGE: Within a vertical yellow rectangle, in black: Madeline | a black and yellow drawing of a little girl | mit Bildern | und Versen von | Ludwig Bemelmans | Blüchert Verlag Stuttgart

PAGINATION: Unpaged. 24 leaves; endpapers. 29.4 x 20.7 cm.

COVERINGS: Original covering not seen.

PUBLISHED: 1954 at DM 9,80. The number of sets of sheets printed cannot be determined, as neither the publisher nor the publisher's records can be found. On *verso of title leaf:* Alle deutschsprachigen Rechte bei Blüchert Verlag, Stuttgart, Silberburgstrasse 152 Die Englische Ausgabe erschien bei Derek Verschoyle Ltd. London Unter dem Titel »Madeline« - Copyright 1939 by Ludwig Bemelmans Printed in Germany *Half-title* on recto of second leaf, in red. Endpapers plain. (The translation, uncredited, is by Heinz Strix.)

ILLUSTRATIONS: There are 39 black and yellow, and 8 full-color, illustrations by the author in addition to the drawing upon the title leaf.

COPY EXAMINED: Detroit Public Library, Detroit, Michigan.

g. Cheap edition ([1954]):

TITLE PAGE: In black: Madeline | Story and Pictures by | Ludwig Bemelmans | a full-color illustration of the Tuileries Gardens facing the Louvre | Simon and Schuster • New York | Copyright 1939, 1954 by Ludwig Bemelmans. All rights reserved, Including the right of reproduction in whole | or in part in any form. Designed and produced by The Sandpiper Press and Artists and Writers Guild, Inc. | Printed in the U.S.A. by Western Printing and Lithographing Company. Published by Simon and Schuster, Inc., | Rockefeller Center, New York 20. Published Simultaneously in Canada by The Musson Book Company, Ltd., Toronto.

PAGINATION: Unpaged. 14 leaves. 20.3 x 16.9 cm.

COVERINGS: Full-color stiff cardboard covers printed on front with illustrations of a nun, twelve little girls in yellow, and the Eiffel Tower, with author and title in yellow. Spine in silver and black. No dust jacket. The inside of the front cover shows multi-colored figures against an orange background.

PUBLISHED: Between March 29 and July 31, 1954 at $0.25. 2,000,000 sets of sheets printed. The *title verso* begins the text.

A Goldencraft version of this edition, in one cloth and two plastic bindings for schools and libraries (the latter two of which read, on spine, The Golden Library), came out between six and twelve months later for $1.00; the number of copies is not known; the books were 31 x 23 cm.

This is Little Golden Books No. 186.

ILLUSTRATIONS: In addition to the title page illustration there are 28 illustrations by the author, all in full-color, and some slightly redrawn from those of the original edition. Also: The illustration on the verso of the third leaf of the original edition is here omitted; the illustrations on the verso of the sixth and recto of the seventh leaves are here omitted; the illustrations on the verso of the eighth and recto of the ninth leaves are here omitted; the two illustrations on the verso of the eleventh leaf and the top illustration on the recto of the twelfth are here omitted; the illustration on the recto of the thirteenth leaf is here omitted; the illustration on the verso of the thirteenth leaf and that on the recto of the fourteenth are combined into a single illustration (which is © Ludwig Bemelmans, 1954, and the reason for the double copyright on the title page); the illustration on the verso of the fifteenth leaf, those on both sides of the sixteenth leaf, and that on the recto of the seventeenth leaf are here omitted; the illustration on the recto of the nineteenth leaf has here been redrawn; all of the illustrations on the twentieth and twenty-first leaves are here omitted; the illustrations on the verso of the twenty-second and all those on the twenty-third leaf are here omitted.

COPY EXAMINED: Mrs. Madeleine Bemelmans.

h. First French edition ([1954]):

TITLE PAGE: In black: Madeleine | Texte et Illustrations de | L. Bemelmans | a full-color illustration of the Tuileries Gardens facing the Louvre | in black, between two magenta roosters: Cocorico | in black: Droits de traduction et d'adaptation réservés pour tous les pays. Copyright 1939, 1954 par Simon and Schuster, Inc., | et Artists and Writers Guild, Inc. - Printed in France.

PAGINATION: Unpaged. 14 leaves. 20 x 16.7 cm.

COVERINGS: Full-color stiff cardboard covers printed on front with illustrations of a nun, twelve little girls in yellow, and the Eiffel Tower; title in yellow, and Un Petit Livre d'Or in white; 85 in black; and on back with publisher's list continued from inside back cover. Spine gilded. No dust jacket.

This is N° 85 of Les Petits Livres d'Or.

PUBLISHED: October, 1954 at an unknown price. Number of sets of sheets printed cannot be determined, as the publisher keeps no records for more than ten years. On *verso of 14th leaf:* Imprimerie M. Déchaux, Paris (C.O.L. 30-01-15) 10-1954- Dépôt légal 4e trimestre 1954 - Cocorico, éditeur (No 225) - No d'impression 42. On *inside of back cover:* Les Éditions Cocorico 25, Boulevard des Italiens - Paris (2e).

Note: This book was reprinted in 1971 under a different imprint. See A24q.

ILLUSTRATIONS: As in A24g.

COPY EXAMINED: MP.

i. Second British edition ([1957]):

TITLE PAGE: Within a vertical yellow rectangle, in black: Madeline | a black and yellow drawing of a little girl | in black: story & pictures by | Ludwig Bemelmans | colophon | André Deutsch

PAGINATION: Unpaged. 24 leaves; endpapers. 30 x 21.8 cm.

COVERINGS: Full-color paper-covered boards printed in white with author and title on front and on spine; in black upon a yellow strip: Madeline by Ludwig Bemelmans; in white upon a black strip: André Deutsch. Full-color dust jacket printed in white.

PUBLISHED: September 16, 1957 at 15s. 6,000 sets of sheets printed. On *verso of title leaf:* First published 1952 by André Deutsch Limited. [Note: this is an error; see A24f.] *Half-title* on recto of second leaf. Endpapers white.

ILLUSTRATIONS: In addition to the title page drawing there are 39 black and yellow and 8 full-color illustrations by the author.

COPY EXAMINED: Mr. André Deutsch, 105 Great Russell Street, London. 7th Impression examined.

j. Second American edition ([1958]):

TITLE PAGE: Within a vertical yellow rectangle, in black: Madeline | a black and yellow drawing of a little girl | in black: story & pictures by |

Ludwig Bemelmans | The Viking Press • New York

PAGINATION: Unpaged. 24 leaves; endpapers. 31.5 x 22.5 cm.

COVERINGS: Paper-covered boards printed on front with a full-color illustration of a nun, twelve little girls in yellow, and the Eiffel Tower, with author and title in white; and on a full-color spine, upon a yellow strip, in black: Madeline by Ludwig Bemelmans. Dust jacket not seen.

PUBLISHED: September 30, 1958 at $3.50. The number of sets of sheets originally printed cannot be determined (see below). On *verso of title leaf*: Copyright 1939 by Ludwig Bemelmans. Published by The Viking Press, Inc. 625 Madison Avenue, New York 22, N.Y. Published in Canada by the Macmillan Company of Canada Limited. Lithographed in the United States of America. *Half-title* in red on recto of second leaf. Endpapers printed with a full-color illustration of the Place de la Concorde.

Some copies of this edition were selected by The Literary Guild in April, 1977 and made available to members at an unknown price and in a format that has not been examined.

Note: There is some mystery surrounding this edition, only the scantiest records of which currently exist. The Viking Press published its first edition of *Madeline* September 30, 1958, having purchased 6,000 leftover copies of the Simon and Schuster 1939 edition from the publisher at a nominal price. Whether these copies were de-stroyed or redistributed with a Viking sticker on the title page is not known. I have never seen a copy of the book with a sticker or with 1958 on the title or title verso.

It is reasonably likely that Viking used the Simon and Schuster plates, except for the title page; although there is some chance new plates were struck for this edition and that no mention of this was made in the text. Yet all subsequent reprintings of this edition bear on the title verso the distinct text (that would have been inaccurate in 1958): New Viking Edition 1960; and it is known at the publisher that no new plates were struck by Viking in 1960. Sales figures were recorded continuously, in fact, from 1958 to 1962, as though only one edition was being tracked: 31,000 copies were sold in that period.

The best that can be said at this point is that it is most likely Viking put out some copies in 1958 and some around 1960 and that the publisher considered these to be parts of a single "New Viking" edition of *Madeline*. I think it reasonable to assume the original printing consisted of the 6,000 Simon and Schuster copies, now put out by Viking; and that in 1960 the edition was reprinted to the extent of 25,000 additional copies which had the title verso information given above. It is this edition that has been regularly reprinted, in fact at least twenty-eight times. As of 1967 the title verso bears the following information: Copyright © renewed 1967 by Madeleine Bemelmans and Barbara Bemelmans Marciano.

An undetermined number of copies of a reprint of this edition was taken by the Book-of-the-Month Club and made available to its membership in spring 1971 singly at $3.50 or in a triple combination with *Madeline's Rescue* and *Madeline and the Gypsies* at $8.75. The books were in the Children's Christmas Catalogue. The book was accompanied by a copy of the *Book-of-the-Month Club News* for Spring 1971, which contained a synopsis.

ILLUSTRATIONS: In addition to the endpapers and the title-drawing, there are 39 black and yellow and 8 full-color illustrations by the author.

COPY EXAMINED: MP.

k. Second Swedish edition ([1963]):

TITLE PAGE: A black and yellow picture of a little girl | Madeline | Ritad och berättad av Ludwig Bemelmans | Översatt av Nils Ludvig | Illustrationsförlaget

Unpaged. 28 leaves. 30.5 x 21.2 cm. Covering as for A24c.

PUBLISHED: 1963 at SKR 12:25. Number of sets of sheets printed and precise publication date cannot be determined as the publisher's record is unavailable. On *title verso:* Nog tycker jag att Madeline | som bok är både bra och fin, | och tror att ingen blir mer glad | för tusen leksaker i rad. | Den stad vår flicka levde i | hon kallade ju själv Pari; | på svenska heter den Paris - | här lär du känna den precis. | Där lekte hon varenda dag | med vänner i ett näpet lag. | Visst råkade hon illa

ut, | men sagan har ett lyckligt slut. | Ja, den är både bra och fin | och kallas - märk väl - Madelin(e). Titeln på den Amerikanska Upplagan (originalupplagan) är Madeline. *Half-title* in red. On verso of half-title: 2:a upplagan A.C. Schmidt A/S Kobenhavn. The recto of the first and verso of the last leaves are glued to the boards; and the verso of the first leaf and recto of the second, and verso of the second-last and recto of the last leaves, are printed as endpapers with a full-color illustration of the Place de la Concorde.

ILLUSTRATIONS: As in A24a.

COPY EXAMINED: Kungliga Biblioteket, Stockholm.

l. Second German edition ([1966]):

TITLE PAGE: Within a vertical yellow rectangle, in black: Madeline | a black and yellow drawing of a little girl | in black: Ein Bilderbuch | von Ludwig Bemelmans | Deutsch von James Krüss | Otto Maier Verlag Ravensburg

PAGINATION: Unpaged. 24 leaves; endpapers. 30 x 21.8 cm.

COVERINGS: Full-color Linson-covered boards printed in white with author and title on front; on spine, in black upon yellow: Otto Maier Verlag Ravensburg Madeline Ludwig Bemelmans. No dust jacket.

PUBLISHED: November 1966 at DM 9,80. 6,000 sets of sheets printed. On *verso of title leaf:* colophon "Bilderbücher der Sechs" Printed in

Hungary 1966 By Kossuth Printing House, Budapest. *Half-title* on recto of second leaf. Endpapers plain.

ILLUSTRATIONS: In addition to the title page drawing there are 39 black and yellow and 8 full-color illustrations by the author.

COPY EXAMINED: Mr. André Deutsch, 105 Great Russell Street, London.

m. First American paperback edition ([1966]):

TITLE PAGE: Within a vertical yellow rectangle, in black: Madeline | a black and yellow drawing of a little girl | in black: by Ludwig Bemelmans | Scholastic Book Services | Published by Scholastic Book Services, a division | of Scholastic Magazines, Inc., New York, N.Y.

PAGINATION: Unpaged. 24 leaves. 23 x 19 cm.

COVERINGS: Full-color paper covers with a blue vertical band on left and an illustration of a nun, twelve little girls, and the Eiffel Tower. Title and author in white. On a green spine in black: TJ 839 Madeline • Bemelmans. The back cover is avocado green. Pages trimmed. No dust jacket.

PUBLISHED: February 1966 at $0.60. The number of sets of sheets originally printed cannot be determined, as the publisher's records are not available, but 140,000 copies appeared between publication and 1988. On *verso of title leaf:* Single copy price 60¢. Quantity prices available on request. This Scholastic Book Services edition is published by arrangement with The Viking Press, Inc. 1st printing February 1966. Printed in the U.S.A.

7,500 copies of a "Big Book" version of this edition, measuring 45.7 x 38.1 cm., and in other respects the same, were published September 1987 at $20.00.

ILLUSTRATIONS: As in A24a.

COPY EXAMINED: Mrs. Madeleine Bemelmans.

n. Children's choice edition ([1967]):

TITLE PAGE: Within a vertical yellow rectangle, in black: Madeline | a black and yellow drawing of a little girl | in black: story & pictures by | Ludwig Bemelmans | The Viking Press • New York | between two reading walruses, within a black rectangle: A Children's Choice® Book Club Edition From Scholastic Book Services (a black design of an open book)

PAGINATION: Unpaged. 24 leaves; endpapers. 26 x 19.7 cm.

COVERINGS: Full-color laminated paper-covered boards, printed on front with an illustration of nun with twelve little girls and the Eiffel tower and author and title in white; on a spine that modulates from red at top through orange, yellow, green and blue to purple at bottom, at top: a waving white walrus, in black: Madeline Bemelmans; at bottom: an open white book. No dust jacket.

Published 1967 at an unknown price. Number of sets of sheets printed cannot be determined, as the publisher's records have been lost. On *verso of title leaf:* Copyright 1939 by Ludwig Bemelmans copyright © renewed 1967 by Madeleine Bemelmans and Barbara Bemelmans Marciano Published by The Viking Press 40 West 23rd Street, New York, N.Y. 10010 Printed in U.S.A. *Half-title* in red. Endpapers as in A24a. The verso of the front free endpaper is printed with a Children's Choice logo of a reading walrus airborne in a balloon that says This Book Belongs to. The balloon basket reads: children's choice®.

ILLUSTRATIONS: As in A24a.

COPY EXAMINED: The University of Florida Baldwin Library Special Collection, Gainesville.

o. British paperback edition ([1968]):

TITLE PAGE: Within a vertical yellow rectangle, in black: Madeline | a black and yellow drawing of a little girl | in black: story & pictures by | Ludwig Bemelmans | dancing bear colophon | Sphere Books | in Association with | André Deutsch

PAGINATION: [1] - 48 pp. 22.7 x 16.7 cm.

COVERINGS: Full-color paper covers printed on front with an illustration of a nun, twelve little girls and the Eiffel Tower, title and author in white; yellow spine is blank. No dust jacket.

PUBLISHED: February, 1968 at 5s. Number of sets of sheets printed cannot be determined, as the publisher kept no records at the time. On *verso of title leaf,* page [4]: First published by André Deutsch Ltd. 1952. [Note: this is an error; see A24f.] Second Impression 1957. Third Impression 1961. Fourth Impression 1966. This Edition first published by Sphere Books Ltd. In association with André Deutsch Ltd. 1968. 40 Park Street, London W.1. Trade Mark (a circle, white on top and black beneath). *Half-title* on page [1], with a black drawing of Madeline and a publisher's blurb which mentions "the film cartoon based on Madeline" [see below]. On page [2]: other books in the *Madeline* series available in Sphere Books: Madeline's Rescue | Madeline and The Bad Hat | Madeline and The Gypsies | Madeline in London. Also: Made and printed in Jugoslavia by ,,Radisa Timotic"— Beograd.

As regards the British cartoon film adaptation of *Madeline* referred to in this edition, absolutely no information can be found. Neither does Sphere currently discover any record of any kind that would suggest *Madeline and the Bad Hat, Madeline and the Gypsies, Madeline in London,* or *Madeline's Rescue* were actually ever published by that company; therefore no entries are made here under A25, A26, A27 or A30.

ILLUSTRATIONS: As in A24a.

COPY EXAMINED: Mrs. Madeleine Bemelmans.

p. Second American paperback edition ([1969]):

TITLE PAGE: Within a vertical yellow rectangle, in black: Madeline | a black and yellow drawing of a little girl | in black: story & pictures by | Ludwig Bemelmans | The Viking Press • New York

PAGINATION: Unpaged. 23 leaves, 1 blank leaf. 22.7 x 18.8 cm.

COVERINGS: Laminated paper-covers printed on front with an illustration of a nun, twelve little girls and the Eiffel Tower, author and title in white; on a blue-green spine, printed in black: VS-23 Ludwig Bemelmans Madeline. Green illustration of a little girl on back cover with title in black and "A Caldecott Honor Book." No dust jacket.

PUBLISHED: 1969 at $1.25. Number of sets of sheets printed cannot be determined, as the publisher's records are lost. On *verso of title leaf:* Viking Seafarer edition issued in 1969 by The Viking Press, Inc. 625 Madison Avenue, New York, N.Y. 10022. Distributed in Canada by The Macmillan Company of Canada Limited. No facsimile endpapers.

This is Viking Seafarer No. VS-23.

Note: Around 10,000 copies of this edition were distributed after February 1975 in a "Seafarer Reading Chest" package, including 8 copies of the book, a cassette with narration, and a teacher's guide by Roy Oakley.

ILLUSTRATIONS: Aside from the title illustration and the facsimile endpapers near the end, there are 8 full-color and 40 yellow and black illustrations by the author.

COPY EXAMINED: College Education Centre Library, North Bay, Ontario.

q. Reprint of First French edition ([1971]):

TITLE PAGE: In magenta: Madeleine | Texte et Illustrations de | L. Bemelmans | a full-color illustration of the Tuileries Gardens facing the Louvre | one magenta rooster facing right | in black: éditions des deux coqs d'or | © 1954 by Éditions des Deux Coqs d'Or, Paris. | Publié en accord avec Western Publishing Company, Inc., Racine, Wisconsin

PAGINATION: Unpaged. 1 blank leaf, 8 leaves. 19 x 16.5 cm.

COVERINGS: Full-color cardboard covers with title in yellow and above, in white upon a green border, Un Petit Livre d'Or and in black, 85. At bottom, in black, within a rectangle, éditions des deux coqs d'or. Spine gold and unprinted. No dust jacket. Green, yellow and black illustration of eleven little girls holding flowers on back cover along with a list of Petit Livres d'Or 333 through 349.

This is N° 85 of Les Petits Livres d'Or.

PUBLISHED: 1971 at approximately 4FF. The exact publication date, price, and number of sets of sheets printed cannot be determined. The *title leaf verso* is the beginning of the text. On verso of final leaf: Dépôt légal 4° Trimestre 1971. Deux Coqs d'Or éditeur, n° A 45357 71 Imprimé en France - Cité-Press-Paris n° 1376. The insides of the covers are printed with a multi-colored Petit Livre d'Or pattern of stars, balloons, barns, sailboats, cowboys, etc.

Note: This is a reprint, over a new imprint, of A24h. Simon & Schuster's Little Golden Books are the responsibility of the Western Publishing Co., formerly the Western Printing Co. Sometime before 1959 Éditions Cocorico, Western's French subsidiary responsible for Les Petits Livres d'Or (French Little Golden Editions), became Éditions des Deux Coqs D'or. Deux Coqs d'Or was subsequently sold by Western to Sphère Diffusion, Paris, which went bankrupt in Spring 1991. In June 1991 Deux Coqs d'Or came under the ownership of Hachette, Paris.

TEXT and ILLUSTRATIONS: As in A24h, with the same translation (uncredited), except that this edition is somewhat abbreviated, and some of the text is slightly altered, as follows: The text and illustrations from the verso of the third leaf, entirety of the fourth leaf, and recto of the fifth leaf of A24h are here omitted. The first two lines on the verso of the fifth leaf, "Madeleine était/ La plus jeune" are here collapsed into a single line; the remaining text on the fifth leaf verso and that on the sixth leaf recto, along with the two accompanying illustrations, are here omitted. The illus-trations on the seventh leaf verso and eighth leaf recto are here omitted. The first two lines on the eighth leaf verso, "Chacun se mit à pleurer:/ Tous les yeux étaient mouillés" are here omitted; the second two lines, "Le docteur dut l'emporter/ Chaudement enveloppée" are here changed to "Dans ses bras, il dut emporter/ Madeleine, chau-dement enveloppée." The illustration on the ninth leaf recto is here omitted; and the remaining three lines along with the four lines on the ninth leaf verso: "Qui tous deux les emmena./ Madeleine s'éveilla/ A quelques heures de là./ Bientôt elle but et mangea./ Et voici ce qui l'amusa:/ Au plafond était un dessin/ Qui représentait un lapin" are collapsed into the following five lines on the fifth leaf recto of this edition: "A quelques heures de là,/ Madeleine s'éveilla, but et mangea./ Et voici ce qui l'amusa:/ Au plafond était un dessin/ Qui repésentait un lapin." The text and illustra-tions on the tenth leaf, and on the eleventh leaf recto, are here omitted; the text is replaced with the top four lines on the current fifth leaf verso: "Les onze petites filles/ Et Mademoiselle Clavel/ Vinrent à la clinique/ Un beau matin." The fifth line of the fifth leaf verso text, originally "« Oh! oh! » s'écrièrent-elles" here reads "« Oh! oh! » sécrièrent-elles."

COPY EXAMINED: Los Angeles Public Library Children's Literature Department.

r. Japanese edition ([1972]):

TITLE PAGE: Within a vertical yellow rectangle, in black: Genkina Madeline | a black and yellow drawing of a little girl | in black: by Ludwig Bemelmans | Translated by Asada Teiji | Fukuinkan Shoten

PAGINATION: [1] - [48] pp.; endpapers. 30.5 x 22.3 cm.

COVERINGS: Lamination on paper-covered boards printed on front with a full-color illustration of a nun, twelve little girls in yellow and the Eiffel Tower, with author and title in white; on an olive green spine, in black: by Ludwig Bemelmans Genkina Madeline and at base Fukuinkan Shoten | colophon. No dust jacket.

PUBLISHED: November 10, 1972 at ¥1130. 224,000 sets of sheets printed. On *verso of title leaf,* page [2]: Madeline, Story and pictures by Ludwig Bemelmans. Copyright 1939 by Ludwig Bemelmans. Originally published by The Viking Press, Inc., New York. Japanese language edition copyright 1972 by Fukuinkan-Shoten, Publishers, Tokyo, by arrangements with Charles E. Tuttle Co. *Index to color plates* on page [47]. *Author's blurb* and *advertisements for other books* in the Madeline series on page [48]. Also on page [48]: Published November 10, 1972. Tokyo-to Chiodaku Mitzuzaki-cho 1-1-9 Fukuinkan Shoten. Printed by Sei Kosha. [colophon]. Book care guidelines. Endpapers as in A24a.

ILLUSTRATIONS: As in A24a.

COPY EXAMINED: Mrs. Madeleine Bemelmans.

s. First South African edition ([1973]):

TITLE PAGE: Within a vertical yellow rectangle, in black: Madeleine | a black and yellow drawing of a little girl | in black: Verhaal en tekeninge deur Ludwig Bemelmans | Afrikaanse beryming deur Leon Rousseau | colophon | Human & Rousseau | Kaapstad en Pretoria

PAGINATION: Unpaged. 24 leaves; endpapers. 30 x 21.9 cm.

COVERINGS: Paper-covered boards printed on front with a full-color picture of a nun and twelve little girls at the Eiffel Tower, with title in black upon a yellow band, and author in white; on spine, in black upon a yellow strip: Madeleine by Ludwig Bemelmans; in white upon a black strip: colophon. Full-color dust jacket reproduces the covering.

PUBLISHED: May 1974 at R2,95. 3,147 sets of sheets printed. On *verso of title leaf:* Die berymer bedank mej Freda Linde vir haar voorstelle en hulp. Oorspronklike titel: *Madeline*. Afrikaanse beryming deur Leon Rousseau. Eerste Afrikaanse uitgawe in 1973 deur Human & Rousseau Uitgewers (Edms.) Bpk., Stategebou, Roosstraat, Kaapstad; Pretoriusstraat 239, Pretoria. Geset deur Human & Rousseau en gedruk in mede-produksie met André Deutsch. Printed Offset Litho in Great Britain by Cox & Wyman Ltd, London, Fakenham and Reading. *Note on pronunciation* on verso of title leaf: *Opmerkings oor die uitspraak* Die korrekte uitspraak van die Franse eienamm Madeleine is „Maddelên", om te rym met Seine (die rivier—uitgespreek „Sên"). Om hierdie rede is „Madeleine" in hierdie kinderboek nooit in 'n rymposisie gebruik waar dit bv. met „skyn" of „fyn" moet ryn nie. 'n Mens wil egter nie té puristies wees nie. Die algemene Afrikaanse uitspraak van die naam is „Maddelyn", en kinders wat dit so wil uitspreek, kan dit gerus maar doen. Dit is 'n veel minder growwe fout as die algemene Suid-Afrikaanse uitspraak „Perie" vir Pierre. Die naam van die suster wat die dogtertjies oppas, juffrou Clavel, word „Klawél" uitgespreek.— L. R. . . . uitgespreek.—L.R. *Half-title* in black on recto of second leaf. The back cover of the dust jacket is plain yellow and a list of the color plates is on the back flyleaf. Endpapers plain.

ILLUSTRATIONS: In addition to the title page drawing there are 39 black and yellow and 8 full-color illustrations by the author.

COPY EXAMINED: MP.

t. **Third American Paperback** edition ([1977]):

TITLE PAGE: Within a vertical yellow rectangle, In black: Madeline | a black and yellow drawing of a little girl | in black: story & pictures by | Ludwig Bemelmans | Puffin Books

PAGINATION: Unpaged. 23 leaves, 1 blank leaf. 22.6 x 18.1 cm.

COVERINGS: Full-color paper covers printed with title and author in white on front; on spine, in black upon yellow: Ludwig Bemelmans Madeline.

PUBLISHED: 1977 at $3.50. Number of sets of sheets printed cannot be determined, as the publisher's record is lost. *On verso of title leaf:* Published in Picture Puffins 1977 Reprinted 1978 (twice), 1980, 1981, 1982, 1983 Printed in the United States of America by Rae Publishing Co., Inc., Cedar Grove, New Jersey Set in Century Expanded. *Blurb* from The New York Times on inside of front cover. *Other Puffin books about Madeline* on inside of back cover.

This book was also made available at $5.65 in 1977 in a Puffin Tote along with *Madeline's Rescue* and *Madeline in London*. The three books were packaged together in a plastic hang-up bag.

In addition, 25,000 copies of the book were released in October, 1991 as part of a box set entitled *My Very First Puffin Library*. The set was priced at $19.95 and in addition to this title included *Make Way for Ducklings* by Robert Mc-

Closkey; *Corduroy* by Don Freeman: *The Story About Ping* by Marjorie Flack and Kurt Wiese; and *The Story of Ferdinand* by Munro Leaf.

ILLUSTRATIONS: In addition to the title page drawing there are 39 black and yellow and 8 full color illustrations by the author.

COPY EXAMINED: MP.

u. Swedish reprint ([1979]):

TITLE PAGE: A black and yellow picture of a little girl | In black: Madeline | Text/bild: Ludwig Bemelmans | Svensk text: Nils Ludvig | Carlsen and, enclosed in a black square: if

PAGINATION: Unpaged. 28 leaves. 29 x 20.5 cm.

COVERINGS: Lamination on paper - covered boards printed on front with a full-color illustration of a nun and twelve little girls with the Eiffel Tower; and with author and title in white. Spine not seen. No dust jacket.

PUBLISHED: Soon after December 15, 1978 at SKR 34:00. 4,000 sets of sheets printed; 3,000 copies bound. On *verso of title leaf:* Madeline © Copyright 1939 by Ludwig Bemelmans Danish text © by Piet Hein Printed 1978 in Italy by New Interlitho. On page [7], beneath a black drawing of a nun and twelve little girls in the Tuileries: De små flickorna och mannen som matar duvorna befinner sig i Tuilerierna vid Louvre. Ludwig Bemelmans har i sin bok om Madeline använt denna och många andra parisiska exteriörer [followed by a listing of illustrations of attractions in

Paris]. On *back cover* in black and blue, with the same illustration from the Tuileries: Nog tycker jag att Madeline | som bok är både bra och fin, | och tror att ingen blir mer glad | för tusen leksaker i rad. | Den stad vår flicka levde i | hon kallade ju själv Pari; | på svenska heter den Paris - | här lär du känna den precis. | Där lekte hon varenda dag | med vänner i ett näpet lag. | Visst råkade hon illa ut, | men sagan har ett lyckligt slut. | Ja, den är både bra och fin | och kallas - märk väl - Madelin. The verso of the first and recto of the second, and again the verso of the second last and recto of the last leaves are printed as endpapers as in A24v.

ILLUSTRATIONS: As in A24a.

COPY EXAMINED: Kungliga Biblioteket, Stockholm.

v. Third German edition ([1979]):

TITLE PAGE: A black and yellow picture of a little girl | in black: Madeline | Erzählt und gezeichnet von Ludwig Bemelmans | Reinbeker Kinderbücher | Carlsen Verlag

PAGINATION: Unpaged. 28 leaves. 29 x 20.5 cm.

COVERINGS: Full-color laminated boards printed on front with an illustration of a nun and twelve little girls with the Eiffel Tower; title and author in white. On a yellow spine, in black: Ludwig Bemelmans Madeline; and at base: Carlsen Verlag. Madeline von Ludwig Bemelmans and at base Carlsen. No dust jacket.

PUBLISHED: Soon after December 15, 1978 at DM 16,80. 3,000 sets of sheets printed; 2,400 copies bound. On *verso of second leaf:* © Carlsen Verlag GmbH • Reinbek bei Hamburg 1979. Lizenzausgabe mit freundlicher Genehmigung des Diogenes Verlags. Titel der amerikanischen Ausgabe Madeline. Die vorliegende Übersetzung stammt von Christian Strich, Werner Minotsch und Alfons Barth. Copyright © 1939/1952 by Ludwig Bemelmans Copyright © 1978 by Diogenes Verlag AG, Zürich Alle deutschen Rechte vorbehalten. [Note: The Diogenes edition appeared in February of 1980. See A25x.] On *recto of fourth leaf:* Description of the author, under a drawing of a nun with twelve little girls in the Tuileries Gardens facing the Louvre. The recto of the first leaf and verso of the last are pasted to the boards, and the verso of the first leaf and recto of the second; and again the verso of the second last leaf and recto of the last are printed as endpapers with a full-color illustration of the Place de la Concorde. The pale blue back cover reads KM ab 4J at top, with a black reproduction of the author's blurb page illustration and a blurb about the illustrations of Paris in the book, and at bottom, Reinbeker Kinderbücher.

ILLUSTRATIONS: Besides the illustrations of the endpapers, the title page, and the author's blurb page there are 39 black and yellow and 8 full-color illustrations by the author.

COPY EXAMINED: Carlsen Verlag GmbH, Hamburg.

w. Danish reprint ([1979]):

TITLE PAGE: In black, dark yellow, and pale yellow, a little girl | in black: Madeline | Tegnet og fortalt af Ludwig Bemelmans | Gendigtet på dansk af Piet Hein | . . . fra Carlsen if

PAGINATION: Unpaged. 28 leaves. 29 x 20.5 cm.

COVERINGS: Full-color paper-covered boards printed on front with title and author in white; and upon a yellow spine, in black: Ludwig Bemelmans Madeline . . . fra Carlsen/if. No dust jacket.

PUBLISHED: Soon after December 15, 1978 at an unknown price. 4,000 sets of sheets printed; 3,000 copies bound. On *verso of title leaf:* Danish text © by Piet Hein Printed in Italy by New Interlitho 5.oplag 4/79. On *recto of second leaf:* a list of identifiable Paris scenes (taken from the flyleaf of the first edition). Included as well is the black drawing of the Tuileries Gardens facing the Louvre and a translation of the explanatory text from the back of the dust jacket of the first edition. The facsimile endpapers are printed with a full-color drawing of the Place de la Concorde, as in A24v.

Note: The title page suggests the original poetic text has been in some way rewritten by Piet Hein.

ILLUSTRATIONS: In addition to the endpapers, the title page drawing, and the drawing on the illustrations list, there are 39 black and yellow and 8 full-color illustrations by the author.

COPY EXAMINED: Carlsen/if publishers, København.

x. *Second Swiss edition* ([1980]):

TITLE PAGE: Upon a double page, within a full-color drawing labelled (in yellow) Place de la Concorde and itself bounded by green leaves, in black: Ludwig Bemelmans | Madeline | Diogenes

PAGINATION: [1] - [56] pp. 19 x 15.5 cm.

COVERINGS: White paper covers printed on front with a full-color illustration of a nun and twelve little girls in the rain at Nôtre Dame and author, title and colophon in black; and on spine, in black: Ludwig Bemelmans, a yellow dot, Madeline, and at base, kinder-detebe 31. No dust jacket.

This is Diogenes Kinder Taschenbuch Nr. 31.

PUBLISHED: February 1980 at DM 7,80 and Swiss fr 7,80. Number of sets of sheets printed cannot be determined, as the publisher's record cannot be located. On *verso of title leaf*, page [4]: Titel der amerikanischen Originalausgabe: > Madeline < (Simon and Schuster, Inc., New York). Copyright © 1939/1952 by Ludwig Bemelmens. Die deutsche Erstausgabe erschien 1947. Die vorliegende Neuübersetzung stammt von Christian Strich, Werner Mintosch und Alfons Barth. Veröffentlicht als Diogenes Kinder Taschenbuch, 1980. Alle deutschen Rechte vorbehalten. Copyright © 1978 by Diogenes Verlag

AG Zürich. *Series half-title* on page [1]: Diogenes Kinder Taschenbuch 31 | [then in black, within a yellow vertical rectangle:] de | te | be. *Half-title* on page [5]. *Note about the author* on page [53], with a black drawing of the Tuileries Gardens facing the Louvre. *Other Diogenes children's books* on pages [54] - [55].

ILLUSTRATIONS: The illustrations in the text are as in A24a.

COPY EXAMINED: Mrs. Madeleine Bemelmans.

y. *French paperback edition* [(1985)]:

TITLE PAGE: Upon a double page, within a full-color drawing labelled (in yellow) Place de la Concorde and itself bounded by green leaves, in black: Ludwig Bemelmans | Madeleine | lutin poche de l'école des loisirs | 11, rue de Sèvres, Paris 6^e

PAGINATION: [1] - 48 pp. 19 x 15 cm.

COVERINGS: Pale yellow paper covers printed with a full color illustration of the Eiffel Tower with a nun and twelve little girls in yellow, the author's name in white and the title in olive; on spine, in black: lutin poche Madeleine Bemelmans. No dust jacket.

PUBLISHED: September 1985 at FF30.00. Number of sets of sheets printed cannot be determined, as the publisher will not release the information. On *verso of title leaf*, page [4]: Première édition dans la collection "lutin poche de l'école des loisirs": septembre 1985. Imprimé en France par Maury à Malesherbes.

ILLUSTRATIONS: As in A24a, though considerably reduced in size, with one "emendation": a spurious twelfth little girl has been excised from the top black and yellow drawing on the verso of the twentieth leaf. On this "correction" see J533.

COPY EXAMINED: MP.

z. Second British paperback edition ([1986]):

Madeline was published at £1.95 in November, 1986 by Penguin Books of Harmondsworth, Middlesex in Picture Puffins. As the publisher will not communicate, it is not possible to determine the number of sets of sheets printed or the precise date of publication. It has not been possible to examine a copy of this edition.

aa. Spanish pop-up edition ([1987]):

TITLE PAGE: Beneath a pop-up little house in Paris covered with vines, surrounded by a fence outside which sits an artist with canvas and palette peered at by a curious gendarme, in black: Madeline | texto e ilustraciones de | Ludwig Bemelmans

The translation into Spanish is uncredited and was done in-house.

PAGINATION: 1 leaf, 4 interior folded and glued "leaves," 1 leaf. 25.3 x 20.2 cm.

COVERINGS: Laminated yellow paper-covered boards printed on front with a full-color illustration of a nun, twelve little girls and the Eiffel Tower, with title in white; in black: Un Libro Basado en el Original de | Ludwig Bemelmans. Printed on a yellow spine, in black: Madeline Bemelmans; at base: Montena, colophon. No dust jacket.

This book is in the "Libros mágicos" series of pop-up books.

PUBLISHED: March 1987 at 1439 pesetas. 3,000 copies printed. On *back cover*: ¡Con vosotros, Madeline! Las aventuras del famoso personaje de Ludwig Bemelmans, presentadas con un atractivo formato lleno de movimiento y color. Un libro tridimensional y divertido para presentar a la pequeña Madeline. Las ventanas del viejo colegio de París se abrea de par en par y aparecen las doce niñas que siempre en fila estaban, siempre en fila cenaban, se cepillaban los dientes y se acostaban. Salían de casa pasadas las nueve siempre en fila, hiciera sol o hubiera nieve. La dulce Madeline era la menor, mas en todo mostraba mucho valor. Así comienza la encantadora historia que fascinatá a niños y a adultos gracias a sus ilustraciones animadas y a los textos llenos de humor. Adaptación de Jody Wheeler Disenio e papiroflexia de David A. Carter © 1987 Editorial Mondiberica Avda. Alfonso XIII, 50 • 28016 Madrid Impreso e encuadernade en Colombia para Intervisual Communications Inc. The recto of the first leaf and verso of the last are glued to the boards and the verso of the first leaf forms part of the title page while the recto of the last contains the last of the text.

ILLUSTRATIONS: There are 17 full-color illustrations by the author, of which 9 are designed for pop-up.

COPY EXAMINED: Mondadori España, Madrid.

bb. Japanese pop-up edition ([1987]):

TITLE PAGE: Beneath a pop-up little house in Paris covered with vines, surrounded by a fence outside which sits an artist with canvas and palette, peered at by a curious gendarme, in black: Chiisana Madoleno | sakue | Ludwig Bemelmans
The title translates as *Little Madeline*.

PAGINATION: 1 leaf, 4 interior folded and glued "leaves," 1 leaf. 25.3 x 20.2 cm.

COVERINGS: Laminated yellow paper-covered boards printed on front with a full-color illustration of a nun, twelve little girls and the Eiffel Tower, with title in English in white, in Japanese in black, and, in black: Shikake Ehon Ludwig Bemelmans Saku ("based on the book written by Ludwig Bemelmans"). Printed on a yellow spine, in black: Chiisana Madoleno Shikake Ehon, and at base, Dainippon Kaiga. No dust jacket.

PUBLISHED: Spring 1987 at ¥ 2400 by Dainippon Kaiga, Tokyo. 5,000 copies printed. On *back cover:* [In Japanese:] a blurb about the author, a blurb about the book; author; title; Trans-

lated by Kinuko Okamatsu. First edition 1987. The publisher's name and address.[In English:] First edition. Text copyright © Madeline Bemelmans and Barbara Bemelmans Marciano, 1987. Adaptation by Jody Wheeler Design and paper engineering by David A. Carter Printed and bound in Colombia S.A. for Intervisual Communications Inc., Los Angeles, CA 90045 U.S.A. The recto of the first leaf and verso of the last are glued to the boards and the verso of the first leaf forms part of the title page while the recto of the last contains the last of the text.

ILLUSTRATIONS: There are 17 full-color illustrations by the author, of which 9 are designed for pop-up.

COPY EXAMINED: Intervisual Communications, Los Angeles.

cc. American pop-up edition ([1987]):

TITLE PAGE: Beneath a pop-up little house in Paris covered with vines, surrounded by a fence outside which sits an artist with canvas and palette, peered at by a curious gendarme, in black: Madeline | story & pictures by | Ludwig Bemelmans

PAGINATION: 1 leaf, 4 interior folded and glued "leaves," 1 leaf. 25.3 x 20.2 cm.

COVERINGS: Laminated yellow paper-covered boards printed on front with a full-color illustration of a nun, twelve little girls and the Eiffel

Tower, with title in white, and in black: A Pop-up Book based on the original by | Ludwig Bemelmans. Printed on a yellow spine, in black: Madeline Bemelmans; at base: Viking Kestrel. No dust jacket.

PUBLISHED: September 11, 1987 at $13.95. 35,000 copies printed. On *back cover:* Viking Kestrel. First edition. Text and illustrations copyright © Madeline Bemelmans and Barbara Bemelmans Marciano, 1987. Art adapted by Jody Wheeler. Design and paper engineering by David A. Carter. First published in 1987 by Viking Penguin Inc., 40 West 23rd Street, New York, New York 10010. Published simultaneously in Canada by Penguin Books Canada Limited. Printed and bound in Colombia, S.A. for Intervisual Communications, Inc., Los Angeles, California. The recto of the first leaf and verso of the last are glued to the boards and the verso of the first leaf forms part of the title page while the recto of the last contains the last of the text.

Note: An undetermined number of copies of this edition were distributed by the Book-of-the-Month Club to its membership in December 1987 at $12.95. The books were in the Children's Christmas Catalogue. The book was accompanied by a copy of the *Book-of-the-Month Club News* for December 1987, which contained a synopsis.

ILLUSTRATIONS: There are 17 full-color illustrations by the author, of which 9 are designed for pop-up.

COPY EXAMINED: MP.

dd. Second South African edition ([1988]):

TITLE PAGE: Within a vertical yellow rectangle, in black: Madeleine | a black and yellow drawing of a little girl | in black: Ludwig Bemelmans | Vertaal deur Freda Linde | Qualitas

PAGINATION: Unpaged. 24 leaves; endpapers. 30 x 21.9 cm.

COVERINGS: Paper-covered boards printed on front with a full-color picture of a nun and twelve little girls at the Eiffel Tower, with title and author in white; on spine in black upon a yellow strip: Madeleine deur Ludwig Bemelmans; at base in white upon a black strip: Qualitas. Full-color dust jacket reproduces the covering.

PUBLISHED: February 1988 at R 14.70. 3,000 sets of sheets printed. *Verso of title leaf* is blank. *Opposite the half-title page:* Oorspronklike titel: *Madeline.* Uitgegee deur Simon & Schuster, New York in 1938 Uitgegee in 1952 deur Andre Deutsch Limited, London Afrikaanse uitgawe © 1987 deur Qualitas (Edms.) Bpk Posbus 26444, Arcadia, Pretoria 0007 Alle regte voorbehou. Vertaal deur Freda Linde Geset, gedruk en gebind deur Colorgraphic, Durban. Endpapers plain.

Note: The notation opposite the half-title, "Uitgegee deur Simon & Schuster, New York in 1938," is erroneous. See A24a.

ILLUSTRATIONS: As in A24s.

COPY EXAMINED: Lydia Snyman, Cape Town.

ee. Mini-box edition ([1989]):

TITLE PAGE: Within a vertical yellow rectangle, in black: Madeline | a black and yellow drawing of a little girl | in black: story & pictures by | Ludwig Bemelmans | Puffin Books

PAGINATION: Unpaged. 32 leaves. 15.6 x 11.3 cm.

COVERINGS: Full-color paper covers printed with title and author in white on front; on spine, in black upon yellow: Ludwig Bemelmans Madeline. The book is packaged together with the similar editions of *Madeline and the Bad Hat* (see A25) and *Madeline's Rescue* (see A30) inside a cardboard replica of the old house in Paris covered with vines.

This edition is known in the trade as *Madeline's House*.

PUBLISHED: September, 1989 at $11.95. 25,000 sets of sheets were printed originally, and a second 25,000 followed by Christmas. On *verso of title leaf:* Published in Picture Puffins 1977 This edition published 1989. *Half-title* on recto of third leaf. *Other Madeline titles* on verso of third leaf and upon back cover. *Second half-title* on recto of fifth leaf. The recto of the first leaf and all of the last are turquoise; the verso of the first leaf and recto of the second, and again the verso of the thirtieth leaf and recto of the thirty-first are printed as facsimile endpapers with a picture of the sun shining on the Place de la Concorde.

Note: An undetermined number of copies of this edition were distributed by the Children's Book-of-the-Month Club to its membership in November 1989 at $10.50.

ILLUSTRATIONS: In addition to the title page drawing there are 39 black and yellow and 8 full color illustrations by the author.

COPY EXAMINED: MP.

A25. Madeline and the Bad Hat [1956/57]

a. Limited First edition:

TITLE PAGE: Within a vertically rectangular, full-color illustration of a youth with barbells and a statue of a lion, in white: Madeline | and the Bad Hat | Written and Illustrated by | Ludwig Bemelmans | The Viking Press • New York

PAGINATION: 3 leaves, [1] - 54 pp., 2 leaves. 30.6 x 22.4 cm.

COVERINGS: Mint green cloth-covered boards stamped on front with a yellow, black and red figure of a youth waving a hat on a bicycle, and printed on spine, in dark green, Bemelmans Madeline and the Bad Hat Viking. Red slip case.

PUBLISHED: December 1, 1956 at $7.50. 985 copies specially bound from a printing of 23,000 sets of sheets. On *recto of third leaf:* a black and yellow drawing of a nun with twelve little girls | in black: Of this autographed, limited first edition, | 985 have been printed, of which | 885 are for sale *Dedication* on verso of third leaf: To | Mimi *Half-title* on page [1] with a black and yellow drawing of a youth waving a hat on a bicycle. *Other books by the author* on page [2], listing five titles. On *verso of title leaf:* Limited, autographed edition, December 1956 First trade edition, March 1957 Lithographed in U.S.A. by Livermore and Knight Co. The recto of the first leaf and verso of the last are pasted down to the insides of the boards. The verso of the first leaf and recto of the second, and again the verso of the second-last leaf and recto of the last, are printed as endpapers with a full-color illustration of a view of Nôtre Dame from beneath the Petit Pont.

ILLUSTRATIONS: In addition to the facsimile endpapers, the title page illustration, the illustration on the third leaf, and the illustration on the half-title, there are 32 black and yellow and 19 full-color illustrations by the author.

COPY EXAMINED: MP.

a (bis). First trade edition ([1957]):

TITLE PAGE: Within a vertically rectangular, full-color illustration of a youth with barbells and a statue of a lion, in white: Madeline | and the Bad Hat | Written and Illustrated by | Ludwig Bemelmans | The Viking Press • New York

PAGINATION: 2 leaves, 1 blank leaf, [1] - 54 pp., 2 leaves. 30.6 x 22.2 cm.

COVERINGS: Red cloth-covered boards stamped on front in black with a drawing of a little girl holding the hand of a youth in a black gown and hat, and printed on spine in black: Bemelmans Madeline and the Bad Hat Viking. Full-color dust jacket printed in white.

PUBLISHED: March 8, 1957 at $3.50. 23,000 sets of sheets printed; 15,000 copies bound. *Verso of title leaf, half-title* and *dedication* as in A25a. Facsimile endpapers as in A25a.

This book was the winner of the New York Herald Tribune Children's Spring Book Festival Award.

15,000 copies of this edition were selected by the Junior Literary Guild in May, 1957 and distributed to membership at an unknown price with slight alteration to binding and book spine.

The book was reprinted in 1984 with the title verso reading as follows: Copyright © renewed Madeleine Bemelmans and Barbara Bemelmans Marciano, 1984.

ILLUSTRATIONS: As in A25a.

COPY EXAMINED: MP.

b. British edition ([1958]):

TITLE PAGE: Within a vertically rectangular full-color illustration of a youth with barbells and a statue of a lion, in white: Madeline | and the Bad Hat | Written and Illustrated by | Ludwig Bemelmans | beneath the rectangle, in black: André Deutsch • London

PAGINATION: Unpaged. 32 leaves. 30 x 22.1 cm.

COVERINGS: Paper-covered boards printed on front with a full-color illustration of the Place de la Concorde and author and title in white, and upon a pale yellow spine, in black: Madeline and the Bad Hat by Ludwig Bemelmans; at base, in yellow upon a black strip: André Deutsch. Dust jacket not seen.

PUBLISHED: September 19, 1958 at 15s. Approximately 10,000 sets of sheets printed. On *verso of title leaf:* First published 1958 André Deutsch Limited 12-14 Carlisle Street Soho Square London W1 (colophon) Printed in The Netherlands by Drukkerij Holland N.V., Amsterdam. *Half-title* on recto of third leaf, in black with a black and yellow drawing of a youth waving a hat upon a bicycle. *Second half-title* on recto of fifth leaf, in black with a black drawing of a little girl. *Other books by the author* on verso of third leaf, listing five titles. Facsimile endpapers as in A25a.

ILLUSTRATIONS: As in A25a.

COPY EXAMINED: MP.

c. German edition ([1958]):

TITLE PAGE: In red: Madeline | in black: und der Böse Bube | in full color: drawing of a youth holding up barbells with a statue of a reclining lion | in black: Text und Illustrationen von | in red: Ludwig Bemelmans | in black: Blüchert Verlag Hamburg

PAGINATION: Unpaged. 32 leaves. 30 x 22 cm.

COVERINGS: Blue cloth-covered boards stamped on front with a yellow, black and red figure of a youth waving a hat on a bicycle; printed on spine, in dark green: Blüchert Verlag Madeline und der Böse Bube von Ludwig Bemelmans. Full-color dust jacket printed in white.

PUBLISHED: 1958 at DM 9,80. Number of sets of sheets printed cannot be determined, as the publisher and the publisher's records are unlocatable. On *verso of title leaf:* Übersetzung ins Deutsche: Maria Berling Die Originalausgabe erschien bei Viking Press, New York unter dem Titel: Madeline and the Bad Hat Printed in Holland 1958. *Half-title* on recto of following leaf, with black and yellow drawing of a child upon a bicycle. Facsimile endpapers as in A25a.

ILLUSTRATIONS: As in A25a.

COPY EXAMINED: Mrs. Madeleine Bemelmans.

d. Danish edition ([1961]):

TITLE PAGE: Upon a vertically rectangular full-color illustration of a youth with barbells next to a statue of a lion, within a white clearing, in black: Madeline | og det Sorte Får | within a second white clearing, at bottom of illustration: Skrevet og illustreret af Ludwig Bemelmans Oversat af Piet Hein | beneath the illustration: Illustrationsforlaget

PAGINATION: Unpaged. 32 leaves. 30 x 20.6 cm. |

COVERINGS: Full-color paper-covered boards printed on front in white with title and author, and upon a yellow spine, in black: Madeline og det Sorte Far af Ludwig Bemelmans. No dust jacket.

PUBLISHED: 1961 at an unknown price. Number of sets of sheets printed cannot be determined, as the publisher's records are lost. On *verso of title leaf:* Titlen på den amerikanske udgave (originaludgaven) er Madeline and the Bad Hat. *Half-title* on recto of third leaf, with black and yellow drawing of a child with a black hat upon a bicycle. On *verso of third leaf:* Printed in Holland. An excerpt from the *author's introduction,* printed on the dust jacket of the first edition, appears on the recto of the fifth leaf. Facsimile endpapers as in A25a.

ILLUSTRATIONS: As in A25a.

COPY EXAMINED: Carlsen/if publishers, Copenhagen, Denmark.

e. Paperback edition ([1968]):

TITLE PAGE: Within a vertically rectangular full-color illustration of a youth with barbells and a statue of a lion, in white: Madeline | and the Bad Hat | Written and Illustrated by | Ludwig Bemelmans | The Viking Press • New York

PAGINATION: Unpaged. 32 leaves. 24.2 x 18 cm.

COVERINGS: Full-color paper cover printed with author, title and Viking Seafarer colophon in white; and printed on spine, in white: VS-1 Madeline and the Bad Hat by Ludwig Bemelmans, and at base, Viking. Pages trimmed. No dust jacket.

PUBLISHED: 1968 at $1.25. Number of sets of sheets printed cannot be determined, as the publisher's record is lost. On *verso of title leaf,* page [4]: Viking Seafarer edition. Issued in 1968 by The Viking Press, Inc. Printed in U.S.A. Third leaf contains on recto a black and yellow drawing of a nun with twelve little girls and on verso the dedication, To | Mimi. *Half-title* on recto of fourth leaf. The verso of the first leaf and recto of the second, and again the verso of the second-last leaf and recto of the last, are printed as endpapers with a full-color illustration of a view of Nôtre Dame from beneath the Petit Pont.

This is Viking Seafarer No. VS-1.

ILLUSTRATIONS: As in A25a.

COPY EXAMINED: Mrs. Madeleine Bemelmans.

f. Japanese edition ([1973]):

TITLE PAGE: Within a vertically rectangular full-color illustration of a youth with barbells and a statue of a lion, in white: Madeline to Ita-zurakko | by Ludwig Bemelmans | Translated by Asada Teiji | Fukuinkan Shoten

PAGINATION: [1] - [56] pp.; endpapers. 30.3 x 22 cm.

COVERINGS: Lamination on paper - covered boards printed on front with a full-color illustration of the Place de la Concorde, and with author and title in white; and on a royal blue spine, in black, by Ludwig Bemelmans Madeline to Ita-zurakko and at base Fukuinkan Shoten | colophon. No dust jacket.

PUBLISHED: May 10, 1973 at ¥700. 40,000 sets of sheets printed. On *verso of title leaf*, page [2]: Madeline and The Bad Hat, Story and pictures by Ludwig Bemelmans. Copyright 1956 by Ludwig Bemelmans. Originally published by The Viking Press, Inc., New York. Japanese language edition copyright 1973 by Fukuinkan-Shoten, Publishers, Tokyo, by arrangements with Charles E. Tuttle Co. *Index to color plates* on page [53]. On page [54]: a black and yellow illustration of a nun with twelve little girls. *Author's blurb on page [55]. Advertisements* for other books in the Madeline series on page [56]. Also on page [56]: Published May 10, 1973. 101 Tokyo-to Chiodaku Mitzuzaki-cho 1-1-9 Fukuin-kan Shoten. Printed by Sei Kosha. Designed by Kobayashi. [colophon]. Book care guidelines. Endpapers as in A25a.

ILLUSTRATIONS: As in A25a.

COPY EXAMINED: Mrs. Madeleine Bemelmans.

g. Second Paperback edition ([1977]):

TITLE PAGE: Within a vertically rectangular full-color illustration of a youth with barbells and a statue of a lion, in white: Madeline | and the Bad Hat | Written and Illustrated by | Ludwig Bemelmans | beneath the illustration, in black: Puffin Books

PAGINATION: Unpaged. 32 leaves. 20.9 x 17.5 cm.

COVERINGS: Full-color paper covers printed on front with title and author in white and on spine, in black upon yellow, Ludwig Bemelmans Madeline and the Bad Hat.

Published 1977 at an unknown price. Number of sets of sheets printed cannot be determined, as the publisher's record is lost. On *verso of title leaf:* Published in Puffin Books 1977 Printed in the United States of America by Georgian Web Off-set, Garden City, New York Set in Bodoni. *Half-title* on recto of fourth leaf. *Drawing* on recto of third leaf, and *dedication* on verso, as in A25e. The verso of the first leaf and recto of the second, and again the verso of the 31st leaf and recto of the 32nd, are printed with full-color illustrations which reproduce the facsimile endpapers of full-sized editions.

ILLUSTRATIONS: In addition to the drawings on the title leaf and with the dedication there are 32 black and yellow and 21 full color illustrations by the author.

COPY EXAMINED: MP.

A26. Madeline and the Gypsies [1958]

a. First edition ([1958]):

TITLE PAGE: Upon a horizontally rectangular full-color illustration of two costumed children upon a prancing circus horse, in yellow: Madeline and the Gypsies | by Ludwig Bemelmans | in black: a McCall's | Christmas gift | for the whole family | [signed:] Bemelmans

Unpaged. 8 leaves. 16.3 x 22.8 cm. No covers.

PUBLISHED: December 1958, at no charge. Approximately 3,000,000 sets of sheets printed. The recto of the first leaf and verso of the 12th act as covers. On *verso of first leaf:* Copyright © 1958 by Ludwig Bemelmans

This is an insert in the Christmas 1958 edition of *McCall's* magazine.

ILLUSTRATIONS: In addition to the title illustration there are 26 illustrations by the author.

Aside from the illustration of the railway station on the eighth leaf recto, which in the trade edition appears on pp. 50-51, all of the illustrations in this edition are altered versions of the illustrations in A26b. An example of a particularly subtle change: on the fifth leaf recto here, there is a drawing of a postcard sent to Miss Clavel, reproduced in the first trade edition on p. 28. The present edition shows the postmark as being from Carcasonne and the first trade edition gives it as Honfleur.

COPY EXAMINED: *McCall's* magazine.

a (bis). First trade edition:

TITLE PAGE: Within a vertically rectangular full-color illustration of a clown balancing two acrobats upon a bicycle balanced on a high wire attached to a table, in white: Madeline and the | Gypsies | upon the tablecloth, in white: by | Ludwig | Bemelmans | at the bottom of the illustration: The Viking Press • New York

PAGINATION: 2 leaves, [1] - 56 pp., 2 leaves. 30.4 x 21.9 cm.

COVERINGS: Mint green linen-weave cloth-covered boards stamped in black on front with a drawing of an equestrienne standing upon a bowing horse and printed on spine, in black: Madeline and The Gypsies by Ludwig Bemelmans at base: The Viking Press. Full-color dust jacket printed in yellow and white.

PUBLISHED: September 11, 1959 at $3.50. 36,000 sets of sheets printed; 20,000 copies bound. On *verso of title leaf,* page [4]: Published in 1959 by The Viking Press, Inc. A shorter version of this story appeared in *McCall's* Lithographed in U.S.A. by Livermore & Knight Co. *Dedication* on page [4]: with a black and yellow drawing of a clown playing a bass drum: To May Massee. *Half-title* on page [1]. The recto of the first leaf and the verso of the last leaf are pasted down upon the insides of the boards. The verso of the first leaf and recto of the second, and again the verso of the second last leaf and recto of the last, are printed as endpapers with a full-color illustration of Le Pont d'Avignon at springtime. A *letter from the author* appears on the front flyleaf; the rear flyleaf contains a *list of illustrations:* The Bridge at Avignon, End-papers; Notre-Dame in a storm, p. 10-11; Chateau de Fontainebleau, 18-19; The pool at Marly-le-Roi, 20; Chartres, with the Cathedral, 21; Mont-Saint-Michel, 22-23; Carcassonne, 26-27; A Normandy farm, 38-39; The seacoast at Deauville, 43; Gare Saint-Lazare in Paris, 50-51.

Note: An undetermined number of copies of a reprint of this edition were taken by the Book-of-the-Month Club and made available to its membership in spring 1971 singly at $4.75 or in a triple combination with *Madeline's Rescue* and *Madeline* at $8.75. The books were in the Children's Christmas Catalogue. The book was accompanied by a copy of the *Book-of-the-Month Club News* for Spring 1971, which contained a synopsis.

The text is here reprinted and expanded from *McCall's,* December 1958; see A26a.

The first two lines of text on p. 1 are, in the original, four lines. The next two lines are omitted in the original. The fifth line, which here ends with a dash, ends with a comma in the original. "He was all alone; his parents were away;" reads originally "Pepito's parents were away,". A comma ending has been added to the eleventh line. The concluding lines on the page, "And so —/ Dear reader —" are absent from the original. The line on p. 6, "Here we go!" is absent from the original. On p. 7, the dash ending of the first line replaces an original comma ending. In the third line the semicolon was originally a dash. The text on pp. 8-11, "A sudden gust of wind/ A bolt of lightning,/ Even the Rooster found it frightening./ The big wheel stops; the passengers land./ How fortunate there is a taxi stand!" read originally "A cloudburst came and sheets of lightning/ And thunderclaps; it got cold and frightening./ The big wheel stopped; the passengers land./ How fortunate there is a taxi stand!" On p. 12, the exclamation point ending of the first line was originally a period ending. In the fourth line, "half-past" was originally "half past". On p. 17 "The big wheel was folded, and the tent" read originally "The wheel was folded and the tent;" and "For Gypsies do not like to stay —" read originally "For Gypsies don't pay rent or stay —" The text on pp. 18-19 is absent in the original. On p. 22-23, "And never —never —/ To go to sleep." was originally "Never, never to go to sleep." On pp. 24-25 "The Gypsies taught them grace/ And speed" was originally "The Gypsies taught them balance and speed"; and the lines on pp. 26-27 were originally one line. On p. 29, the first word was absent in the original; the comma after "because" in the second line was absent in the original; the fourth line had, originally, a period ending; the fifth line, "And suddenly revived" was originally "But suddenly she revived" and originally neither the fifth nor the sixth lines were indented. The exclamation point ending of the seventh line was originally a dash. On p. 30, "They rushed to the scene of the disaster" was originally "She took a train to the scene of the disaster." On p. 32 "The Gypsy Mama said, 'How would you like to try on/ This lovely costume of a lion?' " was originally "She said, 'Come here, my children, and try on/ This lovely costume of a lion.' " On p. 33 the word "both" in the second line was absent in the original and the comma ending was originally a period. The last two lines, "And nobody knew what was inside/ The tough old lion's leathery hide" were absent in the original. On pp. 34-35, "This was a fascinating game./ Compared to this, all else was tame./ A circus lion earns his bread/ By scaring people half to death./ And after doing that, he's fed./ And after that, he's put to bed" were originally "Then the strong man picked the lion up,/ Put him in a cage and snapped the lock./ And there they were until the elephant/ Said, 'They can't do that to my friends, they can't.'/ With a mighty yank the cage came off the truck./ 'Good-by, dear friends, I wish you luck.' " On p. 37 the second line, and the lines on

pp. 38-39, appear somewhat further on as "They smelled sweet flowers,/ They came to a farm,/ They frightened the barnyard,/ Intending no harm." On p. 42, the second line, "In a zoo or circus, we'll surely be shot" was originally "In a zoo or a circus, we'll surely get shot." On pp. 43-45, the text replaces the following: "And then with weary feet they headed/ Back to the lion cage they dreaded./ They said, 'It's not that we want to complain,/ But we'd like to sleep in our own beds again.'/ And said Pepito, 'No work and all play/ Is no fun if you have to do it all day.'/ Just then Madeline cried, 'Oh!/ Look, Pepito, here comes someone we know!' " On p. 46 the exclamation point ending of the first line was originally a period ending. The period ending of the second line was originally an exclamation point ending. On p. 47 the first line was originally indented. The second line ending was originally unpunctuated. And originally there were these lines as well: "Because she had no children of her own,/ And now these two were as good as gone." On p. 48 the first line was originally two lines with an exclamation point ending the second instead of a comma. The second line was two lines ending with "cheeks" instead of "cheek". The third line was two lines. The fourth line was two lines. On pp. 49-56, the present text, "The best part of a voyage—by plane,/ By ship,/ Or train—/ Is when the trip is over and you are/ Home again./ Here is a freshly laundered shirty—/ It's better to be clean than dirty./ In two straight lines/ They broke their bread/ And brushed their teeth/ And went to bed./ 'Good night, little girls, thank the Lord you are well!/ And now PLEASE go to sleep,' said Miss Clavel./ And she turned out the light and closed the door—/ And then she came back, just to count them once more!" read originally, "The nicest part/ Of a voyage,/ By plane,/ By ship,/ Or train,/ Is when/ The trip/ Is over/ And you are/ Happily home again."

14,000 copies of this edition were selected by the Literary Guild, December 1959, and distributed to membership at an unknown price with slight alteration to binding and book spine.

ILLUSTRATIONS: In addition to the endpapers, the title page illustration and the dedication drawing, there are 25 black and yellow and 22 full color illustrations by the author. See also A26a, since most of the illustrations have been altered from the first edition.

COPY EXAMINED: MP.

b. British edition ([1961]):

TITLE PAGE: Within a vertically rectangular full-color illustration of a clown balancing two acrobats upon a bicycle balanced on a high wire attached to a table, in white: Madeline and the | Gypsies | upon the tablecloth, in white: by | Ludwig | Bemelmans | beneath the illustration, in black: André Deutsch • London

PAGINATION: 2 leaves, [1] - 56 pp., 2 leaves. 29.5 x 22 cm.

COVERINGS: Full-color paper boards printed with title in yellow and author in white on front; and on spine, in red upon a yellow strip: Madeline and The Gypsies by Ludwig Bemelmans at base, in white upon a black strip: André Deutsch. Full-color dust jacket printed in yellow and white.

PUBLISHED: August 31, 1961 at 15s. Approximately 10,000 sets of sheets printed. On *verso of title leaf:* First printed 1961 by André Deutsch Limited printed in The Netherlands by Drukkerij Holland N.V. Amsterdam. *Dedication* on verso of title leaf: As in A26a(bis). Facsimile endpapers as in A26a(bis).

ILLUSTRATIONS: As in A26a(bis).

COPY EXAMINED: The British Library, Great Russell Street, London. Dust jacket information from André Deutsch Ltd., Great Russell Street, London.

c. Danish edition ([1962]):

TITLE PAGE: Upon a vertically rectangular full-color illustration of a clown balancing two acrobats upon a bicycle balanced upon a high wire attached to a table, within a white clearing, in black: Madeline Og | Zigøjnerne | upon the tablecloth: Af | Ludwig | Bemelmans | Oversat af | Piet Hein | at the bottom of the illustration: Illustrationsforlaget

PAGINATION: 2 leaves, [1] - 56 pp., 2 leaves. 29.8 x 21 cm.

COVERINGS: Full-color paper-covered boards

printed on front with title in yellow and author in white; and on spine, in yellow Madeline Og Zigøjnerne af Ludwig Bemelmans. No dust jacket.

PUBLISHED: 1962 at an unknown price. Number of sets of sheets printed cannot be determined, as the publisher will not communicate. *Half-title* on page [1]. On *verso of half-title leaf*, page [2]: Titlen på den amerikanske udgave (originaludgaven) er Madeline and The Gypsies Printed in the Netherlands. *List of illustrations* on page [2]: Broen i Avignon, omslaget — Notre-Dame Kirken i Uvejr, side 10-11; Slottet Fontainebleau, 18-19; Svømmebassinet i Marly-leroi, 20; Domkirken i Chartres, 21; Mont-Saint-Michel, 22-23; Carcassonne, 26-27; En Bondegård i Normandiet, 38-39; Kysten Ved Deauville, 43; Saint-Lazare Banegården i Paris, 50-51. *Other Madeline titles* of the publisher on page [2]. *Dedication* on verso of title leaf, page [4], as in A26a. Facsimile endpapers as in A26a(bis).

ILLUSTRATIONS: As in A26a(bis).

Note: The back cover contains the title, the publisher, a black and yellow drawing of a little girl, and a lengthy reader's abstract.

COPY EXAMINED: Carlsen/if publishers, Copenhagen, Denmark.

d. Paperback edition ([1973]):

The Viking Press published *Madeline and the Gypsies* at $1.50 in October 1973 as part of its "Seafarer" series. The publisher's record has been lost,

so there is no way to determine the number of sets of sheets printed. A copy of this edition has not been found for examination.

This is Viking Seafarer No. VS-81.

e. Japanese edition ([1973]):

TITLE PAGE: Within a vertically rectangular full-color illustration of a clown balancing two acrobats upon a bicycle balanced on a high wire attached to a table, in white: Madeline to | Jipushii | upon the tablecloth, in black: Ludwig | Bemelmans by | Translated by Asada Teiji | at the bottom of the illustration: Fukuinkan Shoten

PAGINATION: [1] - [56] pp.; endpapers. 30.3 x 22 cm.

COVERINGS: Lamination on paper - covered boards printed with a full-color illustration of two young acrobats on a black horse and printed on a red spine, in black: By Ludwig Bemelmans Madeline To Jipushii; and at base: Fukuinkan Shoten | colophon. No dust jacket.

PUBLISHED: May 10, 1973 at ¥1130. 27,000 sets of sheets printed. On *verso of title leaf*, page [2]: with a black and yellow drawing of a clown playing a bass drum: To May Massee. Madeline and The Gypsies Story and pictures by Ludwig Bemelmans. Copyright 1958, 1959 by Ludwig Bemelmans. Originally published by The Viking Press, Inc., New York. Japanese language edition copyright 1973 by Fukuinkan-Shoten, Publishers, Tokyo, by arrangements with Charles E.

Tuttle Co. *Index to color plates* on page [55]. *Author's blurb* and *advertisements for other books* in the Madeline series on page [56]. Also on page [56]: Published May 10, 1973. 101 Tokyo-to Chiodaku Mitzuzaki-cho 1-1-9 Fukuinkan Shoten. Printed by Sei Kosha. Designed by Kobayashi (colophon). Book care guidelines. Endpapers as in A26a(bis).

ILLUSTRATIONS: As in A26a(bis).

COPY EXAMINED: Mrs. Madeleine Bemelmans.

f. Second paperback edition ([1977]):

TITLE PAGE: Within a vertically rectangular full-color illustration of a clown balancing two acrobats upon a bicycle balanced on a high wire attached to a table, in white: Madeline and the | Gypsies | upon the tablecloth, in white: by | Ludwig | Bemelmans | beneath the illustration, in black: Puffin Books

PAGINATION: Unpaged. 32 leaves. 20.8 x 17.5 cm.

COVERINGS: Full-color paper covers printed with title in yellow and author in white on front and on spine, in black upon yellow: Ludwig Bemelmans Madeline and the Gypsies.

PUBLISHED: 1977 at an unknown price. Number of sets of sheets printed cannot be determined, as the publisher's record is lost. On *verso of title leaf:* Published in Puffin Books 1977 Printed in the United States of America by Georgian Web

Offset, Garden City, New York Set in Bodoni. *Dedication* on verso of title leaf as in A26a. *Half-title* on recto of third leaf. The verso of the first leaf and recto of the second, and again the verso of the 31st leaf and recto of the 32nd, are printed with full-color illustrations which reproduce the endpapers of full-sized editions. The inside front cover contains a *blurb* from the *Chicago Tribune*.

ILLUSTRATIONS: In addition to the title page and dedication drawings there are 25 black and yellow and 24 full color illustrations by the author.

COPY EXAMINED: MP.

A27. Madeline in London [1961]

a. First edition:

TITLE PAGE: Within a vertically rectangular full-color illustration of a horse guard in uniform, and two children upon a black horse in an archway, in black: Madeline | in | in red: London | by | Ludwig Bemelmans | in black: Viking - New York

PAGINATION: 2 leaves, [1] - 56 pp., 2 leaves. 30.4 x 22.2 cm.

COVERINGS: Red linen-weave cloth-covered boards stamped on front in black with a drawing of two children upon a strutting horse and printed on spine, in black: Bemelmans Madeline in London; at base: Viking. Full-color dust jacket printed in pale green and white; on spine: A Guild Book.

Further printings of this edition have laminated full-color paper-covered boards illustrated on front with a picture of a nun, twelve little girls, and a guard in red topcoat, with title in pale green and author in white; printed on a pale green spine, in red: Madeline in London by Ludwig Bemelmans; at base, in black: The Viking Press.

PUBLISHED: October 6, 1961 at $3.50. Number of sets of sheets printed and bound is unknown by the publisher, but an edition of at least 15,000 can be presumed. On *verso of title leaf:* First published in 1961 by The Viking Press, Inc. Portions of this story appeared in *Holiday,* Copyright © 1961 by The Curtis Publishing Company Printed in the U.S.A. by Livermore & Knight Co. *Half-title* on page [1]. *Other books by the author* on page [2], listing six titles. The recto of the first leaf and the verso of the last leaf are pasted down upon the insides of the boards. The verso of the first leaf and recto of the second, and again the verso of the second last leaf and recto of the last, are printed as endpapers with a full-color illustration of a yellow airplane circling over Westminster in red.

Part of the text is here reprinted from *Holiday,* August 1961; see E194.

14,500 copies of this edition were selected by the Junior Literary Guild between October, 1961 and April, 1962 and distributed to membership at an unknown price with slight alteration to binding and book spine.

ILLUSTRATIONS: In addition to the facsimile endpapers and the title leaf illustration, there are 28 black and yellow and 31 full color illustrations by the author.

COPY EXAMINED: MP.

b. British edition ([1962]):

TITLE PAGE: Within a vertically rectangular full-color illustration of a horse guard in uniform, and two children upon a black horse in an archway, in black: Madeline | in | in red: London | by | Ludwig Bemelmans | in black: André Deutsch

PAGINATION: 2 leaves, [1] - 56 pp., 2 leaves. 29.5 x 22 cm.

COVERINGS: Full-color paper boards printed on front with title in pale green and author in white; on spine, in red: Madeline in London by Ludwig Bemelmans; in black: André Deutsch. Dust jacket not examined.

PUBLISHED: November 30, 1962 at 15s. Approximately 10,000 sets of sheets printed. On *verso of title leaf:* First published 1962 by André Deutsch Limited 105 Great Russell Street London W C 1 Printed in Hungary by Penzjegy Nyomda. *Half-title* on page [1]. *Second half-title* on page [3]. Facsimile endpapers as in A27a.

ILLUSTRATIONS: As in A27a.

Note: In the second impression, the verso of the title leaf reads: First published November 1962

by André Deutsch Limited, 105 Great Russell Street London W C 1 Second impression 1966 Printed in Hungary by Kossuth Printing House.

COPY EXAMINED: Mr. André Deutsch, 105 Great Russell Street, London.

c. Paperback edition ([1972]):

The Viking Press published *Madeline in London* as part of its "Seafarer" edition series in 1972, at $1.50. The publisher's record being lost, it is not possible to determine the precise publication date or the number of sets of sheets printed. A copy of this edition has not been found for examination.

This is Viking Seafarer No. VS-71.

Note: Some copies of this edition were distributed after June 1977 in a "Seafarer Reading Chest" package, including multiple copies of the book, a cassette with narration, and a teacher's guide by Roy Oakley.

d. Second paperback edition ([1977]):

TITLE PAGE: Within a vertically rectangular full-color illustration of a horse guard in uniform, and two children upon a black horse in an archway, in black: Madeline | in | in red: London | by | Ludwig Bemelmans | in black: Puffin Books

PAGINATION: Unpaged. 32 leaves. 23.1 x 19 cm.

COVERINGS: Full-color paper covers printed on front with title in pale aqua and author in white; upon a yellow spine, in black: Ludwig Bemelmans Madeline in London ISBN 0 14 050.199 1. No dust jacket.

PUBLISHED: 1977 at an unknown price. Number of sets of sheets printed cannot be determined, as the publisher's record is lost. On *verso of title leaf:* Published in Puffin Books 1977 Portions of this story appeared in *Holiday*, Copyright © 1961 by The Curtis Publishing Company Printed in the United States of America by Georgian Web Offset, Garden City, New York Set in Bodoni Bold. *Half-title* on recto of third leaf. The verso of the first leaf and recto of the second, and again the verso of the 31st leaf and recto of the 32nd, are printed with full-color illustrations which reproduce the endpapers of the first edition.

ILLUSTRATIONS: In addition to the title page illustration there are 28 black and yellow and 33 full color illustrations by the author.

COPY EXAMINED: MP.

A28. Madeline's Christmas [1956]

a. First edition [(1956)]:

TITLE PAGE: Upon a vertically rectangular full-color illustration of a nun with twelve little girls and the Eiffel Tower decorated like a Christmas tree, in a snowfall, in yellow: Madeline's | Christmas | by | Ludwig Bemelmans | beneath the illustration, in black: A McCall's Book | © Copyright 1956 by Ludwig Bemelmans

PAGINATION: Unpaged. 12 leaves. 18.7 x 13 cm. No covers.

PUBLISHED: December 1956 at no supplemental charge. Approximately 3,000,000 sets of sheets printed. The recto of the first leaf and verso of the 12th act as covers.

This is an insert in the Christmas 1956 edition of *McCall's* magazine.

ILLUSTRATIONS: In addition to the title illustration there are 28 full-color illustrations by the author.

COPY EXAMINED: MP.

a (bis). Reprint (First trade edition) [(1985)]:

TITLE PAGE: In blue: Madeline's Christmas | a full-color illustration of a little girl peeking out from beneath the red ribbon binding a Christmas package | in black, By Ludwig Bemelmans | Viking Kestrel

PAGINATION: Unpaged. 16 leaves; endpapers. 30.5 x 22 cm.

COVERINGS: Full-color paper-covered cardboard covers printed with a full color illustration of a nun with twelve little girls and the Eiffel Tower decorated like a Christmas tree in a snowfall, the author's name and title in white; on spine, in white: Madeline's Christmas Bemelmans; at bottom: Viking Kestrel. No dust jacket.

PUBLISHED: October 1, 1985 at $12.95. 50,000 sets of sheets printed. On *verso of second leaf:* Sincere thanks to Mrs. Ludwig Bemelmans and Barbara Bemelmans for their help and advice in adapting and restoring the text and art for *Madeline's Christmas,* and for lending us the few remaining pieces of original art. For this book, the art has been photographically enlarged and recolored by Jody Wheeler to prepare it for reproduction. Originally published as a special book insert in the 1956 Christmas edition of *McCall's.* This edition first published by Viking Penguin Inc. 1985. Published simultaneously in Canada. Copyright © Madeleine Bemelmans and Barbara Bemelmans Marciano, 1985. Copyright © Ludwig Bemelmans, 1956. Printed in Italy by New Interlitho. *Half-title* on recto of first leaf and on recto of third leaf, in red. *Other books in the* Madeline *series* on verso of first leaf. Plain red endpapers.

TEXT: The text is here emended from the first edition, A28a, as follows: "Madeline just went . . ." from the verso of the first leaf is here changed to, "Madeline just said. . . ." "Nobody was stirring" from the recto of the second leaf is here changed to, "Not a creature was stirring." "Because the mouse was in bed with a cold/ Like everybody else in that house which was old" from the recto of the second leaf is here changed to, "For like everyone else in that house which was old/ The poor mouse was in bed with a miserable cold." "Our little Madeline" from the verso of the second leaf is here changed to, "Our brave little Madeline." "But no . . ." is added at the bottom of the verso of the fourth leaf. " 'These,' said Madeline, 'would just be neat' " on the verso of the fifth leaf is here changed to, " 'Why, these,' said Madeline, 'would be so neat'." " 'Twelve times one thousand makes/ Twelve thousand francs./ Here they are with all our thanks' " from the verso of the sixth leaf is here changed to, "Madeline gave him a handful of francs,/ 'Here they are with all our thanks.' " "The rug merchant got feeling very cold" from the recto of the seventh leaf is here changed to, "The rug merchant got awfully cold." "In fact, he was now so awfully chilly/ He wanted to get his rugs back— but will he?" from the bottom of the sixth leaf verso and seventh leaf recto is here changed to, " 'To sell my rugs,' he cried, 'was silly!/ Without them I am very chilly.'/ He wants to get them back—/ But will he?" "He made it—back to Madeline's at last—/ But, poor man, he was frozen fast" from the verso of the seventh leaf is here changed to, "He made it—back to Madeline's door—/ He couldn't take one footstep more." "Our hero was below zero/ And Madeline was about/ To thaw him out" from the recto of the eighth leaf is here changed to, "And little Madeline set about/ To find a way to thaw him out." "The magician swallowed another pill./ 'Ask me, Madeline, what you will.'/ She said, 'I have no// particular wishes,/ But please, sir, help me with

the dishes' " from the verso of the eighth leaf is here changed to, "The magician, as he took his pill, said/ 'Ask me, Madeline, what you will.'/ Said she, 'I've cooked a dinner nutritious,/ Will you please help me with these dishes?' " " 'While you put them away/ I'll go out and see" from the recto of the ninth leaf is here changed to, " 'If you'll clear up/ I'll go and see'." "At his magic ring he gave a glance/ And after a moment went into a trance./ The dirty dishes washed themselves/ And jumped right back upon their shelves" from the recto of the ninth leaf is here changed to, "His magic ring he gave a glance/ And went into a special trance—/ The dirty dishes washed themselves/ And jumped right back upon the shelves." "He lit incense and mumbled/ words profound and tragic:" from the verso of the ninth leaf is here changed to, "And then he mumbled words profound—" "And suddenly the carpets were magic" from the verso of the ninth leaf is here changed to, "That made the carpets leave the ground—" "So, in Dallas and Rome/ And on the Panamanian Isthmus,/ The little girls were all home . . ." from the bottom of the tenth leaf verso and eleventh leaf recto is here changed to, "And twelve little girls were on their way—" "FOR CHRISTMAS!!!!!" from the verso of the eleventh leaf is here changed to, "To surprise their parents on Christmas Day." "Miss Clavel was herself again and well—/ She thought it time to ring the school bell" from the verso of the eleventh leaf is here changed to, "Miss Clavel again quite well/

Thought it time to ring her bell." And, " 'And here we're back—all twelve no less—/ HAPPY NEW YEAR and TOGETHERNESS!' " from the verso of the twelfth leaf is here changed to, "And now we're back, all twelve right here/ To wish our friends a HAPPY NEW YEAR!"

7,500 copies of this edition were selected by The Literary Guild in October, 1985 and made available to membership at $9.59 with slight modification of book spine.

ILLUSTRATIONS: In addition to the title illustration there are 28 full-color illustrations by the author. There are some illustration changes from the first edition, A28a. The small outdoor scene from the top of the seventh leaf recto, and Miss Clavel with shovel from the bottom of the eleventh leaf verso are here omitted. Then, Miss Clavel and the little girls with the tiger in the zoo, from *Madeline*, A24a, is added in on the new fourth leaf verso; and facing it, on the new fifth leaf recto, is a full-color drawing of the twelve little girls in their beds.

The text of this edition is reproduced in full as an encore in *McCall's*, December 1985, pp. 112-117, see E201. The text is identical except that the dash at the end of the line on the fifteenth leaf recto has been omitted.

COPY EXAMINED: MP.

b. British edition [(1985)]:

TITLE PAGE: In blue: Madeline's Christmas | a full-color illustration of a little girl peeking out from beneath the red ribbon binding a Christmas package | in black: By Ludwig Bemelmans | colophon | André Deutsch

PAGINATION: Unpaged. 16 leaves; endpapers. 29.9 x 21.5 cm.

COVERINGS: Full-color paper-covered cardboard covers printed with a full color illustration of a nun with twelve little girls and the Eiffel Tower decorated like a Christmas tree in a snowfall, the author's name and title in white; on spine, in white: Madeline's Christmas Bemelmans and at bottom, André Deutsch. No dust jacket.

PUBLISHED: October 10, 1985 at £4.95. 50,000 sets of sheets printed. On *verso of second leaf:* Sincere thanks to Mrs. Ludwig Bemelmans and Barbara Bemelmans for their help and advice in adapting and restoring the text and art for *Madeline's Christmas*, and for lending us the few remaining pieces of original art. For this book, the art has been photographically enlarged and recolored by Jody Wheeler to prepare it for reproduction. Originally published as a special book insert in the 1956 Christmas edition of McCall's. This edition first published in Great Britain in 1985 by André Deutsch Limited 105 Great Russell Street London WC1B 3LJ. Copyright © 1985 Madeline Bemelmans and Barbara Bemelmans Marciano. Copyright © 1956 Ludwig

Bemelmans. Copyright renewed © 1984 Madeline Bemelmans and Barbara Bemelmans Marciano. All rights reserved. *Half-title* on recto of first leaf and on recto of third leaf, in red. *Other books in the* Madeline *series* on verso of first leaf, listing five titles. Plain white endpapers.

ILLUSTRATIONS: As in A28a(bis).

COPY EXAMINED: MP.

c. French edition [(1987)]:

TITLE PAGE: In black: Ludwig Bemelmans | in blue: Le Noël de | Madeleine | a full-color illustration of a little girl peeking out from beneath the red ribbon binding a Christmas package | in black: adapté de l'américain | par Michèle et Christian Poslaniec | l'école des loisirs | 11, rue de Sèvres, Paris 6ᵉ

PAGINATION: Unpaged. 15 leaves, 1 blank leaf; endpapers. 30.4 x 21.2 cm.

COVERINGS: Full-color paper-covered cardboard covers printed with a full color illustration of a nun with twelve little girls and the Eiffel Tower decorated like a Christmas tree in a snowfall, the author's name in white and the title in pale blue; on spine, in white: Bemelmans; in pale blue: Le Noël de Madeleine; in white: l'école des loisirs; and a colophon at bottom. No dust jacket.

PUBLISHED: 1987 at FF62.00. Number of sets of sheets printed cannot be determined, as the publisher will not release the information. On *verso of first leaf*: © 1987, l'école des loisirs, Paris,

pour l'édition en langue française. Imprimé en France par Berger-Levrault à Nancy. *Half-title* on recto of first leaf, printed in red. Plain red endpapers.

The text is a translation of that from A28a(bis).

ILLUSTRATIONS: As in A28a(bis).

COPY EXAMINED: MP.

d. American paperback edition ([1988]):

TITLE PAGE: In blue: Madeline's Christmas | a full-color illustration of a little girl peeking out from beneath the red ribbon binding a Christmas package | in black: By Ludwig Bemelmans | Puffin Books

PAGINATION: Unpaged. 16 leaves. 22.5 x 18 cm.

COVERINGS: Laminated paper covers printed on front with a full-color illustration of a nun, twelve little girls, and the Eiffel Tower garbed as a Christmas tree and with author and title in white and colophon in black and white. A 1.5 cm. yellow band at left continues upon the spine, which is printed in black: Ludwig Bemelmans Madeline's Christmas. The back cover reproduces the front cover between two wide yellow bands, the right of which includes the Picture Puffins colophon. No dust jacket.

PUBLISHED: 1988 at $3.95. The precise publication date and number of sets of sheets printed cannot be determined, as the publisher has no records. On *verso of title leaf:* Sincere thanks to Mrs. Ludwig Bemelmans and Barbara Bemelmans for their help and advice in adapting and restoring the text and art for *Madeline's Christmas,* and for lending us the few remaining pieces of original art. For this book, the art has been photographically enlarged and recolored by Jody Wheeler to prepare it for reproduction. Originally published as a special book insert in the 1956 Christmas edition of *McCalls* This edition first published by Viking Penguin Inc., 1985 Published in Picture Puffins 1988. *Half-titles* in red on recto of first leaf and recto of third leaf. *Other books by the author* on verso of first leaf, including the other 5 titles in the *Madeline* series. On inside front cover, blurbs from *Horn Book*, *Parents Magazine* and *ALA Booklist*. On inside back cover, a list of 24 other Puffin titles, including *Madeline and the Gypsies*.

ILLUSTRATIONS: As in A28a(bis).

COPY EXAMINED: MP.

e. Japanese edition ([1989]):

TITLE PAGE: In blue: Madolenu No | Kurisumasu | a full-color illustration of a little girl peeking out from beneath the red ribbon binding a Christmas package | in black: Ludwig Bemelmans • Sakuen - Tawara Machi • Geyakkusu

Machi Tawara is the translator into Japanese.

PAGINATION: Unpaged. 16 leaves; endpapers. 30.3 x 21.1 cm.

COVERINGS: Full-color paper-covered cardboard covers printed with a full color illustration of a nun with twelve little girls and the Eiffel Tower decorated like a Christmas tree in a snowfall, the title in yellow, and author and translator in white; on a blue spine, vertically, in yellow: Madolenu No Kurisumasu; in white: Ludwig Bemelmans Sakuen • Tawara Machi Geyakkusu and at bottom, [colophon] Yugaku-sha. The back cover is pale blue with the title page illustration repeated. Publisher and price are in black. No dust jacket.

PUBLISHED: December 15, 1989 at ¥ 1,200. 6,000 sets of sheets printed. On *verso of title leaf:* Madeline's Christmas by Ludwig Bemelmans [Copyright statements] Published in Japan by Yugaku-sha Ltd., Tokyo Japanese translation rights arranged with Viking Penguin Inc., New York through Tuttle-Mori Agency Inc., Tokyo. *Half-title* on recto of second leaf, in red. On *verso of* final leaf: notes about the author and translator and also: Mitsui Kazumi, President. The title, author, translator, publisher, publisher's address and telephone numbers and ISBN number are also given, as is the fact that the book was printed by Dainippon Kaiga; and: © 1989 Machi Tawara. Plain red endpapers.

ILLUSTRATIONS: As in A28a(bis).

COPY EXAMINED: MP.

A29. Madeline's Christmas in Texas [1955]

TITLE PAGE: Upon a periwinkle blue background, in white: madeline's christmas in texas | a black and red drawing of a nun with twelve little girls and a dog | in black: by ludwig bemelmans

PAGINATION: 10 leaves. Unpaged. 12.6 x 17.7 cm.

COVERINGS: The first and last leaves function as a cover. Staple bound.

PUBLISHED: 1955 at an unknown price. Number of sets of sheets printed cannot be determined as the company's records are lost. On *verso of title leaf:* written and illustrated just for Neiman-Marcus by Ludwig Bemelmans [with a line of blue stars]. On *verso of rear cover:* this book is a christmas gift to you from Neiman-Marcus copyright © by Ludwig Bemelmans 1955

The contents of this booklet appeared in radically different form as "Madeline's Christmas," in *Good Housekeeping*, December 1955, see E168. (There is no relation between that material and the text of *Madeline's Christmas*, A28.) The text of A29 for the first three stanzas: John Cowan Moneystacker Fogg/ Said: "I'm about to close my log./ I have no children and no wife./ Before I say 'Goodbye' to life,/ My Texas goods and my ura-

nium mine,/ I leave to my great grandchild, Madeline."// And then, Great Grandpa closed his eyes/ And departed for Texas Paradise./// Mr. Crockett, his lawyer, sat down at the table/ And figured what to put in a cable,/ And the telegrapher took a glance/ To check the rates to Paris, France./ In an old house in Paris/ That was covered with vines/ Lived twelve little girls/ In two straight lines./ In two straight lines they broke their bread/ And brushed their teeth and went to bed./ And the very next/ day at half past nine/ A telegram was delivered/ For Madeline./ Little Madeline cried, "Booohooo!/ I won't go alone to Texacooo!"/ "Don't worry, Madeline, we'll all go with you./ And now, to sleep, for at the crack/ Of dawn, we must rise to pack." reads in *Good Housekeeping* as follows: In an old house in Paris/ That was covered with vines/ Lived twelve little girls/ In two straight lines,/ Including Mlle. Madeline Fogg/ And Genevieve, her beloved dog./// Two days before Christmas/ At half past nine/ A cable came for Madeline./ Her great-grandpapa, in bad health,/ Had willed her all his earthly wealth./ Then Great-grandpapa closed his eyes/ And departed for Paradise./// To Texas Madeline was bid./ When she heard it she ran and hid;/ The little girls cried;/ Genevieve moaned;/ Miss Clavel groaned./ And so/ They *all* decided to go.

ILLUSTRATIONS: In addition to the cover illustration there are 14 black and blue illustrations by the author. Two of the illustrations: Miss Clavel and her twelve little girls riding in Crockett's car; and the ushering in of the gusher; appeared in the *Good Housekeeping* version, with slight alterations, the car illustration being aligned a little more horizontally in the first and Crockett's jacket being inked in, in the second. The part of the illustration of Madeline looking at her cattle which shows Madeline on horseback appeared in *Good Housekeeping* with the armadillo, Madeline's scarf, and Geneviève's scarf inked in. Madeline sitting still and listening to her great-grandfather's will appeared in *Good Housekeeping* in a differently-drawn version, essentially more cramped. And the penultimate picture of Miss Clavel and the girls returning to the house in Paris appeared in *Good Housekeeping* left-right reversed.

COPY EXAMINED: University Library, University of Colorado at Boulder, Boulder, Colorado.

A30. Madeline's Rescue [1953]

a. First edition:

TITLE PAGE: In black: Madeline's | Rescue | a full-color drawing of a nun with twelve little girls at a street corner next to a clock | Story and pictures by | Ludwig Bemelmans | The Viking Press • New York • 1953

PAGINATION: 2 leaves, [1] - 56 pp., 2 leaves. 30.5 x 22.2 cm.

COVERINGS: Taupe linen-weave cloth-covered boards stamped in red on front with a drawing of a dog and a youth in water and printed on spine, in red: Madeline's Rescue by Ludwig Bemelmans; at base: The Viking Press. A variant binding has cherry red linen-weave cloth-covered boards stamped in black. Full-color dust jacket printed in white.

PUBLISHED: April 3, 1953 at $3.00. 21,000 sets of sheets printed; 11,000 copies bound. On *verso of title leaf:* Published by The Viking Press in April 1953. Published on the same day in the Dominion of Canada By The Macmillan Company of Canada Limited. This story first appeared in *Good Housekeeping*. Lithographed in the U.S.A. by Livermore and Knight Co. *Half-title* on page [1]. *Second half-title* on page [5]. The recto of the first leaf and verso of the last leaf are pasted down upon the insides of the boards. The verso of the first leaf and recto of the second, and again the verso of the second last leaf and recto of the last, are printed as endpapers with a full-color illustration of the Île de la Cité. The dust jacket shows the Pont des Arts facing the Institut de France, and the rear flyleaf has information about the color illustrations.

This book is the recipient of the Caldecott Medal.

Note: An undetermined number of copies of a reprint of this edition were taken by the Book-of-the-Month Club and made available to its membership in spring 1971 singly at $3.95 or in a triple combination with *Madeline* and *Madeline and the Gypsies* at $8.75. The books were in the Children's Christmas Catalogue. The book was accompanied by a copy of the *Book-of-the-Month Club News* for Spring 1971, which contained a synopsis.

The text is here reprinted from *Good Housekeeping*, December 1951, see E138. On page 7, the first two lines of the text are extended from the first four lines of the original; the fourth line, "In two straight lines in rain or shine," was originally two lines, "In two straight lines,/ Rain or shine"; the eighth line originally had a comma ending; and the "Pooh pooh!" of the ninth line were originally "Pooh! Pooh!" On page 9, the "—" ending of the second line is absent in the original. The text on pp. 10-13, "Poor Madeline would now be dead/ But for a dog/ That kept its head," read originally, "But for a dog that kept its head/ Madeline might now be dead." The text on page 14, "And dragged her safe from a watery grave" is absent from the original. The text on p. 16 was originally in two lines. The text on p. 17 was originally in two lines. The text on p. 18, " 'Good night, little girls—I hope you sleep well.'/ 'Good night, good night, dear Miss Clavel!' " read originally, " 'Good night, little girls. Sleep well.'/ 'Good night, good night, Miss Clavel.' " There was originally a comma after the third word of

the second line of p. 19. The final line on p. 19, "About where the dog should sleep that night" was originally two lines, "To determine on whose bed/ The dog would sleep that night." The text on p. 20, "The new pupil was ever/ So helpful and clever" read originally, "The next day in school,/ The new pupil was no fool." The text on p. 21, "The dog loved biscuits, milk, and beef/ And they named it Genevieve" read originally, "She ate candy and beef./ They named her Genevive." There was originally a comma after the line printed on p. 22. The word "enjoyed" on p. 23 was originally, "she came for". The text on p. 24 is omitted in the original. The " 'Tap, tap!' " beginning the first two lines on p. 28 was originally, "Tap, tap." The "!" at the end of the second line on that page was originally a "." The text from the middle of p. 28 to the end of p. 29, " 'Dear me, it's a dog! Isn't there a rule/ 'That says DOGS AREN'T ALLOWED IN SCHOOL?/ 'Miss Clavel, get rid of it, please,'/ Said the president of the board of trustees./ 'Yes, but the children love her so,'/ Said Miss Clavel. 'Please don't make her go.' " did not appear in the original at all. On p. 30, the comma after the second word was originally a dash. Opening quotation marks appearing at the beginning of the third and fourth lines on that page were not used in the original, and the fourth line, " 'This creature of uncertain race!" was originally, "A creature of most doubtful race!" The text on p. 31, " 'Off with you! Go on—run! scat!/

'Go away and don't come back!' " was originally, " 'Be off,/ old fleabag. Scat!/ Go away and/ don't come back!' " The text on p. 32, "Madeline jumped on a chair./ 'Lord Cucuface,' she cried, 'beware!/ 'Miss Genevieve, noblest dog in France,/ 'You shall have your VEN-GE-ANCE!' " was originally, "Madeline jumped on a/ chair./ 'Cucu-face,' she cried,/ 'beware!/ Miss Genevive, no-blest/ dog in France,/ You shall have your/ ven-ge-ance!' " The text on p. 33, " 'It's no use crying or talking./ 'Let's get dressed and go out walk-ing./ 'The sooner we're ready, the sooner we'll leave—/ 'The sooner we'll find Miss Gene-vieve.' " was originally, " 'Dear children, get dressed./ The sooner we leave,/ The sooner we'll find Genevive.' " The text from pp. 34-39, "They went looking high/ and low/ And every place a dog might go./ In every place they called her name/ But no one answered to the same" is en-tirely absent from the original. The text on p. 40, "The gendarmes said, 'We don't believe/ 'We've seen a dog like Genevieve.' " was originally, "The police joined the search./ But at last said, 'We grieve/ To state we can't find Genevive.' " The two lines of text on p. 41 were originally four lines; the word "home" is absent in the original; and the word "broken-hearted" was originally unhyphenated. The text on p. 42, " 'Oh, Gene-vieve, where can you be?/ 'Genevieve, please come back to me." is absent from the original. On p. 43, where there is no punctuation at the end of

the first line there was originally a comma; and where at the end of the second line there is a period there was originally no punctuation. On p. 44 the second line, "On Miss Genevieve out-side" was originally, "On Miss Genevive, who was outside." The text on p. 46 is emended here exactly as is the text on p. 18. The text on p. 47, "Miss Clavel turned out the light,/ And again there was a fight,/ As each little girl cried,/ 'Genevieve is *mine* tonight!' " was origi-nally, "Miss Clavel turned out the light./ After she left, there was a fight/ About where the dog should sleep at night." The text on pp. 48-50, "For a second time that night/ Miss Clavel turned on her light,/ And afraid of a disaster,/ She ran fast—/ And even faster" was originally, "For the second time that night,/ Miss Clavel turned on her light,/ And ran to stop a riot." On p. 51 the comma ending the first line was orig-inally a dash and the spelling of the dog's name is changed as throughout; the second line open-ing quotation mark is absent in the original. The text on pp. 52-54, "That was the end of the riot—/ Suddenly all was quiet./ For the third time that night/ Miss Clavel turned on the light,/ And to her surprise she found" was originally, "Miss Genevive worried a lot that night/ But Genevive was very bright,/ And soon she set things right—" The text on p. 55, "That sud-denly there was enough hound" was originally, "And suddenly there was enough hound/ to go all around." The text on p. 56, "To go all around" was originally, "The End".

13,500 copies of this edition wee selected by the Junior Literary Guild in August, 1953 and distributed to membership at an unknown price with slight alteration to binding and book spine.

ILLUSTRATIONS: In addition to the facsimile endpapers and the title page drawing there are 40 black and yellow and 8 full-color illustrations by the author. The illustrations on p. 7, 8, 10-11, 12, 14, 15, 22, 24, 26, 27, 30, 34, 35, 36, 37, 38-39, 42, 43, and 53 (including all of the full-color illustrations) were absent from the original appearance. The illustrations on pages 18, 20, 25, 29, 32, 46, 51, and 54 appeared in the original in somewhat different form; the illustration on p. 48 is here in a new position; the illustration on p. 55 is here reversed. In addition, 5 black drawings from the original story are absent from this edition.

Note: Part of this first edition was printed, as well, by A. Hoen & Co., Inc., and part by R. R. Heywood Co., Inc.

COPY EXAMINED: MP.

b. First British edition ([1953]):

TITLE PAGE: In black: Madeline's | Rescue | a full-color drawing of a nun with twelve little girls at a street corner next to a clock | Story and pictures by | Ludwig Bemelmans | Derek Verschoyle | 13 Park Place, St. James's, London, S.W.1

PAGINATION: As in A30a. 30.6 x 22.1 cm.

COVERINGS: Cherry red cloth-covered boards stamped in black as in A30a; on spine, in black upon a yellow strip: Madeline's Rescue by Ludwig Bemelmans; at base, in yellow upon a black strip: Derek Verschoyle. Full-color dust jacket printed in white.

PUBLISHED: November 23, 1953 at 12s 6d. Approximately 10,000 sets of sheets printed. On *verso of title leaf:* First published in Great Britain by Derek Verschoyle Ltd. Thirteen Park Place, St. James's London, S.W.1 Made and printed in Great Britain by D. R. Hillman and Sons, Ltd. Frome. *Half-titles* and facsimile endpapers as in A30a.

ILLUSTRATIONS: As in A30a.

COPY EXAMINED: MP.

c. German edition ([1954]):

TITLE PAGE: In black: Madelines | Rettung | a full-color drawing of a nun with twelve little girls at a street corner next to a clock | Mit Bildern und nach Versen von | Ludwig Bemelmans | Blüchert Verlag Stuttgart

PAGINATION: [1] - 56 pp.; endpapers. 30.6 x 21.7 cm.

COVERINGS: Red linen-weave cloth-covered boards stamped on front in brown with a drawing of a dog and a youth in water; and printed on spine: Madelines Rettung Von Ludwig Bemelmans. Full-color dust jacket printed in black and white.

PUBLISHED: 1954 at DM 9,80. Number of sets of sheets printed cannot be determined, as the publisher's records have been lost. On *verso of title leaf:* Deutsche Übersetzung Heinz Strix. Printed in Germany. *Half-title* on page [1]. *Second half-title* on page [5]. Endpapers as in A30a.

ILLUSTRATIONS: As in A30a.

COPY EXAMINED: Mrs. Madeleine Bemelmans.

d. British reprint ([1957]):

TITLE PAGE: In black: Madeline's | Rescue | full-color illustration of a nun with twelve little girls near a clock | in black: story and pictures by | Ludwig Bemelmans | colophon | André Deutsch

PAGINATION: 2 leaves, [1] - 56 pp., 2 leaves. 30 x 21.8 cm.

COVERINGS: Full-color paper-covered boards with a picture of the Institut de France on the front. Printed on front with author and title in white; and on spine, in black upon a yellow strip: Madeline's Rescue by Ludwig Bemelmans at base, in yellow upon a black strip: André Deutsch. Full-color dust jacket printed in white.

PUBLISHED: September 16, 1957 at 15s. 6,000 sets of sheets printed. On *verso of title leaf:* First published 1953 printed in Yugoslavia. *Half-title* on page [1]. *Second half-title* on page [5]. Facsimile endpapers as in A30a.

ILLUSTRATIONS: As in A30a.

COPY EXAMINED: Mr. André Deutsch, 105 Great Russell Street, London. 5th Impression, 1972, examined.

e. Danish edition ([1960]):

TITLE PAGE: A full-color drawing of a nun with twelve little girls at a street corner next to a clock | in black: Madelines | Redning | Tegnet og fortalt af Ludwig Bemelmans | Oversat af Piet Hein | Illustrationsforlaget

PAGINATION: [1] - 56 pp.; endpapers. 29.9 x 20.4 cm.

COVERINGS: Full-color paper-covered boards showing the Pont des Arts facing the Institut de France, with author and title in white. The yellow spine is printed in black: Madelines Redning af Ludwig Bemelmans. No dust jacket.

PUBLISHED: 1960 at an unknown price. The number of sets of sheets printed cannot be determined, as the publisher's record is lost. On *verso of title leaf,* page [4]: Titlen på den amerikanske udgave (originaludgaven) er Madeline's Rescue Copyright Ludwig Bemelmans. *Half-title* on page [1]. On page [5]: A listing of the Parisian scenes illustrated in the book. As in A30a the endsheets are pasted down upon the boards and the endpapers are printed in full-color with an illustration of the Île de la Cité.

ILLUSTRATIONS: As in A30a.

COPY EXAMINED: University of Minnesota, Kerlan Collection.

f. First American paperback edition ([1967]):

TITLE PAGE: In black: Madeline's | Rescue | a full-color drawing of a nun with twelve little girls at a street corner next to a clock | by Ludwig Bemelmans | colophon | Scholastic Inc. | New York Toronto London Auckland Sydney

PAGINATION: Unpaged. Twenty-four leaves. 22.8 x 19.1 cm..

COVERINGS: Full-color paper cover printed with an illustration of the Pont des Arts facing the Institut de France against a red sky, with author and title in white; and printed on a yellow spine, in black: 0-590-08908-0 Madeline's Rescue; and at base: Bemelmans. No dust jacket.

PUBLISHED: 1967 at an unknown price. The number of sets of sheets originally printed cannot be determined, as the publisher's records are lost; but 225,000 copies were printed between 1967 and 1988. On *verso of title leaf:* Copyright 1951, 1953 by Ludwig Bemelmans. This edition is published by Scholastic Book Services, a divison of Scholastic Magazines, Inc., by arrangement with The Viking Press, Inc. Printed in the U.S.A.

ILLUSTRATIONS: There are 40 black and yellow and 8 full-color illustrations by the author.

COPY EXAMINED: MP.

g. South African edition ([1972]):

TITLE PAGE: In black: Madeleine Se | Redding | a full-color drawing of a nun with twelve little girls at a street corner next to a clock | Verhaal en tekeninge deur Ludwig Bemelmans | Afrikaanse beryming deur Leon Rousseau | Human & Rousseau Kaapstad en Pretoria

PAGINATION: [1] - 56 pp.; endpapers. 29.7 x 21.4 cm.

COVERINGS: Paper-covered boards printed with a full-color drawing of a nun with twelve little girls and a dog on the Pont des Arts facing the Institut de France, with title in black on a yellow band and author in white; on a yellow spine, in black: Ludwig Bemelmans Madeleine se Redding; and at base: colophon. The dust jacket reproduces the covering. A list of Paris scenes illustrated is on the rear flyleaf.

PUBLISHED: December, 1972 at R 2,50. 2,975 sets of sheets printed. On *verso of title leaf,* page [4]: Die berymer bedank mnr. Kobus van Zyl vir sy wenke en voorstelle. Fonetiese uitspraak van die Franse name: Madeleine: Maddelên. Seine: Sên. Clavel: Klawél. Geneviève: Zjênewi-êw. Oorspronklike titel: Madeline's Rescue. Afrikaanse beryming deur Leon Rousseau. Eerste Afrikaanse uitgawe in 1972 deur Humen & Rousseau Uitgewers (Edms.) Bpk. Stategebou, Roosstraat, Kaapstad; Pretoriusstraat 235, Pretoria. Geset deur Human & Rousseau en gedruk in mede-produksie met André Deutsch. *Half-title* on page [1]. *Second half-title* on page [5]. The endpapers contain a full-color illustration of the Île de la Cité.

ILLUSTRATIONS: Aside from the endpapers and title drawing, there are 8 full-color and 40 black and yellow illustrations by the author.

COPY EXAMINED: MP.

h. Second American paperback edition ([1973]):

TITLE PAGE: In black: Madeline's | Rescue | a full-color drawing of a nun with twelve little girls at a street corner next to a clock | Story and pictures by | Ludwig Bemelmans | The Viking Press • New York

PAGINATION: Unpaged. 1 blank leaf, 29 leaves, 2 blank leaves. 22.7 x 18.3 cm.

COVERINGS: Laminated paper-covers bearing on front a full-color illustration of the Pont des Arts facing the Institut de France and with author and title in white; and on a yellow spine, printed in black: VS-76 Ludwig Bemelmans Madeline's Rescue. Printed in black on yellow back cover: Winner of the Caldecott award, A Seafarer Book. No dust jacket.

PUBLISHED: 1973 at $1.50. Number of sets of sheets printed cannot be determined, as the publisher's records are lost. On *verso of title leaf*: Viking Seafarer edition issued in 1973 by The Viking Press, Inc. 625 Madison Avenue, New York, N.Y. 10022. Distributed in Canada by The

Macmillan Company of Canada Limited. This story first appeared in *Good Housekeeping*. *Half-title* in black on recto of third leaf. The recto of the first and verso of the final blank leaves are pasted to the boards. The twenty-ninth leaf verso and thirtieth leaf recto are printed with an illustration in full-color of the Île de la Cité.

This is Viking Seafarer No. VS-76.

ILLUSTRATIONS: Aside from the title illustration and the facsimile endpapers near the end, there are 8 full-color and 40 yellow and black illustrations by the author.

COPY EXAMINED: Clemson University Library.

i. Japanese edition ([1973]):

TITLE PAGE: In black: Madeline To Inu | a full-color drawing of a nun with twelve little girls at a street corner next to a clock | by Ludwig Bemelmans | Translated by Asada Teiji | Fukuinkan Shoten

PAGINATION: [1] - [56] pp.; endpapers. 30.2 x 22 cm.

COVERINGS: Lamination on paper - covered boards printed with a full-color illustration of the Pont des Arts facing the Institut de France, printed with author and title in white. Printed on a yellow spine, in black: By Ludwig Bemelmans Madeline To Inu; and at base: Fukuinkan Shoten | colophon.

PUBLISHED: May 10, 1973 at ¥ 1130. 171,000

sets of sheets printed. On *verso of title leaf,* page [2]: Madeline's Rescue Story and pictures by Ludwig Bemelmans. Copyright 1951, 1953 by Ludwig Bemelmans. Originally published by The Viking Press, Inc., New York. Japanese language edition copyright 1973 by Fukuinkan-Shoten, Publishers, Tokyo, by arrangements with Charles E. Tuttle Co. *Index to color plates* on page [53]. On page [54]: a black and yellow drawing of a girl and dog in the water. *Author's blurb* on page [55]. *Advertisements for other books in the* Madeline *series* on page [56]. Also on page [56]: Published May 10, 1973. 101 Tokyo-to Chiodaku Mitzuzaki-cho 1-1-9 Fukuinkan Shoten. Printed by Sei Kosha. Designed by Kobayashi. [colophon] Book care guidelines. Endpapers as in A30a.

ILLUSTRATIONS: As in A30a.

COPY EXAMINED: Mrs. Madeleine Bemelmans.

j. Third American paperback edition ([1977]):

TITLE PAGE: In black: Madeline's | Rescue | full-color illustration of a nun with twelve little girls near a clock | in black: Story and pictures by | Ludwig Bemelmans | Puffin Books

PAGINATION: Unpaged. 32 leaves. 22.6 x 18.1 cm.

COVERINGS: Full-color paper covers printed

with author and title in white and a picture of the Institut de France on front; on spine, in black; Ludwig Bemelmans Madeline's Rescue. No dust jacket.

PUBLISHED: 1977 at an unknown price. Number of sets of sheets printed cannot be determined, as the publisher's records are lost. On *verso of title leaf:* Published in Picture Puffins 1977 Reprinted 1978, 1979, 1981, 1983 Printed in the United States of America by Rae Publishing Co., Inc., Cedar Grove, New Jersey Set in Bodoni. *Half-title* on recto of third leaf. *Second half-title* on recto of fifth leaf. The verso of the first leaf and recto of the second, and again the verso of the 31st leaf and recto of the 32nd, are printed with full-color illustrations which reproduce the facsimile endpapers of the first edition.

ILLUSTRATIONS: In addition to the title page drawing there are 40 black and yellow and 10 full-color illustrations by the author.

COPY EXAMINED: MP. 1983 reprint examined.

k. Children's Choice edition ([1982]):

TITLE PAGE: In black: Madeline's | Rescue | a full-color drawing of a nun with twelve little girls at a street corner next to a clock | Story and pictures by | Ludwig Bemelmans | The Viking Press • New York

PAGINATION: [1] - 56 pp; endpapers. 29.8 x 20 cm.

COVERINGS: Full-color laminated paper-covered boards, printed on front with an illustration of the Pont des Arts facing the Institut de France and with author and title in white; on a yellow spine, at top, in black: Madeline's Rescue by Ludwig Bemelmans; at bottom: The Viking Press. No dust jacket.

PUBLISHED: 1982 at an unknown price by Scholastic Book Services, New York. Number of sets of sheets printed cannot be determined, as the publisher's records have been lost. On *verso of title leaf*, page [4]: Copyright 1951, 1953 by Ludwig Bemelmans A Children's Choice Book Club Edition. *Half-title* in black on page [1]. *Second half-title* in black on page [5]. Endpapers as in A30a.

ILLUSTRATIONS: As in A30a.

COPY EXAMINED: Scholastic Books, New York.

1. French edition [(1986)]:

TITLE PAGE: In black: Ludwig Bemelmans | Le Sauvetage de | Madeleine | adapté de l'américain par Michèle et | Christian Poslaniec | a full-color drawing of a nun with twelve little girls at a street corner next to a clock | lutin poche de l'école des loisirs | 11, rue de Sèvres, Paris 6e

PAGINATION: [1] - [56] pp. 19 x 15 cm.

COVERINGS: Pale yellow paper covers printed

with a full color illustration of the Pont des Arts facing the Institut de France, the author's name in black and the title in olive; on spine, in black: lutin poche Le sauvetage de Madeleine Bemelmans. No dust jacket.

PUBLISHED: March 1986 at FF30.00. Number of sets of sheets printed cannot be determined, as the publisher will not release the information. On *verso of title leaf*, page [4]: Première édition dans la collection "lutin poche de l'école des loisirs": mars 1986. Imprimé en France par Maury à Malesherbes. *Biographical note* about the author on page [56].

ILLUSTRATIONS: As in A30a, though considerably reduced in size.

COPY EXAMINED: MP.

A31. Marina [1962]

TITLE PAGE: In red: Marina | a full-color drawing of two seals upon a bicycle on a high wire | in turquoise: by | in black: Ludwig Bemelmans | Harper & Row, Publishers, New York and Evanston

PAGINATION: Unpaged. 20 leaves. 25.3 x 31.8 cm.

COVERINGS: One-sixteenth navy cloth-covered, and fifteen-sixteenths full-color paper-covered boards printed on front with a seal in a yellow hat, title in white, and author in black. Spine plain. Full-color dust jacket printed in white and black.

PUBLISHED: December 19, 1962 at $3.95. 25,000 sets of sheets printed. On *verso of title leaf:* Marina Copyright © 1962, by Harper & Row, Publishers, Incorporated. Two lines reading Marina | Copyright © 1962 by Ludwig Bemelmans are cancelled. *Half-title* on recto of fourth leaf, within an oval of six full-color dolphins. The recto of the first leaf and verso of the last are pasted down upon the insides of the boards. The verso of the first leaf and recto of the second, and again the verso of the 19th leaf and recto of the 20th, are printed as endpapers in aqua with creatures of the sea in black and Marina in white, black and red.

This edition was distributed in The United Kingdom at 26s.

ILLUSTRATIONS: In addition to the facsimile endpapers, the title drawing, and the half-title drawing, there are 28 full-color illustrations by the author.

COPY EXAMINED: MP.

A32. My Life in Art [1958]

a. First edition:

TITLE PAGE: Within a black drawing of a canvas upon an easel, in black: My Life | in | Art | Bemelmans | beneath the drawing: Harper & Brothers, Publishers | New York

PAGINATION: [1] - [64] pp., 16 leaves; endpapers. 32 x 24.5 cm.

COVERINGS: One-eighth black cloth-covered, and seven-eighths marbled sienna paper-covered boards. Upon the front is pasted a full-color tip-in showing houseboats in the Seine beneath the Louvre. The spine is printed in white: Bemelmans, in gold: My Life in Art; in white, at base: Harper. White dust jacket with a full-color illustration, lettered in black.

PUBLISHED: October 29, 1958 at $5.95. 12,500 sets of sheets were printed and bound; 9,000 sets were delivered for publication. On *verso of title leaf,* page [4]: Printed in the United States of America. Library of Congress catalog card number: 58-8821. *Half-title* on page [1], plain. *Second half-title* on page [5], with a black drawing of a dog sleeping. *Frontispiece* on page [2]: A tipped-in full-color illustration of Schloss Ort. Gmunden, Austria. The endpapers are robin's egg blue printed with a brown drawing of a swan and a kiosk beneath leafy trees.

The chapter entitled "Swan Country" appeared earlier in *Vogue*, September 1, 1958 as "When You Lunch with the Emperor;" see E182.

ILLUSTRATIONS: In addition to the endpapers, the title drawing, and the drawing upon the second half-title, there are 27 black drawings by the author and full-color reproductions of his paintings. The full-color reproductions number 35, as follows: 1 glued down upon the outside of the front cover; 1 tipped in as frontispiece; 1 tipped in on page [59]; and 32 printed one per page upon the last 16 leaves of the book, which are made of glossy paper.

COPY EXAMINED: MP.

a (bis). Photoreproduction ([on demand]):

TITLE PAGE: Within a black drawing of a canvas upon an easel, in black: My Life | in | Art | Bemelmans | beneath the drawing: Harper & Brothers, Publishers | New York

PAGINATION: [1] - [64] pp., 16 leaves. 32 x 24.5 cm.

COVERINGS: In paperback or cloth-covered boards. Published on demand by Ann Arbor Microfilms Books on Demand, 300 North Zeeb Road, Ann Arbor, Michigan 48106. No. OP47228.

b. British edition ([1958]):

TITLE PAGE: Within a black drawing of a canvas upon an easel, in black: My Life | in | Art | Bemelmans | beneath the drawing: André Deutsch : London

PAGINATION: As in A32a. 32.2 x 24 cm.

COVERINGS: One eighth navy cloth-covered, and seven-eighths white paper-covered boards. The front is printed with a full-color illustration of houseboats in the Seine beneath the Louvre and with author and title in black. The spine is printed in gold: Bemelmans (facsimile signature); My Life in Art; at base: colophon. Dust jacket as in A32a.

PUBLISHED: November 14, 1958 at 35s. The number of sets of sheets printed cannot be determined, as the publisher's records were lost in transit to the United States. On *verso of title leaf*, page [4]: First published 1958 by André Deutsch Limited 12-14 Carlisle Street Soho Square London 1I Printed in Great Britain by D. R. Hillman and Sons Ltd Frome Somerset. *Half-title, second half-title* and *frontispiece* as in A32a. The endpapers are on pale blue paper, printed as in A32a.

ILLUSTRATIONS: As in A32a.

COPY EXAMINED: MP.

c. German edition ([1959]):

TITLE PAGE: Within a black drawing of a canvas upon an easel, in black: Bemelmans | Mein | Leben | Als | Maler | beneath the drawing: Blüchert Verlag Hamburg

PAGINATION: [1] - [64] pp., 16 leaves; endpapers. 32 x 23.6 cm.

COVERINGS: Wheat colored linen-weave cloth-covered boards stamped in black with author's signature on front; on spine: Mein | Leben | Als | Maler. White dust jacket with a full-color illustration, lettered in black.

PUBLISHED: 1959 at DM 28,50. Number of sets of sheets printed cannot be determined, as neither the publisher nor the publisher's records can be located. On *verso of title leaf,* page [4]: Aus dem Amerikanischen: Nino Erné. Die Originalausgabe dieses Buches erschien 1958 unter dem Titel My Life in Art bei Harper & Brothers in New York. Printed in Germany 1959.

ILLUSTRATIONS: As in A32a.

COPY EXAMINED: Mrs. Madeleine Bemelmans.

A33. My War With the United States [1937]

a. First edition:

TITLE PAGE: In black: Ludwig Bemelmans | My War With the United States | Illustrated by the Author | The Viking Press | New York | 1937 | a black drawing of a cannon beside a rampart with six cannonballs

PAGINATION: [1] - 151 pp., 3 blank leaves; endpapers. 23.4 x 14.3 cm.

COVERINGS: Beige linen-weave cloth-covered boards stamped on front in turquoise with a cannon and six cannonballs on spine, in turquoise: Bemelmans • My War With the United States • Viking Press. Top, front and bottom edges stained red. Yellow dust jacket printed in black, red and turquoise.

PUBLISHED: July 2, 1937 at $2.50. 5,000 sets of sheets printed; 5,000 copies bound. On *verso of title leaf,* page [4]: Printed in the United States of America by The Duenewald Printing Corporation First published in July 1937. *Half-title* on page [1]. *Second half-title* on page [7]. Endpapers plain.

CONTENTS on page [5]: *Foreword*, 9; Please Don't Shoot, 11; The Operation, 21; Summer Sprouts, 27; The Good Prisoners, 33; Mad Maître d'Hôtel, 39; To the Left, 53; Tirol in Buffalo, 65; David, 73; The Mess in Order, 79; The Buttermachine, 87; Night on Guard, 91; A Trip to Mississippi, 101; Leave of Absence, 113; The Widow from Scranton, 121; Polish Kate's, 129; The Army Is Like a Mother, 139; Bayonet School, 143.

"Bayonet School" contains a section entitled "The Elephant Cutlet" which appeared as well in Town & Country (see E9) and which is reproduced in A9.

ILLUSTRATIONS: In addition to the title page drawing there are 18 black drawings by the author, 17 of which are on the chapter heads.

COPY EXAMINED: MP.

b. British edition ([1938]):

TITLE PAGE: In black: Ludwig Bemelmans | My War With the United States | Illustrated by the Author | Victor Gollancz Ltd | London | 1938 | a black drawing of a cannon beside a rampart with six cannonballs

PAGINATION: [1] - 149 pp., 1 blank leaf; endpapers. 23.5 x 14 cm.

COVERINGS: Black cloth-covered boards plain on the front, stamped in gold on spine: My War | With the | United | States | Ludwig | Bemelmans | at base: Gollancz. Yellow and magenta dust jacket printed in black.

PUBLISHED: July 4, 1938 at 9s. 2,000 sets of sheets printed. On verso of title leaf: Printed in

Great Britain by Purnell and Sons, Ltd. (T.U.) Paulton (Somerset) and London. Half-title on page [1]. Endpapers plain.

CONTENTS on page [5]: Foreword, 7; Please Don't Shoot, 9; The Operation, 19; Summer Sprouts, 25; The Good Prisoners, 31; Mad Maître d'Hôtel, 37; To the Left, 51; Tirol in Buffalo, 63; David, 71; The Mess in Order, 77; The Buttermachine, 85; Night on Guard, 89; A Trip to Mississippi, 99; Leave of Absence, 111; The Widow from Scranton, 119; Polish Kate's, 127; The Army Is Like a Mother, 137; Bayonet School, 141.

ILLUSTRATIONS: In addition to the drawing on the title page there are 17 black illustrations by the author on the chapter heads.

COPY EXAMINED: The book was seen at The British Library, Great Russell Street, London. The dust jacket was seen at Victor Gollancz Ltd, 14 Henrietta Street, Covent Garden, London.

c. Cheap edition ([1939]):

My War With the United States was published October 9, 1939 at 89¢ by The Sun Dial Press. It has not been possible to examine a copy of the book. The number of sets of sheets printed cannot be determined, as publisher's records cannot be found for this title.

d. Second cheap edition ([1941]):

TITLE PAGE: In black: Ludwig Bemelmans | My War With the United States | Illustrated by the Author | The Modern Library | New York | a black drawing of a cannon beside a rampart with six cannonballs

PAGINATION: 1 blank leaf, [1] - 151 pp., 3 blank leaves; endpapers. 17.8 x 11.9 cm.

COVERINGS: Royal blue linen-weave cloth-covered boards stamped on front with title and author's last name in gold within a scarlet, gold-edged rectangle; within a gold rectangle, a colophon in gold. Stamped on spine in gold: colophon | within a gold-edged scarlet rectangle, in gold: My War | With the | United | States | by | Ludwig | Bemelmans | • | Modern | Library. Top edges stained red. Yellow dust jacket printed in black and turquoise.

This is Modern Library Edition No. 175.

PUBLISHED: October 1, 1941 at 95¢. Number of sets of sheets printed cannot be determined, as the publisher's records are lost. On *verso of title leaf*, page [4]: First Modern Library Edition, 1941. *Half-title* on page [1], including the text, "The Modern Library of the World's Best Books." *Second half-title* on page [7], plain. Gray and white endpapers are printed with the Modern Library colophon. The inside of the dust jacket has a list of Modern Library titles, including Modern Library Giants as far as No. G66.

CONTENTS on page [5]: As in A33a.

Note: There is a variant binding with a thicker paper and slightly paler cloth covers, where the inside of the dust jacket has a list of Modern Library titles, including Modern Library Giants as far as No. G67. The variance is rare in Modern Library editions.

ILLUSTRATIONS: As in A33a.

COPY EXAMINED: MP.

A34. Now I Lay Me Down to Sleep [1943]

a. First trade issue:

TITLE PAGE: In black, with the first letter enlarged and decorated: Now I Lay Me Down to Sleep | by Ludwig Bemelmans | New York : The Viking Press : 1943

PAGINATION: 1 blank leaf, 4 leaves, 1 - 299 pp., 1 blank leaf; endpapers. 20.2 x 13.5 cm.

COVERINGS: Tan linen-weave cloth-covered boards stamped on front with an olive green and sienna horizontal rectangle through which the author and title appear in tan between two rules; on spine, at head: two olive green rules | in tan showing through an olive green rectangle: Bemel- | mans | in tan showing through a sienna rectangle: Now | I Lay | Me | Down | to | Sleep | an olive green rule | an olive green rule | in tan, between two tan rules, upon an olive green rectangle: Viking. Full-color dust jacket printed in olive green.

PUBLISHED: October 25, 1943 and issued February 18, 1944 at $2.50 [see below]. 32,600 sets of sheets printed; 32,050 copies bound. On *verso of title leaf:* This edition is produced in full compliance with all War Production Board conservation orders. Copyright 1942-3 by Ludwig Bemelmans Printed in U.S.A. by American Book-Stratford Press Published by the Viking Press in October 1943 Published on the same day in the Dominion of Canada by The Macmillan Company of Canada Limited. *Acknowledgment* on verso of title leaf: The author's thanks are given to Harry Bull, editor of *Town and Country*, in which portions of this story appeared serially, partly under the present title and partly under the title "Man of the World." *Other books by the author* on recto of first leaf, listing six titles. *Half-title* on recto of fourth leaf.

Note: According to the publisher's current record, the deluxe edition of this book appeared October 25, 1943; see A34a(bis). The trade— officially, the first—edition was published at the same time but *appeared* later, February 18, 1944. The subsequent 1944 reprint is significantly different, having involved new plates and new binder's dyes, and is here described as A34b.

CONTENTS on recto of third leaf: 1. Biarritz, 1; 2. Miss Graves, 18; 3. The *S. S. Monte Cristi*, 36; 4. Casablanca, 47; 5. The Good Samaritan, 65; 6. The Salamander, 78; 7. The Jews Are to Blame, 102; 8. The Kiss Royale, 116; 9. Bon Voyage, 149; 10. *La Reina del Pacifico*, 197; 11. Man in Tears, 210; 12. The Laughter of the Indians, 223; 13. Call It Love, 236; 14. Do Good to the Poor, 256; 15. The Feast of the Holy Waters, 273; 16. Now I Lay Me Down to Sleep, 290.

Parts of "Biarritz" and "Miss Graves" appeared originally in *Town & Country*, October 1942, as "Man of the World;" see E73. Parts of "Miss Graves" and much of "The *S. S. Monte Cristi*" appeared originally in *Town & Country*, November 1942, as "Man of the World;" see E74. "The Good Samaritan," in somewhat different form, appeared originally in *Town & Country*, February 1943, as "Man of the World;" see E75. "The Salamander and The Jews Are to Blame, in slightly different form, appeared originally in *Town & Country*, May 1943, as "Man of the World;" see E76. "The Kiss Royale," in somewhat different form, appeared originally in *Town & Country*, June 1943, as "The Royal Kiss, Which is the 5th Episode of Man of the World;" see E78. Part of "Bon Voyage," in somewhat different form, appeared originally in *Town & Country*, August 1943, as "The Panama Canal, Which is the Sixth Episode of Man of the World;" see E80. *"La Reina del Pacifico,"* "Man in Tears," and part of "The Laughter of the Indians," all in somewhat different form, appeared originally in *Town & Country*, September 1943, as "Now I Lay Me Down to Sleep;" see E81. "The Feast of the Holy Waters" and "Now I Lay Me Down to Sleep," in somewhat different form, appeared originally in *Town & Country*, October 1943, as "Now I Lay Me Down to Sleep;" see E82.

COPY EXAMINED: MP.

a (bis). Deluxe illustrated edition ([1943]):

TITLE PAGE: In black, with the first letter enlarged and decorated: Now I Lay Me Down to Sleep | By Ludwig Bemelmans | New York : The Viking Press : 1943

PAGINATION: 1 blank leaf, 6 leaves, 1 - 299 pp., 1 blank leaf; endpapers.

COVERINGS: Full-color illustrations on unnumbered glossy pages are inserted after pages 6, 22, 80, and 282. 20.2 x 13.5 cm. Gray buckram-covered boards. The front contains a full-color illustration, pasted down, of the Place Vendôme. On the spine, stamped in gold upon a rectangular burgundy leather patch: a double rule | Bemel- | mans | a double rule | Now | I Lay | Me | Down | to | Sleep | a double rule | Viking | a double rule. Top, front, and bottom edges stained olive green. Black slip case with facsimile of front cover from A34a pasted down on front.

PUBLISHED: between October 25 and November 12, 1943 at $7.50. 526 copies specially bound from a printing of 32,600 sets of sheets. The recto of the first printed leaf is a signature page printed in olive green as follows: This illustrated edition of | Now I Lay Me Down to Sleep | is limited to four hundred copies | for sale, numbered 1 to 400, and | one hundred copies for private | distribution, numbered I to C | this copy is number | numbered in ink | author's signature | This edition is dedicated to | Isa de Rivas *Other books by the author* on recto of second printed leaf; *verso of title leaf;* and *contents* all as in A34a. *Half-title* on recto of sixth printed leaf. The fifth printed leaf is on glossy paper and contains a list of the color illustrations, see below. Olive green endpapers printed in black with an drawing of the Reina del Pacifico and crocodiles by the author.

ILLUSTRATIONS for the Limited Edition on recto of fifth printed leaf, with a full-color illustration of a gentleman upon a park bench: "Place Vendome," facing page 6; "Restaurant Robinson," facing page 22; "The Plaza," facing page 80; "The Farewell of Miss Graves," following page 282.

COPIES BOUND: Of the 526 copies of this edition, four hundred were for public sale; one hundred were for private distribution; and twenty-six were special copies labelled A to Z upon the signature page.

COPY EXAMINED: MP.

b. Reprint ([1944]):

TITLE PAGE: In black, with the first letter enlarged and decorated: Now I Lay Me Down to Sleep | by Ludwig Bemelmans | New York : The Viking Press : 1944

PAGINATION: 1 blank leaf, 3 leaves, [1] - 245 pp., 1 blank leaf; endpapers. 20.3 x 13.6 cm.

COVERINGS: Covering as in A34a. Top edges stained olive green. Full-color dust jacket printed in olive green. Top of front flyleaf is printed in black: Now I Lay Me Down To Sleep $2.50.

PUBLISHED: February 18, 1944 at $2.50. Number of sets of sheets printed cannot be determined, as the publisher's records have lapsed. On *verso of title leaf:* This edition is produced in full compliance with all War Production Board conservation orders. Copyright 1942-3 by Ludwig Bemelmans Printed in U.S.A. by H. Wolff Book Mfg. Co. Limited Edition published by The Viking Press in October 1943 First Regular Edition (October 1943) issued in February 1944 Second Printing February 1944. *Acknowledgment* on verso of title leaf, as in A34a. *Half-title* on recto of first leaf. *Second half-title* on page [1]. *Other books by the author* on verso of first leaf, listing six titles. Endpapers plain.

Note: An undetermined number of copies of this edition were made available in March 1944 to membership by the Book-of-the-Month Club, singly at $2.50 or as part of a Dual Selection at approximately $3.00. They included a synopsis by Henry Seidel Canby reprinted from the February edition of the *Book-of-the-Month Club News.* These copies have pages trimmed to 19.7 x 13.5 cm. and covered in tan linen-weave cloth-covered boards stamped on front with an olive green rectangle through which author and title show in tan between two rules; and on spine, as in A34a, but with all stamping in olive green only. Top edges stained olive green or red. Full-color dust jacket printed in pale green. Front flyleaf is printed in black at top, Now I Lay Me Down To Sleep. On *verso of title leaf:* Copyright 1942, 1943 by Ludwig Bemelmans Printed in U.S.A. by H. Wolff, New York, N.Y. Published on the same day in the Dominion of Canada by The Macmillan Company of Canada Limited This edition is produced in full compliance with all War Production Board conservation orders.

CONTENTS on recto of third leaf: 1. Biarritz, 3; 2. Miss Graves, 17; 3. The *S. S. Monte Cristi,* 32; 4. Casablanca, 41; 5. The Good Samaritan, 56; 6. The Salamander, 67; 7. The Jews Are to Blame, 86; 9. Bon Voyage, 124; 10. *La Reina del Pacifico,* 163; 11. Man in Tears, 174; 12. The Laughter of the Indians, 184; 13. Call It Love, 195; 14. Do Good to the Poor, 211; 15. The Feast of the Holy Waters, 224; 16. Now I Lay Me Down to Sleep, 238.

COPY EXAMINED: MP.

c. British edition ([1944]):

TITLE PAGE: In black: Ludwig Bemelmans | a rule | Now I | Lay Me Down | to Sleep | colophon | Hamish Hamilton | London

PAGINATION: [i] - [vi] pp., 1 - 234 pp.; endpapers. 18.5 x 12.5 cm.

COVERINGS: Sienna cloth - covered boards

stamped with title in gold on front; on spine, in gold; now I lay me down to sleep • ludwig bemelmans; at base: colophon | Hamish | Hamilton. Full-color dust jacket printed in olive green. (There is a variant dust jacket with the spine printed in sienna.)

PUBLISHED: Between November 24 and December 15, 1944 at 8s 6d. The number of sets of sheets printed cannot be determined, as the publisher cannot withdraw old records from storage. On *verso of title leaf*, page [iv]: First published 1944 Printed in Great Britain by William Clowes and Sons, Limited, London and Beccles. *Half-title* on page [i]. *Other books by the author* on page [ii], listing five titles. Endpapers plain.

The edition was reprinted in January 1945 at 9s 6d. The number of sets of sheets printed cannot be determined.

CONTENTS on page v: 1. Biarritz, 1; 2. Miss Graves, 14; 3. The S. S. *Monte Cristi*, 28; 4. Casablanca, 36; 5. The Good Samaritan, 51; 6. The Salamander, 61; 7. The Jews Are to Blame, 79; 8. The Kiss Royale, 90; 9. Bon Voyage, 116; 10. *La Reina del Pacifico*, 154; 11. Man in Tears, 164; 12. The Laughter of the Indians, 174; 13. Call It Love, 185; 14. Do Good to the Poor, 100; 15. The Feast of the Holy Waters, 213; 16. Now I Lay Me Down to Sleep, 226.

COPY EXAMINED: MP.

d. Australian edition ([1945]):

TITLE PAGE: In black: Ludwig Bemelmans | Now I | Lay Me Down | to Sleep | Hamish Hamilton | London | George Jaboor | Melbourne

PAGINATION: [1] - 240 pp.; endpapers. 18.3 x 12.2 cm.

COVERINGS: Dark royal blue linen-weave cloth-covered boards, plain on front; stamped on spine, in dark indigo: Now I | lay me | down | to | sleep | a sweeping line | Bemelmans; and at base Hamilton | Jaboor. Full-color dust jacket printed in yellow with Hamilton Jaboor in red on spine.

PUBLISHED: 1945 at 10s 6d. The number of sets of sheets printed cannot be determined, as the publisher cannot withdraw old records from storage. On *verso of title leaf*, page [4]: Registered in Australia for transmission by Post as a Book. First published 1944 Australian Edition 1945 Wholly set up and printed in Australia by Wilke and Co. Pty. Ltd., Melbourne, for George Jaboor, 431 Bourke Street, Melbourne, Australasian representative of Hamish Hamilton Ltd., London. *Half-title* on page [1]. *Other books by the author* on page [2], listing five titles. No table of contents. Endpapers plain.

COPY EXAMINED: MP.

e. Cheap edition ([1946]):

TITLE PAGE: In black, with the first letter enlarged and decorated: Now I Lay Me Down to Sleep | by Ludwig Bemelmans | The Sun Dial Press-Garden City, New York

PAGINATION: 3 leaves, [1] - 245 pp., 2 blank leaves; endpapers. 19.9 x 14 cm.

COVERINGS: Turquoise cloth-covered boards stamped with author and title on a maroon rectangle on front; on spine, in maroon: a double rule | on a maroon rectangle, in turquoise: Bemel- | mans | a single rule | Now | I Lay | Me | Down | to | Sleep | in maroon: a single rule | a single rule | Sun Dial | Press | a double rule. Full-color dust jacket printed in chartreuse. On *inside of front flyleaf*: This book is printed from the plates of the original edition. The text is complete and unabridged. The low price is made possible by the elimination of original production costs and the author's acceptance of a reduced royalty. On *inside of rear flyleaf*, in red: No. 724.

PUBLISHED: March 4, 1946 at $1.00. 20,000 sets of sheets printed. On *verso of title leaf*: Sun Dial Press Reprint Edition, 1946, by special arrangement with the Viking Press. Printed in the U.S.A. *Acknowledgement* on verso of title leaf, as in A34a. *Half-title* on recto of first leaf. *Second half-title* on page [1]. *Other books by the author* on verso of first leaf, listing six titles. Endpapers plain.

CONTENTS on recto of third leaf: As in A34b.

COPY EXAMINED: MP.

f. Italian edition ([1948]):

TITLE PAGE: In black: E Ora Andiamo | A Letto | di Ludwig | Bemelmans | in black: two crossed sabres and a star | Longanesi & C. | Milano

PAGINATION: [1] - [340] pp. 17.6 x 12 cm.

COVERINGS: Dark gray-brown cardboard covers with a horizontal beige band stippled with white and printed in black on front: Bemelmans; on back: Longanesi & C; printed on spine, at top, in black: 31; then on continuation of the beige band: E ora andiamo | a letto. Edges trimmed and unstained. Full-color dust jacket printed on front with part of a full-color illustration, "Luchow's Restaurant on a Sunday Evening," from between pages 112 and 113 of *The Donkey Inside*, A8; and with title, author and publisher in black and white; and on back with the names of twenty-one titles in the "La Gaja Scienze" series. The inside of the dust jacket is printed with other titles from the publisher.

This is No. 31 of the La Gaja Scienza series.

PUBLISHED: January 1948 at 700 Lire. 3,000 sets of sheets printed. On *verso of title leaf*: Proprietà Letteraria Riservata Longanesi E C. 1948, Milano, Via Borghetto, 5 Traduzione Dall'Inglese di Marcella Hannau Titolo Originale Dell'Opera Now I Lay Me Down to Sleep Stampato in Italia. *Half-title* on page [7]. *Series title* on page [3]: "La Gaja Scienza" | Volume 31. *Colophon* on page [339]: Finito di Stampare Il 15 Gennaio 1948 Nello Stabilimento Grafico R. Scotti Milano.

CONTENTS (INDICE) on page [337]: I, Biarritz, 9; II, Miss Graves, 28; III, Lo Jacht Monte Cristi, 48; IV, Casablanca, 59; V, Il buon Samaritano, 79; VI, La salamandra, 92; VII, La colpa e degli Ebrei, 118; VIII, Il Kiss Royale, 133; IX, Bon Voyage, 169; X, La Reina del Pacifico, 222; XI, Uomo in lacrime, 237; XII, Gli Indiani ridono, 251; XIII, Chiamiamolo amore, 265; XIV, Fate del bene ai poveri, 287; XV, La festa delle acque sante, 305; XVI, Ed ora mi pongo a dormire, 324.

COPY EXAMINED: Library of Congress, Washington, D.C.; Biblioteca Querini Stampalia, Venezia.

g. Hungarian edition ([1948]):

TITLE PAGE: In black: Ludwig Bemelmans | in red: Szertelen Élet | in black: Bibliotheca

PAGINATION: [1] - [256] pp.; endpapers. 20.5 x 14.2 cm.

COVERINGS: Black paper-covered boards stamped on front in silver with a cherub bearing harp. Spine is covered in white cloth and stamped in gray: Bemelmans | Szertelen | Élet; and at base: Bibliotheca. White dust jacket printed in white and turquoise.

PUBLISHED: 1948 at a price now unknown. Number of sets of sheets printed cannot be determined, as the publisher and the publisher's records have vanished. On *verso of title leaf,* page [4]: A mü eredeti címe: Now I Lay Me Down to Sleep. Forditotta: Székely Beéta. A fedölapot Csillag Vera tervezte. Budapest 1948. *Colophon* on page [1]. *Note about the author* on pages 5 - [6]. On page [256]: Felelös kiadó: Pap László. Igazság nyomda Budapest, VI., Horn Ede-utca 9-11.— Felelös vezetö: Falus József.

COPY EXAMINED: Mrs. Madeleine Bemelmans.

h. Paperback edition ([1950]):

Now I Lay Me Down to Sleep was published in an abridged edition March 24, 1950, at 25¢, by New American Library in New York. It has not been possible to examine a copy of this edition. The number of sets of sheets printed cannot be determined, as the publisher's records were lost during acquisition by a new owner.

This is Signet Books No. 776.

A35. On Board Noah's Ark [1962]

a. First edition:

TITLE PAGE: Upon a drawing of an easel next to three children, in black: On Board | Noah's Ark | by | Ludwig Bemelmans | The Viking Press | New York

PAGINATION: 2 leaves, [1] - 48 pp., 2 leaves, 49 - 80 pp., 2 leaves, 81 - [168] pp., 2 leaves, 169 - [188] pp., 2 blank leaves; endpapers. 21.1 x 14.1 cm.

COVERINGS: One-eighth red linen-weave cloth-covered, and seven-eighths two-tone gray paper-covered boards stamped in dark gray with a sailboat on front; on spine, in gold: Bemelmans On Board Noah's Ark Viking. The papered boards have a wave pattern. Top edges stained gray. Full-color dust jacket printed in red and white.

PUBLISHED: May 18, 1962 at $5.00. 12,000 sets of sheets printed; 12,000 copies bound. On *verso of title leaf*, page [2]: First published in 1962 by The Viking Press, Inc. 625 Madison Avenue, New York 22, N.Y. Part of this book appeared in *Holiday* under the title "My Riviera Cruise," copyright © 1961 by The Curtis Publishing Co. Printed in the U.S.A. *Half-title* on recto of first leaf. *Other books by the author* on verso of first leaf, listing twenty-three titles. *Frontispiece* on verso of second leaf, a full-color illustration of the *Arche de Noé* in harbor. An *author's note*, unsigned, is on page [3]. A facsimile of the author's Foreign Vessel Passport is printed in black and brown on page [5]. Pink endpapers printed with a black drawing titled, "Interior Restaurant of the Hotel Arche de Noé on the Island of Porquerolles."

Note: An undetermined number of copies of this edition were distributed by the Book-of-the-Month Club to its membership in mid-summer 1962 at $5.00. The book was accompanied by a copy of the *Book-of-the-Month Club News* for Mid-Summer 1962, which contained a synopsis.

CONTENTS on page [7]: Part One: l. The Riviera, 13; 2. Ship-Owner, 36; 3. Mayday, 65; 4. The Feast of San Giorgio, 71; 5. The Good One, 87. Part Two: 6. The Etruscan Vase, 101; 7. Napoli, 109; 8. Valse Triste, 153; 9. Ischia, 161; 10. Return, 174.

The text is here reprinted from "My Riviera Cruise," *Holiday*, June 1961; see E193.

List of Color Illustrations on page [9]: The *Arche de Noé*, Frontispiece; *Passeport de Navires Etrangers*, following page 6; The Old Port of Antibes and the *Arche de Noé*, following page 48; Antibes Vacationers, following page 48; The Yellow House, following page 48; The Promenade *"des Anglais"* in Nice, following page 48; The Harbor of Monaco, the *Christina*, and the *Arche de Noé*, following page 80; San Fruttuoso, following page 80; The Disaster in Portofino, following page 80; Fishermen with a Shark at Capri, following page 80; Ischia (the painting that fell in the water), following page 168; Departure from Ischia, following page 168; Isle Rousse, Corsica-Sunset, following page 168; The Isle of Porquerolles, following page 168.

ILLUSTRATIONS: In addition to the endpapers, the title page drawing, and the color illustrations listed, there are 61 black drawings by the author.

COPY EXAMINED: MP.

b. British edition ([1962]):

TITLE PAGE: Upon a drawing of an easel next to three children, in black: On Board | Noah's Ark | by | Ludwig Bemelmans | Collins | London

PAGINATION: as in A35a. 21 x 14.3 cm.

COVERINGS: Red linen-weave cloth-covered boards stamped on spine, in gold: On Board Noah's Ark Bemelmans; at base: Collins. Dust jacket as in A35a.

PUBLISHED: November 1962 at 21s. Approximately 7,000 sets of sheets printed. On *verso of title leaf*, page [2]: Printed in Great Britain Collins Clear-type Press: London and Glasgow. *Other books by the author* on verso of first leaf, listing fourteen titles. *Frontispiece, author's note, passport, contents*, and *list of color illustrations* as in A35a. Endpapers as in A35a.

ILLUSTRATIONS: As in A35a.

COPY EXAMINED: MP.

c. German edition ([1965]):

TITLE PAGE: In black: Ludwig Bemelmans | a black drawing of three children watching a sailboat, with an easel, upon which: Noahs Arche | at bottom: Kiepenheuer & Witsch

PAGINATION: [1] - [184] pp.; endpapers. 22 x 14 cm.

COVERINGS: Brick red linen-weave cloth-covered boards plain on front. There is a white sticker at the top of the spine on which is printed in black: Ludwig | Bemelmans | in green: Noahs | Arche. The dust jacket is yellow on back and contains on front a full-color painting by the author of two women in bikinis; author in yellow, title in white, and publisher in black.

PUBLISHED: 1965 at DM 14,80. Number of sets of sheets printed cannot be determined, as the publisher cannot release the information. On *verso of title leaf*, page [6]: Titel der Originalausgabe On Board Noah's Ark © 1962 by Ludwig Bemelmans. Aus dem Amerikanischen von Nino Erné. Alle deutschsprachigen Rechte 1965 bei Verlag Kiepenheuer & Witsch · Köln · Berlin. Gesamtherstellung: Kleins Druck- und Verlagsanstalt GmbH Lengerich (Westfalen) Printed in Germany 1965. *Colophon* on page [1]. *Half-title* on page [3]. An *author's note*, unsigned, is on page [9]. A facsimile of the author's Foreign Vessel Passport is printed in black on page [11]. Taupe endpapers printed as in A36a.

CONTENTS (INHALT) on page [7]: Erster Teil: Komplette Riviera, 15; Herr eines Bootes, 36; Erneuter Kommandowechsel, 63; Das San Giorgio-Fest, 69; Der rechte Kapitän, 83; Zweiter Teil: Die Etruskische Vase, 97; Napoli, 105; Capri, 114; Der Herr der Iphigenia, 127; Valse Triste, 148; Ischia, 157; Stürmische Heimkehr, 170.

ILLUSTRATIONS: There are 57 black illustrations by the author in addition to the title page drawing and the endpapers. There are no color reproductions in this edition.

COPY EXAMINED: Mrs. Madeleine Bemelmans.

A36. Parsley [1955]

a. First edition:

TITLE PAGE: Within a full-color wildflower border, in black: Parsley | by | Ludwig Bemelmans | Harper & Brothers New York

PAGINATION: [1] - [48] pp.; endpapers. 25.4 x 31.7 cm.

COVERINGS: Mint green linen-weave cloth-covered boards with gray cloth-covered spine. The front is stamped with the title and a drawing of a stag in dark green. The spine is stamped in dark green: Bemelmans Parsley; at bottom: Harper. There is a full-color dust jacket bearing an illustration of a woebegone stag munching wildflowers in the woods while an owl sleeps upon its antler and other animals frolic nearby; printed with author and title in white; with a yellow spine printed with author in red and title and publisher in black. On front flyleaf, in green: Parsley; in black: Instead of reading about this book, just turn the pages and take a look. (sig-

nature of the author and full-color illustration of forget-me-not). Rear flyleaf contains four critical blurbs about *The High World*, A16, with a black illustration by the author.

PUBLISHED: September 21, 1955 at $3.50. 25,000 sets of sheets printed. On *verso of title leaf*, page [4]: This story was published in *Woman's Day*, the A & P Magazine, under the title "The Old Stag and the Tree." Reprinted by permission. *Half-title* on page [1] contains a full-color drawing of Shepherd's-purse. *Second half-title* on page [5] contains a full-color drawing of cowslip. *Author's acknowledgment* on page 46: The author wishes to thank Mabel Souvaine in whose magazine, *Woman's Day*, this story first appeared. The endpapers are plain.

This edition was distributed in The United Kingdom at 29s.

15,000 copies of this edition were selected by the Literary Guild between October, 1955 and April, 1956 and distributed, with minor alteration to the spine, at $1.00.

The text appeared originally as "The Old Stag and the Tree" in *Woman's Day*, January 1954; see E160.

ILLUSTRATIONS: Besides those on the half-title pages, there are full-color drawings of herbs on every even-numbered page from 6 to 46 inclusive, and there is a listing of the names of these herbs, within a full-color herbal border, on page [47]. All of the odd-numbered pages from

7 to 45 inclusive are printed with full-color full-page illustrations.

Note: The book was reprinted in 1980 at $8.95, with the following title page: Within a full-color wildflower border, in black: Parsley | by | Ludwig Bemelmans | Harper & Row, Publishers | New York, Evanston, and London

COPY EXAMINED: MP.

b. First South African edition ([1980]):

TITLE PAGE: Within a full-color wildflower border, in black: Die Bok en die Boom | deur | Ludwig Bemelmans | Qualitas-Uitgewers

PAGINATION: [1] - [48] pp. 20.3 x 24.6 cm.

COVERINGS: Full-color paper-covered boards printed on front with an illustration of a woebegone stag munching wildflowers in the woods while an owl sleeps upon its antler and other animals frolic nearby, and with title and author in silver; upon a pale yellow spine, in dark brown: Die Bok en die Boom; at base: Qualitas. There is a full-color dust jacket reproducing the cover.

PUBLISHED: July 1980 at R 5.20. The number of sets of sheets printed is not known but is likely to have been approximately 3,000. The translation into Afrikaans is by Lydia Pienaar. On *verso of title leaf*: Oorspronklik uitgegee onder die titel *Parsley* deur Harper & Row, New York Die verhaal het oorspronklik in 'n tydskrif *Woman's Day* verskyn onder die titel *The Old Stag and*

the Tree Kopiereg © 1953, 1955 deur Ludwig Bemelmans Afrikaanse uitgawe kopiereg © 1980 Qualitas-Uitgewers Posbus 26444, Arcadia, Pretoria 0007 Alle regte voorbehou Vertaal deur Lydia Pienaar Gedruk en gebind deur Werdadrukkers, Fabriekstelle 5 & 6, Isithebe, Natal.

ILLUSTRATIONS: As in A36a, except that the note about the author within a flowered border on page [47] replaces the list of wildflowers presented in A36a.

COPY EXAMINED: Lydia Snyman, Cape Town.

c. Zulu edition ([1980]):

Parsley was published as *I-Parsley* in July 1980 by Qualitas of Arcadia and Pretoria at R 5.20. The number of sets of sheets printed is not known but is likely to have been around 3,000. The book was in paper covers and measured approximately 21 x 26 cm. The translation into Zulu is by A. A. Khuzwayo. A copy of this edition has not been found for examination.

d. Second South African edition ([1990]):

TITLE PAGE: Within a full-color wildflower border, in black: Die Bok en die Boom | deur Ludwig Bemelmans | colophon | Anansi-Uitgewers

PAGINATION: [1] - [48] pp. 22 x 27.7 cm.

COVERINGS: Paper-covered boards printed on

front with a full-color illustration of a woebegone stag munching wildflowers in the woods while an owl sleeps upon its antler and other animals frolic nearby, with title and author in white; on a yellow spine, in black: Die Bok en die Boom Ludwig Bemelmans; at base: Anansi-Uitgewers. The back cover has a full-color illustration of the stag looking through binoculars attached to a yellow tree (as on page [45]). The full-color dust jacket reproduces the cover. Printed on the front flyleaf, in green: Die Bok en die Boom; in black: Moenie hier iets óór die verhaal probeer soek nie. Blaai liewer die blaaie om en leer dit self ken; (signature of the author and full-color drawing of forget-me-not). Back flyleaf contains a blurb about a book by Theodor Fontane.

PUBLISHED: December 1990 at R28.95. 3,000 sets of sheets printed. On *verso of title leaf*, page [4]: (colophon) Oorspronklik uitgegee onder die title *Parsley* deur Harper & Row, New York Die verhaal het vir die eerste keer verskyn in die tydskrif *Woman's Day* onder die titel *The Old Stag and the Tree* Uitgegee met hulle toestemming Kopiereg © 1953, 1955 Ludwig Bemelmans Hierdie uitgawe kopiereg © 1990 Anansi-Uitgewers, Forestweg 10, Oranjezicht 8001 Alle regte voorbehou Vertaal deur Lydia Snyman (Translated by Lydia Snyman) Setwerk en reproduksie Unifoto, Kaapstad. Page [1] contains a full-color drawing of shepherd's-purse. *Half-title* on page [5] contains a full-color drawing of cowslip. On page 46: Die skrywer wil graag Mabel Souvaine bedank in wie

se tydskrif *Woman's Day* die verhaal vir die eerste keer verskyn het. *Note about the author* on page [47] within the same full-color wildflower border as is used on the title page.

ILLUSTRATIONS: As in A36a. The note about the author on page [47] replaces the list of wildflowers presented in A36a.

COPY EXAMINED: Mrs. Madeleine Bemelmans.

A37. Quito Express [1938]

TITLE PAGE: Over a sienna drawing of a train running toward a mountain behind which the sun is shining, in black: Quito Express | Story & Pictures by | Ludwig | Bemelmans | Published by The Viking Press • New York • 1938

PAGINATION: [1] - [48] pp.; endpapers. 17.9 x 23.5 cm.

COVERINGS: Paper-covered boards with a sienna cloth-covered spine. There is a sienna drawing upon the front covering of an Ecuadorian child with two chickens and some corn; upon the back covering, a drawing of the two chickens, the corn, mountains and the sun. The front is printed in black: Quito Express | by Ludwig Bemelmans; the spine is plain. The sienna, black and white dust jacket reproduces the board covers.

PUBLISHED: September 30, 1938 at $1.00.

10,000 sets of sheets printed; 5,000 copies bound. On *verso of title leaf,* page [4]: Copyright 1938 by Ludwig Bemelmans. Lithographed in U. S. A. by William C. D. Glaser. There is a sienna drawing of a conductor's whistle, a punch, and some railway tickets. *Half-title* on page [1]: contains a sienna drawing of a child, two chickens, a tree and the sun. The endpapers are plain.

This edition was reprinted in 1965 at $2.00, with the title verso containing this information: First published September 1938. Copyright 1938 by Ludwig Bemelmans. Reissued (from new plates) 1965. Distributed in Canada by The Macmillan Company of Canada, Ltd. Printed in U.S.A.

ILLUSTRATIONS: In addition to the drawings upon the title, title verso and half-title pages there are 43 sienna drawings by the author.

COPY EXAMINED: MP.

A38. Rosebud
[1942]

TITLE PAGE: In blue: Rosebud | Bemelmans | a drawing of an irate fuchsia rabbit with a blue book: | Random House - New York

PAGINATION: [1] - 32 pp.; endpapers. 25.5 x 20.5 cm.

COVERINGS: Cornflower blue paper-covered boards printed with a white hatched border and the title in white, the title page drawing in fuchsia and blue, and the author's last name in black. The blue spine is printed in black: Rosebud Bemelmans; and at bottom: Random House. The dust jacket reproduces the covering of the boards.

PUBLISHED: October 1, 1942 at $1.00. The number of sets of sheets printed cannot be determined, as the publisher's records have been lost. On *verso of title leaf,* page [2]: Printed in the United States of America by Western Printing and Lithographing Company. The cornflower blue endpapers are printed with a multitude of white rabbits.

ILLUSTRATIONS: In addition to the title drawing there are 29 other drawings by the author, printed in black, cornflower blue, fuchsia, and lavender. In addition, page 25 contains colored highlighting which is not actually a figure drawing.

COPY EXAMINED: MP.

A39. Small Beer
[1939]

a. First edition:

TITLE PAGE: Upon a drawing of a tuba in an armchair next to a table with a glass of wine beneath a hanging light, in black: Small Beer | Ludwig | Bemelmans | The Viking Press • MCMXXXIX • New York

PAGINATION: [1] - 186 pp., 1 leaf; endpapers. 21 x 13 cm.

COVERINGS: Cherry cloth-covered boards blind-stamped with a violin on front; on spine, within a black rectangle, in gold: Small | Beer | Bemelmans; at bottom, in black: Viking Press. Top edges stained yellow. Yellow and white dust jacket, with a drawing of a baby and dog in a park, printed in black.

PUBLISHED: August 28, 1939 at $2.50. 2,850 sets of sheets printed; 2,675 copies bound. On *verso of title leaf*, page [4]: Published in August 1939. Copyright 1935, 1936, 1937, 1939 by Ludwig Bemelmans. Printed in U.S.A. by Vail-Ballou Press. *Half-title* on page [1]. *Other books by the author*, listing *Life Class* and *My War with the United States*, on page [2]. Endpapers printed with a black drawing of a writer busy at his table in a cluttered studio with a dozing dog.

Some copies of this edition were selected by the Dollar Book Club after February 1, 1942 and distributed to membership at $1.00.

CONTENTS on page [5]: "No Trouble at All" 9; Dog Story, 29; My English Suit in Paris, 49; Putzi, 65; Fancy Green, 81; Theodore and "The Blue Danube," 99; The Isle of God, 113; Sacre du Printemps, 133; Dear General, What a Surprise!, 147; A Christmas Story, 169.

"No Trouble at All" is here reprinted from *Vogue*, March 1, 1937; see E5; it was reprinted in *Town & Country*, June 1957; see E175. "Dog Story" is here reprinted from *The New Yorker*, Vol.

XV, August 12, 1939; see E27 and as well A43. "My English Suit in Paris" is here reprinted from *Town & Country*, March 1939; see E21. As "Inside, Outside," "Putzi" first appeared in *Story*, October 1936; see E4. "The Isle of God" is here reprinted from *The New Yorker*, Vol. XV, August 5, 1939; see E26. "Theodore and *The Blue Danube*" is here reprinted from *Story*, May, 1936; see E2. "Sacre du Printemps" is here reprinted from *Story*, June, 1937 and May-June, 1941; see E7 and E56. "Dear General, What a Surprise!" is here reprinted from *Town & Country*, August 1939; see E24.

ILLUSTRATIONS: There is a full page black drawing by the author on the recto of the leaf preceding each chapter. In addition to these, to the endpapers, and to the title page drawing, there are 86 black drawings by the author.

COPY EXAMINED: MP.

a (bis). Deluxe limited edition ([1939]):

TITLE PAGE: Upon a drawing of a tuba in an armchair, next to a table with a glass of wine, beneath a hanging light, in black: Small Beer | Ludwig | Bemelmans | The Viking Press • MCMXXXIX • New York

PAGINATION: 2 leaves, [1] - 186 pp., 1 leaf; endpapers. 21 x 13 cm.

COVERINGS: Red linen-covered boards, stamped in gold, upon a black band, in between two golden angels: Small Beer. Stamped in gold upon spine: Bemelmans | upon the black band: Small | Beer | then: Viking Press. Within a black slipcase printed in black upon a gold band, Bemelmans. Edges stained red all around. No dust jacket.

PUBLISHED: August 28, 1939 at $5.00. 175 copies specially bound from a printing of 2,850 sets of sheets. *Verso of title leaf, contents, endpapers* and *illustrations* are as in A40a. The *half-title* is on recto of first leaf. The recto of the second leaf bears the text, in red: One hundred and seventy-five copies of the first edition have been specially bound with an original illustration in color This copy is number [hand-numbered in black ink]. Page [1] contains an original water-colored drawing by the author and his signature in black ink.

COPY EXAMINED: MP.

b. British edition [(1940)]:

TITLE PAGE: Upon a drawing of a tuba in an armchair, next to a table with a glass of wine, beneath a hanging light, in black: Small Beer | Ludwig | Bemelmans | London | John Lane The Bodley Head

PAGINATION: [3] - 186 pp., endpapers. 18.6 x 12.5 cm.

COVERINGS: Pale blue linen-covered boards with multicolored flecks. A white sticker on spine is printed in blue: Small | Beer | • | Ludwig |

Bemelmans | • | The Bodley Head. Top edges stained gray. Dust jacket not seen.

PUBLISHED: May 1940 at 7s 6d. Number of sets of sheets printed cannot be determined, as the publisher's records were lost during the Second World War. On *verso of title leaf:* First published in England 1940. Printed in Great Britain by Lowe and Brydone Printers Ltd., London, N.W.10. *Half-title* on page [3], *contents* on page [7], as in A39a.

ILLUSTRATIONS: As in A39a.

COPY EXAMINED: MP.

c. Cheap edition [(1945)]:

TITLE PAGE: Within a black rectangle, upon a drawing of a tuba in an armchair, next to a table with a glass of wine, beneath a hanging light, in black: Small Beer | Ludwig | Bemelmans | beside the Pocket Books logo: Pocket Books, Inc. | New York, N.Y.

PAGINATION: 3 leaves, [1] - 134 pp., 2 leaves; endpapers. 16.1 x 10.5 cm.

COVERINGS: White, ochre, blue and orange paper cover printed in black. Edges stained red all around.

This is Pocket Book No. 306.

PUBLISHED: August, 1945 at 25¢. Number of sets of sheets printed cannot be determined, as the publisher's records have been lost. *Verso of title leaf* contains printing history and the text: This Pocket Book edition is published by arrangement with The Viking Press, Inc. On recto of first leaf: a selection of press clippings. On verso of first leaf: This is a wartime book[.] This Pocket Book includes every word contained in the original, higher-priced edition. It is printed from brand-new plates made from completely re-set, large, clear, easy-to-read type, and is produced in full compliance with the Government's regulations for conserving paper and other essential materials. *Half-title* on page [1] contains the black drawing which is printed on the endpapers of A40a. Publisher's advertisement on recto of second-last leaf; U. S. Victory Waste Paper Campaign advertisement on verso of second-last leaf. List of Pocket Books on last leaf. Plain red endpapers.

Contents on recto of third leaf: "No Trouble At All," 3; Dog Story, 17; My English Suit in Paris, 31; Putzi, 42; Fancy Green, 53; Theodore and "The Blue Danube," 66; The Isle of God, 76; Sacre du Printemps, 91; Dear General, What a Surprise!, 102; A Christmas Story, 117.

ILLUSTRATIONS: As in A39a.

COPY EXAMINED: MP.

d. Paperback edition [(1961)]:

TITLE PAGE: Upon a drawing of a tuba in an armchair, next to a table with a glass of wine, beneath a hanging light, in black: Small Beer | Ludwig | Bemelmans | Capricorn Books, New York

PAGINATION: [1] - 186 pp., 3 leaves. 18.5 x 10.7 cm.

COVERINGS: Yellow paper covers printed in black; on spine, in black: Bemelmans • Small Beer (logo) Cap | 49.

This is Capricorn Books No. 49.

PUBLISHED: April 1961 under licence from The Viking Press, at $0.95. The number of sets of sheets printed cannot be determined, as the publisher's records are not available. On *verso of title leaf*, Capricorn Books Edition, 1961. *Half-title* on page [1], *contents* on page [5] as in A39a. Capricorn titles on second-last leaf.

This book was distributed in The United Kingdom at 9s by H. Jonas & Company Ltd, 33-37 Moreland Street, London EC1.

ILLUSTRATIONS: As in A39a.

COPY EXAMINED: MP.

A40. The Street Where the Heart Lies [1963]

a. First edition:

TITLE PAGE: In black: Ludwig Bemelmans | The Street Where the Heart Lies | beside a black drawing of rooftops with a black cat: colophon | The World Publishing Company | Cleveland and New York

PAGINATION: [1] - 236 pp., 2 leaves; endpapers. 20.2 x 13.5 cm.

COVERINGS: Kelly green linen-covered boards stamped with the author's signature in gold and an underline in blue; on spine, in gold: The | Street | Where | the | Heart | Lies | in blue: * | in gold: Bemelmans | upon a blue figure of a woman on a rooftop, in gold: World. Top edges stained dark blue. Full color dust jacket printed in red, black and white.

PUBLISHED: January 7, 1963 at $3.95. Number of sets of sheets printed and exact publication date cannot be determined, as the publisher and the publisher's records have vanished. The *title* occupies pages [2] and [3]. On *verso of title*, page [4]: First Edition. WP1162. *Half-title* on page [1]. *Author's disclaimer* on page [5]. Ochre endpapers printed with a black drawing of a quai in Paris.

Note: An undetermined number of copies of this edition were distributed by the Book-of-the-Month Club to its membership in January 1963 at $3.95. The book was accompanied by a copy of the *Book-of-the-Month Club News* for January 1963, which contained a synopsis.

CONTENTS on pages [7] and [8]: Part One: 1. Under the Bridge, 11; 2. Liberty, 19; 3. Perfect Service, 28; 4. Sleepless Night, 40; 5. The Rehearsal, 47; 6. Save Himself Who Can, 57; 7. The Tourist, 67. Part Two: 8. The Tour d'Argent, 83; 9. Turn Over, Please, 103; 10. Aisha and Ali, 112; 11. Just the Family, 119; 12. Opening Night, 125; 13. Mohammed, 135. Part Three: 14. Silent Night, 147; 15. The Radio Taxi, 156; 16. The Gift, 164; 17. The Virgin, 183; 18. The Little White Horse, 197; 19. Relaxez-Vous, 204; 20. Celebration, 212; 21. The Friend of the Family, 224; 22. Long Past Your Bedtime, 232.

"The Tour d'Argent" appeared as "Gala at the Tour d'Argent" in *Playboy*, December 1962; see E197.

ILLUSTRATIONS: In addition to the title drawing and endpapers, there is a black drawing by the author on the first page of every chapter and on the three section title pages, and a drawing of a violin on the final page.

COPY EXAMINED: MP.

b. German edition [(1961)]:

TITLE PAGE: In black: Ludwig Bemelmans | Die Strasse in der mein Herz wohnt | beside a black drawing of rooftops with a black cat: Kiepenheuer & Witsch

PAGINATION: [1] - [276] pp.; endpapers. 19 x 11.5 cm.

COVERINGS: Yellow linen weave cloth-covered boards. A white sticker on the spine is printed, in black: Die Strasse | in der mein | Herz wohnt. Full color dust jacket printed in red, black and white.

PUBLISHED: 1963 at DM 15,80. 4,000 sets of sheets printed. The *title* occupies pages [4] and [5]. On *verso of title*, page [6]: Titel der amerikanischen Originalausgabe The Street Where

The Heart Lies Einzig autorisierte Übertragung von Nino Erné. *Half-title* on page [3]. *Colophon* on page [1]. *Author's disclaimer* on page [7]. Red endpapers printed with a black drawing of a quai in Paris.

CONTENTS on pages [9] and [10]: I—Unter der Brücke, 13; Freiheit, 22; Perfekte Bedienung, 33; Schlaflose Nacht, 47; Im Kabarett, 55; Rette Sich Wer Kann, 66; Der Tourist, 77. II—Ente auf Silberner Schale, 95; Umdrehen, Bitte!, 119; Aischa und Ali, 129; Im Engsten Kreis, 137; Premiere, 144; Mohammed, 156. III—Monsieur Finsterwald, 171; Der Taxichauffeur, 178; Das Geschenk, 188; Eine Glückliche Ehe, 212; Das Kleine Weisse Pferd, 229; Relaxez-Vous!, 238; Hochzeit, 247; Ein Freund der Familie, 260; Unter der Brücke, 271.

ILLUSTRATIONS: As in A40a.

COPY EXAMINED: MP.

c. Cheap edition [(1964)]:

TITLE PAGE: In black: The | Street | Where | the Heart | Lies | Ludwig Bemelmans | Illustrated by the author | A MacFadden-Bartell Book

PAGINATION: [1] - 159 pp. 18.1 x 10.7 cm.

COVERINGS: Paper cover printed in yellow. Edges stained red all around.

This is MacFadden-Bartell Book No. 60-153.

PUBLISHED: The week of March 23, 1964 at 60¢. Number of sets of sheets printed and exact publication date cannot be determined, as neither the publisher nor the publisher's records can be located. On *verso of title*, page [4]: This book is the complete text of the hardcover edition. A MacFadden Book . . . 1964. *Publisher's blurb* on page [1]. *Critics' comments* on page [2]. *Author's disclaimer* on verso of title leaf.

CONTENTS on page [5]: Part One: 1. Under the Bridge, 9; 2. Liberty, 14; 3. Perfect Service, 20; 4. Sleepless Night, 27; 5. The Rehearsal, 32; 6. Save Himself Who Can, 38; 7. The Tourist, 44. Part Two: 8. The Tour d'Argent, 55; 9. Turn Over, Please, 68; 10. Aisha and Ali, 74; 11. Just the Family, 79; 12. Opening Night, 83; 13. Mohammed, 90. Part Three: 14. Silent Night, 99; 15. The Radio Taxi, 105; 16. The Gift, 111; 17. The Virgin, 123; 18. The Little White Horse, 132; 19. Relaxez-Vous, 137; 20. Celebration, 142; 21. The Friend of the Family, 150; 22. Long Past Your Bedtime, 156.

ILLUSTRATIONS: As in A40a with two exceptions. First, the final drawing of a violin has been replaced with a drawing of a guitar. And on page [6] there is a frontispiece of a clochard lifting his hat that does not appear in the first edition.

COPY EXAMINED: MP.

A41. Sunshine: A Story About the City of New York [1950]

TITLE PAGE: Upon the right front endpaper (which is full-colored), within a black blimp, in yellow "lights": Sunshine | a story about the city of New York | by Ludwig Bemelmans | at the bottom of the page, upon a yellow sandwich board, in black: Simon | and | Schuster | Publishers

PAGINATION: [1] - [40] pp.; endpapers. No page is numbered. The verso of the right front endpaper is printed, as is the recto of the left rear endpaper; giving the impression that there are in fact 44 pages with the title on page [1]. 30.5 x 22.7 cm.

COVERINGS: Full-color paper-covered boards showing the Statue of Liberty and Manhattan from the Staten Island Ferry, printed in yellow with the title and author's name. The spine is printed in green upon a yellow band: Sunshine by Ludwig Bemelmans; and in white at bottom upon a black band: Simon and Schuster 817. The full-color dust jacket reproduces the board coverings; the rear fly-leaf contains a listing of all the New York landmarks illustrated in the book.

PUBLISHED: May 15, 1950 at $2.50. The number of sets of sheets printed cannot be deter-mined, as the publisher keeps no records for more than ten years. *Verso of title leaf* contains a black and yellow drawing of Grant's Tomb (which appears as well on the rear board covering) and the text, "The author wishes to thank Mr. Herbert R. Mayes, Editor of *Good Housekeeping*, in which this story first appeared." And also, "Portions reprinted from *Good Housekeeping* magazine. Copyright 1949 by Hearst Magazines, Inc. Designed and produced by the Sandpiper Press and Artists And Writers Guild, Inc. Printed in the U.S.A. by Western Printing and Lithographing Company." The endsheets are printed with a full-color illustration of Midtown Manhattan from the East River in a snowfall.

This book was the winner of the New York Herald Tribune Children's Spring Book Festival Award.

The text appeared originally as "Sunshine Sunshine Go Away: A Story About the City of New York" in *Good Housekeeping*, December, 1949 (see E125) somewhat other than it is to be found here, including a different division of lines throughout. More particularly: on the recto of the second leaf the advertisement now printed, in a box: "Two Cheerful Rooms with bath/ in a building that truly hath atmosphere/ and old world charm: in summer cool,/ in winter warm, venetian blinds, open/ fireplace, cross-ventilation, ample closet/ space, refrigerator and hardwood floor./ A lovely view. Bus stops at door" originally read, upon a facsimile of a tear-out from the want ads: "Two

Cheerful Rooms/ with Bath/ In a building that truly hath atmos-/ phere and old world charm. In summer/ cool, in winter warm. Venetian Blinds,/ open fireplace, Cross Ventilation, ample/ closet space. Refrigerator and hard-/ wood floor. A lovely view. Bus stops at/ door." On the verso of the second leaf, the second line, "And rushed out into the street," read originally, "And rushed into the street;" the third line, " 'Go,' he said with angry face" read originally, " 'Go,' he said, with angry face;" originally a comma followed the eleventh line; the twelfth line was in quotes; the thirteenth line had a comma ending. On the recto of the third leaf, the first line originally had a comma after the second word; the third line had a semi-colon ending; the fourth line had a comma following the final word; the seventh line had a comma ending; in the fifteenth line the word "indeed" was surrounded by commas and the dash was absent from the ending; and the quotation mark after the sixteenth line was absent. Before the text on the verso of the third leaf there was originally this couplet: "This is where my troubles cease./ I'll nail her with an airtight lease!' " On the verso of the third leaf the first line ended with a comma; on the second line the word "whiskbroom" was originally two words. On the recto of the fourth leaf, the first two lines, "Quietly as a mouse/ She came into the house," were originally, "Sunshine, with old-fashioned charm,/ Offered the lady his right arm;" the fifth line had no quotation mark at the beginning; the eighth

line had no quotation mark at the end; the ninth line had no quotation mark at the beginning; the word "heaven-sent" in the twelfth line was originally two words; and the last two lines appeared originally in one line. On the recto of the fifth leaf the fifth line is incorporated originally into the fourth line, and originally "the Stars and Stripes" is *The Stars and Stripes* and "William Tell" is *William Tell.* The first two lines on the verso of the fifth leaf, "Miss Moore was totally immersed/ In music whenever she rehearsed" appeared originally after the following couplet, and that couplet was originally a quatrain. On the seventh leaf recto, Mr. Sunshine's lawyer originally had no name; the second line ended with a question mark; and the word "awful" in the last line was originally "dreadful." On the seventh leaf verso, the fifth through eighth lines, "This is an unhappy hour./ You underestimated the power/ Of a woman,/ Whom no Judge would dare to summon" were absent from the original; the ninth line had a comma ending; the eleventh line had a comma ending. On the eighth leaf verso the first line originally had a comma ending. On the ninth leaf verso, the ending of the ninth line was originally an exclamation mark. On the tenth leaf verso, the ending of the first line was originally a dash; the second line had a comma following the penultimate word; in the eighth line, the period after "lady" was originally a comma and the word "All" was "all;" the ninth line had no comma after the first word. Prior to the text on the eleventh leaf verso, there was a quatrain, "Miss Moore sadly paid,/ And with a deep sigh she said:/ 'I really don't see/ Why such things must always happen to me.' " On the same page the colon after the first word of the sixth line was originally a comma. On the twelfth leaf verso, the seventh line ended with a dash originally. On the thirteenth leaf recto there was no quotation mark at the beginning of the first line. On the thirteenth leaf verso there was no quotation mark beginning the first line; the fourth line had a period ending; the seventh line ended with quotation marks; the eighth line began with quotation marks; the word "again" in the ninth line was originally "back;" the next two lines, "In answer to the powerful prayers/ Of the son of an Irish cop" read originally, "They were led in powerful prayers/ By the son of an Irish cop." On the fourteenth leaf recto the word "clouds" originally had no following comma. On the fifteenth leaf recto the words "like out of" read originally, "as if from." The fifteenth leaf verso appeared originally somewhat later, with the word "pity" capitalized; before it came what is now on the seventeenth leaf recto, "Miss Moore ascended to Columbia Heights/ And sold umbrellas to Brooklynites" but with the word "Columbia" reading only "the;" and then "Little Sarah Hellman/ Sold her first to Cardinal Spellman;" and then "The management of a store called Mazy/ Was not at all crazy/ To see that there were many more/ Umbrellas sold outside than inside the store;" and then what is now on

the sixteenth leaf recto, "This customer is a United Nations delegate;/ The tall building is called the Empire State" with a period instead of a semi-colon ending the first line; and then what is now on the sixteenth leaf verso, "It was windy, cold, and showery,/ And tough work down on the Bowery." On the nineteenth leaf recto "played" in the first line was originally "gave a concert;" and the second line, "And gave a concert in Carnegie Hall" read originally, "And played under Toscanini in Carnegie Hall." On the twentieth leaf verso the period at the end of the second line was originally a dash. On the recto of the final flyleaf, a couplet originally preceded what is now the first line: "His nose was red, his hands were blue,/ He mumbled: 'I have something to say to you." And then, the "is" at the end of the current first line originally read, "was;" there were originally no quotation marks at the beginning of the third line. Before the next line there was originally a quatrain: "I live in a dark and drafty room/ In a place that has never seen a broom./ It's lonesome there, and still and cold./ My bones are aching, I'm getting old." The dash at the end of the fifth line was originally absent; and the sixth line, "Is that my own lawyer hates me" read originally, "Is that even my lawyer hates me." Six original lines have now been omitted: "I couldn't stand it any more tonight./ I said to myself: 'You've got to make things right.'/ I'll let you have this old house for a song./ That's what I came to tell you—so long.["]/ He turned to go after he had told of his grief./ Miss Moore said, 'Poor man, please don't leave.' " " 'But' " at the beginning of the seventh line was originally, " 'Oh,' ". The semi-colon at the end of the ninth line was originally a period. The comma at the end of the eleventh line was originally a period. In the original, this couplet followed what is now the concluding line: "His nose no longer red, his hands not blue,/ And here's a Merry Christmas to all of you."

ILLUSTRATIONS: In addition to the endsheets and the title verso there are 42 other illustrations by the author, some in full-color, some in black and yellow, some in pink and black, and some in lavender and black; and page [39] contains the score of "O holy night!" Some of the illustrative work is particularly interesting because of layout exigencies: the full-color illustration on the verso of the fourth leaf reproduces only a little more than half of the original illustration, which includes the fence and trees of Gramercy Park at left; some of the two-page full-color illustration of Miss Moore conducting the children, printed on the verso of the fifth and recto of the sixth leaves, was originally cropped; the map of the New York Subway on the verso of the tenth and recto of the eleventh leaves was not in the original; the two-page illustration of La Guardia airport on the verso of the seventeenth and recto of the eighteenth leaves has been printed in full-color on the right and in black and yellow on the left. Further: there are illustrations in each version which are absent from the other and some of the black and yellow illustrations in this edition have been re-drawn from earlier versions printed in *Good Housekeeping*.

COPY EXAMINED: MP.

A42. A Tale of Two Glimps [1947]

TITLE PAGE In black: A Tale | of Two Glimps | a color picture of two glimps dancing | by Ludwig Bemelmans

PAGINATION: Unpaged. 25 leaves, 1 blank leaf; endpapers. 19.4 x 22.6 cm.

COVERINGS: Paper-covered boards printed with a half full-color, half black drawing of two glimps upon the grass, with the title in red and author's name in black. Spine blank. The rear cover is printed in red: The Columbia | Broadcasting System | 485 Madison Avenue | New York 22, N.Y. No dust jacket.

PUBLISHED: 1947 and distributed without charge to associates of the Columbia Broadcasting System. The precise publication date and number of sets of sheets printed cannot be determined, as the publisher has no records of this publication. *Verso of title leaf* is blank. *Dedication* from Columbia Broadcasting System on recto of second leaf: This book is dedicated/ to the young in heart,/ for it is their vision/ that has given us/ the miracle of television. Endpapers plain.

ILLUSTRATIONS: Aside from the title page drawing there are 21 black and 26 full-color illustrations by the author.

COPY EXAMINED: MP.

A43. To the One I Love the Best [1955]

a. First edition:

TITLE PAGE: In black: To The | One I Love | the Best | A flourish: | By | Ludwig Bemelmans | A flourish: | The Viking Press | New York | 1955

PAGINATION: 5 leaves, [1] - [256] pp.; endpapers. 21.4 x 14.3 cm.

COVERINGS: Gray cloth-covered boards stamped on front in green with a sculpture upon a plinth; and upon a green spine, in gold: To | the One | I Love | the Best | Bemelmans; at bottom: Viking. Top edges stained green. Full-color dust jacket printed in black.

PUBLISHED: February 24, 1955 at $3.75. 15,000 sets of sheets printed; 15,000 copies bound. On *verso of title leaf:* An excerpt from this book appeared in *Vogue.* Typography by Ervine Metzl. *Half-title* on recto of first leaf. *Other books*

by the author on verso of half-title. *Frontispiece,* a black drawing of Lady Mendl upon a sofa, is on verso of second leaf. *Dedication* on recto of fourth leaf: "To Mother and Charles from Stevie with Love." The endpapers are printed with a green and white drawing of a garden with elephant topiary by moonlight.

CONTENTS on fifth leaf: Part One, Elsie at Home, 1.1 Invitation, 3; 2. The Footstool of Madame Pompadour, 8; 3. At Home, 19; 4. Benedict Canyon, 24; 5. The Snake Charmer, 29; 6. To the One I Love the Best, 42; 7. You Shall Have Music, 54; 8. A Thing of Beauty Is a Joy Forever, 66; 9. The Iron Will, 76; 10. The Little Red Clock, 89; 11. The Prospect of Tara, 97; 12. Central Casting, 106; 13. The Anniversary, 111; 14. Mad Dogs and Englishmen, 124; 15. Kitty Cats and Puthy Cats, 130; 16. Late for Dinner, 140; 17. The Visit to San Simeon, 151; Part Two, Elsie Abroad: 18. Little Old New York, 175; 19. The Cyanide Pill, 188; 20. The Villa in Versailles, 197; 21. The Kindergarten, 209; 22. Old Friends, 214; 23. Thirteen at Table, 222; 24. Dog Story, 236; 25. Aboard the Future, 244; Postscript, 255.

"The Footstool of Madame Pompadour" is here reprinted from *Holiday,* May 1951, where it appeared as "Madame Takes the Count;" see E134. "To the One I Love The Best" is here reprinted from *Vogue,* February 15, 1955; see E165. "Dog Story" is here reprinted from *The New Yorker,* August 12, 1939; see E27.

ILLUSTRATIONS: There are two black drawings, one on each of the section titles, pages [1]
and [173].

COPY EXAMINED: MP.

b. British edition ([1955]):

To the One I Love the Best was published July 28,
1955 at 15s by Hamish Hamilton, London. The
number of sets of sheets printed cannot be determined, as the published cannot retrieve old
records from storage. A copy of this edition has
not been found for examination.

c. German edition ([1956]):

TITLE PAGE: Ludwig Bemelmans | Alte Liebe
Rostet Nicht | Kiepenheuer & Witsch | Köln •
Berlin

PAGINATION: [1] - [284] pp.; endpapers. 20.5
x 12.2 cm.

COVERINGS: Plum red linen-weave cloth-
covered boards stamped on front in black with a
sculpture upon a plinth; on spine: Ludwig |
Bemelmans | a rule | Alte Liebe | Rostet | Nicht.
Top edges stained gray. Full-color dust jacket
printed in black.

PUBLISHED: 1956 at DM 14,80. Number of
sets of sheets printed cannot be determined, as the
publisher cannot release the information. On *verso
of title leaf*, page [6]: Titel der Originalausgabe: To
the One I love the Best. Deutsch von Rudolf
Rocholl. Schutzumschlag nach einem Entwurf

des Verfassers. 1. - 4. Tausend • 1956. Alle deutschsprachigen Rechte bei Verlag Kiepenheuer &
Witsch, Köln • Berlin. Druck: Kölnische Verlags-
druckerei. *Colophon* on page [1]. *Half-title* on page
[3]. *Frontispiece*, a black drawing of Lady Mendl
upon a sofa, is on page [4]. *Dedication* on page [7]:
Für Mutter und Charles | in dankbarem gedenken
| von Stevie. *Author's postscript* on page [281],
signed "L.B." and "Paris 1954." Endpapers plain.

CONTENTS (INHALT) on page [283]: Erster
Teil, Elsie Daheim: 1. Die Einladung, 11; 2. Die
Fussbank der Madame Pompadour, 16; 3. Zu
Hause, 28; 4. Benedict Canyon, 34; 5. Die Schlan-
genbeschwörerin, 39; 6. To the One I love the
Best, 52; 7. Auf jeden Fall Musik, 64; 8. Etwas
Schönes bedeutet ewige Freude, 77; 9. Der eis-
erne Wille, 88; 10. Die kleine rote Uhr, 102; 11.
Das Unternehmen Tara, 111; 12. Die grosse
Besetzung, 121; 13. Der Hochzeitstag, 126; 14.
Engländer und tollwütige Hunde, 139; 15. Miezek-
ätzchen und Pussikätzchen, 146; 16. Zu spät zum
Essen, 156; 17. Die Reise nach San Simeon, 168;
Zweiter Teil, Elsie in der Fremde: 18. Kleines
altes New York, 195; 19. Die Giftpille, 209; 20.
Die Villa in Versailles, 219; 21. Der Kindergarten,
231; 22. Alte Freunde, 237; 23. Dreizehn bei
Tisch, 246; 24. Eine Hundegeschichte, 261; 25.
An Bord der Zukunft, 269; Postskriptum, 281.

ILLUSTRATIONS: There is a black drawing
with each of the two section half-titles.

COPY EXAMINED: Mrs. Madeleine Bemelmans.

d. Swedish edition ([1957]):

TITLE PAGE: In black: Ludwig Bemelmans | Till den | Jag Älskar | Högst | colophon | a rule | Gebers

PAGINATION: [1] - [276] pp. 21 x 13.5 cm.

COVERINGS: Gray paper covers printed with a white drawing of a sculpture in a garden, with author in black and title in black and magenta. Printed on spine, in black: L. Bemelmans; in magenta: Tell Den Jag Älskar Högst. Pages uncut and untrimmed. No dust jacket.

PUBLISHED: 1957 at SKR 17:50. The precise date of publication and number of sets of sheets printed cannot be determined, as the publisher will not communicate. On *verso of title leaf*, page [4]: Originalets titel: To the One I Love the Best. Till svenska av Carl Sundell. Omslag efter Bemelmans av Åke Nilsson. © 1955 Ludwig Bemelmans. Almqvist & Wiksell / Gebers Förlag Ab. Printed in Sweden by Almqvist & Wiksells Boktryckeri Aktiebolag Uppsala 1957. *Half-title* on page [1]. *Frontispiece* on page [2], as in A44a. *Dedication* on page [5]: Till Mamma och Charles | med tillgivenhet | från Stevie. *Author's postscript* on page [276], signed "L.B." *Section half-titles* on pages [9] and [189].

Note: There is some suggestion on the back cover that a hard-cover edition of this book was also published at 22 kr 50 öre, but there is no formal record of it in any catalogue seen, nor does the Royal Library in Stockholm, which would normally have come into possession of such a book, have record of one.

CONTENTS (INNEHALL) on page [7]: Invitation, 11; Madame Pompadours fotpall, 15; Hemma, 27; Benedict Canyon, 33; Ormtjuserskan, 38; Till den jag älskar högst, 51; Du slipper inte ifrån musik, 63; Det sköna är en fröjd för evigt, 76; Järnviljan, 86; Den lilla röda pendylen, 101; >>Projekt Tara<<, 109; I rampljuset, 119; Bröllopsdagen, 124; Galna hundar och engelsmän, 137; Kissemissar och missekissar, 143; Sen till middag, 153; Ett besök på San Simeon, 165; Lilla kära gamla New York, 191; Cyanidpillret, 204; Villan i Versailles, 214; Kindergarten, 226; Gamla vänner, 232; Tretton till bordet, 240; En hundhistoria, 256; Med kurs på framtiden, 264; Postskriptum, 276.

ILLUSTRATIONS: There is a black drawing by the author on each of the two section half-title pages.

COPY EXAMINED: Mrs. Madeleine Bemelmans.

e. Austrian edition ([1973]):

To the One I Love the Best was published in June, 1973 at OS 80,— by Buchgemeinde Alpenland, Klagenfurt, under the title *Alte Liebe Rostet Nicht*. 5,000 sets of sheets were printed. It has not been possible to find a copy of this edition for examination.

A44. Welcome Home! [1960]

TITLE PAGE: Upon a gray drawing of woodland fowl and beasts, in red: Welcome Home! | by Ludwig Bemelmans | in black: After a poem by Beverley Bogert | Harper & Brothers | Publishers New York

PAGINATION: Unpaged. 1 blank leaf, 12 leaves, 1 blank leaf. 25.3 x 31.2 cm.

COVERINGS: Paper-covered boards printed with a full-color picture of a sly fox and, in black: Welcome Home! by Ludwig Bemelmans Harper & Brothers Established 1817. The spine is covered in green cloth and is blank. The full-color dust jacket reproduces the board coverings.

PUBLISHED: September 28, 1960 at $3.95. 21,000 sets of sheets printed. On *verso of title leaf:* This story originally appeared in *Mademoiselle* under the title "Randy." *Half-title* on recto of first printed leaf. *Second half-title* on recto of third printed leaf.

This edition was distributed in The United Kingdom at 26s.

The text appeared as "Randy" in *Mademoiselle,* December 1959; see E191.

ILLUSTRATIONS: There are 17 full-color illustrations by the author.

COPY EXAMINED: MP.

A45. The Woman of My Life [1957]

a. First edition:

TITLE PAGE: With a black drawing of a rose, in black: The | Woman | of My Life | by | Ludwig Bemelmans | 1957 | The Viking Press • New York

PAGINATION: [1] - 218 pp., 3 leaves; endpapers. 21.2 x 14.3 cm.

COVERINGS: Blue linen-weave cloth-covered boards blind-stamped on front with the drawing from the title page; on spine, in red: Ludwig Bemelmans, and in white: The Woman of My Life The Viking Press. Top edges stained red. Full color dust jacket printed in white.

PUBLISHED: October 10, 1957 at $3.50. 20,000 sets of sheets printed; 20,000 copies bound. On *verso of title leaf,* page [4]: Printed in the U.S.A. by The Colonial Press Inc. *Half-title* on page [1]. *Second half-title* on page [7]. *Other books by the author* on page [2]. Unillustrated. Endpapers plain.

CONTENTS on page 5: 1. Evelyn, 9; 2. French Lesson, 20; 3. Engagement, 32; 4. The Institut Truffaut, 39; 5. Wine for the Prisoner, 48; 6. Chez Madame Poupon, 53; 7. 13 Rue St.-Augustin, 64; 8. Transfiguration, 72; 9. Château de Plaisir, 84; 10. Paris la Nuit, 96; 11. Chambre d'Amour, 102; 12. The Sleepwalker, 109; 13. The

Truth Game, 118; 14. Reveillon, 133; 15. The Angel, 160; 16. Voyage of Discovery, 176; 17. Of Pigs and Truffles, 187; 18. The New Duchess, 192; 19. Revenge, 199; 20. The Wedding, 207; 21. The Woman of My Life, 213.

"13 Rue St.-Augustin" appeared as "No. 13 Rue St. Augustin" in *Town & Country*, May 1947; see E105. It appears as well in A3.

COPY EXAMINED: MP.

b. First British edition ([1957]):

TITLE PAGE: In black: The | Woman | of | My Life | By | Ludwig Bemelmans | colophon | Hamish Hamilton | London

PAGINATION: [1] - 160 pp.; endpapers. 21.5 x 13.8 cm.

COVERINGS: Red cloth - covered boards stamped upon spine, in silver, between flourishes: The Woman of My Life; then Ludwig Bemelmans, with a colophon at bottom. Full color dust jacket printed in white.

PUBLISHED: November 7, 1957 at 12s 6d. Number of sets of sheets printed cannot be determined, as the publisher cannot retrieve old records from storage. On *verso of title leaf*, page [6]: Made and Printed by Wyman and Sons, Ltd. London, Fakenham and Reading. *Half-title* on page [3]. *Other titles by the author* on page [4]. Unillustrated. Endpapers plain.

CONTENTS on page [7]: 1. Evelyn, 9; 2. French Lesson, 17; 3. Engagement, 26; 4. The

Institut Truffaut, 31; 5. Wine for the Prisoner, 38; 6. Chez Madame Poupon, 41; 7. 13 Rue St.-Augustin, 49; 8. Transfiguration, 55; 9. Château de Plaisir, 64; 10. Paris la Nuit, 73; 11. Chambre d'Amour, 77; 12. The Sleepwalker, 82; 13. The Truth Game, 88; 14. Reveillon, 99; 15. The Angel, 119; 16. Voyage of Discovery, 130; 17. Of Pigs and Truffles, 138; 18. The New Duchess, 142; 19. Revenge, 147; 20. The Wedding, 153; 21. The Woman of My Life, 157.

COPY EXAMINED: MP.

c. German edition ([1958]):

TITLE PAGE: In black: Ludwig Bemelmans | Die Frau meines Lebens | Roman | Kiepenheuer & Witsch • Köln • Berlin

PAGINATION: [1] - [184] pp.; endpapers. 20.5 x 12.5 cm.

COVERINGS: Pale blue linen-weave cloth-covered boards stamped on front with a smiling red mouth and on spine, in red: Bemelmans • Die Frau meines Lebens. Top edges stained yellow. Yellow dust jacket printed in red, blue, black and white.

PUBLISHED: 1958 at DM 12,80. 5,000 sets of sheets printed. On *verso of title leaf*, page [6]: Titel der Originalausgabe The Woman of My Life. Deutsch von Jeannie Ebner. Schutzumschlag Werner Labbé. 1. - 5. Tausend 1958. Alle deutschsprachigen Rechte bei Verlag Kiepenheuer & Witsch, Köln • Berlin. Gesamtherstellung Kleins

Druck- und Verlagsanstalt Lengerich, Westfalen. *Colophon* on page [1]. *Half-title* on page [3]. On page [184]: Im gleichen Verlag erschienen von | Ludwig Bemelmans | Alte Liebe rostet nicht | ✻ | Hotel Splendid | ✻ | Mit Kind und Krümel nach Europa. Endpapers plain.

CONTENTS (INHALT) on page [183]: 1. Evelyn, 7; 2. Französisch-Unterricht, 16; 3. Die Verlobung, 26; 4. Das Institut Truffaut, 32; 5. Wein für den Häftling, 40; 6. Bei Madame Poupon, 44; 7. Rue St.-Augustin Nummer 13, 53; 8. Wandlungen, 60; 9. Château de Plaisir, 70; 10. Paris bei Nacht, 80; 11. Chambre d'Amour, 85; 12. Der Schlafwandler, 91; 13. Das Wahrheitsspiel, 98; 14. Die Erweckung, 111; 15. Der Engel, 134; 16. Eine Entdeckungsreise, 147; 17. Von Schweinen und Trüffeln, 156; 18. Die neue Herzogin, 160; 19. Rache, 165; 20. Die Hochzeit, 172; 21. Die Frau meines Lebens, 177.

COPY EXAMINED: Mrs. Madeleine Bemelmans.

d. German reprint ([1960]):

TITLE PAGE: In black: Ludwig Bemelmans | Die Frau meines Lebens | Roman | Deutscher Bücherbund

PAGINATION: [1] - [262] pp., 1 blank leaf; endpapers. App. 19.4 x 11.8 cm.

COVERINGS: Light gray linen-covered boards stamped on front with a light blue and black picture (not by Bemelmans) of a prisoner, on spine, within a black rectangle between two black rules, in gold: Ludwig | Bemelmans | Die Frau | meines | Lebens. Top edges stained gray. White dust jacket printed with an illustration (not by the author) in black, yellow, brown, pink and blue with author in blue and title in white.

PUBLISHED: 1960 at an unknown price. Number of sets of sheets printed, publication price, and exact publication date cannot be determined, as the publisher's records are lost. On *verso of title leaf*, page [4]: Titel der Originalausgabe >> The woman of my life <<. Deutsch von Jeannie Ebner. Mit Genehmigung des Verlages Kiepenheuer & Witsch und des Autors Ludwig Bemelmans. Schutzumschlag und Einband: Team 60, München. Druck: Badendruck GmbH, Karlsruhe.

CONTENTS (INHALT) on page [261]: 1. Evelyn, 5; 2. Französisch-Unterricht, 18; 3. Die Verlobung, 33; 4. Das Institut Truffaut, 41; 5. Wein für den Häftling, 52; 6. Bei Madame Poupon, 57; 7. Rue St.-Augustin Nummer 13, 71; 8. Wandlungen, 81; 9. Château de Plaisir, 96; 10. Paris bei Nacht, 111; 11. Chambre d'Amour, 118; 12. Der Schlafwandler, 127; 13. Das Wahrheitsspiel, 138; 14. Die Erweckung, 157; 15. Der Engel, 191; 16. Eine Entdeckungsreise, 210; 17. Von Schweinen und Trüffeln, 223; 18. Die neue Herzogin, 229; 19. Rache, 237; 20. Die Hochzeit, 247; 21. Die Frau meines Lebens, 253.

COPY EXAMINED: Deutscher Bibliothek, Frankfurt.

e. First British paperback edition [(1961)]:

TITLE PAGE: In black: The | Woman | of | My Life | By | Ludwig Bemelmans | Colophon: | Arrow Books

PAGINATION: [1] - 160 pp. 17.7 x 11 cm.

COVERINGS: The covers are printed in red and black with a figure of a woman and with the author and title in black; on spine, in black, within a white band: The Woman of My Life, and then in white: Ludwig Bemelmans with a colophon at bottom, and in red: G76.

PUBLISHED: July 3, 1961 at 3s 6d. Number of sets of sheets printed cannot be determined, as the publisher's records have been lost. On *verso of title leaf*, page [6]: An imprint of The Hutchinson Group. Grey Arrow edition 1961. This book has been printed in Great Britain by litho-offset at Taylor Garnett Evans & Co. Ltd., Watford, Herts. and bound by them. *Half-title* on page [3]. *Other books by the author* on page [4].

This is Grey Arrow No. G76.

CONTENTS on page [7]: As in A45b.

COPY EXAMINED: MP.

f. Second British paperback edition [(1968)]:

TITLE PAGE: In black: Ludwig Bemelmans | a rule | The Woman of My Life | colophon | Arrow Books

PAGINATION: [1] - 192 pp. 17.7 x 11 cm.

COVERINGS: Black paper covers printed on front with a picture of a woman in a fur coat and with title and author in yellow and a brief blurb in white; upon a yellow spine, in black, at top: 101 The Woman of My Life | Ludwig Bemelmans, at bottom: colophon. Back cover is blue.

PUBLISHED: September 1968 at 5s. Number of sets of sheets printed cannot be determined, as the publisher's records have been lost. On *verso of title leaf*, page [6]: Arrow Books Ltd 178-202 Great Portland Street, London W1 An Imprint of The Hutchinson Group First published in this edition 1968 Made and printed in Great Britain by The Anchor Press Ltd., Tiptree, Essex.

CONTENTS on page [7]: 1. Evelyn, 7; 2. French Lesson, 17; 3. Engagement, 28; 4. The Institut Truffaut, 34; 5. Wine for the Prisoner, 42; 6. Chez Madame Poupon, 46; 7. 13 Rue St.-Augustin, 56; 8. Transfiguration, 63; 9. Château de Plaisir, 74; 10. Paris la Nuit, 85; 11. Chambre d'Amour, 91; 12. The Sleepwalker, 97; 13. The Truth Game, 105; 14. Reveillon, 118; 15. The Angel, 142; 16. Voyage of Discovery, 156; 17. Of Pigs and Truffles, 165; 18. The New Duchess, 170; 19. Revenge, 176; 20. The Wedding, 183; 21. The Woman of My Life, 188.

COPY EXAMINED: Tiptree Book Services Limited.

g. German paperback edition ([1975]):

TITLE PAGE: In black: Ludwig Bemelmans | Die Frau meines Lebens | Roman | colophon, in white within a black castle: Bastei | Lübbe

PAGINATION: [1] - 190 pp., 1 printed leaf. 17.5 x 10.8 cm.

COVERINGS: Red, orange, black and white paper covers printed on front with a full-color photograph of a young woman with chrysanthemums, author in white and title in black; on spine (from base upward), in white on black: colophon; and in black, Ludwig Bemelmans • Die Frau meines Lebens and at top, Heiterer | Roman, then 16006 | a rule | two stars.

PUBLISHED: April 1975 at DM 3,80. Number of sets of sheets printed cannot be determined, as the publisher's records are lost. On *verso of title leaf*, page [4]: Titel der amerikanischen Originalausgabe: The Woman of My Life. Deutsch Übersetzung: Jeannie Ebner. © Copyright der deutschen Ausgabe: Verlag Kiepenheuer & Witsch, Köln/Berlin. Lizenzausgabe: Bastei-Verlag Gustav H. Lübbe, Bergisch Gladbach. Printed in Western Germany 1975. Einbandgestaltung: Manfred Peters. Titelfoto: Lagarde. Gesamtherstellung: Ebner, Ulm. *Half-title* on page [1]. On the final printed leaf: Publisher's advertisements for other books in the Heitere Romane series.

CONTENTS (INHALT) on page [5]: 1. Evelyn, 7; 2. Französisch-Unterricht, 17; 3. Die Verlobung, 23; 4. Das Institut Truffaut, 34; 5. Wein für den Häftling, 42; 6. Bei Madame Poupon, 46; 7. Rue St.-Augustin Nummer 13, 56; 8. Wandlungen, 63; 9. Château de Plaisir, 74; 10. Paris bei Nacht, 85; 11. Chambre d'Amour, 90; 12. Der Schlafwandler, 96; 13. Das Wahrheitsspiel, 105; 14. Die Erweckung, 117; 15. Der Engel, 141; 16. Eine Entdeckungsreise, 155; 17. Von Schweinen und Trüffeln, 164; 18. Die neue Herzogin, 168; 19. Rache, 174; 20. Die Hochzeit, 181; 21. Die Frau meines Lebens, 186.

COPY EXAMINED: University of Victoria Library, Victoria, B.C.

A46. The World of Bemelmans [1955]

TITLE PAGE: In black: The World of | a black drawing of a ship: | Bemelmans | An omnibus by | Ludwig Bemelmans | New York | The Viking Press • 1955

PAGINATION: [i] - viii, [1] - [504] pp.; endpapers. 20.9 x 14.1 cm.

COVERINGS: Paper-covered boards printed with pink rectangles and a blue figure of two swans. The spine, covered with rust-colored cloth, is stamped, at top, in a blue rectangle: The

| World | of; and then, Bemelmans in plain blue; and at bottom, in a blue rectangle, Viking. Top edges stained gray. Full-color dust jacket printed in red and black. There is an alternate binding: the book measures 21.2 x 14.2 cm.; the boards are covered with beige linen-weave cloth stamped with the swans in pink; and the spine stamping is pink.

PUBLISHED: October 7, 1955 at $4.95. 12,000 sets of sheets printed; 12,000 copies bound. On *verso of title leaf,* page [iv]: A number of the stories and sketches in this book originally appeared in *The New Yorker, Holiday, Harper's Bazaar, Town & Country, Vogue, This Week,* and *Story,* some of them in somewhat different form. *Half-title* on page [i]. *Other books by the author* on page [ii]. The beige endpapers are printed with a black drawing of an artist busy in his studio with a pair of snoozing dogs—a slight variant on the endpaper drawing for A40a.

CONTENTS on page [v]: (This omnibus prints the complete contents, with illustrations included, of A33a, A39a, A8a, and A21a, followed by five new stories.) *My War With The United States* — Foreword, 2; Please Don't Shoot, 3; The Operation, 11; Summer Sprouts, 16; The Good Prisoners, 20; Mad Maître d'Hôtel, 25; To the Left, 36; Tirol in Buffalo, 44; David, 49; The Mess in Order, 54; The Buttermachine, 60; Night on Guard, 63; A Trip to Mississippi, 71; Leave of Absence, 80; The Widow from Scranton, 85; Polish Kate's, 91; The Army Is Like a Mother, 99;

Bayonet School, 103. *Small Beer*—"No Trouble at All", 113; Dog Story, 121; My English Suit in Paris, 129; Putzi, 136; Fancy Green, 142; Theodore and "The Blue Danube," 149; The Isle of God, 153; Sacre du Printemps, 162; Dear General, What a Surprise!, 168. *The Donkey Inside* — The S.S. *Mesias,* 181; On a Bench in a Park, 189; The Guayaquil and Quito Railway, 199; Quito, 204; About the Inhabitants of Quito, 209; The Morale of the Natives, 216; The Boots of General Altamir Pereira, 223; Benitin and Eneas, 230; The Ride with Rain, 239; The Ride with the Long Night, 246; The Day with Hunger, 251; This Is Romance, 256; Dream in Brooklyn, 264; The Headhunters of the Amazon, 270; Adolf in Quito, 280; Prison Visit, 287; Poor Animal, 293; The Promised Land, 297; Buenos Días, Gran Hotel, 306; The Painted Grapes, 312; The Friends of Ecuador, 319; To a White Rose, 324; The S.S. *Santa Lucía,* 330; Author's Note, 333. *I Love You, I Love You, I Love You*—Souvenir, 337; I Love You, I Love You, I Love You, 346; Star of Hope, 351; Pale Hands, 356; Watch the Birdie, 368; Bride of Berchtesgaden, 378; Chagrin d'Amour, 386; Headhunters of the Quito Hills, 391; Vacation, 401; Cher Ami, 408; Camp Nomopo, 414; Sweet Death in the Electric Chair, 421. *New Stories*—"The Golden Opportunity," 433; Down Where the Würzburger Flows, 465; The Dog of the World, 471; The Street Where the Heart Lies, 476; The Paris Underworld, 483.

"Down Where the Würzburger Flows" appeared in *Town & Country*, June 1953, as "That Old World Flavor Down Where the Würzburger Flows;" see E150. "The Dog of The World" appeared in *Holiday*, May 1955; see E167. "The Street Where The Heart Lies" is not the same as material in A40; see instead E164.

ILLUSTRATIONS: Aside from the title page drawing there are 60 black illustrations by the author.

COPY EXAMINED: MP.

Special Publications Authored by Ludwig Bemelmans

Special Publications Authored by Ludwig Bemelmans

Section "B" lists titles authored by Ludwig Bemelmans and offered for private distribution. It is set out exactly as is "A."

B1. Een Kerst Geschiedenis [1946]

TITLE PAGE: Two black angels | in red: Een Kerst Geschiedenis | two black angels | in black: De geschiedenis van een Schoenlapper, | de Schoenlappersvrouw, Graaf César de la Tour | de la Tour-Midi en zijn huisknecht Joseph, | de Schoenlapperskinderen, een veelbelovende Baby, | hun Schoenen en een Kerstboom, | verteld en getekend door | Ludwig Bemelmans | dit alles gemaakt tot een typografisch grapje | en in het Nederlands overgebracht voor | Het Model voor den Uitgever | a red star in black: Kerstmis 1946 a red star

A Christmas Story | The Story of a Cobbler, | The Cobbler's Wife, Count César de la Tour | de la Tour-Midi and his butler Joseph, | the cobbler's children, a promising baby, | their shoes and a Christmas tree, | told and drawn by | Ludwig Bemelmans | this all made to a typographical joke | and translated into Dutch for | The Model of the Editor | Christmas 1946

PAGINATION: 1 blank leaf, eleven leaves. 22.5 x 16.5 cm.

COVERINGS: Red paper cover upon laminated paper boards, with title printed in blue. Spine not printed. No dust jacket. The Dutch translation is uncredited.

PUBLISHED: For Christmas 1946 and distributed without price by C.G.A. Corvey in Amsterdam. Number of copies printed unknown. The *title verso* is blank. The recto of the final leaf is blank and a *Publisher's Colophon* is on the verso, page 24, as follows, in black: Verantwoording. Deze tekst, gezet ter gelegenheid van Kerstmis, uit letterallerhande, werd afgedrukt op Houtvrij Offset en voor het omslag werd een restantje kerstrood Egmont gebruikt. De cliché's werden vervaardigd door Pax Holland, Amsterdam. De typografie is van Johan H. van Eikeren; a red star, in black: C.G.A.Corvey's Papiergroothandel Amsterdam Rotterdam Groningen den Haag Utrecht Almelo, die deze modellen verspreidt, wenst vrienden en relaties met dit laatste nummer in 1946 een voorspoedig Nieuw Jaar; a red star, in black: Meijer's Boek- en Handelsdrukkerij te Wormerveer, die deze modellen zet en drukt, brengt hiermee de beste wensen voor 1947 over en hoopt van harte weer alle opdrachten te kunnen uitvoeren; a red star. The colophon translates: Account: this text, composed at the occasion of Christmas, out of all kinds of characters, was printed on "Houtvrij Offset" and for the cover a vest of Christmas-red Egmont was used. The clichés were made by Pax Holland, Amsterdam. The typography is of Johan H. van Eikeren. C.G.A.Corvey's Paper Wholesale Amsterdam Rotterdam Groningen The Hague Utrecht Almelo who distributes this model, wishes friends and relations with this last number in 1946 a Happy New Year. Meyer's Book and Tradeprinter in Wormerveer who sets off and who prints this model, puts across with it best wishes for 1947 and hopes for the best to be able to execute every order again for the future.

The contents appeared originally as "The Count and the Cobbler" in *Harper's Bazaar*, December 1935; see E1.

ILLUSTRATIONS: Aside from those on the title page, there are 16 black, 2 red, 1 black and red, and 1 black, green and red illustrations by the author.

COPY EXAMINED: Koninklijke Bibliotheek, 's-Gravenhage, Netherlands. For translations from the Dutch I am indebted to Astrid Vrehen.

B2. The Kind Peasant, the Big Bear and the Little Birdie [c. 1960]

TITLE PAGE: In black: The | Kind Peasant | the | Big Bear | and | the Little Birdie | a black drawing of a big bear and a little birdie in a tree | A Fable | by | Ludwig Bemelmans

PAGINATION: 15 leaves. Approximately 8 x 5½ inches.

COVERINGS: No cover. No binding. This is a monograph printed (apparently by photo-offset) in black on heavy white paper for private distribution only. One sheet of paper has been folded to act as a set of "covers," while the remaining seven sheets have been roughly cut in half to provide the interior 13 leaves.

Printed c. 1960, not for publication or sale. Number printed unknown. The monograph is believed to have been given without charge to friends of the author. Text is printed only on the recto of each of the first fourteen leaves and, in the style of a children's book, each page of text except the second from the end incorporates a black drawing.

ILLUSTRATIONS: There are 13 black drawings by the author.

COPY EXAMINED: MP.

Collections of Work by Bemelmans Edited by Others

Collections of Work by Bemelmans Edited by Others

SECTION "C" LISTS TITLES containing collections of the work of Ludwig Bemelmans, but arranged and edited by others. It is set out exactly as is "A."

C1. La Bonne Table [1964]

a. First edition:

TITLE PAGE: Upon a periwinkle blue page; within a curtained white window, upon the sill of which perches a black cat, observed by an aging serving maid, in black: Ludwig Bemelmans | La Bonne Table | Selected and Edited by | Donald and Eleanor Friede | at bottom: | Simon and Schuster • New York • 1964

PAGINATION: [1] - [448] pp.; endpapers. 23.3 x 15.2 cm.

COVERINGS: Four-fifths periwinkle blue paper-covered, and one-fifth white cloth-covered boards, stamped with a waiter arranging a vase upon a pedestal in blue and the author's signature in red; on spine, in blue: waiter examining wine with bucket | in red: Ludwig | Bemelmans | La | Bonne | Table | in blue: Chef stirring sauce | Simon and | Schuster. Top edges stained gray. The white dust jacket has the author in red, the title in green, the phrase "His lifetime love affair with the art of dining—in his own words and his own pictures, from behind the scenes and at table" in blue and a sketch of a table with a fruit bowl and candelabrum in black. The rear of the jacket contains a photograph captioned, "Ludwig Bemelmans (with walking stick) on the steps of his studio at an inn near Paris—surrounded by his secretary, the chef, and the others who happily cooked for him, served him at table, and continually voiced their opinions of his art."

PUBLISHED: October 28, 1964 at $8.95. Number of sets of sheets printed cannot be determined, as the publisher keeps no records for longer than ten years. On *verso of title leaf*, page [4]: Copyright © 1962, 1963 by Madeleine Bemelmans and Barbara Bemelmans as co-executrices of the estate of Ludwig Bemelmans. First Printing. Manufactured in the United States of America by Rand McNally & Company, Chicago, Illinois. Designed by Eve Metz. *Publishers' permissions* on verso of title leaf, page [4]. *Half-title* on page [1]. Page [2], facing the title, is periwinkle blue. White endpapers printed in blue with sketches of, among other things, La Colombe (Bemelmans' bar in Paris). Pages [19], [145], [275], and [291] are periwinkle blue.

Note: An undetermined number of copies of this edition were distributed by the Book-of-the-Month Club to its membership in January 1965 at $8.95. The book was accompanied by a copy of the *Book-of-the-Month Club News* for January 1965, which contained a review by Gilbert Highet, including: "And what beautiful, smooth, witty English he wrote! It is all but impossible to remember, as one reads, that he was brought up speaking German, and Bavarian German at that."

CONTENTS on pages 5 - 9, including two black, and one black and blue, illustrations by the author: Introduction by Donald and Eleanor

"Adieu to the Old Ritz" appeared in *Town and Country*, December 1950; see E131. "Monsieur Victor" is here reprinted from A23 and A17. "The Problem of Seating People . . ." appeared in *Holiday*, February 1953, under the title, "On Innkeeping;" see E146. "Grapes for Monsieur Cape" and "Herr Otto Brauhaus" are here reprinted from A23 and A17. "Beau Maxime" appeared in A23 as a part of "Grapes for Mr. Cape." "The Education of a Waiter" appeared in A23 as a part of "Mr. Sigsag Goes to Sea." "Dinner Out" and "Old Luchow" appeared in A23 as parts of "Dinner Out." All were reprinted in A17. "Art at the Hotel Splendide" is here reprinted from A18 and A17. "The Brave Commis" is here reprinted from A23 and A17. "'The Army Is Like a Mother . . .'" and "The Buttermachine" are here reprinted from A33 and A46. "No Trouble at All" is here reprinted from A39, A17, and A46. "Affair; All Maîtres d'Hotel Love to Eat . . ." and "Coming Out" are here reprinted from A23 and A17. "My First Visit to Paris . . ." appeared in *Holiday*, January 1954, as "Bemelmans' Magic Cities;" see E158. "Theodore and 'The Blue Danube'" is here reprinted from A39 and A46. "'Most Swindles in Austria . . .'" appeared in *Holiday*, August 1962, as "The Soul of Austria;" see E196. "The Kitchen of the Golden Basket" is here reprinted from A13. "Lady Mendl's Chef" is here reprinted from A11. "The Survivors" and "Monsieur Albert of Maxim's" are here reprinted from A3. "The Chef I Almost Hired" is here reprinted from A33. "Monsieur Dumaine" appeared in *Town and Country*, January 1959, as "A Quick One;" see E184. "Monsieur Soulé" appeared in *Holiday*, February 1953; see E147. "Down Where the Würzberger Flows" is here reprinted from A46. "Grandfather and the Zipperl" is here reprinted from A23 and A17. "'Among the Birds That Make Good Eating . . .'" is here reprinted from A16. "Filet de Sole Colbert" is here reprinted from A23 and A17. "The S.S. Mesias" and "A Day with Hunger" are here reprinted from A8 and A46. "Apples" is here reprinted from A34. "Vacation" is here reprinted from A21 and A46. "You Shall Have Music" is here reprinted from A43. "'What Has Happened to the Famous Vintages . . .'" is here reprinted from A3. "Les Saucissons d'Arles," "Baked Clams Chez Georges" and "The Treasured Client" are here reprinted from A3. "To Be a Gourmet" appeared in *Holiday*, February 1953; see E148. "'Princes, Generals, Deep-Sea Captains . . .'" appeared in *Town and Country*, August 1958, as "Gala in Monte Carlo"; see E181. "The Spaghetti Train" is here reprinted from A11. "Poulets de Bresse" is here reprinted from A20. "Lady Mendl's Dining Room" is here reprinted from A43. "Lunch with Bosy" is from an unpublished manuscript. "Luchow's" is here reprinted from G23. "'Lady Mendl Liked Dogs and People Slim . . .'" is here reprinted from A11. "Among the Arabs" appeared in *Holiday*, October 1953, as "Road to Marrakech;" see E154. "Caviar" appeared in *Playboy*, January 1961; see E192. "At The Mediterranée" is here reprinted from A20. "Recipe for Cockles or Clams" appeared in *Town & Country*, September 1959, as part of "Invitation to a Castle;" see E189.

"Texas Legend" appeared in *McCall's*, August 1956, as "The Texas Legend;" see E171. " 'Second Door to Your Right . . .' " is here reprinted from A43. "The Best Way to See Cuba" appeared in *Holiday*, December 1957; see E179. "Chez René" is here reprinted from A35. "The Best Way to See Rio" appeared in *Holiday*, December 1958; see E183. "Shipowner" is here reprinted from A35. "The Island of Porquerolles" is from an unpublished manuscript, 1961. "Toni and Rocco" is here reprinted from A35. "How I Took the Cure" appeared in *Holiday*, June 1959; see E187. "Letter to a Restaurateur" is from unpublished correspondence, 1962. "The French Train," "Hotel de Paris, Monte Carlo," "L'Oustau de Baumanière," and "The First Cherries" are from an unpublished journal, 1962. "The Elephant Cutlet" is here reprinted from A33 and A46; and also appeared as A9; see as well E9. "Christmas in Tyrol" and "Glow Wine" are here reprinted from A16. "About Clouds and Lebkuchen" is here reprinted from A14. "Wedding in Tyrol" is here reprinted from A10. "Schweinerei" is here reprinted from A4. "Tales of the South American General" is here reprinted from A34. "Pepito" is here reprinted from A25. "Germiny a L'Oseille" is here reprinted from A43. "Romanoff's for Lunch" is here reprinted from A7. "Romanoff's: Two Views" is here reprinted from A43 and A7. "The Commissary," "Servant Trouble," "Snowy Night in Malibu," "Come Rain, Come Shine," and "Mocambo" are here reprinted from A7.

"Hunger Dream" is here reprinted from A11. "Guten Appetit" is here reprinted from A1. "Twelve Little Girls" is here reprinted from A24. "Madame L'Ambassadrice" is here reprinted from A20. "The International" is here reprinted from A35. "The Woman of My Life," "Wedding Breakfast," and "Of Pigs and Truffles" are here reprinted from A45. "Perfect Service," "Heavenly Soup," and "The Tour d'Argent" are here reprinted from A40. "When You Lunch with the Emperor" is here reprinted from A32.

ILLUSTRATIONS: Aside from the title drawing and those on the cover and with the contents there are 216 black and 22 black and periwinkle blue illustrations by the author. Some of the menus between pages [276] and [289] are also illustrated, but not by Bemelmans.

COPY EXAMINED: MP.

b. British edition [(1964)]:

TITLE PAGE: Upon a periwinkle blue page, within a curtained white window, upon the sill of which perches a black cat observed by an aging serving maid, in black: Ludwig Bemelmans | La Bonne Table | Selected and Edited by | Donald and Eleanor Friede | at bottom: | Hamish Hamilton • London • 1964

PAGINATION: [1] - [448] pp.; endpapers. 23.3 x 15.5 cm.

COVERINGS: Black and blue "tweed" weave cloth-covered boards plain on the cover; stamped on spine, at top, in gold upon black: La | Bonne | Table | fancy rule | Ludwig | Bemelmans, and at bottom: gold colophon. Top edges stained black. Dust jacket not seen.

PUBLISHED: November 30, 1964 at 42s. Number of sets of sheets printed cannot be determined, as the publisher's records were lost in transit to the United States. On *verso of title leaf*, page [4]: First published in Great Britain 1964 by Hamish Hamilton Ltd. Manufactured in the United States of America by Rand McNally & Company, Chicago, Illinois. Designed by Eve Metz. *Half-title* on page [1]. Page [2] is periwinkle blue. Endpapers as in C1a. Periwinkle blue pages as in C1a.

CONTENTS on pages 5 - 9, including two black and one black and periwinkle blue drawing by the author: As in C1a.

ILLUSTRATIONS: As in C1a.

COPY EXAMINED: The British Library.

c. Reprint [(1989)]:

TITLE PAGE: In black: La Bonne Table | flourish Ludwig Bemelmans, flourish | four diamonds | Selected and Edited by Donald and Eleanor Friede | a drawing of a chef with his hands folded behind his back: | colophon: | David R. Godine, Publisher | Boston

PAGINATION: [1] - [448] pp. 23 x 15 cm.

COVERINGS: Paper covers printed in mauve, cream and blue with a floral motif, and, within a diamond, a drawing of a waiter presenting cigars at table to two diners, and, in black, within mauve bands, the title and author; on spine: Bemelmans, gold flourish, La Bonne Table and at bottom Nonpareil | Books | Godine.

This is Nonpareil Book No. 58.

PUBLISHED: September 15, 1989 at $12.95. 7,167 sets of sheets printed. On *verso of title leaf*, page [4]: This is a Nonpareil book First published in 1989 by David R. Godine, Publisher, Inc. Horticultural Hall 300 Massachusetts Avenue Boston, Massachusetts, 02115. First published in 1964 by Simon and Schuster, Inc., New York. First Printing. *Publishers' permissions* on verso of title leaf, page [4]. *Half-title* on page [1].

CONTENTS on pages [5] - 9, with three black illustrations by the author: As in C1a.

ILLUSTRATIONS: Aside from the title drawing and those on the cover and with the contents there are 238 black illustrations by the author. Some of the menus between pages [276] and [289] are also illustrated, but not by Bemelmans.

COPY EXAMINED: MP.

C2. Tell Them It Was Wonderful [1985]

a. First edition:

TITLE PAGE: In black: • • • • • • | Tell Them | It Was | Wonderful | • • • • • • | Selected Writings by | Ludwig Bemelmans | Edited and with | an Introduction by | Madeleine Bemelmans | Foreword by | Norman Cousins | Colophon | Viking

PAGINATION: [i] - [xx], [1] - [316] pp.; endpapers. 22.8 x 15.2 cm.

COVERINGS: Robin's egg blue paper covered boards, plain, with a maroon cloth-covered backbone; stamped on spine, in silver: Ludwig Bemelmans • • • • • • Tell Them It Was Wonderful and at base, between two rules: Viking. Lilac dust jacket printed with author and title in maroon and with a reproduction of two Indians in a canoe spying the Statue of Liberty in New York Harbor, with subway, Indians, the Staten Island Ferry and Manhattan in the background (hand-tinted by Orna Benesh).

PUBLISHED: November, 1985 at $19.95. The number of sets of sheets printed is not known by the publisher. On *verso of title*, page [iv]: Copyright © Madeleine Bemelmans and Barbara Bemelmans Marciano, 1985. First published in 1985 by Viking Penguin Inc. Published simultaneously in Canada. The illustration which appears on the jacket of this book originally appeared in the February 1941 issue of *Glamour* magazine. Page 316 constitutes an extension of this copyright page. Printed in the United States of America by R. R. Donnelley & Sons Company, Harrisonburg, Virginia. Designed by Robin Hessel. *Dedication* on page [v]. *Half-title* on page [i], with colophon. *Foreword* on pages [vii] - [ix].

CONTENTS on pages [xi] - [xiii]: Foreword by Norman Cousins, vii; Introduction by Madeleine Bemelmans, xv; Childhood • 1; Swan Country, 3; *Lausbub*, 12; Arrival in America, 28; The Hotel Years, 1915-1917 • 31; My First Actress, 33; The Splendide, 40; Herr Otto Brauhaus, 43; Mr. Sigsag, 51; Art Class, 65; The Brave Commis, 67; The Army • 73; Please Don't Shoot, 75; Fort Porter, 83; Night on Guard, 93; The Mess in Order, 98; Leave of Absence, 104; Bayonet School, 109; The Hotel Years, 1919-1929 • 115; If You're Not a Fool, 117; The Ballet Visits the Magician, 124; The Homesick Bus Boy, 131; The Simple Life • 139; Bavaria, 141; Sawmill in Tirol, 148; Success at Last • 155; The Old Ritz, 157; The Isle of God (or Madeline's Origin), 163; Barbara • 167; Camp Nomopo, 169; Little Bit and the *America*, 176; Hollywood • 195; Invitation, 197; The Footstool of Madame Pompadour, 201; The Visit to San Simeon, 210; Lust for Gold, 227; Moses Fable, 240; Fresh Paint, 247; Adventures Abroad (1950-1962) • 253; Cher Ami, 255; My Favorite City, 262; The Dog of the World,

268; La Colombe, 273; Ship-Owner, 293; May-day, 305; Last Visit to Regensburg, 309.

"Swan Country" is here reproduced from *Vogue*, September 1, 1958, where it appeared as "When You Lunch With the Emperor"; see E182. *Lausbub* is here reproduced from A23, where it appeared as prologue; it was reprinted in A17. "Arrival in America" is here reproduced from A33, where it appeared as author's Foreword. "My First Actress" is here reproduced from *Stage*, May 1938 and from *Theatre Arts*, May 1949; see E14 and E117. It appears as well in A23. "The Splendide" is here reproduced from *Town & Country*, September 1941, where it appeared as "The Splendide: The Perfect Behavior of a Crazy Fool;" see E60. It appeared in different form in A23 as part of "Monsieur Victor," and was reprinted in A17. "Herr Otto Brauhaus" is here reproduced from *Life Class*; see A23. It was reprinted in A17. "Mr. Sigsag" is here reproduced from *Town & Country*, July 1938, where it appeared in somewhat different form as "Busboy's Holidays: Dinner at Luchow's and a Trip to the Sea;" see E16. It was reprinted in *Life Class*, A23, and in A17, as "Mr. Sigsag Goes to Sea." "Art Class" is here reproduced from A23, where it formed a portion of "Life Class;" it was reprinted in A17. "The Brave Commis" is here reproduced from A23. It was reprinted in A17. "Please Don't Shoot, Fort Porter" (originally "Mad Maître d'Hôtel"), "Night on Guard," "The Mess in Order," "Leave of Absence" and "Bay-

onet School" are here reproduced from A33. "If You're Not a Fool" is here reproduced from A23; it was reprinted in A17. "The Ballet Visits The Magician" is here reproduced from *The New Yorker*, July 6, 1940, where it appeared as "The Ballet Visits the Splendide's Magician;" see E39. It appeared as well in A18. "The Homesick Bus Boy" is here reproduced from *The New Yorker*, November 9, 1940, where it appeared as "The Homesick Bus Boy of the Splendide;" see E46. It appeared as well in A18. "Bavaria" is here reproduced from *Life Class*, where it appeared as "Seven Hundred Brides;" see A23. It was reprinted in A17. "Sawmill in Tirol" is here reproduced from A23; it was reprinted in A17. A portion of "The Old Ritz" appeared as "A Gemütliche Christmas" in *Town & Country*, December, 1957; see E180. "The Isle of God" is here reproduced from *The New Yorker*, August 5, 1939; see E26. It appeared as well in A39 and in slightly different form in A3. "Camp Nomopo" is here reproduced from *Town & Country*, July 1942, where it appeared as "Little Girl with a Headache [Camp No Mo Pie];" see E72. It appeared as well in A21. "Little Bit and the *America*" is here reproduced from *Collier's*, January 10, 1953, where it appeared as "The Dog That Travelled Incognito;" see E145. It appeared as well in A11. "Invitation" is here reproduced from A43. "The Footstool of Madame Pompadour" is here reproduced from *Vogue*, February 15, 1955, where it appeared in different form as "The One I Love

Best; Lady Mendl;" see E165. It appeared as well in A43. "The Visit to San Simeon" is here reproduced from A43. "Lust for Gold" is here reproduced from *Town & Country*, June 1946, where it appeared as part of "Servant Trouble;" see E91. As "Fat Canary" it appeared in A7. "Moses Fable" and "Fresh Paint" are here reproduced from A7. "Cher Ami" is here reproduced from *Vogue*, October 15, 1941, where it appeared as "Cher Ami: The Servant Problem of Ludwig Bemelmans;" see E63. It appeared as well in A21. "My Favorite City" is here reproduced from *Holiday*, where it appeared in different form as "Paris: City of Rogues," April 1953; and as "Bemelmans' Magic Cities," January 1954; see E149 and E158. "The Dog of the World" is here reproduced from *Holiday*, May 1955; see E167. It appeared as well in A46. La Colombe" is here reproduced from A32. "Ship-owner" and "Mayday" are here reproduced from A35. "Last Visit to Regensburg" appears here for the first time (and may have been the last material written by the author).

ILLUSTRATIONS: There are 24 black illustrations by Ludwig Bemelmans.

COPY EXAMINED: MP.

b. Paperback edition [(1987)]:

TITLE PAGE: In black: • • • • • | Tell Them | It Was | Wonderful | • • • • • | Selected Writings by | Ludwig Bemelmans | McGraw-Hill Book Company | New York St. Louis San Francisco Auckland | Bogotá Hamburg Johannesburg London Madrid | Mexico Milan Montreal New Delhi Panama Paris | São Paulo Singapore Sydney Tokyo Toronto

PAGINATION: [i] - [xx], [1] - [316] pp. 20.5 x 13.5 cm.

COVERINGS: Lilac paper covers printed with author and title in maroon and illustration as in C2a; on spine, black colophon and in maroon: Bemelmans Tell Them It Was Wonderful, and at base, in black: McGraw-Hill.

PUBLISHED: June, 1987 at $7.95. 8,160 sets of sheets printed. On *verso of title leaf*, page [iv]: Reprinted by arrangement with Viking Penguin Inc. First McGraw-Hill Paperback edition, 1987. (Cover illustration, copyright extension, and design notes as for C2a.) *Half-title* on page [i]. *Dedication* on page [v]. *Foreword* as in C2a.

CONTENTS on pages [xi] - [xiii]: as in C2a.

ILLUSTRATIONS: As in C2a.

COPY EXAMINED: MP.

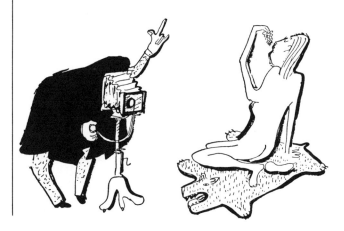

Collections
Edited by Bemelmans of
Work by Others

Collections
Edited by Bemelmans of
Work by Others

Section "d" lists titles edited by Ludwig Bemelmans, but containing the work of other writers as well as himself. It is set out exactly as is "A."

D1. Holiday in France [1957]

a. First edition:

TITLE PAGE: Occupying a two-page spread, upon a black drawing of a crowd gawking at the Eiffel Tower, in black: Holiday in France | Collected and Illustrated | by Ludwig Bemelmans | Houghton Mifflin Company Boston | The Riverside Press Cambridge •

PAGINATION: [i] - [xiv], [1] - [336] pp., 2 blank leaves; endpapers. 21.3 x 14 cm.

COVERINGS: Four-fifths gray-blue paper-covered, and one-fifth beige linen-weave cloth-covered boards; stamped in front with a pale blue figure of a tourist with camera; on spine, in red: Holiday in France, in dark blue: Bemelmans; and at bottom, in red: H M Co. Top edges stained red. Full-color dust jacket (with a Bemelmans drawing) printed in red with title, black with list of authors, and in white, at bottom, "Selected and decorated by Ludwig Bemelmans."

PUBLISHED: November 13, 1957 at $5.00. 6,000 sets of sheets printed, with an additional 2,500 on a second printing later. On *verso of title leaf*, page [iv]: All articles in this collection, with the exception of Mr. Bemelmans' Introduction, appeared originally in *Holiday* magazine. *Half-title* on page [i]. *Second half-title* on page [ix]. *Introduction by Ludwig Bemelmans* on page [x], including a collage incorporating a photograph of La Co-

lonne de la place Vendôme with a black drawing by Bemelmans and the first phrase of his text. The gray-blue endpapers are printed with a light blue drawing of motorists under a bridge in Paris.

Note: The dust jacket text notwithstanding, Ludwig Bemelmans did not make the selection of pieces to be included in this volume.

CONTENTS on pages [v] - viii: Ludwig Bemelmans, "Introduction," x; the ways of france: Colette, "French Women," 2; Ludwig Bemelmans, "French Rogues," 13; Ruth McKenney, "French Children," 30; Paul Bowles, "Artists in Paris," 44; Art Buchwald, "The Night Life," 59; André Maurois, "The Forty Immortals," 66; Paul E. Deutschman, "How to Buy a Dior Original," 77; Ludwig Bemelmans, "The Best Way to See France," 92; Joseph Wechsberg, "France's Three-Star Restaurants," 109; the places of france: John Steinbeck, "One American in Paris," 142; Irwin Shaw, "Paris! Paris!", 154; Francis Steegmuller, "Notre Dame de Paris," 189; Francis Steegmuller, "Château d'Amour," 202; Sam Boal, "Monte Carlo," 216; Francis Steegmuller, "France's Grande Corniche," 232; S. J. Perelman, "Riviera Revisited," 245; Alan Moorehead, "Incorrigible Marseilles," 252; Robert Capa, "Deauville and Biarritz," 269; Paul E. Deutschman, "Magnificent Versailles," 287; savoir faire: Paul E. Deutschman, "Where to Stay," 303; Paul E. Deutschman, "Getting About," 309; Paul E. Deutschman, "The French Touch," 317; Mario Pei, "How to Speak French," 320.

"French Rogues" is here reprinted from *Holiday*, April 1953, where it appeared as "Paris: City of Rogues;" see E149. "The Best Way to See France" is here reprinted from *Holiday*, May 1952; see E140.

ILLUSTRATIONS: Aside from the drawings on the dust jacket, title page, and with the introduction, there are 24 black illustrations by Bemelmans.

COPY EXAMINED: MP.

b. British edition ([1958]):

TITLE PAGE: Occupying a two-page spread, upon a black drawing of a crowd gawking at the Eiffel Tower, in black: Holiday in France | collected and illustrated by | Ludwig Bemelmans | André Deutsch, Colophon

PAGINATION: [1] - 288 pp.; endpapers. 20.9 x 13.3 cm.

COVERINGS: Red cloth-covered boards plain in front and stamped on spine, in gold: Holiday | in | France | * | Ludwig | Bemelmans | colophon | and at base: André | Deutsch. Dust jacket not examined.

PUBLISHED: June 6, 1958 at 18s. Number of sets of sheets printed cannot be determined, as the publisher's records were lost in transit to the United States. On *verso of title leaf*, page [4]: First published 1958 by André Deutsch Limited 12-14 Carlisle Street Soho Square. Printed in Holland by Drukkerij Holland and N.V. Amsterdam.

Half-title on page [1]. The robin's egg blue endpapers are plain.

CONTENTS on page 5: Ludwig Bemelmans, "Introduction," 9; the ways of france: Colette, "French Women," 13; Ludwig Bemelmans, "French Rogues," 21; Ruth McKenney, "French Children," 35; Paul Bowles, "Artists in Paris," 47; Art Buchwald, "The Night Life," 60; André Maurois, "The Forty Immortals," 66; Paul E. Deutschman, "How to Buy a Dior Original," 75; Ludwig Bemelmans, "The Best Way to See France," 87; Joseph Wechsberg, "France's Three-Star Restaurants," 100; the places of france: John Steinbeck, "One American in Paris," 131; Irwin Shaw, "Paris! Paris!", 141; Francis Steegmuller, "Notre Dame de Paris," 169; Francis Steegmuller, "Château d'Amour," 180; Sam Boal, "Monte Carlo," 191; Francis Steegmuller, "France's Grande Corniche," 204; S. J. Perelman, "Riviera Revisited," 214; Alan Moorehead, "Incorrigible Marseilles," 220; Robert Capa, "Deauville and Biarritz," 235; Paul E. Deutschman, "Magnificent Versailles," 249; savoir faire: Paul E. Deutschman, "Where to Stay," 263; Paul E. Deutschman, "Getting About," 267; Paul E. Deutschman, "The French Touch," 273; Mario Pei, "How to Speak French," 276.

ILLUSTRATIONS: Aside from the title page drawing there are 22 black illustrations by Bemelmans.

COPY EXAMINED: Mr. André Deutsch, London.

Publications in Periodicals

Publications in Periodicals

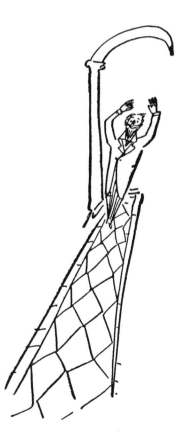

THE "E" SECTION CONTAINS all of the periodical publications with Bemelmans as author, *whether these are stories or articles* and whether they are in pictures or in English. It is very often difficult to be sure whether one is reading pure fiction, pure autobiography, or a mix with these pieces as with Bemelmans' books.

Periodical contributions by Bemelmans involving only his career as an artist are listed separately, in section "G." Pieces by others *about* Bemelmans' art are in "I."

The "E" listings are given chronologically, not alphabetically. When a magazine published only in a given month, as in "April, 1944" I have taken the liberty of assigning a hypothetical publication date for the first of the month in order to place the material in sequence with other stories. I have tried to indicate whether there were accompanying illustrations and if so, what kind. I have described the illustrations where they seemed of some particular interest.

Some of the stories were reprinted later in book form. The rule of thumb for Bemelmans was: half the time, the book chapter would have the same title as the magazine article from which it was drawn; half the time the title would be changed completely or slightly altered. Rarely the book chapter would be a word-for-word reprint, usually it was re-written. In many cases the re-writing was extensive. Names were changed — Lady Mendl in "The Fat Canary" became Lady Graveline in *Dirty Eddie*; or the spellings of names — Miss Prinzip in "The Fat Canary" became Miss Princip in *Dirty Eddie*; Eddie himself, indeed, was at first Eddy. Sometimes the periodical publication came later than the book chapter. Sometimes magazines printed stories more than once, or stories printed in one magazine were reprised in another.

It was very difficult indeed to keep track of all this, since the magazine pages do not invariably contain the same titles as the *Reader's Guide* suggests they did. Often something indexed under one title actually appeared under another; and was reprinted in a book or later an anthology under still another. Bemelmans wrote the way he drew, working and re-working as though with verbal sketches.

There is mention in the *Herald Tribune* obituary, J495, that Bemelmans wrote for *Esquire*. I can find no evidence that this is so and, indeed, *Esquire* denies it. Although I have not examined hard copies of Esquire prior to January 1948 I believe it unlikely there was a publication in that magazine.

1. "The Count and the Cobbler," *Harper's Bazaar*, December 1935, pp. 52-53. With 21 illustrations by the author. See also B1.

2. "Theodore and 'The Blue Danube'," *Story*, Vol. VIII No. 46, May 1936, pp. 37-44. With 13 illustrations by the author.

3. "May Massee: As Her Author-Illustrators See Her," *The Horn Book Magazine*, Vol. 12 No. 4, July-August 1936, p. 231. May Massee was Bemelmans' editor for children's books at Viking Press. The trade edition of *Madeline and the Gypsies* is dedicated to her; see A26a(bis). See as well J332 and J336.

4. "Inside, Outside," *Story*, Vol. IX No. 51, October 1936, pp. 65-74. With 14 illustrations by the author.

5. " 'No Trouble at All'," *Vogue*, March 1, 1937, pp. 74-153. With 8 illustrations by the author. See as well E176.

6. "Postkarten aus Wien," *Vogue*, May 15, 1937, pp. 68-69. With 8 full-color illustrations by the author.

7. "Sacre du Printemps," *Story*, Vol. X No. 59, June 1937, pp. 40-46. With 6 illustrations by the author.

8. "Jungles, Beards, Pythons, Parrots and How to Influence People," *Vogue*, September 1, 1937, pp. 110-158. With 1 illustration by the author.

9. "The Elephant Cutlet," *Town & Country*, Vol. 92 No. 4180, September 1937, p. 73. With 7 illustrations in black with color wash. Illustrated especially for *Town & Country*. The story appeared originally in A33. See as well A9.

10. "Quito," *The New Yorker*, Vol. XIII, October 30, 1937, p. 88. In *Our Footloose Correspondents*.

11. "Prison? It's Wonderful," *Globe*, Vol. II No. 2, November, 1937, pp. 6-11. With seven black illustrations by the author, four of which are titled, "Panoptico," "Flower," "The Cactuses in Back of the Prison," and "Cellblock."

12. "Poor Animal!," *Globe*, Vol. II No. 3, December, 1937 - January, 1938, pp. 25-27. With one black illustration by the author. An editor's note appears on p. 24.

13. "Chile con Amore: a sentimental journey from Valparaiso to Quito," *Vogue*, April 1, 1938, pp. 92-136. With 1 full-color illustration by the author, "Plaza Independencia—Quito."

14. "My First Actress," *Stage*, May 1938, pp. 18-19. With 1 black and yellow illustration by the author.

15. "Garden Spots," *Stage*, June 1938, pp. 22-23. With 1 black illustration by the author of a waiter with a menu in a garden.

16. "Busboy's Holidays: Dinner at Luchow's and a Trip to the Sea," *Town & Country*, Vol. 93 No. 4190, July 1938, pp. 38-66. With 1 full-color illustration by the author.

17. "The Coming Out Party," *Town & Country*, Vol. 93 No. 4192, September 1938, pp. 48-85. With 1 full-color illustration by the author.

18. "Why Doesn't Somebody . . .," *The New Yorker*, Vol. XIV, December 10, 1938, pp. 91-93. In *Our Footloose Correspondents*.

19. "Transgressor in Galapagos," *Town & Country*, Vol. 94 No. 4196, January 1939, pp. 24-25. The story is told entirely by means of illustrations, of which there are 10 in black with color wash.

20. "Back to Quito," *House Beautiful*, Vol. 81 No. 2, February 1939, pp. 30-31. With 2 black illustrations by the author.

21. "My English Suit in Paris," *Town & Country*, Vol. 94 No. 4198, March 1939, pp. 44-100. With 1 full-color illustration by the author.

22. "Speaking of Ashes," *Stage*, June 1939, p. 42. With 1 black illustration by the author.

23. "Have You a Reservation?," *Reader's Digest*, Vol. 35 No. 208, August 1939, pp. 36-38. Condensed from *Life Class*, A23.

24. "Dear General, What a Surprise!," *Town & Country*, Vol. 94 No. 4203, August 1939. The story is an account of Bemelmans' experience rehearsing, but never actually performing, the role of General Liebfrau in the play, *Good Hunting*, by Nathanael West and Joseph Schrank, Produced by Jerome Mayer and Leonard Field, staged by Mr. Mayer and starring Estelle Winwood, George Tobias, and Aubrey Mather. The play opened at the Hudson Theater, New York, November 21, 1938, to a short run. General Liebfrau was played in fact by Alfred Kappeler. The photograph of Bemelmans reproduced with the story is printed as well in J96.

25. "He Couldn't Write About the Fair," a letter on the World's Fair, *Vogue*, August 1, 1939, pp. 64-65. With 4 black illustrations by the author.

26. "The Isle of God," *The New Yorker*, Vol. XV, August 5, 1939, pp. 46-47. In *Our Footloose Correspondents*.

27. "Dog Story," *The New Yorker*, Vol. XV, August 12, 1939, pp. 18-20.

28. "True Love Story," *Town & Country*, Vol. 94 No. 4204, September 1939. With title art and 15 illustrations by the author. The story is told exclusively by means of the illustrations.

29. "The Bride of Berchtesgaden," *The New Yorker*, Vol. XV, September 23, 1939, pp. 18-21.

30. "Italian Paradise," *Town & Country*, Vol. 94

No. 4205, October 1939. With illustration in full-color by the author.

31. "I Love America," *Town & Country*, Vol. 95 No. 4209, February 1940, pp. 34-75. With 1 black illustration by the author.

32. "Buenas Días, Gran Hotel," *Town & Country*, Vol. 95 No. 4210, March 1940, pp. 56-58. With 4 black and 2 full-color illustrations by the author.

33. "La Spécialité de la Maison: a happy attack on the Specialities of most Restaurants including '21,' Louise's and Luchow's," *Vogue*, March 15, 1940, pp. 72-73. With 4 black illustrations by the author.

34. "The Donkey Inside: Escape and Farewell," *Town & Country*, Vol. 95 No. 4212, May 1940, pp. 61-114. With 1 full-color illustration by the author.

35. "Mespoulets of the Splendide," *The New Yorker*, Vol. XVI No. 13, May 11, 1940, pp. 17-19. With 1 black illustration by the author.

36. "Art at the Hotel Splendide," *The New Yorker*, Vol. XVI No. 16, June 1, 1940, pp. 28-32. With 1 black illustration by the author.

37. "S. S. Mesias," *Town & Country*, Vol. 95 No. 4213, June 1940, pp. 46-75. With 1 black illustration by the author.

38. "I love you—I love you—I love you—," *Vogue*, June 1, 1940, pp. 59-104. With 1 full-color illustration by the author. (See also G64.) This piece was reprinted in the August 1940 issue of British *Vogue*, with the same full-color illustration, as "Episode from the Paris of the Past."

39. "The Ballet Visits the Splendide's Magician," *The New Yorker*, Vol. XVI No. 21, July 6, 1940, pp. 20-22. With 1 black illustration by the author.

40. "The Splendide's Magician Does a New Trick," *The New Yorker*, Vol. XVI No. 24, July 27, 1940, pp. 19-21. With 1 black illustration by the author.

41. "Fifi," *Town & Country*, Vol. 95 No. 4215, August 1940, pp. 29-32. With 1 full-color illustration by the author.

42. "The Painted Grapes," *Town & Country*, Vol. 95 No. 4216, September 1940, pp. 55-91. With 1 black and 1 full-color illustration by the author.

43. "Easy Money at the Splendide," *The New Yorker*, Vol. XVI No. 31, September 14, 1940, pp. 21-23. With 1 black illustration by the author.

44. "Adolf in Ecuador," *The New Yorker*, Vol. XVI No. 33, September 28, 1940, pp. 50-52. In *Our Footloose Correspondents*.

45. "The Morale of the Natives," *Town & Coun-*

try, Vol. 95 No. 4218, November 1940, pp. 63-118. With 1 black illustration by the author.

46. "The Homesick Bus Boy of the Splendide," *The New Yorker*, Vol. XVI No. 39, November 9, 1940, pp. 20-23. With 1 black illustration by the author.

47. "Peruvian Legend," *Town & Country*, Vol. 95 No. 4219, December 1940, pp. 59-60. With 3 black and 1 full-color illustrations by the author.

48. "The Splendide's Night in Granada," *The New Yorker*, Vol. XVI No. 45, December 21, 1940, pp. 17-20. With 1 black illustration by the author.

49. "This is Romance," *Town & Country*, Vol. 96 No. 4220, January 1941, pp. 49-75. With 1 black illustration by the author.

50. "Sweet Land of Liberty," *Glamour*, February 1941.

51. "'Dance for Charity'," *Vogue*, February 1, 1941, pp. 62-63. With 1 black and 1 full-color illustration (entitled, "War Relief Ball at the Ritz") by the author.

52. "The Splendide's Hispano," *The New Yorker*, Vol. XVII No. 6, March 22, 1941, pp. 22-24. With 1 black illustration by the author.

53. "The Donkey Inside," a condensation of the novel, A8, *Reader's Digest*, Vol. 38 No. 228, April 1941, pp. 125-143. With 1 black and orange and 1 orange illustration by the author.

54. "Vacation," *Town & Country*, Vol. 96 No. 4223, April 1941, pp. 58-90. With 3 full-color illustrations by the author.

55. "The Head-Hunters of the Quito Hills," *The New Yorker*, Vol. XVII No. 9, April 12, 1941, pp. 37-44. In *A Reporter at Large*.

56. "Sacre du Printemps," *Story*, Vol. XVIII No. 89, May-June 1941, pp. 94-99. With 5 black illustrations by the author. A republication of E7.

An unauthorized, somewhat "re-written," unillustrated version of this story appeared again, as "It All Depends on How You Want It," by Martin H. Mack, in *Circle*, 7-8, 1946, pp. 128-132. *Circle* counted among its subscribers Aldous Huxley and Jean Renoir; Henry Miller, along with Robert Duncan, Darius Milhaud and Kenneth Patchen, contributed to the same issue. Allene Talmey, then features editor of *Vogue*, sent Bemelmans the magazine along with a note (February 28, 1946) saying, "I must tell you how much I enjoyed Mr. Mack's story and I am writing this to you especially because, dear, you wrote it first. It is your own wonderful piece about Emile Kratzig, who got the seventh class funeral."

Mack is described in the contributor's notes: ". . . a retired member of the New York Fire Dept. He is now 58 years old and this is his first attempt at writing—quite unconsciously arrived at. He alleges that the incidents of the story were dreamed." Indeed, Bemelmans' Kratzig is described in the piece as "a retired, eccentric fireman."

Correspondence passed between Bemelmans and George Leite, the editor and publisher of *Circle*, and Bemelmans hinted at "making with lawyers." But what Leite called "this horrible state of affairs" was apparently settled with amity.

57. "That's Panama," *McCall's*, Vol. 68, June 1941, pp. 20-93. With 1 full-color illustration and 1 composite, made up of 13 small color pictures, by the author. In the composite, one of the images shows the Panama Canal, with the water flowing in the wrong direction. [On Bemelmans reversing the flow, see as well the conclusion to "The Isle of God" in C2a.]

58. "Air Mail to Barbara: Caribbean Letters to His Daughter," *Town & Country*, Vol. 96 No. 4226, July 1941, pp. 33-61. With 1 full-color illustration by the author.

59. "The Lost Mandolin of the Splendide," *The New Yorker*, Vol. XVII No. 22, July 12, 1941, pp. 16-19. With 1 black illustration by the author.

60. "The Splendide: The Perfect Behavior of a Crazy Fool," *Town & Country*, Vol. 96 No. 4228, September 1941, pp. 63-64. With 2 black and 1 full-color illustrations by the author. This story

appears as "Monsieur Victor" in both A23, C1 and C2.

61. "Pale Hands Beside the Circular Bar," *The New Yorker*, Vol. XVII No. 30, September 6, 1941, pp. 15-19.

62. "The Valet of the Splendide," *The New Yorker*, Vol. XVII No. 35, October 11, 1941, pp. 23-26. With 1 black illustration by the author.

63. "Cher Ami: The Servant Problem of Ludwig Bemelmans," *Vogue*, October 15, 1941, pp. 68-107. With 1 black illustration by the author.

64. "The Murderer of the Splendide," *The New Yorker*, Vol. XVII No. 42, November 29, 1941, pp. 19-23. With 1 black illustration by the author.

65. "Le Chagrin d'Amour Est Formidable," *Town & Country*, Vol. 96 No. 4230, December 1941, pp. 94-95. With 9 black illustrations by the author.

66. "The Splendide's Meringue Glâcée," *The New Yorker*, Vol. XVII No. 50, January 24, 1942, pp. 23-24. With 1 black illustration by the author.

67. "Sweet Death in the Electric Chair," *Harper's Bazaar*, No. 2762, March 1, 1942, pp. 40-98. With 5 black illustrations by the author.

68. "How to Almost Open a Musical," *Town &*

Country, Vol. 97 No. 4234, March 1942, pp. 55-58. With 10 black illustrations by the author.

69. "Ludwig Bemelmans' Splendide Apartment," *Vogue*, April 1, 1942, pp. 60-105. With 4 full-color illustrations by the author and 2 black and white photographs.

70. "Souvenir: Memory of the Normandie, the 'Femme Fatale' of Ships," *Vogue*, June 1, 1942, pp. 49-79. With 1 black illustration by the author.

71. "Watch the Birdie," *The New Yorker*, Vol. XVIII No. 16, June 6, 1942, pp. 15-18.

72. "Little Girl with a Headache [Camp No Mo Pie]," *Town & Country*, Vol. 97 No. 4238, July 1942, pp. 25-27. With 5 black illustrations by the author. See "Camp Nomopo" in C2.

73. "Man of the World," *Town & Country*, Vol. 97 No. 4241, October 1942, pp. 57-82. With 2 black illustrations by the author. (First episode) The blurb reads, "Ludwig Bemelmans has just finished a play in collaboration with Charles MacArthur." The play, never published or produced, was *My War With the United States*.

74. "Man of the World," *Town & Country*, Vol. 97 No. 4242, November 1942, pp. 60-82. With 1 black illustration by the author, titled "Miss Graves is rescued from a watery one." (Second episode)

75. "Man of the World," *Town & Country*, Vol. 98 No. 4245, February 1943, pp. 46-75. With 1 black illustration by the author, titled "Frightened at first by the sound of twigs breaking beneath his robust boots as he hastened into the glade, she breathed a sigh of relief as she noted that this was a man of obvious respectability." (Third episode)

76. "Man of the World," *Town & Country*, Vol. 98 No. 4247, May 1943, pp. 64-100. With 1 full-color illustration by the author. (Fourth episode)

77. "Post Card Home," *Vogue*, May 1, 1943, pp. 42-86. With 4 full-color illustrations by the author.

78. "The Royal Kiss, Which is the 5th Episode of Man of the World," *Town & Country*, Vol. 98 No. 4248, June 1943, pp. 56-92. With 2 black illustrations by the author, titled, "At last General Leonidas Erosa and the Spanish beauty arrived at the Royal Kiss. Cyrano ran to the door. 'Bon soir, mon Général. Bon soir, Madame. Psst, psst! Table sixty-seven! Psst, psst! The wine!" and "In the center of the floor was a human pie, slowly turning, a mass of pressed-together arms, faces, elbows, and backsides. Here and there a couple tried a few leaping steps to get out of it and moved to the edge for a second or two, but every time the pool of dancers sucked them in again."

79. "Yolanda and the Thief," with Jacques

Théry, *Town & Country*, Vol. 98 No. 4249, July 1943, pp. 58-83. See also H13.

80. "The Panama Canal, Which is the Sixth Episode of Man of the World," *Town & Country*, Vol. 98 No. 4250, August 1943, pp. 74-89. With 2 black illustrations by the author, titled "On the bridge: the vain and susceptible Captain Gulbransson with photokinetic Mme. Farah. Far left in Second Class: Vitasse, the General's chef, with Mrs. Losch and her daughter Hilda" and " 'Ah! How intelligent you are, my sweet!' "

81. "Now I Lay Me Down to Sleep," *Town & Country*, Vol. 98 No. 4251, September 1943, pp. 92-135. With 2 black illustrations of La Reina del Pacifico by the author, one including this blurb: "Notice to Passengers; in midstream, the erratic and unpredictable Señor Bemelmans has informed us that he no longer likes the title "Man of the World," and henceforth will call his story "Now I Lay Me Down to Sleep."

82. "Now I Lay Me Down to Sleep," *Town & Country*, Vol. 98, No. 4252, October 1943, pp. 104-130. With 1 black and 1 colored illustration by the author, and the blurb " 'Now I Lay Me Down to Sleep,' Ludwig Bemelmans' first novel, herewith completed in *Town & Country*, will be published by Viking this month."

83. "Joyride," *Town & Country*, Vol. 99 No. 4265, October 1944, pp. 98-101. With 8 full-color illustrations by the author.

84. "Through the Eye of the Needle," *Town & Country*, Vol. 99 No. 4267, December 1944, pp. 107-147. With 4 full-color illustrations by the author.

85. "Knife and Fork in Hollywood," *Town & Country*, Vol. 100 No. 4269, February 1945, pp. 106-130. With 4 full-color illustrations by the author.

86. "The Blue Danube," *Town & Country*, Vol. 100 No. 4270, March 1945, pp. 92-148. With 3 black and 3 full-color illustrations by the author.

87. "The Blue Danube, II," *Town & Country*, Vol. 100 No. 4271, April 1945, pp. 85-139. With 6 black illustrations by the author.

88. "Art for Art's Sake," *Town & Country*, Vol. 100 No. 4274, July 1945, pp. 54-109.

89. "Irons in the Fire," *Town & Country*, Vol. 100 No. 4276, September 1945, pp. 112-179. With 1 black and 1 full-color illustration by the author.

90. "Gramercy Nocturne," *Town & Country*, Vol. 100 No. 4282, March 1946, pp. 105-165. With 5 black illustrations by the author.

91. "Servant Trouble," *Town & Country*, Vol. 100 No. 4285, June 1946, pp. 66-85. With 2 full-color illustrations, one titled "He worried about when his suits would come back from the tailor— especially the double-breasted cashmere"; and 1

line drawing, all by the author. See "Lust for Gold" in C2.

92. "The Fat Canary," *Town & Country*, Vol. 100 No. 4286, July 1946, pp. 82-122. With a title illustration and 6 black illustrations by the author, titled "Miss Prinzip exemplified Wildgans efficiency," "Vashvily painted from his hospital window the nest which a bird had made from the hair of another patient, Hedy Lamarr," "He finally chose one of the exquisite products of Cuba," "The 'King of Ease' was a very intelligent piece of furniture," "With his harmonious system he soon gained ten pounds," and "As if in his favorite listening pose, he relaxed and fell asleep."

93. "The Reluctant Waiter," *Boston Herald News Week*, July 21, 1946. See "The Animal Waiter" in *Hotel Splendide*, A18.

94. "The Reluctant Waiter," *Oregon Journal News Week*, July 21, 1946. See E86.

95. "The Fat Canary," *Town & Country*, Vol. 100 No. 4287, August 1946, pp. 103-151. With a title illustration and 3 black illustrations by the author, titled " 'That is the one we had the teeth straightened, isn't it?' 'Yes, and capped,' " " 'We want you to be happy here," and 'Our principal aim is not belles lettres.' "

96. "The Fat Canary," *Town & Country*, Vol. 100 No. 4288, September 1946, pp. 158-252. With 2 full-color illustrations by the author, titled

" 'That's a swell ending. The little woman at the oven. She runs to the door. The door opens. There's the chaplain,' " and " 'The similarity between that last time and now is astonishing.' "

97. "The Fat Canary," *Town & Country*, Vol. 100 No. 4289, October 1946, pp. 178-273. With 1 full-color illustration by the author, titled "The twelfth pig was black, and because of that his mother called him Dirty Eddy."

98. "The Fat Canary," *Town & Country*, Vol. 100 No. 4290, November 1946, pp. 116-246. With 3 black illustrations by the author, titled "Holding his nose, he jumped into the pool. They were again 'just like a couple of kids,' " "Moses Fable jumped up with a wild cry of pain," and " 'No,' said Cassard sadly. 'Tonight I sleep alone." A blurb at the end of the story reads, "The Fat Canary" will be published by Viking Press in 1947 under the title "Will You Marry Me?" In fact the five stories of that title appeared in that year as parts of *Dirty Eddie*, A7.

99. "Introducing Ludwig Bemelmans," *Holiday*, Vol. 1 No. 10, December 1946, pp. 68-75. With 4 black and 3 full-color illustrations by the author.

100. "Come, Fly With Me to Paris," *Holiday*, Vol. 2 No. 1, January 1947, pp. 66-73. With 1 black and 5 full-color illustrations by the author.

101. "Back Again in Paris," *Holiday*, Vol. 2 No.

2, February 1947, pp. 91-117. With 2 black and yellow and 5 full-color illustrations by the author.

102. "Switzerland," *Holiday*, Vol. 2 No. 3, March 1947, pp. 75-135. With 5 full-color illustrations by the author.

103. "Under a Tyrolean Hat," *Holiday*, Vol. 2 No. 4, April 1947, pp. 87-141. With 6 full-color illustrations by the author.

104. "Return to Munich," *Holiday*, Vol. 2 No. 5, May 1947, pp. 67-155. With 4 full-color illustrations by the author.

105. "No. 13 Rue St. Augustin," *Town & Country*, Vol. 101 No. 4296, May 1947, pp. 86-136. With 1 black and 1 full-color illustration by the author.

106. "The Antlers of the Alpenrose," *The New Yorker*, Vol. XXIII No. 14, May 24, 1947, pp. 27-31.

107. "Story of a Bavarian," *Holiday*, Vol. 2 No. 6, June 1947, pp. 67-161. With 3 full-color illustrations by the author.

108. "The Story of a Bavarian and His Travels: I," *The New York Herald Tribune*, Paris, July 1, 1947, p. 6. With 1 black illustration by the author.

109. "The Story of a Bavarian and His Travels: II," *The New York Herald Tribune*, Paris, July 8, 1947, p. 7. With 1 black illustration by the author.

110. "The Story of a Bavarian and His Travels: III," *The New York Herald Tribune*, Paris, July 15, 1947, p. 7. With 1 black illustration by the author.

111. "Gypsy Music," *Holiday*, Vol. 3 No. 4, April 1948, pp. 107-110. With 3 full-color illustrations by the author.

112. "Folie de Grandeur," *Holiday*, Vol. 3 No. 5, May 1948, pp. 46-127. With 3 black and 9 full-color illustrations by the author and 1 color collage.

113. "Venice," *Holiday*, Vol. 4 No. 2, August 1948, pp. 60-127. With 1 black and 3 full-color illustrations by the author.

114. "Promenade Sur Mer," *Holiday*, Vol. 4 No. 3, September 1948, pp. 110-117. With 1 black and orange and 2 full-color illustrations by the author.

115. "Mademoiselle Regrets," *Holiday*, Vol. 4 No. 4, October 1948, pp. 116-120. With 2 full-color illustrations by the author.

116. "The Wicked Ironmonger," *Theatre Arts*, Vol. 33 No. 2, March 1949, pp. 28-33. With 10 black illustrations by the author.

117. "My First Actress," *Theatre Arts*, Vol. 33 No. 4, May 1949, pp. 28-31. With 3 black illus-

trations by the author. This is a second publishing of E14.

118. "The Master of the Alpenrose," *Town & Country*, Vol. 103 No. 4321, June 1949, pp. 43-93. With 2 black and 1 full-color illustrations by the author.

119. "Serpents in Aspen," *Town & Country*, Vol. 103 No. 4322, July 1949, pp. 37-89. With 1 black and 2 full-color illustrations by the author.

120. "Vienna Revisited," *Holiday*, Vol. 6 No. 2, August 1949, pp. 60-128. With 1 black and 2 full-color illustrations by the author.

121. "Holiday for Heroes," *Town & Country*, Vol. 103 No. 4323, August 1949, pp. 63-87. With 4 black and 1 full-color illustrations by the author.

122. "Diary With a Blank Page," *Holiday*, Vol. 6 No. 3, September 1949, pp. 110-128. With 3 black and 2 full-color illustrations by the author.

123. "The Turn of the Tide," *Town & Country*, Vol. 103 No. 4324, September 1949, pp. 107-162. With 1 black illustration by the author.

124. "Isle of Capri," *Holiday*, Vol. 6 No. 5, November 1949, pp. 60-150. With 3 black and 3 full-color illustrations by the author.

125. "Sunshine, Sunshine, Go Away," *Good Housekeeping*, Vol. 129 No. 6, December 1949, pp. 63-76. With 40 illustrations by the author, many in full color. See also A41.

126. "Cinderella Isle," *Holiday*, Vol. 6 No. 6, December 1949, pp. 126-139. With 4 full-color illustrations by the author.

127. "The Film Test," *Town & Country*, Vol. 104 No. 4332, May 1950, pp. 61-105. With 1 black illustration by the author.

128. "Road to Salerno," *Holiday*, Vol. 8 No. 4, October 1950, pp. 90-111. With 1 full-color illustration by the author.

129. "To Elsie With Love," *Town & Country*, Vol. 104 No. 4337, October 1950, pp. 128-179. With 1 black and 1 full-color illustration by the author.

130. "Christmas in Tyrol," *Holiday*, Vol. 8 No. 6, December 1950, pp. 64-170. With 2 black and 1 full-color illustrations by the author.

131. "Adieu to the Old Ritz," *Town & Country*, Vol. 104 No. 4339, December 1950, pp. 90-93. With 21 full-color illustrations by the author.

132. "How to Be a Prince," *Holiday*, Vol. 9 No. 4, April 1951, pp. 19-134. With 6 black and 1 black and yellow illustrations by the author.

133. "The Happy Place," *Woman's Home Companion*, Vol. 78, April 1951, pp. 28-86. With 5 full-color and 8 black and tinted illustrations by the author. See also A15.

134. "Madame Takes the Count," *Holiday*, Vol. 9 No. 5, May 1951, pp. 70-79. With 4 black and 1 black and pink illustrations by the author.

135. "The Perfect Marriage," *Holiday*, Vol. 9 No. 6, June 1951, pp. 75-133. With 4 black and 1 black and turquoise illustrations by the author.

136. "Mad Masquerade," *Holiday*, Vol. 10 No. 1, July 1951, pp. 65-71. With 3 black, 1 black and pink, and 3 full-color illustrations by the author.

137. "Fingerprints, Monsieur?," *Vogue*, September 15, 1951, pp. 157-202.

138. "Madeline's Rescue," *Good Housekeeping*, Vol. 133 No. 6, December 1951, pp. 55-60. With 32 illustrations by the author. See also A30.

139. "Mighty Vesuvius!," *Holiday*, Vol. 11 No. 1, January 1952, pp. 102-107. With 2 full-color illustrations by the author.

140. "The Best Way to See France," *Holiday*, Vol. 11 No. 5, May 1952, pp. 68-93. With 1 black and 8 full-color illustrations by the author.

141. "The Color of Spain," *Holiday*, Vol. 11 No. 6, June 1952, pp. 56-119. With 1 black and 5 full-color illustrations by the author.

142. "Remember Me?," *Woman's Day*, 16th year, 8th issue, June 1952, pp. 48-123. With one black and yellow illustration by the author. This is a sequel to "The Bride of Berchtesgaden," E29.

143. "The Borrowed Christmas," *Holiday*, Vol. 12 No. 6, December 1952, pp. 110-168. With multiple full-color Santa Clauses by the author. See as well A5. From the Hôtel Ritz, Place Ven-dôme, Paris early in 1952 Bemelmans wrote to Sam Golden, "I just got a call from the Holiday People, to do a page with Santa Clauses along Fifth Avenue, Such a thing might be a good Christmas card also, but what I am asking for and, I will gladly pay for the expenses, is to have sent to me First class Mail, via a fast boat, documentation; I mean pictures of Santa Clauses, and the way they stand on Fifth Ave, some have I think a Chimney and others a kind of a ring with three poles, I am not altogether sure of the details. I shall be very obliged if the detail of the costume, beard, boots, and the way they stand and ring the bell can be shown." Then again, on 28 April 1952, in a postscript, "Thanks for the Santa Clice." Golden was head of the American Artists Group.

144. "Fröhliche Weihnachten," *Town & Country*, Vol. 106 No. 4363, December 1952, pp. 93-129. With 4 black illustrations by the author.

145. "The Dog That Travelled Incognito," *Collier's*, Vol. 131, January 10, 1953, pp. 22-25. See "Little Bit and the *America* " in *Father, Dear Father*, A11.

146. "On Innkeeping," *Holiday*, Vol. 13 No. 2, February 1953, pp. 46-89. With 2 black and 1 full-color illustrations by the author.

147. "Monsieur Soulé," *Holiday*, Vol. 13 No. 2, February 1953.

148. "To Be a Gourmet," *Holiday*, Vol. 13 No. 2, February 1953.

149. "Paris: City of Rogues," *Holiday*, Vol. 13 No. 4, April 1953, pp. 60-87. With 2 black and 1 full-color illustrations by the author. See "My Favorite City" in C2.

150. "That Old World Flavor Down Where the Würzburger Flows," *Town & Country*, Vol. 107 No. 4369, June 1953, pp. 41-110.

151. "Madeline at the Coronation," *Collier's*, Vol. 131, June 6, 1953, pp. 18-19.

152. "Two-Faced Tangier," *Holiday*, Vol. 14 No. 3, September 1953, pp. 44-84. With 1 black and yellow and 2 full-color illustrations by the author.

153. "Father, Dear Father," an excerpt of A11, *New York Herald Tribune This Week*, September 13, 1953, pp. 22-59. With 3 black illustrations by the author.

154. "Road to Marrakech," *Holiday*, Vol. 14 No. 4, October 1953, pp. 106-142. With 1 full-color illustration by the author. Also known as "Among the Arabs."

155. "Ludwig Bemelmans," an autobiographical sketch, *New York Herald Tribune This Week*, October 11, 1953. "I like painting more than anything. I hate writing."

156. "Paris in the Snow," *New York Herald Tribune This Week*, December 20, 1953, pp. 14-15.

With 1 black and 1 full-color illustration by the author.

157. "A Texan, a Parisian and a Baby," *New York Herald Tribune*, Paris, December 25, 1953, p. 7. From *Father, Dear Father*, A11.

158. "Bemelmans' Magic Cities," *Holiday*, Vol. 15 No. 1, January 1954, pp. 56-119. With 2 full-color, 1 blue and 1 brown illustrations by the author.

159. "My First Visit to Paris," *Holiday*, Vol. 15 No. 1, January 1954.

160. "The Old Stag and the Tree," *Woman's Day*, 17th year, 4th issue, January 1954, p. 20.

161. "In the Heart of Paris," *Town & Country*, Vol. 108 No. 4379, May 1954, pp. 80-108. With 2 full-color illustrations by the author.

162. "Voyage," *New York Herald Tribune This Week*, May 9, 1954, pp. 15-43. With 1 full-color illustration by the author.

163. "Caldecott Award Acceptance," *The Horn Book Magazine*, Vol. XXX No. 4, August 1954, pp. 270-275. Bemelmans received the Caldecott Award for *Madeline's Rescue*, A30.

164. "The Street Where the Heart Lies," *Boston Sunday Herald This Week*, Feb. 13, 1955. This story is unrelated to A40. See as well A46.

165. "The One I Love the Best," *Vogue*, February 15, 1955, pp. 60-113.

166. "My Craziest Tour of Paris," *Coronet*, Vol. 37, March 1955, pp. 59-64.

167. "The Dog of the World," *Holiday*, Vol. 17 No. 5, May 1955, pp. 81-128. With 2 black and 2 brown illustrations by the author.

168. "Madeline's Christmas," *Good Housekeeping*, Vol. 141 No. 6, December 1955, pp. 74-75. With 7 black and red illustrations by the author. See also A29. Note: This is not the same as A28, even though the titles are identical.

169. "Deck the Halls with Boughs of Holly, 'Tis the Season to Be Jolly, FaLaLaLa?," *Town & Country*, Vol. 109 No. 4397, December 1955, pp. 86-87. With 1 black and 1 full-color illustration by the author.

170. "Midas Tour of Italy," *Holiday*, Vol. 19 No. 1, January 1956, pp. 44-119. With 2 brown and 1 full-color illustrations by the author.

171. "The Texas Legend," *McCall's*, Vol. 83, August 1956, pp. 6-30; with 12 illustrations by the author.

172. "I Love Paris in the Wintertime," *Town & Country*, Vol. 110 No. 4409, December 1956, p. 134. With 1 black illustration by the author.

173. "The Austrian Emperor's Favorite Dishes," *Woman's Day*, 20th year, 3rd issue, December 1956, pp. 32-66.

174. "Hotel Splendide Revisited," *Town & Coun-*try, Vol. 111 No. 4415, June 1957, pp. 34-37. With 2 black and 1 full-color illustrations by the author.

175. " 'No Trouble at All'," *Town & Country*, Vol. 111 No. 4415, June 1957, pp. 88-97. With 3 black illustrations by the author. See as well E5.

176. "Love at the Splendide," *Town & Country*, Vol. 111 No. 4417, August 1957, pp. 46-47.

177. "Otto Kahn's Top Hat," *Town & Country*, Vol. 111 No. 4417, August 1957, pp. 80-86.

178. "Moving Day," *Town & Country*, Vol. 111 No. 4418, September 1957, pp. 127-128.

179. "The Best Way to See Cuba," *Holiday*, Vol. 22 No. 6, December 1957, pp. 66-229. With 7 full-color illustrations by the author.

180. "A Gemütliche Christmas," *Town & Country*, Vol. 111 No. 4421, December 1957. With 1 illustration by the author.

181. "Gala in Monte Carlo," *Town & Country*, Vol. 112 No. 4429, August 1958, pp. 64-65. With 10 black illustrations by the author.

182. "When You Lunch With the Emperor," *Vogue*, September 1, 1958, pp. 208-255. With 3 black illustrations by the author.

183. "The Best Way to See Rio," *Holiday*, Vol. 24 No. 6, December 1958, pp. 76-161. With 1 black and 4 full-color illustrations by the author.

184. "A Quick One," *Town & Country*, Vol. 113 No. 4434, January 1959, pp. 30-97. With 3 black illustrations by the author.

185. "Brazil's Fantastic New Capital," *Holiday*, Vol. 25 No. 3, March 1959, pp. 46-52.

186. "But I Like Mexico!," *Town & Country*, Vol. 113 No. 4437, April 1959, pp. 76-146. With 2 black and 1 full-color illustrations by the author.

187. "How I Took the Cure," *Holiday*, Vol. 25 No. 6, June 1959, pp. 64-122. With 1 black illustration by the author.

188. "Sao Paulo: Skyscrapers and Poison Toads," *Holiday*, Vol. 26 No. 3, September 1959, pp. 28-31.

189. "Invitation to a Castle," *Town & Country*, Vol. 113 No. 4442, September 1959, pp. 118-166. With 2 black illustrations by the author.

190. "Bemelmans Paints New York," *Holiday*, Vol. 26 No. 4, October 1959, pp. 64-71. With 7 full-color illustrations by the author.

191. "Randy," *Mademoiselle*, Vol. 50, December 1959, pp. 42-45.

192. "Caviar: The Noblest Roe of them All," *Playboy*, Vol. 8 No. 1, January 1961, pp. 41-103. With one full-color illustration by the author: a mustachioed violinist serenades diners in a busy restaurant with palms; a red-jacketed waiter holds high a tin of Beluga while in the foreground another spoons more from its resting place in a tin that rides the back of a ice-sculpture goose. A photograph of Ludwig Bemelmans is on p. 1.

193. "My Riviera Cruise," *Holiday*, Vol. 29 No. 6, June 1961, pp. 50-125. With 3 full-color illustrations by the author.

194. "Madeline in London," *Holiday*, Vol. 30 No. 2, August 1961, pp. 50-55. With 22 full-color and 8 black and yellow illustrations by the author. See as well A28.

195. "Cinderella Isle," *Argosy*, Vol. XXIII No. 6, June 1962, pp. 45-53.

196. "The Soul of Austria," *Holiday*, Vol. 32 No. 2, August 1962, pp. 26-110. Also known as "Most Swindles in Austria." With 7 full-color illustrations by the author.

197. "Gala at the Tour d'Argent," *Playboy*, Vol. 9 No. 12, December 1962, pp. 122-164. There are 3 black and one color illustration by the author. The color illustration is a portrait of Gala, titled, "It was Gala's habit to tilt her head away from him to avoid his loose hand as much as possible." A photograph of Ludwig Bemelmans is on p. 3.

198. "Visit to an Irish Castle," *Holiday*, Vol. 33 No. 4, April 1963, pp. 33-39. With 1 black illustration by the author.

199. "Franz Josef: A Habsburg Marriage," *Holiday*, Vol. 35 No. 1, January 1964, pp. 68-88.

200. "The Marvelous Mission to Moscow," *Holiday*, Vol. 35 No. 2, February 1964, pp. 108-118.

201. "Madeline's Christmas," *McCall's*, Vol. 113, December 1985, pp. 112-117, including full-color illustrations. This is an encore publication of the original *McCall's* magazine insert booklet, listed as A28a; but the text is that of the first trade edition, A28a(bis). This is not the same as E168.

202. "Shirt Tale of Paris," *Travel Holiday*, October 1991, p. 134, including one full-color illustration by Alexa Grace. This is an excerpt from E158.

Contributions by Bemelmans to Anthologies Edited by Others

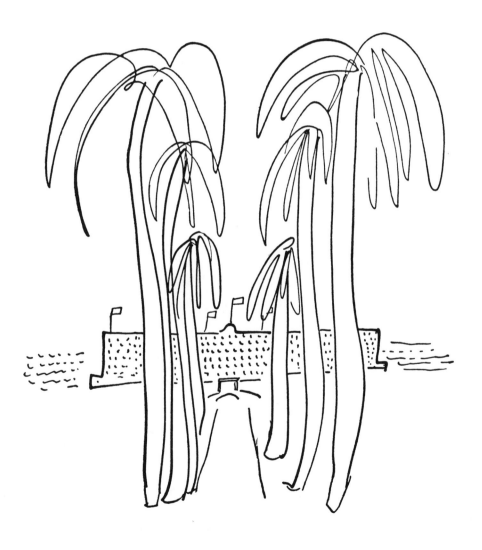

Contributions by
Bemelmans to Anthologies
Edited by Others

SECTION "F" CONTAINS anthologizations of Ludwig Bemelmans' material. The anthologies are listed in alphabetical order according to title, with subsidiary listings for reprints or subsequent editions. Although from some points of view this is an eccentric way of listing anthologies it is in keeping with the overall aim of this book, which is to permit a reader holding a volume containing Bemelmans' work to determine the placement of that volume in the general oeuvre.

The researching of anthologization is taxing at best. There are only two primary catalogued sources of information, the not very thorough *Essay and General Literature Index* and whatever rather spotty references one may find in the *Readers' Guide to Periodical Literature*. Only about five of the numerous pieces

listed in this section are referred to in either of these. The researcher is therefore left to hunt through what anthologies of prose, humor, or topical material can be found on the shelves of libraries and antiquarian booksellers.

F1. Adventures for Readers [1963]

"Dog Overboard," in Elizabeth C. O'Daly and Egbert W. Nieman, eds., *Adventures for Readers: Book Two*, New York: Harcourt, Brace and World, 1958, pp. 118-129. Reprinted 1963 and 1968. With six illustrations by the author.

This piece appeared in *Father, Dear Father*, A11, as "Little Bit and the *America*." See also E145.

F2. All-Star Cast [1947]

"My First Actress," in Sally Deutsch, ed., *All-Star Cast: A Footlight Anthology*, Chicago: Ziff-Davis Publishing Co., and Toronto: Ambassador Books, 1947, pp. 5-9.

The story appeared originally in *Stage* magazine; see E14; and subsequently in *Theatre Arts*; see E117. [*Copy examined:* The University of Toronto Library]

F3. American Authors Today [1947]

"The Valet of the Splendide," in Whit Burnett and Charles E. Slatkin, eds., *American Authors Today*, Boston and New York: Ginn and Company, 1947, pp. 155-163. There is a photograph of Ludwig Bemelmans by Fred Stein, as well as an editors' blurb and nine study questions.

The story appeared originally as "My Valet Lustgarten" in *Hotel Splendide*, A18. [*Copy examined:* Toronto Public Library]

F4. Bedside Tales [1945]

"Watch the Birdie," in Peter Arno, ed., *The Bedside Tales*, New York: William Penn Publishing Company, 1945, pp. 11-20. [The spine reads TUDOR.]

The story appeared originally in *The New Yorker*, June 6, 1942; see E71; and was reprinted in *I Love You. I Love You. I Love You*, A21. [*Copy examined:* Joint Fiction Reserve, Barrie Public Library, Barrie, Ontario]

F5. Best American Short Stories [1942]

"The Valet of the Splendide," in Martha Foley, ed., *The Best American Short Stories 1942*, Boston: Houghton Mifflin Co. and Toronto: Allen, 1942, pp. 19-27.

The story appeared originally in *The New Yorker*, October 11, 1941; see E62. As "My Valet Lustgarten" it was part of *Hotel Splendide*, A18. [*Copy examined:* The University of Toronto Library]

F6. Best of Both Worlds [1968]

"Little Bit and the *America*," in Georgess McHargue, comp., *The Best of Both Worlds: An Anthology of Stories for All Ages*, Garden City, N.Y.: Doubleday, 1968, pp. [162] - 181. With one black design by Paul Bacon.

The story appeared originally in *Father, Dear Father*, A11. [*Copy examined:* Library of Congress]

F7. Best of Modern Humor [1951]

a. *First edition:* "The Homesick Bus-Boy," in P. G. Wodehouse and Scott Meredith, eds., *The Best of Modern Humor*, New York: Medill McBride Company Inc., 1951, pp. 170-180.

"The Homesick Bus-Boy" appeared originally in *The New Yorker*, November 9, 1940; see E46; and was part of *Hotel Splendide*, A18. It was reprinted in *Hotel Bemelmans*, A17. No illustrations. [*Copy examined:* Boston Public Library]

b. *Reprint:* "The Homesick Bus-Boy," in P. G. Wodehouse and Scott Meredith, eds., *The Best of Modern Humor*, New York: Metcalf Associates, Inc. (Formerly Medill McBride Co., Inc.), 1952, pp. 170-179. No illustrations. [*Copy examined:* Boston Public Library]

F8. Caldecott Medal Books [1957]

"And So Madeline Was Born," in Bertha Mahony Miller and Elinor Whitney Field, eds., *Caldecott Medal Books, 1938-1957, with the Artist's Acceptance Papers and Related Material Chiefly from* the *Horn Book Magazine*, *Horn Book Papers*, Vol. 2, Boston: Horn Book, 1957, pp. 254-265. See as well E163.

F₉. Caravan of Music Stories
[1947]

"Putzi," in Noah Daniel Fabricant and Heinz Werner, eds., *A Caravan of Music Stories by the World's Great Authors*, New York: Frederick Fell, Inc. and Toronto: Saunders, 1947, pp. 49-54.

The story appeared originally as "Inside, Outside" in *Story*, October 1936; see E4. It was part of *Small Beer*, A39. [*Copy examined:* Toronto Public Library]

F₁₀. Carnival of Modern Humor
[1967]

a. *First edition:* "The Ballet Visits the Splendide's Magician," in P. G. Wodehouse and Scott Meredith, eds., *A Carnival of Modern Humor*, New York: The Dial Press, 1967, pp. 7-13. A Delacorte Press Book.

The story appeared originally in *The New Yorker*, July 6, 1940; see E39; and was part of *Hotel Splendide*, A18. [*Copy examined:* York University Library]

b. *British edition:* "The Ballet Visits the Splendide's Magician," in P. G. Wodehouse and Scott Meredith, eds., *A Carnival of Modern Humour*, London: Herbert Jenkins, 1968, pages unknown.

F₁₁. City of Love
[1955]

"My English Suit in Paris," in Daniel Talbot, ed., *City of Love: Stories of the Gaiety, the Excitement, the Spirit of Paris*, New York: Dell Publishing Co., 1955, pp. 78-88. With four black illustrations by the author.

The story appeared originally in *Small Beer*, A39.

F₁₂. Dogs
[1964]

"Dog Story," in Florence K. Peterson, ed., *Dogs: Heroes, Adventurers, Friends; A Collection of 30 Outstanding Stories*, with Foreword by Farley Mowat, New York: Platt and Munk, 1964, pp. 98-106.

There is one black illustration by Hamilton Greene.

The story appeared originally in *The New Yorker*, August 12, 1939, see E27 and also A43. [*Copy examined:* Library of Congress]

F13. Empire City [1955]

"In Defense and Praise of Brooklyn: II," in Alexander Klein, ed., *The Empire City: A Treasury of New York*, New York and Toronto: Rinehart and Co. Inc., 1955, pp. 156-157.

The story, which is paired here with another piece about Brooklyn by Truman Capote, originally appeared in *Father, Dear Father*, A11. [*Copy examined:* Toronto Public Library]

F14. 55 Short Stories [1949]

a. *First edition:* "The Ballet Visits the Splendide's Magician," in The New Yorker Magazine, *55 Short Stories from The New Yorker*, New York: Simon and Schuster, 1949, pp. 80-85.

The story appeared originally in *The New Yorker*, July 6, 1940; see E39; and was part of

Hotel Splendide, A18. [*Copy examined:* The University of Toronto Library]

b. *British edition:* "The Ballet Visits the Splendide's Magician," in The New Yorker Magazine, *55 Short Stories from The New Yorker*, London: Victor Gollancz and Toronto: Musson, 1952, pages unknown.

F15. Fireside Treasury [1963]

a. *First edition:* "The Homesick Bus Boy," in Scott Meredith, ed., *The Fireside Treasury of Modern Humor*, New York: Simon and Schuster, 1963, pp. 113-118.

The story appeared originally in *The New Yorker*, November 9, 1940; see E46; and *Hotel Splendide*, A18, and was reprinted in *Hotel Bemelmans*, A17. [*Copy examined:* MP]

b. *British edition:* "The Homesick Bus Boy," in Scott Meredith, ed., *The Fireside Treasury of Modern Humour*, London: Hamish Hamilton, 1964, pages unknown.

F16. Firsts of the Famous [1962]

a. *First edition:* "Theodore and the Blue Danube," in Whit Burnett, ed., *Firsts of the Famous*, New York: Ballantine Books, 1962, pp. 20-28. Ballantine Books No. F598. With fifteen black illustrations by the author. A note about Ludwig Bemelmans is on p. 19.

The story first appeared in *Story*, May 1936, see E2, and is also to be found in *Small Beer*, A39. [*Copy examined:* Library of Congress]

b. *Dutch edition:* "Theodore en De Blauwe Donau," in Whit Burnett, ed., *Zo begonnen ze*, Amsterdam: M. M. Meulenhoff, 1964, pp. 25-33. Meulenhoff Pockets No. 142. With 13 black illustrations by the author. [*Copy examined:* Stadsbibliotheek Haarlem]

F17. Food for Thought [1987]

"Pêche Melba" excerpts, in Joan and John Digby, eds., *Food for Thought*, New York: William Morrow and Co. Inc., 1987, pp. 439-440. The material first appeared in *Are You Hungry Are You Cold*, A1. [*Copy examined:* Mrs. Madeleine Bemelmans]

F18. French Collection [1975]

"Gala at the Tour d'Argent," in Playboy Magazine, *The French Collection*, Chicago: Playboy Press, 1975, pp. 126-144.

The story appeared first in *Playboy*, December 1962; see E197. [*Copy examined:* Mrs. Madeleine Bemelmans]

F19. Great Stories about Show Business [1957]

"Dear General, What a Surprise!," in Jerry D. Lewis, ed., *Great Stories About Show Business*, New York: Coward-McCann, Inc., 1957, pp. 9-16.

The story first appeared in *Town & Country*, August 1939; see E24; as well as *Small Beer*, A39. [*Copy examined:* The University of Toronto Library]

F20. Home Book of Christmas [1941]

"About Three Kings, Uncle Herman's Uniform and Christmas Night in the Tyrol," in May Lamberton Becker, ed., *The Home Book of Christmas*, New York: Dodd Mead & Co., 1941, pp. 519-522.

The material first appeared in *Hansi*, A14. [*Copy examined:* Toronto Public Library]

F21. Humorous Short Stories [1960]

"Little Bit and the 'America,' " in Greta A. Clark, comp., *Humorous Short Stories*, New York: Hart Publishing Company, Inc., 1960, pp. 31-46. With one black drawing, unattributed, not by Bemelmans. The story appeared originally in *Father, Dear Father*, A11. [*Copy examined:* MP.]

F22. I Am an American [1941]

"I am an American," in Robert Spiers Benjamin, ed., *I am an American by Famous Naturalized Americans*, New York: Alliance Book Corporation and Toronto: Ambassador Books, 1941, pp. 169-176. "This book had its origin in broadcasts . . . given on a program prepared by the Immigration and Naturalization Service of the United States Department of Justice."

F23. Laughing Space [1982]

"Putzi," in Isaac Asimov and J. O. Jeppson, eds., *Laughing Space: Funny Science Fiction*, Boston: Houghton Mifflin Co., 1982, pp. 100-104.

The story first appeared as "Inside, Outside" in *Story*, October 1936; see E4. It was part of *Small Beer*, A39. [*Copy examined:* The University of Toronto Library]

F24. Majority [1952]

"The Animal Waiter," and "Art at the Hotel Splendide," in *Majority 1931-1952: An Anthology of 21 Years of Publishing*, by the editors at Hamish Hamilton, London: Hamish Hamilton, 1952, pp. 881-893.

The material first appeared, respectively, in *Boston Herald News Week* and *Oregon Journal News Week* for July 21, 1946; see E93 and E94; and *The New Yorker*, June 1, 1940; see E36; and was part of *Hotel Splendide*, see A18d.

F25. Murder [1948]

"Murderer of the Splendide," in James Sandoe, ed., *Murder: Plain & Fanciful with Some Milder Malefactions*, New York: Sheridan House and Toronto: McLeod, 1948, pp. 364-374.

The story first appeared in *The New Yorker*, November 29, 1941; see E64; and was part of *Hotel Splendide*, A18. [*Copy examined:* Toronto Public Library]

F26. Normandie [1985]

"Souvenir" excerpt, in Harvey Ardman, *Normandie Her Life and Times*, New York and Toronto: Franklin Watts, 1985, pp. 231-233.

The material first appeared in *Vogue*, June 1, 1942 as "Souvenir: Memory of the Normandie, the 'Femme Fatale' of Ships"; see E70; and as "Souvenir" was part of *I Love You, I Love You, I Love You*, A21. [*Copy examined:* Mrs. Madeleine Bemelmans]

F27. Opinions and Attitudes [1948]

"Quito," in Stewart Morgan, ed., *Opinions and Attitudes in the Twentieth Century*, New York: The Ronald Press Company, 1948, pp. 231-243.

The material has not been examined but is most likely from *The Donkey Inside*, A8.

F28. Pageant of American Humor [1948]

"The Murderer of the Splendide," in Edwin Seaver, ed., *Pageant of American Humor*, Cleveland and New York: The World Publishing Company, 1948, pp. 472-483.

The story first appeared in *The New Yorker*, November 29, 1941, see E64 and *Hotel Splendide*, A18. [*Copy examined:* Toronto Public Library]

F29. Pause to Wonder [1944]

" 'No Trouble at All' " and "Sacre du Printemps," in Marjorie Fischer and Rolfe Humphries, eds., *Pause to Wonder: Stories of the Marvelous Mysterious and Strange*, New York: Julian Messner Inc. and Toronto: Smithers, 1944, pp. 455-461.

" 'No Trouble at All' " first appeared in *Vogue*, March 1, 1937; see E5; and later in *Town & Country*, June 1957; see E175. "Sacre du Printemps" first appeared in *Story*, June 1937 and *Story*, May-June 1941; see E7 and E56 respectively. Both were part of *Small Beer*, A39.

F30. Reading I've Liked [1941]

a. *First edition:* "Putzi," in Clifton Fadiman, *Reading I've Liked*, New York: Simon and Schuster and Toronto: Musson, 1941, reprinted 1943, pp. 22-29.

The story first appeared as "Inside, Outside" in *Story*, October 1936; see E4. It was part of *Small Beer*, A39.

b. *British edition:* "Putzi," in Clifton Fadiman, *Reading I've Liked*, London: Hamish Hamilton, 1946, pages unknown.

F31. Story Jubilee [1965]

a. *First edition:* "Inside, Outside," in Whit and Hallie Burnett, eds., *Story Jubilee*, Garden City, N.Y.: Doubleday and Co. Inc., 1965, pp. 50-54.

Under this title the story first appeared in *Story*, October 1936, see E4. As "Putzi," it appeared in *Small Beer*, A39. [*Copy examined:* MP]

b. *British edition:* "Inside, Outside," in Whit and Hallie Burnett, eds., *Story Jubilee*, London: Souvenir Press, 1965, pages unknown.

c. *British reprint:* "Inside, Outside," in Whit and Hallie Burnett, eds., *Story Jubilee*, London: Trans-world Publishers, 1967, pages unknown. Corgi Books No. EN7620.

F32. Story Pocket Book [n.d.]

"Sacre du Printemps," in Whit Burnett, ed., *The Story Pocket Book*, New York: Pocket Books, n.d., pp. 133-140. This is Pocket Book No. 276. Probably 1945.

The story first appeared in *Story*, June 1937, and *Story*, May-June 1941; see E7 and E56, and in *Small Beer*, A39. [*Copy examined:* MP]

F33. Subtreasury of American Humor [1945]

a. *First edition:* "The Ballet Visits the Splendide's Magician," in E. B. White and Katharine S. White, eds., *A Subtreasury of American Humor*, New York: Tudor Publishing Co. and Toronto: Musson, 1945, pp. 799-804.

The story first appeared in *The New Yorker*, July 6, 1940; see E39; and in *Hotel Splendide*, A18.

b. *Reprint:* "The Ballet Visits the Splendide's Magician," in E. B. White and Katharine S. White, eds., *A Subtreasury of American Humor*, New York: Modern Library and Toronto: Random House Canada, 1948, pages unknown.

F34. Tales of Christmas [1963]

"Christmas Eve in the Tyrolean Alps," in Herbert H. Wernecke, ed., *Tales of Christmas From Near and Far*, Philadelphia: The Westminster Press and Toronto: Ryerson Press, 1963, pp. 7-10.

The story appeared earlier in *Told Under the Christmas Tree*, © 1950 by The Macmillan Co., see F38. [*Copy examined:* Toronto Public Library]

F35. This Is My Best [1942]

a. *First edition:* "Sacre du Printemps," in Whit Burnett, ed., *This Is My Best*, New York: Burton C. Hoffman—The Dial Press, 1942, pp. 878-885. With six black illustrations by the author. Includes a blurb entitled, "Why He Selected 'Sacre du Printemps' ".

The story first appeared in *Story*, June 1937 and *Story*, May-June 1941; see E7 and E56. [*Copy examined*: MP]

b. *Reprint*: "Sacre du Printemps," in Whit Burnett, ed., *This Is My Best*, Garden City, N.Y.: Garden City Publishing Co. and Toronto: Blue Ribbon Books, 1944, pages unknown.

c. *Second edition*: "Sacre du Printemps," in Whit Burnett, ed., *This Is My Best*, Cleveland: The World Publishing Company, 1944, pages unknown.

F36. This Is My Best Humor [1955]

a. *First edition*: "Inside, Outside," in Whit Burnett, ed., *This Is My Best Humor*, New York: The Dial Press, 1955, pp. 353-364. With fourteen black illustrations by the author.

The material first appeared in *Story*, October 1936; see E4. As "Putzi" it was part of *Small Beer*, A39.

b. *Abridged edition*: "Inside, Outside," in Whit Burnett, ed., *This Is My Funniest (An Abridged Edition)*, New York: Perma Books (Pocket Books), 1957, pp. 116-127. With fourteen black illustrations by the author.

F37. Time to Be Young [1945]

"Camp Nomopo," in Whit Burnett, ed., *Time To Be Young: Great Stories of the Growing Years*, Philadelphia and New York: J. B. Lippincott Co., and Toronto: Longmans, 1945, pp. 81-86.

This story first appeared in *Town & Country*, July 1942 as "Little Girl with a Headache [Camp No Mo Pie]"; see E72; and as "Camp Nomopo" was part of *I Love You, I Love You, I Love You*, A21.

F38. Told Under the Christmas Tree [1948]

"Christmas Eve in the Tyrol," in Literature Committee for the Association for Childhood Education International, *Told Under the Christmas Tree*, New York: Macmillan, 1948, pp. 200-205. With one black illustration by the author.

This story first appeared in *Hansi*, A14.

F39. Treasury of Laughter [1946]

"The Elephant Cutlet," in Louis Untermeyer, ed., *A Treasury of Laughter*, New York: Simon and Schuster and Toronto: Musson, 1946, pp. 34-36. Includes a biography of Ludwig Bemelmans on p. 34.

The story first appeared in *My War With the United States*, A33. See also A9. [*Copy examined:* Toronto Public Library]

F40. Treasury of Short Stories [1947]

"Sacre du Printemps," in Bernardine Kielty, ed., *A Treasury of Short Stories*, New York: Simon and Schuster and Toronto: Musson, 1947, pp. 729-732.

The story first appeared in *Story*, June 1937 and *Story*, May-June 1941; see E7 and E56; and was part of *Small Beer*, A39. [*Copy examined:* Library of Congress]

F41. Vogue's First Reader [1942]

a. *First edition:* "Souvenir," "I Love You—I Love You—I Love You," "Chile Con Amore," " 'No Trouble at All' ", and "Splendide Apartment," in Frank Crowninshield, ed., *Vogue's First Reader*, New York: Julian Messner, 1942, pp. 61-69; 194-198; 240-245; 403-410; and 503-508.

"Souvenir" appeared originally in *Vogue*, June 1, 1942, as "Souvenir: Memory of the Normandie, the 'Femme Fatale' of Ships"; see E70; and, as "Souvenir," was part of *I Love You, I Love You, I Love You*, A21. "I Love You—I Love You—I Love You" appeared originally in *Vogue*, June 1, 1940; see E38; and was part of *I Love You, I Love You, I Love You*, A21. "Chile Con Amore" appeared originally as "Chile con Amore: A Sentimental Journey from Valparaiso to Quito" in *Vogue*, April 1, 1938; see E13; and as a portion of "The Boots of General Altamir Pereira" appeared in *The Donkey Inside*, A8. " 'No Trouble at All' " appeared originally in *Vogue*, March 1, 1937; see E5; was reprinted in *Town & Country*, June 1957; see E175; and was part of *Small Beer*, A39. And "Splendide Apartment" appeared originally as "Ludwig Bemelmans' Splendide Apartment" in *Vogue*, April 1, 1942; see E69. [*Copy examined:* MP]

b. *British edition:* "Souvenir," "I Love You—I Love You—I Love You," "Chile Con Amore," " 'No Trouble at All' ", and "Splendide Apartment," in Frank Crowninshield, ed., *Vogue's First Reader*, London: Hammond, Hammond & Company Limited, 1944, pp. 45-51; 149-151; 183-187; 309-314; and 385-389.

c. *Limited British edition:* "Souvenir," "I Love You—I Love You—I Love You," "Chile Con Amore," " 'No Trouble at All' ", and "Splendide Apartment," in Frank Crowninshield, ed., *Vogue's First Reader*, London: Hammond, Hammond & Company Limited, 1944, pp. 45-51; 149-151; 183-187; 309-314; and 385-389.

d. *Reprint:* "Souvenir," "I Love You—I Love You—I Love You," "Chile Con Amore," " 'No Trouble at All' ", and "Splendide Apartment," in Frank Crowninshield, ed., *Vogue's First Reader*, Garden City, N.Y.: Halcyon House and Toronto: Blue Ribbon Books, 1944, pp. 61-69; 194-198; 240-245; 403-410; and 503-508.

e. *Australian edition:* "Souvenir," "I Love You—I Love You—I Love You," "Chile Con Amore," " 'No Trouble at All' ", and "Splendide Apartment," in Frank Crowninshield, ed., *Vogue's First Reader*, Victoria: Georgian House and Toronto: Smithers, 1944, pages unknown.

F42. Week-end Book [1952]

a. *First edition:* "Herr Otto Brauhaus," in P. G. Wodehouse and Scott Meredith, eds., *The Week-End Book of Humor*, New York: Ives Washburn, 1952, pp. [190]-199.

The story first appeared in *Life Class*, A23. [*Copy examined:* York University Library]

b. *British edition:* "Herr Otto Brauhaus," in P. G. Wodehouse and Scott Meredith, eds., *The Week-End Book of Humour*, London: Herbert Jenkins, 1954, pages unknown.

c. *British reprint:* "Herr Otto Brauhaus," in P. G. Wodehouse and Scott Meredith, eds., *The Week-End Book of Humour*, London: World Distributors, 1960, pp. 202-211.

d. *Second American edition:* "Herr Otto Brauhaus," in P. G. Wodehouse, ed., *P. G. Wodehouse Selects the Best of Humor*, New York: Grosset & Dunlap, 1965, pp. 202-211.

e. *Reprint:* "Herr Otto Brauhaus," in P. G. Wodehouse and Scott Meredith, eds., *The Week-End Book of Humor*, Freeport: Books for Libraries Press, 1971, pp. 190-199.

F43. World of Business [1962]

"The Elephant Cutlet," in Edward C. Bursk, ed., *The World of Business, Vol. III*, New York: Simon and Schuster, 1962, pp. 1873-1874.

The story first appeared in *My War With the United States*, A33. It appeared as well in *Town & Country*; see E9. See also A9. [*Copy examined:* Mrs. Madeleine Bemelmans]

F44. World's Shortest Stories [1961]

"The Buttermachine," in Richard Gibson Hubler, ed., *The World's Shortest Stories: An Anthology*, New York: Duell, Sloan and Pearce, 1961, pp. 54-56.

The story first appeared in *My War With the United States*, A33.

Illustrations by Bemelmans

Illustrations by Bemelmans

S<small>ECTION</small> "G" <small>IS A LISTING OF</small> Bemelmans' illustrative work, including (a) magazine covers, (b) illustrations from his own works published in magazines in another context, (c) editorial illustrations, (d) illustrations for works authored by others, (e) advertising work, (f) cartoons, and (g) illustrative ephemera. I have tried to be as descriptive as possible where images were available to me, but there is no way to use words to capture the vivacity of Ludwig Bemelmans' visual style. If he referred to himself once as a "daffy Dufy" it is surely also possible to detect the influence of Vlaminck, of Matisse, of Klee, of Modigliani, even strains of the Katzenjammer Kids.

I. MAGAZINE COVER
ILLUSTRATIONS
BY LUDWIG BEMELMANS

G1. for Gastronome

A drawing from *La Bonne Table*, C1, was used as the cover of the Autumn 1990, Vol. XII No. 2, issue of *Gastronome*.

G2. for Holiday

a. The issue of *May, 1951:*
A full-page full-color drawing of an alfresco party in the country. A Great Dane sleeps in the foreground. (*Copy examined:* MP.)

   b. The issue of *December, 1952:*
A street corner Santa Claus is using his pocket lighter to ignite the cigarette of a shopper burdened with Christmas presents. This is one of the series of Santas originally intended for inclusion with *The Borrowed Christmas*, included with this issue with other Santas and later published as A5. (*Copy examined:* Toronto Public Library.)

   c. The issue of *September, 1955:*
Gammelstrand Fish market, Copenhagen. Included are the steeple of Nikolai Church, the equestrian statue of Bishop Absalon, fishwives, Danish housewives doing the shopping, and perky sea gulls. (*Copy examined:* Toronto Public Library.)

   d. The issue of *December, 1957:*
Five small full-color drawings titled, from top, "North America" (children carolling at a church in the woods in a snowfall), "Asia" (street musicians and palms), "North Europe" (a sleigh-ride among wintry pines), "Latin America" (street musicians with monkey, and mountains in distance) and "The Mediterranean" (shepherd with sheep). See as well G21. (*Copy examined:* MP.)

   e. The issue of *August, 1961:*
A reduced color drawing of Madeline and Pepito on horse- back. (*Copy examined:* MP.)

   f. The issue of *August, 1962:*
Motorists are driving all sorts of vehicles in every direction and going nowhere. (*Copy examined:* MP.)

G3. for The New York Herald Tribune Magazine

The issue of *October 7, 1959:*

   A color reproduction of a painting included in the Museum of the City of New York "Bemelmans' New York" show. See I16.

G4. for The New Yorker

Except for G4z, G4ee, and G4ff, the titles of the drawings were provided by *The New Yorker*. The descriptions are paraphrased from descriptions provided to the author by *The New Yorker*. All of these covers are reproduced in *The Complete Book of Covers of The New Yorker 1925-1989*, New York: Alfred A. Knopf, 1989.

a. The issue of *March 21, 1942:* "Child at Blackboard." A child is drawing planes in combat, instead of ABCs, at a blackboard. We see flaming Stukas and American pursuit models. (*Copy examined: The New Yorker.*)

b. The issue of *January 2, 1943:* "New Year's Eve (Morning After)." Party hats and balloons are strewn around a night spot being put together again by waiters. (*Copy examined: The New Yorker.*)

c. The issue of *March 6, 1943:* "Italian Restaurant." Typical Italian restaurant interior with a very prominent American flag. (*Copy examined: The New Yorker.*)

d. The issue of *June 12, 1943:* "Bird Sanctuary (Zoo)." A sanctuary attendant is feeding a tropical bird. (*Copy examined: The New Yorker.*)

e. The issue of *August 21, 1943:* "Camp for Girls." A flag is being raised in front of little girls in formation. (*Copy examined: The New Yorker.*)

f. The issue of *October 16, 1943:* "Restaurant." All the tables are empty but one. A waiter dozes behind a screen, at an elegant table from which fabulous food has been eaten. (*Copy examined: The New Yorker.*)

g. The issue of *November 6, 1943:* "Hunting and Fishing." A man fishes, surrounded by wild game; another man hunts, surrounded by choice fish. (*Copy examined: The New Yorker.*)

h. The issue of *March 25, 1944:* "Nightclub (Restaurant)." Waiters are buzzing around a crowded restaurant with menus and tables held high. (*Copy examined: The New Yorker.*)

i. The issue of *April 8, 1944:* "Circus." A clown is tying a bow tie on his dog. We see seals and the world's tallest man as well. (*Copy examined: The New Yorker.*)

j. The issue of *May 11, 1946:* "Wedding cake." A chef decorates a huge wedding cake. (*Copy examined: The New Yorker.*) This illustration originated as a black-and-white drawing in *Small Beer*, A39, and was later re-drawn in color by the artist for this cover. It became the jacket illustration for *Hotel Bemelmans*, A17.

k. The issue of *July 13, 1946:* "Beach scene." A crowd on the sand. (*Copy examined: The New Yorker.*)

l. The issue of *May 10, 1947:* "Ocean voyage." Stewards deliver bouillon to seasick travellers. (*Copy examined: The New Yorker.*)

m. The issue of *January 3, 1948:*
"New Year's Eve at a nightclub." In the foreground a waiter holds out a check. (*Copy examined: The New Yorker.*)

n. The issue of *July 3, 1948:*
"Coney Island." A hot dog stand. (*Copy examined: The New Yorker.*)

o. The issue of *May 28, 1949:*
"Boats in dry dock." Boat owners are living on the boats, not on land: some picnic, some clean, some paint. (*Copy examined: The New Yorker.*)

p. The issue of *July 30, 1949:*
"Girl campers." Girls are being read to by a counsellor as they sit around the cabin fireplace. (*Copy examined: The New Yorker.*)

q. The issue of *April 1, 1950:*
"Mural being painted on wall of Italian restaurant." The proprietor, his wife and a waiter look on in admiration. (*Copy examined: The New Yorker.*)

r. The issue of *June 24, 1950:*
"Paris street scene." A man and woman from New York are getting a traffic ticket. (*Copy examined: The New Yorker.*)

s. The issue of *November 25, 1950:*
"Chefs and waitresses in the kitchen of a restaurant on Thanksgiving Day." One chef carves a turkey. (*Copy examined: The New Yorker.*)

t. The issue of *March 24, 1951:*
"Greenhouse." In a greenhouse full of Easter plants and flowers a man is preparing to turn on sprays. (*Copy examined: The New Yorker.*)

u. The issue of *June 9, 1951:*
"Steamship sailing." Crowd on dock waving farewell. (*Copy examined: The New Yorker.*)

v. The issue of *January 3, 1953:*
"New Year's Eve." Waiters in a nightclub blowing up balloons and setting out party favors for the evening's clientèle. (*Copy examined: The New Yorker.*)

w. The issue of *March 6, 1954:*
"Nightclub pianist." He is spotlit in a crowded nightclub. (*Copy examined: The New Yorker.*)

x. The issue of *June 26, 1954:*
"Foreign-looking restaurant." The tables are outdoors under an arbor of grapes. Waiters serve; desserts wait on a stand. (*Copy examined: The New Yorker.*)

y. The issue of *October 9, 1954:*
"Horseback riding." Instructor with small children on horseback in Central Park. (*Copy examined: The New Yorker.*)

z. The issue of *February 5, 1955:*
"Ski slope." Skiers going in every direction at a crowded slope. (*Copy examined: The New Yorker.*)

aa. The issue of *March 12, 1955:*
"Riding school." Children of many ages riding around a ring. (*Copy examined: The New Yorker.*)

bb. The issue of *November 26, 1955:*
"Thanksgiving dinner." Dinner is served in a restaurant. (*Copy examined: The New Yorker.*)

cc. The issue of *November 10, 1956:*
"Seals in the Central Park Zoo." It is raining. A keeper is throwing fish to the seals. (*Copy examined: The New Yorker.*)

dd. The issue of *October 3, 1959:*
"Grant's Tomb." Part of the George Washington Bridge is in the background. (*Copy examined: The New Yorker.*)

ee. The issue of *June 11, 1960:*
"Restaurant." Very colorful interior. (*Copy examined: The New Yorker.*)

ff. The issue of *August 25, 1962:*
"Chef." A chef prepares a chicken next to an attractive young woman. (*Copy examined: The New Yorker.*)

G5. for Story

The issue of *March-April, 1963* (No. 2 Vol. 36):
A Normandy gypsy with her dog. This is described as possibly one of Bemelmans' last paintings in a brief reminiscence on p. 128, which also includes the black drawing from the chapter, "I have always wanted to meet a humorist," from *The Literary Life and the Hell With It* by Whit Burnett, editor of *Story*. (*Copy examined: MP*)

G6. for Theatre Arts

The issue of *March, 1947:*
A very plump diner sips champagne while a disgruntled chef and waiter look on. From *Now I Lay Me Down to Sleep*, A34. (*Copy examined: MP.*)

G7. for Town & Country

a. The issue of *January, 1938:*
Winter scene, with horse-drawn carriage loaded with skis, and a trudging man with a riding crop. (*Copy examined: Town & Country.*)

b. The issue of *February, 1940:*
The hallway of a grand hotel, with shoes outside the doors. (*Copy examined: Town & Country.*)

c. The issue of *February, 1942:*
A winter scene in the mountains, with a little railway station and a beaming sun. (*Copy examined: Town & Country.*)

d. The issue of *June, 1942:*
From a hotel bedroom with flowered wall-paper, an armchair and a bed with a "Buy War Bonds" leaflet on the coverlet we look through an open window at a battleship upon the waves and an aircraft caught in searchlight beams. (*Copy examined: New York Public Library.*)

e. The issue of *February, 1951:*
A snowfall is upon New York and two affluent

lovers snuggle in a Model-T. (*Copy examined:* New York Public Library.)

f. The issue of *December, 1960:*
A jet aircraft hovers by moonlight over a European city with a prominent cathedral, a Christmas tree, and a child being born in a manger. (*Copy examined: Town & Country.*)

II. ILLUSTRATIONS BY LUDWIG BEMELMANS FROM HIS OWN WORKS

G8. from The Blue Danube

Illustrations from *The Blue Danube*, A4, in *Studio*, Vol. 141, March 1951, p. 77.

G9. from Father, Dear Father

A black reproduction of the cover illustration from *Father, Dear Father*, A11, in *American Artist*, Vol. 18 No. 1, January 1954, p. 33.

G10. from Hansi

Illustrations from *Hansi*, A14, in *Design*, Vol. 53, November 1951, p. 32.

G11. from Madeline

a. One black illustration from *Madeline*, A24, in *Parnassus*, Vol. 11 No. 7, November 1939, p. 40.
b. Endpapers from the *Madeline* series, in *Graphis*, Vol. 11 No. 61, 1955, p. 412.

G12. from Madeline's Rescue

One black illustration from *Madeline's Rescue*, A30, in *Art News*, Vol. 53 No. 8, December 1954, p. 44.

G13. from Now I Lay Me Down To Sleep

A black and white reproduction of the book jacket illustration from *Now I Lay Me Down to Sleep*, A34, in *American Artist*, Vol. 12 No. 4, April 1948, p. 51.

G14. from A Tale of Two Glimps

A layout containing five black drawings, the cover illustration and four inside drawings, from

A Tale of Two Glimps, A42, in *Graphis*, Vol. 5 No. 26, 1949, pp. 140-141. (*Copy examined:* Toronto Public Library)

III. EDITORIAL ILLUSTRATIONS BY LUDWIG BEMELMANS

G15. "The Bookshelf" [1950]

a. A black drawing of four pigeons for the anonymous column, "The Bookshelf," *Theatre Arts*, Vol. 34 No. 7, July 1950, p. 9. (*Copy examined:* Toronto Public Library)

b. A black drawing of four pigeons for the anonymous column, "The Bookshelf," *Theatre Arts*, Vol. 34 No. 8, August 1950, p. 11. (*Copy examined:* Toronto Public Library)

G16. "Endpapers" [1936-1938]

a. Editorial illustrations for the editors' "Endpapers," *Story*, Vol. 8 No. 44, March 1936, pp. 4, 6, 97 and 100. (*Copy examined:* Toronto Public Library)

b. Editorial illustrations for the editors' "Endpapers," *Story*, Vol. 8 No. 45, April 1936, pp. 4-15. (*Copy examined:* Toronto Public Library)

c. Editorial illustrations for the editors' "Endpapers," *Story*, Vol. 9 No. 48, July 1936, p. 4. From *The Literary Life and the Hell With It* by Whit Burnett, editor of *Story*. (*Copy examined:* Toronto Public Library)

d. Editorial illustrations for the editors' "Endpapers," *Story*, Vol. 9 No. 49, August 1936, p. 5. From *The Literary Life and the Hell With It* by Whit Burnett, editor of *Story*. (*Copy examined:* Toronto Public Library)

e. Editorial illustrations for the editors' "Endpapers," *Story*, Vol. 9 No. 50, September 1936, pp. 2-6. From *The Literary Life and the Hell With It* by Whit Burnett, editor of *Story*. (*Copy examined:* Toronto Public Library)

f. Editorial illustrations for the editors' "Endpapers," *Story*, Vol. 12 No. 69, April 1938, p. 5. From *The Literary Life and the Hell With It* by Whit Burnett, editor of *Story*, "A couple of haggises in amorous dalliance as drawn by Captain Bone." (*Copy examined:* Toronto Public Library)

Note: A very Bemelmansian illustration of a man with an umbrella walking with a woman, in *Story*, Vol. XII No. 66, January 1938, p. 7, is captioned, "An illustration done by a Russian in the last century for an early Chekhov humorous story, 'The Man in the Case' (and not an illustration by Story's familiar early Bavarian humorist, Ludwig Bemelmans."

G₁₇. "The Literary Scene" [1949]

A black drawing of a dog in a parked car, to illustrate the anonymous, "The Literary Scene," *Theatre Arts*, Vol. 33 No. 8, September 1949, p. 107. (*Copy examined:* Toronto Public Library)

G₁₈. "Theatre Arts Editorial" [1949-1950]

a. A black drawing of a reindeer with menswear upon its antlers, in *Theatre Arts*, Vol. 33 No. 8, September 1949, p. 111. Then, a black drawing of a family on a beach with a dog, on p. 112. (*Copy examined:* Toronto Public Library)

b. A black drawing of a reindeer with menswear upon its antlers, in *Theatre Arts*, Vol. 33 No. 10, November 1949, p. 9. Then, a black drawing of a woman by a window in an opera box on p. 29; a reduced version of the same drawing is on p. 96. (*Copy examined:* Toronto Public Library)

c. A black boxed drawing of a reindeer, in *Theatre Arts*, Vol. 33 No. 11, December 1949, p. 94; with a note on p. 98 that this is the "Rum Reindeer," the one who did not receive a sub-scription to *Theatre Arts*. Then, a black drawing of a dog in a parked car is on p. 96. (*Copy examined:* Toronto Public Library)

d. A black drawing, "Rum Reindeer", in *Theatre Arts*, Vol. 34 No. 2, February 1950, p. 91. Then, a black drawing of a man and a hat check girl is on p. 93. (*Copy examined:* Toronto Public Library)

e. A black drawing of a standing poodle, in *Theatre Arts*, Vol. 34 No. 5, May 1950, p. 8. Then, a black drawing of a waiter holding a flower is on p. 9. (*Copy examined:* Toronto Public Library)

f. A black drawing of a waiter looking cross-eyed at a butterfly, in *Theatre Arts*, Vol. 34 No. 10, October 1950, p. 9. Then, a black drawing of a woman basting a chicken is on p. 91. (*Copy examined:* Toronto Public Library)

g. A black drawing of a lion tamer and his wife with a lion, in *Theatre Arts*, Vol. 34 No. 11, November 1950, p. 91. (*Copy examined:* Toronto Public Library)

h. A black drawing of a lion tamer and his wife with a lion, in *Theatre Arts*, Vol. 34 No. 12, December 1950, p. 93. As in G18g. (*Copy examined:* Toronto Public Library)

G19. "What of the Night" [1939]

a. A black drawing accompanying the "What of the Night" column, *Stage*, March 15, 1939, p. 17. (*Copy examined:* Toronto Public Library)

b. A black drawing accompanying the "What of the Night" column, *Stage*, April 1, 1939, p. 15. (*Copy examined:* Toronto Public Library)

c. A black drawing accompanying the "What of the Night" column, *Stage*, April 15, 1939, p. 17. (*Copy examined:* Toronto Public Library)

d. A black drawing accompanying the "What of the Night" column, *Stage*, May 1, 1939, p. 15. (*Copy examined:* Toronto Public Library)

e. A black drawing accompanying the "What of the Night" column, *Stage*, May 15, 1939, p. 13. (*Copy examined:* Toronto Public Library)

f. A black drawing accompanying the "What of the Night" column, *Stage*, June, 1939, p. 15. (*Copy examined:* Toronto Public Library)

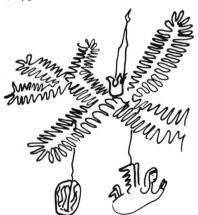

IV. ILLUSTRATIONS BY LUDWIG BEMELMANS FOR WORKS AUTHORED BY OTHERS

G20. "Among My Favorites" [1958]

"Among My Favorites: A Massachusetts Coast Scene by Ludwig Bemelmans," by Eleanor Roosevelt, *Art in America*, Vol. 46, No. 1, Spring 1958, p. 39.

1 black reproduction of a painting by Bemelmans with commentary by Roosevelt. In the "Celebrities Choice" section of the magazine. (*Copy examined:* Robarts Library, University of Toronto)

G21. "A Child's World of Music" [1960]

"A Child's World of Music," by Elizabeth Coatsworth in Elizabeth Coatsworth, *The Children Come Running*, New York: Golden Press, 1960, pp. 82-90.

"The Shepherd's Pipe" on p. 82; "The Sleighbells" on p. 85; "The Organ Grinder" on p. 87;

"The Carol Singers" on p. 88; "Pipes and Drums" on p. 90. See also G1d. These were originally greeting cards for the United Nations Children's Fund. (*Copy examined:* Mrs. Madeleine Bemelmans)

G22. "George of the Ritz" [1958]

"The Secrets of George of the Ritz," as told to A. E. Hotchner, *Town & Country*, Vol. 112, No. 4426, May, 1959, pp. 104-105.

1 full-color illustration. (*Copy examined: Town & Country* Magazine, New York.)

G23. The Literary Life and the Hell With It [1939]

a. First edition:

The Literary Life and the Hell with It by Whit Burnett with Drawings by Bemelmans, New York: Harper Publishers, 1938.

Not seen.

Advertised in *Story*, Vol. XIV No. 75, January-February 1939, p. 1, with the text, "Many pictures by Ludwig Bemelmans".

b. Second edition:

The Literary Life and the Hell with It by Whit Burnett with Drawings by Bemelmans, New York and London: Harper & Brothers Publishers, 1939. Published simultaneously in Canada by Musson.

Whit Burnett was Editor of *Story* magazine. A black drawing of a man in a hammock graces the title page; a sad rose in a flowerpot is on the half-title; a moose peering through a window at a woman on a couch and an Indian chief is on the second half-title; the contents have a picture of a little chapel; and the frontispiece, on verso of second half-title, has a man holding out his hat to another behind a desk, captioned, "I have always wanted to meet a humorist". The endpapers show a man on a hammock. The beige cloth-covered boards are printed in black and red with a man in a hammock, a typewriter, and a smiling sun. "Rocky Mountain Shark" is on page [8]; "Graebisch was unique" is on page [34]; "Hammock Writing," the endpaper drawing, is on page [72]; "Gesellschaftsbuchdruckerei" is on page [116]; "Fourth Avenue" is on page [125]; "Man's initiative over Nature" is on page [159]; "Dr. Irish looked at me curiously" is on page [245]; "Haggi in Amorous Dalliance: Capt. Bone Fecit" is on page [259]. In addition there are 13 more black drawings. (*Copy examined:* Robarts Library, University of Toronto)

G24. Lüchow's German Cookbook [1952]

Lüchow's German Cookbook: The Story and the Favorite Dishes of America's Most Famous German Restaurant, by Jan Mitchell, with an Introduction and Illustrations by Ludwig Bemelmans, Garden City, New York: Doubleday & Company, 1952.

The yellow endpapers are printed with a black drawing of Lüchow's dining room. A black drawing of Lüchow's building is on pp. [18]-[19]. Pages [96]-[97] contain a black drawing of diners in ecstasy. "Bock beer festival" is on pages [210]-[211]. In addition to the above, there are 12 black illustrations by Bemelmans.

Bemelmans' Introduction, "Prosit!" is on pages [11] - 13 and contains one black illustration. The text of the concluding chapter, "The Wines, Beer, and Festivals at Lüchows, or *Down Where the Würzburger Flows*" is completely different from the text of Bemelmans' "Down Where the Würzburger Flows," which appears as a 'new story' in A46 and again, in abbreviated form, in C1.

The dust jacket is printed with "Lüchow's Restaurant on a Sunday Evening," used originally in *Town and Country*, and appearing as well in A8. (*Copy examined:* MP.)

G25. "Ludwig Bemelmans" [1954]

One black illustration from *Hansi*, A14, to illustrate the tribute, "Ludwig Bemelmans," by May Massee, *The Horn Book Magazine*, Vol. 30 No. 4, August, 1954, p. 266.

The article itself runs from p. 263 to p. 269. It is followed by a list of books authored by Bemelmans which is illustrated by a small drawing from *The Castle Number Nine*, A6. The publication of the Massee tribute is inspired by the award to Bemelmans of a Caldecott Award for *Madeline's Rescue*, 1953 (see A30).

G26. "The Man Who Came to Dinner" [1939]

"The Man Who Came to Dinner," by Virginia Faulkner, *Town & Country*, December 1939.

Black line drawings upon red background.

G27. "Minnie and Mr. Clark" [1949]

"Minnie and Mr. Clark," by Robert Downing, *Theatre Arts*, Vol. 33 No. 8, September, 1949, p. 11.

A black drawing of a cat on a rug. There is a reduced version of the same drawing on p. 102. (*Copy examined:* Toronto Public Library)

G28. "Modernist Viewpoint" [1949]

"A Modernist Viewpoint," by Ralph Pearson, *Art Digest*, Vol. 24 October 1, 1949, p. 10.

A drawing of the opera in black.

G29. "Music Al Fresco" [1949]

"Music al Fresco . . .," anon., *Theatre Arts*, Vol. 33 No. 7, August, 1949, p. 4.

A man with a violin case, seen from behind. (*Copy examined:* Toronto Public Library)

G30. "New York Column" [1939]

"Notes for a New York Column," by Katharine Brush, *Stage*, February, 1939, pp. 18-19.

4 black drawings: (*Copy examined:* Toronto Public Library)

G31. Noodle [1937]

a. First edition:

Noodle, Story by Munro Leaf, Pictures by Ludwig Bemelmans, New York: Frederick A. Stokes Company, 1937.

A brown drawing of a dachshund graces the title page. The endpapers show a black poodle and a brown dachshund. The tan cloth-covered boards are stamped in front with a brown and black dachshund. There are 23 additional black and brown drawings, and the dedication on recto of second leaf is garnished with a brown drawing. The brown and black dust jacket is illustrated by Bemelmans. (*Copy examined:* MP)

b. British edition [(1938)]:

Noodle, Story by Munro Leaf, Pictures by Ludwig Bemelmans, London: Hamish Hamilton, 1938. Not seen.

c. Swedish edition [(1940)]:

Snuff, Berättelse av Munro Leaf, Illustrationer av Ludwig Bemelmans, Stockholm: Albert Bonniers Förlag, 1940.

Illustrations as in G31a. (*Copy examined:* The Royal Library, Stockholm)

d. American reprint [(1969)]:

Noodle, Story by Munro Leaf, Pictures by Ludwig Bemelmans, New York: Four Winds Press, 1969.

Illustrations as in G31a. (*Copy examined:* The Free Library of Philadelphia)

e. Swedish reprint [(1989)]:

Snuff, Berättelse av Munro Leaf, Illustrationer av Ludwig Bemelmans, Stockholm: Bonniers Junior Förlag AB, 1989.

Illustrations as in G31a. (*Copy examined:* The Royal Library, Stockholm)

G32. "Now I Lay Me Down to Sleep" [1950]

"Now I Lay Me Down to Sleep," by Elaine Ryan, *Theatre Arts*, Vol. 34 No. 7, July 1950, pp. 57-88.

This is the full reading script of the stage adaptation, H10b, of *Now I Lay Me Down to Sleep*, A34. There are four black illustrations on page 57: a dog, a man sitting on a coffin, a cook reading, and a ship on a bay. Page 58 contains text about the play and about Elaine Ryan, the playwright. The reading text is on pp. 59-88, including repeats of three of the black illustrations: the man on coffin on p. 69, the cook reading on p. 77, the dog on p. 88. (*Copy examined:* Toronto Public Library)

G33. "One on the Isle" [1949]

"One on the Isle," by William A. Leonard, *Theatre Arts*, Vol. 33 No. 8, September, 1949, p. 97.

A begging poodle. (*Copy examined:* Toronto Public Library)

G34. "Razing Cain's" [1938]

"Razing Cain's," by Frank Sullivan, *Stage*, April, 1938, pp. 10-11.

1 black and green illustration. (*Copy examined:* Toronto Public Library)

G35. Review of Madeline and the Bad Hat [1957]

A black illustration of the "Bad Hat" fishing from a roof on p. 295; and another of the "Bad Hat" riding a bicycle on p. 316, to illustrate the anonymous review of *Madeline and the Bad Hat* (see A25). *The Horn Book Magazine*, Vol. 33 No. 4, August 1957. See J389. [*Copy examined:* Toronto Public Library.]

G36. "Tomato Surprise" [1938]

"Tomato Surprise or the Mystery of the French Frogs," by Nina Wilcox Putnam, illustrated by Bemelmans, *Town & Country*, Vol. 93 No. 4188, May 1938, pp. 82-83. With 6 full-color illustrations.

G37. "Twin Cities" [1936]

"Twin Cities," *Fortune*, Vol. XIII, No. 4, April 1936, pp. 114-115.

3 full-color paintings illustrating an article about Minneapolis and St. Paul. The work was done for *Fortune* magazine. See as well J12. (*Copy examined:* Robarts Library, University of Toronto)

G38. "Vogue's Eye View" [1940]

"Vogue's Eye View of Fashions for Big and little Evenings," anon., *Vogue*, Nov. 15, 1940, p. 37.

2 black illustrations and designed title. [*Copy examined:* Rochester Public Library.]

V. ADVERTISEMENTS

G39. for The American Rayon Institute

A black drawing as advertisement for The American Rayon Institute, in *Graphis*, Vol. 12 No. 64, March 1956, p. 124. (*Copy examined:* Toronto Public Library)

G40. for Arrow Shirts [1935]

Advertising for Arrow shirts, 1935.

This was handled through the firm of Cluett Peabody.

G41. for Borden [1934]

Advertising for The Borden Company, 1934.

G42. for Columbia Broadcasting System [1947, 1953]

Illustration for the house organ of the Columbia Broadcasting System, 1947 and 1953.

G43. for Dubonnet [1943]

Advertising for Dubonnet, 1943.

G44. for General Foods [1932]

A full-color drawing of a baby leopard smacking his lips, in advertisement for Jell-O. "When I'm eating Jell-O I wish I were a leopard." (*Copy examined:* MP)

G45. for Harper Publishers

a. An illustration of hikers, to advertise *The High World* by Ludwig Bemelmans. See A16. *The Horn Book Magazine*, Vol. 30 No. 6, December, 1954, p. 389. (*Copy examined:* Toronto Public Library.)

b. A black illustration of a stag and a tree, to advertise *Parsley* by Ludwig Bemelmans. See A36. *The Horn Book Magazine*, Vol. 31 No. 4, August, 1955, p. 237. (*Copy examined:* Toronto Public Library.)

c. A black illustration of a stag and a tree, to advertise *Parsley* by Ludwig Bemelmans. Same as G43b. *The Horn Book Magazine*, Vol. 31 No. 6, December, 1955, p. 417. (*Copy examined:* Toronto Public Library.)

G46. for Holeproof Hosiery

A full-color drawing of a girl with many parcels in a balloon dress. "Only 5 more days for shopping." (*Copy examined:* MP)

G47. for Italian Line [1955]

Advertisement for Italian Line, 1955.

G48. for Little, Brown Publishers

a. A tiny illustration of two elephants, to advertise *The Happy Place* by Ludwig Bemelmans. See A15. *The Horn Book Magazine*, Vol. 28 No. 3, June 1952, p. 146. (*Copy examined:* Toronto Public Library.)

b. Two elephants dancing, to advertise *The Happy Place*, as in G47a, but enlarged. *The Horn Book Magazine*, Vol. 28 No. 5, October 1952, p. 312. (*Copy examined:* Toronto Public Library.)

G49. for Mars Chocolate [1954]

a. Full-color illustration: A pink egg eats a Mars bar while a green egg, a blue egg and a yellow egg lick their lips behind. "smart egg . . ." (*Copy examined:* MP)

b. Full-color illustration: A happy football eats a Mars bar. "All-American." (*Copy examined:* MP)

c. Full-color illustration: A jolly pumpkin eats a Mars bar. "smart punkin." (*Copy examined:* MP)

G50. for McIlhenny Co. [1957-1958]

A series entitled, "A well seasoned traveler's guide to Tabasco." Each advertisement contains recipes.

a. Full-color illustration: a couple being served in a Swedish restaurant. "I find a 'hint of home' in a famous Swedish dish." (*Copy examined:* MP)

b. Full-color illustration: a couple being served in a Swedish restaurant. "An unexpected adventure in Stockholm." Similar to G48a but with different recipes. (*Copy examined:* MP)

c. Full-color illustration: a couple chatting before dinner overlooking Hong Kong harbor. "Hong Kong magic makes an omelet unforgettable." (*Copy examined:* MP)

d. Full-color illustration: diners with chef in restaurant in front of painting of Golden Gate Bridge. "San Francisco, where chicken attains new glory in a Chick-n-que." (*Copy examined:* MP)

e. Full-color illustration: a diner fixes his napkin. "The sauces and gravies of Paris." (*Copy examined:* MP)

f. Full-color illustration: diners ogle a platter offered by a waiter while in background a girl brandishes a fruit tray over her head. "Reunion in Tahiti." (*Copy examined:* MP)

g. Full-color illustration: a curly-haired chef cooks at table. "Italy, home of fine arts . . . and the art of fine cooking." (*Copy examined:* MP)

G51. for The New York Times [1956]

A black and white poster for promotion of *The New York Times*, in *Graphis*, Vol. 13 No. 70, March 1957, p. 115. (*Copy examined:* Toronto Public Library)

G52. for Owens-Corning [1957-1958]

A full-color illustration showing a man, blue in the face, shivering near a heating duct. "Nobody's going to tell *me* it's time to change my furnace filter." Advertisement for Fiberglas Dust Stop Air Filters. (*Copy examined:* MP)

G53. for Radio

Radio advertisements in *Graphis*, Vol. 5 No. 26, 1949, pp. 140-141. (*Copy examined:* Toronto Public Library)

G54. for Saks Fifth Avenue [1941]

Advertising for Saks Fifth Avenue, 1941.

G55. for Strathmore Co. [1951]

Advertising for Strathmore Paper Company, 1951.

G56. for Theatre Arts Magazine

Four black drawings in vertical strip, advertising subscription to *Theatre Arts* magazine. "Now . . . is the time . . . for all good men . . . to subscribe to . . . Theatre Arts." *Theatre Arts*, Vol. 33 No. 4, May 1949, p. 96. (*Copy examined:* Toronto Public Library)

G57. for T.W.A. [1961]

Advertising for Trans-World Airlines, 1961.

G58. for The Viking Press

A black illustration of a girl falling from a bridge to advertise *Madeline's Rescue* by Ludwig Bemelmans. See A30. *The Horn Book Magazine*, Vol. 29 No. 2, April 1953, p. 78.

The advertisement without the illustration is repeated in Vol. 29 No. 3, June 1953. (*Copies examined:* Toronto Public Library.)

G59. for Hiram Walker & Sons, Inc. [1957-1958]

These advertisements were printed four-color and prepared by Foote, Cone & Belding, 155 East Superior St., Chicago, Illinois. They were award-winning in 1958.

a. A full-color illustration of three relaxing yachtsmen and a steward on the stern deck of a yacht with huge yachts moored in the background. Advertisement for Walker's DeLuxe Whiskey. "No whiskey anywhere is more deluxe than Walker's DeLuxe." (*Copy examined:* MP)

b. A full-color illustration of a club's butler secretly taking a nip while clubmembers mingle in the other room. A framed oil of an eighteenth century hunter with noble dog is behind the butler's shoulder. Advertisement for Walker's DeLuxe Whiskey. "Agreed! No whiskey anywhere is more deluxe than Walker's DeLuxe." (*Copy examined:* MP)

c. A full-color illustration of two old gentlemen in chaises being served by a pensive steward under the glares of animal heads hung upon the walls. The tiger rug is apparently in transports of maddened ecstasy. Advertisement for Walker's DeLuxe Whiskey. "Agreed! No whiskey anywhere is more deluxe than Walker's DeLuxe." (*Copy examined:* MP)

d. A full-color illustration of scarlet-jacketed waiters with noses high and a crowd of socializing men in a high-ceilinged bar. The chandelier candles have scarlet hoods. Advertisement for Walker's DeLuxe Whiskey. "No whiskey anywhere is more deluxe than Walker's DeLuxe." (*Copy examined:* MP)

e. A full-color illustration of a gentleman in a sports jacket being catered to in a fancy restaurant. One waiter snaps his fingers while a second pours whiskey. At a table behind a chef carves a capon while a waiter tosses a salad. Advertisement for Walker's DeLuxe Whiskey. "Agreed! No whiskey anywhere is more deluxe than Walker's DeLuxe." (*Copy examined:* MP)

f. A full-color illustration: a mustachioed Scotsman is served whiskey on one side by a waiter in black; on the other a Hindu in turban is served the same by two turbaned retainers. Advertisement for Walker's DeLuxe Whiskey. "Agreed! No whiskey anywhere is more deluxe than Walker's DeLuxe." (*Copy examined:* MP)

g. A full-color illustration: a plump balding valet in a white suit ministers to two men at poolside. One speaks on a black telephone; the other, in the water, holds the receiver of a red one. Advertisement for Walker's DeLuxe Whiskey. "Agreed! No whiskey anywhere is more deluxe than Walker's DeLuxe." (*Copy examined:* MP)

h. A full-color illustration: the lord of the manor in red smoking jacket and with monocle inspects whiskey held by sommelier under the light offered by a butler with a sumptuous candle. The iron gate to the wine celler is open in background. Advertisement for Walker's DeLuxe Whiskey. "Agreed! No whiskey anywhere is more deluxe than Walker's DeLuxe." (*Copy examined:* MP)

i. A full-color illustration: three oilmen confabulate beneath an umbrella while their chauffeurs lean upon vehicle hoods in the background. Advertisement for Walker's DeLuxe Whiskey. "Agreed! No whiskey anywhere is more deluxe than Walker's DeLuxe." (*Copy examined:* MP)

j. A full-color illustration: A white-haired waiter carrying a whiskey tray smirks at a bell-boy running an elevator. The elevator interior is flamboyant turquoise. Advertisement for Walker's DeLuxe Whiskey. "No whiskey anywhere is more deluxe than Walker's DeLuxe." (*Copy examined:* MP)

k. A full-color illustration: While a Scotsman considers the lie of his golfball his butler and chauffeur break out the whiskey from a travelling bar. Advertisement for Walker's DeLuxe Whiskey. "Agreed! No whiskey anywhere is more deluxe than Walker's DeLuxe." (*Copy examined:* MP)

l. A full-color illustration: Gentlemen are being served by waiters who climb to their kiosks perched in a great tree. It is night. High up, an owl observes. Advertisement for Walker's DeLuxe Whiskey. "Agreed! No whiskey anywhere

is more deluxe than Walker's DeLuxe." (*Copy examined:* MP)

VI. CARTOONS

G60. Saturday Evening Post

7 black cartoons in the "Post Scripts" column of *The Saturday Evening Post*, Philadelphia, 1933. These pen-and-ink drawings are referred to in "A Gemütliche Christmas," E180. (*Copies examined:* Toronto Public Library)

a. "Noodles, the Trained Seal," April 29, 1933, p. 22. Six frames. Noodles comes with his manager to see the impresario and gets into a discussion with the latter. Finally, the manager is bouncing a ball on his nose and Noodles has become the manager. This piece is signed BEMELMANS; not the artist's typical signature.

b. A Maître d'Hôtel is directing a pastry chef who has just completed a prodigious five-tiered wedding cake, "You may tear it down, Adolphe. Madame has changed her mind again." December 16, 1933, p. 24.

G61. World Magazine

A comic strip, "The Thrilling Adventures of Count Bric à Brac," published weekly on Sundays in *The World Magazine*, a part of *The New York World* newspaper, beginning July 4, 1926, p. 8-9.

(The strip was also syndicated through the *New York World*'s own service.) This first publication of the cartoon has no signature and no reference to Ludwig Bemelmans. Later the cartoon was signed "Bemelmans." The entry for August 22, 1926 was headed, "Thrilling Adventures of Count Bric à Brac By Bemelmans." "Count Bric à Brac" ran continuously at least until a piece on January 7, 1927 about the unveiling of a statue of Ridikolas II; but possibly longer. The typical technique was heavy pen and ink with a blue wash to tell the engraver where to put Benday (gray tone) shading. At least one episode involved escapades in Moscow.

The July 4, 1926 episode can be described in detail and it is perhaps worth doing this because it is Ludwig Bemelmans' first publication, as far as I know. A header image showing a tiny Alpine village contains the title in a box at left and the following text in a box at right: Today the Count climbs Mount Simplon. In 1806 Napoleon constructed the first road across its forbidding heights; just a century later the 12 Miles Long Tunnel—one of the world's greatest engineering feats—was opened. In the first frame the Count and a friend are atop a grassy crag: "Gee! We forgot the glasses;" "Never mind that—I drink out of the bottle." The tunnel entrance is far be-

low. The two have some trouble maneuvering between mountains— "Gee I never worked so hard in all my life!"—and finally encounter a rather enormous woman holding a pail: "How did SHE get up here" "Easy! She's *born* here."

G62. Young America

A series of "Silly Willy" cartoons in *Young America*, New York, edited by Stuart Scheftel; beginning with "Silly Willy, the Trained Seal" in the first issue, March 8, 1935.

The Silly Willy cartoons continued for about two years. They occupied 6-8 frames at a time, at first in black and then in four colors. The magazine published weekly. Produced for schoolchildren, it was entirely in rhyme. A typical sample of the text: "I'm sure that I'd get more wages/ If I could keep away from stages." Another extolled the virtues (from a seal's point of view) of using an umbrella in the shower.

VII. MISCELLANY

G63. Art Directors Annual

Upon pink board, maroon and black drawings to illustrate the menu for the Art Directors Annual Awards Luncheon, Waldorf Astoria Hotel, New

York, May 27, 1957. Disgruntled but snobby waiters have the menu offerings inscribed upon their shirt fronts or upon the serving dishes they carry. (*Copy examined:* MP)

G64. Portrait of a Paris Square
[1940]

"Portrait of a Paris Square," with text by the editors and a full-color illustration of the Place Vendôme by Bemelmans, *Vogue*, June 1, 1940, p. 58 and reprised August, 1940.

The illustration accompanies, and is referred to in, the story, "I love you—I love you—I love you—"(see E38) but with an independent caption by the editors; and was used as the jacket illustration for *The Best of Times*; see A3a.

SECTION H

Adaptations by Others of Material Authored by Ludwig Bemelmans

Adaptations by Others
of Material Authored by
Ludwig Bemelmans

MANY ADAPTATIONS HAVE BEEN MADE of Bemelmans' work; sometimes of actual published material and sometimes of characters or situations found in published material but developed along different lines. It has seemed clearest to list in section "H" all known adaptations of Bemelmans' works, whether completed publications or characters drawn from these, made in any medium by other people. In the entertainment business time flies; it is often very difficult to trace records of old materials, and many of these materials are old indeed. The listing is alphabetical by the title of the work adapted; and then chronological within each work.

Included here are adaptations with a wide range of fidelity: from the extremely faithful (see for example H9l) to the pastiche (see H9a). Even when illustrations have clearly been done

by commercial artists hired to make reproductions, one can see that some understand and care about the principles by which Bemelmans' characters operate (see for example H4m and H4n) while others seem uninterested (see H9a). Sometimes, of course, the material is directly from Bemelmans (the illustration in H4j and H4k, for example) and sometimes vast changes have needed to be made by the adapter (as in the massive stage production of *Now I Lay Me Down to Sleep*, H10).

In the late 1980s material from the *Madeline* series went into corporate licencing. There has been a recent flood of adaptations in a number of fields—puzzles, posters, videos to name but three—and there is every reason to suspect, as this goes to print, that licencing will continue. Much interest is being shown in *Madeline* materials specifically; and Bemelmans in general. I have tried to include all productions which have been brought to my knowledge and which have either appeared already or are scheduled to appear as of early 1992.

One of the chagrins of doing this work has been hearing of intriguing adaptations that died in the planning stages. *My War With the United States* and *Hotel Splendide* were both in preparation for the New York stage, the former in collaboration with Charles MacArthur and the latter as a Richard Rogers and Dwight Deere Wiman musical comedy. Neither production came through; *My War* was not completed at the script stage; *Splendide* ran into casting difficulties (see E68 and E69). There was also an uncompleted collaboration for the stage with Anita Loos, *To the One I Love the Best*, from A43; which was being written for Helen Hayes as Elsie de Wolfe. Bemelmans was reported to have been working on a musical adaptation of *The Street Where the Heart Lies* at the time of his death; it was spoken of in connection with both David Susskind and Alan Jay Lerner. And much, much later, *Madeline* almost became a Broadway musical, too.

Some adaptations, or purported adaptations, have been impossible to find. There is discussion in correspondence about *Madeline* greeting cards coming out from the American Artists Group to coincide with the publication of the first edition, A24a (undated 1939 note to Sam Golden). The American Artists Group may, as well, have published cards based on Munro Leaf's *Noodle*, which was illustrated by Bemelmans, see G31. (Note from Bemelmans to Golden, March 18, 1938, in which Bemelmans asks for a contract adjustment in order that half the card royalties go to Leaf.) In a note from Mount Kisco, New York dated June 22, 1939, Bemelmans writes to Golden, "Attached you will find a letter from . . . Chicago—it should help us to determine the size of the Quito Picture edition": presumably, then, there were also images from *Quito Express*, A37 or *The Donkey Inside*, A8. However, it has not been possible to find, or otherwise assure the existence of, any of these materials.

Similarly, it has not been possible to locate copies of either (a) greeting cards produced by Hart Vance of St. Louis, Missouri (although a contract was drawn up giving him rights to produce Bemelmans' art in cards, exclusive of Christmas cards) or (b) a greeting card from an unknown producer which contained the full text of *Madeline*.

I. ADAPTATIONS OF MATERIAL
AUTHORED BY
LUDWIG BEMELMANS

H1. The Best of Times

Ile d'Yeu, 1959. 26" x 34" signed silkscreen print of the full-color illustration printed on pp. 184-185 of *The Best of Times*, A3. An edition of 300 was printed by Ary and Sheila Marbain at The Maurel Press, New York, and was made available at $25.00.

H2. The Borrowed Christmas

The Borrowed Christmas. Adapted for television by Joseph Schrank. New York: Compass Productions, 1959. Duration: approx. 20:00.

Appeared December 13, 1959, 5:30 - 6:30 p.m., on *The Hallmark Hall of Fame* in a show entitled, "A Christmas Festival," written and conceived by Carl Beier. NBC Television. Broadcast live and simultaneously filmed and kinephotographed.

Produced and directed by George Schaefer. Original music by Philip J. Lang. Musical direction by Franz Allers. Costumes by Noel Taylor. Scenic design by Jan Scott. With Walter Slezak as Mr. Reallybig, Jules Munshin as the Manager, Alice Pearce as Miss Talmay, David Fran-

cis as Billy, John C. Becher as Officer Flannelly and Hiram Sherman as Santa Claus. See as well A5.

Reviewed in *The New York Times*, December 14, 1959.

H3. Hansi and Other Stories

a. *Hansi* • *Parsley* • *Marina* • *Welcome Home* by Ludwig Bemelmans, read by Carol Channing. New York: Caedmon Records, 1976. Caedmon TC 1515.

Directed by Ward Botsford. Music by Die Engelkinder. Studio recording by Howard W. Harris. See also A14, A36, A31 and A44.

b. *Hansi* • *Parsley* • *Marina* • *Welcome Home* by Ludwig Bemelmans, read by Carol Channing. New York: Caedmon Records, n.d. Caedmon Cassette CDL 51515.

Directed by Ward Botsford. Running time 57:50. See also A14, A36, A31 and A44.

H4. Madeline

a. *Madeline*, an animated film by Stephen Bosustow, Los Angeles: United Productions of America, 1952.

Released October 21, 1952 by Columbia Pictures. 35 mm. color cartoon with sound. Duration: 7:30. One of the "Jolly Frolics." Copyright © Columbia Pictures.

A 16 mm. print is available, released in 1955 through the International Film Bureau.

The film was selected for the Edinburgh Festival. It is No. 33 of the U.P.A. Cartoon Festival, which included as well "Mr. Magoo" and "Gerald McBoing-Boing" cartoons. There was some talk of a full-length *Madeline* cartoon feature but one was not made.

Hart Vance of St. Louis, Missouri wrote to Bemelmans on October 30, 1952: "You will be interested to know that I went to see the animation of 'Madeline' and enjoyed it enormously. From friends of mine who had seen it at other times, I received confirmation of the fact that frequently the audience applauds the picture."

b. *Madeline*. Long-playing phonograph recording. RCA Victor. Reported in *Time*, December 24, 1956.

A story accompanied by a symphonic score.

c. *"Madeline at the Zoo" Screen Print*. New York: The Maurel Press, 1959. An edition of 300 of a 26" x 34" silkscreen print, signed, of Madeline saying "Pooh-pooh" to the tiger at the zoo was printed by Ary and Sheila Marbain and made available at $25.00.

The print was advertised in *The New Yorker*.

d. *Madeline and Other Bemelmans*, told by Carol Channing. New York: Caedmon Records, 1960. Caedmon TC 1113.

Contains *Madeline, Madeline's Rescue, Madeline*

and the Bad Hat, Fifi, and *The Happy Place*. Directed by Howard Sackler. Accordion music for *Madeline* by Bill Costa. See also A24, A30, A25, A12, and A15.

e. *Madeline*. Adapted from the Ludwig Bemelmans books by Sol Saks. Appeared October 16, 1960, 7:00 - 8:00 P.M., on *The Shirley Temple Show*. NBC Television. Color videotape.

Executive Producer: William H. Brown, Jr. Produced by William Asher. Directed by David Green. With Gina Gillespie as Madeline, Imogene Coca as Miss Clavel, Michel Petit as Pepito, Billy Gilbert as the Gypsy Father, and Jane Rose, Rusty Stevens, Kirk Kirkham, Lou Krugman, Terry Gekler, Shari Bernath, and Adele Wynkoop.

The *TV Guide* blurb described the plot as follows: "Madeline is an imaginative nine-year old who lives in Paris with 10 other girls and a stern governess named Miss Clavel." It is worth noting that Madeline is nowhere else given an age; that there are usually 11 other girls; and that Miss Clavel is not typically seen out of habit.

Though the program was titled "Madeline" it seems clear from the casting that the plot followed that of other Madeline titles as well, certainly including some reference to *Madeline and the Gypsies*.

f. *Madeline and Other Bemelmans*, told by Carol Channing. New York: Caedmon Records, 1988. Caedmon Cassette CPN 1113.

Contains *Madeline, Madeline's Rescue, Madeline*

and the Bad Hat, Fifi, and *The Happy Place*. Running time: 52:00. Directed by Howard Sackler. Accordion music for *Madeline* by Bill Costa. See also A24, A30, A25, A12, and A15.

g. *Madeline*, by Judy Rothman, from the book by Ludwig Bemelmans. Burbank: DIC Animation City, 1988. "Hi-Tops Video" MO 22194.

Executive Producers: Saul Cooper, Andy Heywood, Pancho Kohner, Rick Rosen. Produced by Cassandra Schafhausen. Directed by Stephan Martinière. The title song is by Joe Raposo. Narrated by Christopher Plummer. Running time: 30:00. Distributed by Media Home Entertainment, Inc. See also A24. Emmy nomination.

h. *Madeline*, by Ludwig Bemelmans. New York: Puffin, 1989. Puffin Story-Tapes.

Produced by Parachute Press, Inc. Directed by Bernice Chardiet. Contains one Puffin book and a read-along cassette with songs in French and English. See also A24.

i. *Madeline Dolls*. New York: Eden Toys, 1990-1993.

(a) 14″ fabric doll: with blue coat and yellow dress collar, red ascot, yellow hat, pantaloon, embroidered appendectomy scar. Released 1990. (b) 18″ fabric doll: with blue removable buttoned coat and yellow removable dress, red ascot, yellow hat, pantaloon, embroidered appendectomy scar. Released 1990. (c) 4′ fabric display doll: same in design as H4i(b). Released 1991. (d) Christmas Doll: 18″ fabric doll, with holiday plaid red-green-black-and-gold foil dress with black velvet collar; red coat with shoulder cape trimmed in black; black hat with red, green, and gold ribbon; removable fur muff. Released 1991. (e) The Madeline Book and Toy Box, containing a copy of A24t and a special 9″ fabric doll [in a blue smock but otherwise similar to H4i(a)], produced by Puffin Books and Eden Toys in association. Released 1991. (f) Spring Time Doll: with powder blue and yellow searsucker party dress trimmed with eyelet lace; embroidered roses on dress and white party shoes; white gloves; and straw hat trimmed in powder blue. (g) 15″ Madeline skating doll, with green polar fleece coat, gray fur collar and hat, flannel leggings and undershirt, and leather skates with plastic blades. Released Fall, 1992. (h) 12″ Madeline hand puppet, in traditional French schoolgirl costume. Released Fall, 1992. (i) 13″ pajama Madeline, with a two-piece mint and white dotted pajama set (the ones Madeline wore after her appendix operation), and white quilted slippers. Forthcoming Spring 1993.

i (bis). *Madeline Toys and Accessories*. New York: Eden Toys, 1992-1993.

(a) Madeline play house, in cotton, with Madeline, Miss Clavel, Genevieve and Pepito small dolls. Released Fall, 1992. (b) Madeline Melamine, including plate with design of Madeline, the old house, and Genevieve, bowl with design of the Eiffel Tower and sippy cup. Released Fall, 1992. (c) Madeline fork and spoon set, for children, in stainless steel with design of the Eiffel Tower and Madeline. Released Fall, 1992. (d) Madeline puppet theater, including 4" finger puppets of Madeline, Genevieve, Pepito, with stage and changeable scenery. Forthcoming Spring. 1993.

j. *Madeline Poster*, 1990. Berkeley: Peaceable Kingdom Press.

15 x 21 in. Full-color reprint of the cover art from *Madeline*, a nun and twelve little girls with the Eiffel Tower. Art director and publisher is Olivia Hurd.

k. *Madeline Greeting Cards*, 1990. Berkeley: Peaceable Kingdom Press.

2 yellow-and-black, and 1 full-color, greeting cards from *Madeline* material. In yellow and black: (i) Madeline in the hospital bed, while the girls play with her presents, from *Madeline*, see A24a; with the text, "Hope you're feeling better!" or blank inside. (ii) The girls buying flowers before visiting Madeline in hospital, from *Madeline*, see A24a; blank inside. In full-color: (iii) Madeline and the girls ice-skating, from *Madeline*, see A24a; with the text, "Merry Christmas" or blank inside. Art director and publisher is Olivia Hurd.

These cards were available with a fourth, from *Madeline and the Gypsies*; see H6g.

l. *Madeline*. Adapted by James Still from the *Madeline* books of Ludwig Bemelmans. The Emmy Gifford Children's Theater of Omaha, Nebraska. November 23-December 29, 1990.

Directed by James Larson. Music by Jacques Offenbach. Set design by Larry Kaushansky. The cast included Tom Gellatly as Mr. Bemelmans; Pam Carter as Miss Clavel; Kevin Ehrhart as Jean-Pierre the Mouse; Amy Kunz as Isabel the Tiger; Tracy Iwersen as Geneviève the Dog; Keven Barratt as Lord Cucuface and Young Ludwig Bemelmans; Keith Hale as Pepito; and Heather Woodruff and Natasha Arens as both Madeline and Barbara Bemelmans.

All of the *Madeline* books except *Madeline's Christmas* were used for this adaptation.

m. *Madeline Frame Puzzle*. Riverdale, N.J.: International Playthings, 1991.

Designer-illustrator: Sean Platter. Art Director: Martine Redman. A Ravensburger frame puzzle. Madeline and Pepito are walking Geneviève in a park beside the Eiffel Tower. Miss Clavel has flowers, a gendarme watches, a bicyclist rides by and a flower seller smiles at a kiosk in the background. Released January 1991.

n. *Madeline Jigsaw Puzzles*. Riverdale, N.J.: International Playthings, 1991.

2 different jigsaw puzzles based on *Madeline*. Designer-illustrator: Sean Platter. Art Director: Martine Redman. Ravensburger puzzles. (a) "Picnic on the Seine" shows Madeline with a toy sailboat and eleven happy little girls with her on a quai underneath the Petit Pont. Miss Clavel has a basket with two baguettes and Nôtre Dame is in the background. (b) "Toys" shows Madeline and the girls playing with toys under Miss Clavel's supervision in the playroom. Released August 1991.

o. *Madeline Licenced Clothing*. New York: Axelrod and Axelrod Sales and Design, Inc. Forthcoming.

The specific designs are as yet undetermined but are likely to involve t-shirts. The material will be labelled inside, "Funstuff NY." Executive Producer, Deena Axelrod. The licence is not completed at this writing.

p. *Madeline's Friends*. Riverdale, N.J.: International Playthings, 1992. A small (6000 series) vinyl press-and-peel activity set featuring Madeline, Pepito, Geneviève, Miss Clavel, Dr. Cohn, and other figures, all to be set upon a drawing of the old house covered with vines and the Eiffel Tower. Illustrated by Sean Platter. Produced by Uniset, of Roskilde, Denmark. Fall, 1992.

q. *Madeline Card Game*. Riverdale, N.J.: International Playthings, 1993.

A card game featuring Madeline and friends, illustrated by Sean Platter: Forthcoming, 1993. Manufacturer unknown at time of writing.

H5. Madeline and the Bad Hat

a. *Madeline and the Bad Hat*, from the book by Ludwig Bemelmans. New York: Rembrandt Films, 1960.

16 mm. non-theatrical color animated film. Producer: William L. Snyder. Animated by J. Bart, S. Smetana, A. Booresh, B. Shade, V. Coodren, B. Dvorak, V. Maresh. Directed by V. Bedrick. Released 1973 by Macmillan Films.

b. *Madeline and the Bad Hat*, by Stephan Martinière and Peter Landecker, from the book by Ludwig Bemelmans. Montreal: CINAR and France Animation, 1991.

Executive Producers: Saul Cooper and Pancho Kohner. Produced by Ronald A. Weinberg. Directed by Stephan Martinière. Produced in association with Crayon Animation, Global Television Network, Family Channel, FR3, and Hi-Tops Video. The title song is by Joe Raposo. Narrated by Christopher Plummer. Running time: 30:00. See also A25.

c. *Madeline et le petit barbare*, by Stephan Martinière and Peter Landecker, from the book by Ludwig Bemelmans. Montréal: CINAR and France Animation, 1991.

Executive Producers: Saul Cooper and Pancho Kohner. Produced by Ronald A. Weinberg. Directed by Stephan Martinière. French adaptation by Michel Trouillet. Produced in association with Crayon Animation, Global Television Network, Family Channel, FR3, and Hi-Tops Video. The title song is by Joe Raposo. Narrated by Christopher Plummer. Duration: 30:00. See also A25.

d. *Madeline and the Bad Hat*. Weston, Connecticut: Weston Woods Studios, 1991.

16 mm. film. Produced by Morton Schindel and William Snyder, a revision by means of new sound track of the Rembrandt Films motion picture, see H5a. Duration: 8:00.

e. *Madeline and the Bad Hat*. Weston, Connecticut: Weston Woods Studios, 1991.

Videocassette version of H5d. Available worldwide.

H6. Madeline and the Gypsies

a. *Madeline and the Gypsies*, from the book by Ludwig Bemelmans. New York: Rembrandt Films, 1960.

16 mm. non-theatrical color animated film. Producer: William L. Snyder. Animated by J. Bart, B. Dvorak, V. Coodren, R. Mann and S. Smetana. Directed by V. Bedrick. Released 1973 by Macmillan Films.

b. *Carol Channing Reads Madeline and the Gypsies • Madeline in London • Quito Express • The Castle Number Nine*. New York: Caedmon Records, 1970. Caedmon TC 1304.

No production information given. See also A26, A27, A37, and A6.

c. *Carol Channing Reading Madeline and the Gypsies, Madeline in London, Quito Express, The Castle Number Nine by Ludwig Bemelmans*. New York:

Caedmon Records, n.d. Caedmon Cassette CDL 51304.

Running time: 55:27. No production information given. See also A26, A27, A37, and A6.

d. *Madeline and the Gypsies*, adapted for the stage by John Clark Donahue from the book by Ludwig Bemelmans. Minneapolis: Children's Theatre Company of Minneapolis, opened April 15, 1972.

Produced and directed by John Clark Donahue. Music by Hiram Titus. Scenic Design by Jack Barkla after the Bemelmans drawings. With Mary Ann Raymond as Madeline and Matt Brassil as Pepito.

e. *Madeline and the Gypsies*. Color filmstrip with sound track on either record or cassette; with a teacher's guide. H. M. Stone Productions, 1972.

f. *Madeline and the Gypsies*, adapted for the stage by John Clark Donahue from the book by Ludwig Bemelmans. Minneapolis: Children's Theatre Company of Minneapolis, October 19, 1984-February 14, 1985.

Produced by the Children's Theatre Company of Minneapolis. Directed by Barry L. Goldman. Music by Hiram Titus. Scenic Design by Jack Barkla after the Bemelmans drawings. With Jolayne Berg as Madeline and Nathaniel Newhall as Pepito. A reprise of H6d.

g. *Madeline and the Gypsies Greeting Card*, 1990. Berkeley: Peaceable Kingdom Press.

In black and yellow, the circus ring, with Madeline on the tightrope, from *Madeline and the Gypsies*, see A26a(bis); with the text, "Happy Birthday" or blank inside. Art director and publisher is Olivia Hurd. This card was available with 3 *Madeline* cards, see H4k.

h. *Madeline and the Gypsies*, by Stephan Martinière and Peter Landecker, from the book by Ludwig Bemelmans. Montreal: CINAR and France Animation, 1991.

Executive Producers: Saul Cooper and Pancho Kohner. Produced by Ronald A. Weinberg. Directed by Stephan Martinière. Produced in association with Crayon Animation, Global Television Network, Family Channel, FR3, and Hi-Tops Video. The title song is by Joe Raposo. Narrated by Christopher Plummer. Running time: 30:00. See also A26.

i. *Madeline et les tziganes*, by Stephan Martinière and Peter Landecker, from the book by Ludwig Bemelmans. Montréal: CINAR and France Animation, 1991.

Executive Producers: Saul Cooper and Pancho Kohner. Produced by Ronald A. Weinberg. Directed by Stephan Martinière. Produced in association with Crayon Animation, Global Television Network, Family Channel, FR3, and Hi-Tops Video. The title song is by Joe Raposo. Narrated by Christopher Plummer. Duration: 30:00. See also A26.

j. *Madeline and the Gypsies*. Weston, Connecticut: Weston Woods Studios, 1991.

16 mm. film. Produced by Morton Schindel and William Snyder, a revision by means of new sound track of the Rembrandt Films motion picture, see H6a. Duration: 7:00.

k. *Madeline and the Gypsies*. Weston, Connecticut: Weston Woods Studios, 1991.

Videocassette version of H6j. Available worldwide.

l. *Madeline's Circus Adventure*. Riverdale, N.J.: International Playthings, 1992.

A large (7000 series) vinyl press-and-peel activity set recalling Madeline and Pepito's tour with the gypsy circus. Illustrated by Sean Platter. Produced by Uniset of Roskilde, Denmark. Fall 1992.

m. *Madeline at the Circus*. Riverdale, N.J.: International Playthings, 1992.

A see-inside frame puzzle, for children aged 3–5. Illustrated by Sean Platter. Manufactured by Otto Maier Verlag, Ravensburg under the Ravensburger brand name.

H7. Madeline in London

a. *Madeline in London*, by Stephan Martinière and Peter Landecker, from the book by Ludwig Bemelmans. Montreal: CINAR and France Animation, 1991.

Executive Producers: Saul Cooper and Pancho Kohner. Produced by Ronald A. Weinberg.

Directed by Stephan Martinière. Produced in association with Crayon Animation, Global Television Network, Family Channel, FR3, and Hi-Tops Video. The title song is by Joe Raposo. Narrated by Christopher Plummer. Running time: 30:00. See also A27.

b. *Madeline à Londres*, by Stephan Martinière and Peter Landecker, from the book by Ludwig Bemelmans. Montréal: CINAR and France Animation, 1991.

Executive Producers: Saul Cooper and Pancho Kohner. Produced by Ronald A. Weinberg. Directed by Stephan Martinière. Produced in association with Crayon Animation, Global Television Network, Family Channel, FR3, and Hi-Tops Video. The title song is by Joe Raposo. Narrated by Christopher Plummer. Duration: 30:00. See also A27.

H8. Madeline's Christmas

a. *Madeline's Christmas*, by Stephan Martinière and Peter Landecker, from the book by Ludwig Bemelmans. Montreal: CINAR and France Animation, 1990.

Executive Producers: Saul Cooper and Pancho Kohner. Produced by Ronald A. Weinberg. Directed by Stephan Martinière. Produced in association with Crayon Animation, Global Television Network, Family Channel, FR3, and Hi-

Tops Video. The title song is by Joe Raposo. Narrated by Christopher Plummer. Running time: 30:00. See also A28.

b. *Le Nöel de Madeline*, by Stephan Martinière and Peter Landecker, from the book by Ludwig Bemelmans. Montréal: CINAR and France Animation, 1990.

Executive Producers: Saul Cooper and Pancho Kohner. Produced by Ronald A. Weinberg. Directed by Stephan Martinière. Produced in association with Crayon Animation, Global Television Network, Family Channel, FR3, and Hi-Tops Video. French adaptation by Michel Trouillet. The title song is by Joe Raposo. Narrated by Christopher Plummer. Duration: 30:00. See also A28.

H9. Madeline's Rescue

a. *Madeline & Geneviève*. New York: Dell Publishing Company, 1957. Comic No. 796.

Paper-covered comic book. Unpaged. 16 leaves. 25.5 x 18 cm. This is No. 796 in the Dell Four-Color Series. These were printed monthly and this number appeared in May 1957 at 10¢. This was a "one-shot" (one-time) publication.

On *verso of cover*: Ludwig Bemelmans' *Madeline & Geneviève*, No. 796. Published by Dell Publishing Co., Inc., 261 Fifth Ave., New York 16, N.Y.; George T. Delacorte, Jr., President; Helen Meyer, Vice-President; Albert P. Delacorte, Vice-President. © 1957, by Ludwig Bemelmans.

All rights reserved throughout the world. Authorized edition. Printed in U.S.A. Designed and produced by Western Printing & Lithographing Co. At bottom right corner of the first page, in black: Madeline O.S. #796-575. *Front cover* is printed entirely with a full-color illustration showing twelve little girls in yellow outfits — Madeline at the front left patting Geneviève who is wearing a red bow — and Miss Clavel smiling, with a bouquet of pink roses. *Back cover* has Miss Clavel in blue with Madeline under one arm and Geneviève under the other.

Although the characters are clearly from *Madeline's Rescue* the development is not. The book contains three cartoon tales: (A) "Madeline and Geneviève," in which the dog is sprayed by a skunk one night and has to be bathed, along with all of the little girls, by Miss Clavel; (B) "Madeline and the Carousel," in which Madeline imagines that a carousel horse she is riding can actually fly — over Paris and especially the Eiffel Tower — but it turns out she has fallen and acquired for her head a lump the other little girls are willing to pay 2¢ each to touch; and (C) "Madeline and Eclaire the Frog," in which an unknown admirer named Herman sends a frog in a white package wrapped in a red bow. Miss Clavel faints. Geneviève befriends the frog, but the amphibian finally hops away.

Illustrations not credited.

b. *Madeline's Rescue Screen Print*, New York: The Maurel Press, 1959. An edition of 300 of a 26" x 34" silkscreen print, signed, of the hunt for Madeline from p. 34 of *Madeline's Rescue*, A30, was made by Ary and Sheila Marbain and sold for $25.00

This print was advertised in *The New Yorker*.

c. *Madeline's Rescue*, from the book by Ludwig Bemelmans. New York: Rembrandt Films, 1960.

16 mm. non-theatrical color animated film. Producer: William L. Snyder. Animated by S. Smetana, B. Shade, V. Coodren, J. Bart, B. Dvorak, A. Booresh, V. Maresh, K. Mann. Directed by V. Bedrick. Duration: 15:00

d. *Madeline's Rescue*. Weston, Connecticut: Weston Woods Studios, 1960. Filmstrip. 50 frames, color 35 mm. transparency.

Part of Picture Book Parade Series 4. Executive Producer: Morton Schindel.

e. *Madeline's Rescue*. Weston, Connecticut: Weston Woods Studios, 1961. Sound recording. Weston Woods LTC-30.

Available alone or in combination with H9d as a sound filmstrip. Read by Owen Jordan.

f. *Madeline's Rescue*. New York: Viking Penguin, 1989. Puffin Story-Tapes.

Produced and directed by Bernice Chardiet. Performed by Jean Richards and Paul Lazarus. Music by Bruce Coughlin. One "Picture-Puffin" book and a read-along cassette. See also A30.

g. *Madeline's Rescue*, from the book by Ludwig Bemelmans. Minneapolis: Children's Theatre Company of Minneapolis, September 2 November 11, 1990.

Produced by the Children's Theatre Company of Minneapolis. Directed by Jon Cranney. Book and Lyrics by Constance Congdon. Music by Mel Marvin. Choreographed by Vance Holmes. Scenic and Costume Design by Ann Sheffield. With Libby Winters as Madeline and Katherine Ferrand as Miss Clavel.

h. *Madeline's Rescue*, by Stephan Martinière and Peter Landecker, from the book by Ludwig Bemelmans. Montreal: CINAR and France Animation, 1991.

Executive Producers: Saul Cooper and Pancho Kohner. Produced by Ronald A. Weinberg. Directed by Stephan Martinière. Produced inassociation with Crayon Animation, Global Television Network, Family Channel, FR3, and Hi-Tops Video. The title song is by Joe Raposo. Running time: 30:00. See also A30.

i. *Madeline sauvée des eaux*, par Stephan Martinière et Peter Landecker, tiré du livre par Ludwig Bemelmans. Montréal: CINAR et France Animation, 1991.

Executive Producers: Saul Cooper and Pancho Kohner. Produced by Ronald A. Weinberg. Directed by Stephan Martinière. Produced in association with Crayon Animation, Global Television Network, Family Channel, FR3, and Hi-Tops Video. Title song by Joe Raposo. Duration: 30:00. See also A30.

j. *Madeline's Rescue*. Weston, Connecticut: Weston Woods Studios, 1991.

16 mm. film. Produced by Morton Schindel and William Snyder, a revision by means of new sound track of the Rembrandt Films motion picture, see H9c. Duration: 7:00.

k. *Madeline's Rescue*. Weston, Connecticut: Weston Woods Studios, 1991.

Videocassette version of H9j. Available worldwide.

l. *Madeline's Rescue and Other Stories about Madeline*. Videocassette. Distributed by CC Studios as No. 24 of the Children's Circle Home Video Library, 1991.

Included are *Madeline's Rescue*, *Madeline and the Bad Hat*, and *Madeline and the Gypsies*, in revisions by means of new sound track of the Rembrandt Films, see H9c, H5a, and H6a. Duration: 23:00. Producer: William L. Snyder. Narrated by Louise Roberts.

In 1990 some advance copies were made available to subscribers of the Children's Circle Video Reading Program through Early Advantage, Norwalk, Connecticut.

m. *Madeline Game: Help Madeline Find Her Puppies!* Ravensburg: Otto Maier Verlag, 1992.

A game based loosely on *Madeline's Rescue* in which players help the little girls searching Paris for Geneviève's lost puppies. Author: Martine Redman. Illustrator: Sean Platter. This is part of the Ravensburger puzzles and games line, No. 21057 2, published by Otto Maier Verlag, Ravensburg, and distributed in North America by International Playthings of Riverdale, N.J. Released January, 1992.

H10. Now I Lay Me Down to Sleep

a. *Now I Lay Me Down to Sleep*. A radio adaptation. Aired on "This Is My Best," October 10, 1944, 9:30 -10:00 P.M., CBS Radio Network.

Produced by Homer Fickett. Directed by Dave Titus with Whit Burnett. Orchestra conducted by Robert Armbruster. Starring Akim Tamiroff and Mildred Natwick.

A dramatic series presenting stars of radio, stage and screen in adaptations of stories, novels etc. selected by the author as his or her own favorite work. The show's debut was Tuesday September 5, 1944.

b. *Now I Lay Me Down to Sleep*, by Elaine Ryan, from the novel by Ludwig Bemelmans. Palo Alto: Stanford University Memorial Auditorium, opened July 22, 1949.

Produced and staged by Hume Cronyn. With Jessica Tandy and Akim Tamiroff. World Première. See also A34 and G32.

Reviewed in *The New York Times*, July 23, 1949.

c. *Now I Lay Me Down to Sleep*, by Elaine Ryan, from the novel by Ludwig Bemelmans. New York: Broadhurst Theater, opened March 2, 1950.

Broadway production. Produced and staged by Hume Cronyn. With Florence Eldridge and Frederick March. See also A34 and G32.

Typescript: New York: P. Foster and M. H. Schloss, c.1947. Reading script: New York: Hart Stenographic Bureau, 1949, © 1947.

Portrait in *Theatre Arts*, Vol. 34, May 1950, p. 15; and portrait with critical note in *Theatre Arts*, Vol. 34, July 1950, pp. 57-88. Other criticism appeared in: *Catholic World*, Vol. 171, April 1950, p. 171; *Commonweal*, Vol. 51, March 24, 1950, p. 629; *The New Republic*, Vol. 122, March 27, 1950, p. 23; *The New Yorker*, Vol. 26, March 11, 1950, beginning p. 52; *Newsweek*, Vol. 35, March 13, 1950, p. 71; and *Time*, Vol. 55, March 13, 1950, p. 65.

H11. The Street Where the Heart Lies

The Street Where the Heart Lies. Screenplay by Menno Meyjes and Edward Lewis, 1991.

Scheduled for commencement of principal photography after June 1992 for later release. Specific production arrangements are unavailable at this writing, but may involve at least Carthago Films and Columbia Pictures (see *Cahiers du Cinéma*, September 1991, p. 40).

H12. Sunshine

Sunshine. Motion picture, from *Sunshine, Sunshine Go Away: A Story About the City of New York* by Ludwig Bemelmans. New York: Rembrandt Films, 1960.

Produced by Bill Snyder. Released 1973 by Macmillan Films. See also A41 and E125.

II. ADAPTATIONS OF MATERIAL CO-AUTHORED BY LUDWIG BEMELMANS

H13. Yolanda and the Thief

Yolanda and the Thief, musical screenplay by Irving Brecher adapted from the story by Ludwig Bemelmans and Jacques Théry. Metro-Goldwyn-Mayer. Opened October 9, 1945.

Technicolor. 108 min. Produced by Arthur Freed. Directed by Vincente Minnelli. Music by Harry Warren. Lyrics by Arthur Freed. With Fred Astaire, Lucille Bremer, Mildred Natwick. The material first appeared in *Town & Country*; see also E79.

Cutting continuity: Culver City, CA: Loew's Inc., 1945.

III. ADAPTATIONS COLLABORATED UPON BY LUDWIG BEMELMANS OF MATERIAL BY OTHERS

H14. Noah

Noah, by André Obey, translated by Arthur Wilmurt. New York: Longacre Theater, opened February 13, 1935.

Produced and staged by Jerome Mayer. With Pierre Fresnay. The preparation of costumes, animals and scenery was under the personal supervision of Ludwig Bemelmans.

H15. The Passionate Pasha

Le Cadi, or *The Passionate Pasha,* by Christoph Willibald Gluck was performed at the first public appearance of the American Chamber Opera Society. New York. Date not known.

Produced and translated into English by Allen Sven Oxenburg. Musical director: Arnold U. Gamson. Sets executed by Paul Sherman after designs by Ludwig Bemelmans.

NOTE: In 1960 or shortly thereafter a reading of *Madeline* was given by Bob Keeshan as one of the Reading Stories on "The Captain Kangaroo Show," CBS Television, weekdays, 8:00 - 9:00 A.M. Eastern time. The specific date of the broadcast cannot be determined from available records.

In the summer and fall of 1985 Orson Welles

recorded twelve hours of his favorite stories on audio tape for an independent producer in Japan. The tape was to have been used to help in the instruction in English of Japanese schoolchildren. Among the stories was "Grapes for Mr. Cape," originally "Grapes for Monsieur Cape,"

see E42. The recording took place in Welles' bedroom in Hollywood and in a Hollywood recording studio, and the final tapes were never formally released. This is likely the last completed work of Orson Welles.

SECTION I

Exhibitions of Bemelmans' Visual Work

Exhibitions of
Bemelmans' Visual Work

SECTION "I" LISTS GALLERY shows of Bemelmans' work and includes reference to catalogues accompanying the shows and
published articles reviewing or announcing such shows. The
shows are listed chronologically, insofar as the dates could be
determined.

This seems an appropriate place to state formally that there
has been no attempt in compiling this bibliography to make a
systematic listing of the artistic production of Ludwig Bemelmans. There are certainly drawings and watercolors in the thousands; a very substantial number of oils and gouaches; and a
tremendous number of sketches; many of which are related to
Bemelmans' published books and many of which are not. He
sketched and painted virtually everywhere he went, often—*very
often*—repeating workups of similar subject matter. It will be

possible for the reader, studying the descriptions of A28 and A29 alone, to learn how the artist routinely made repeat versions of illustrations which were commonly substituted one for another as books were reprinted from periodical publications or from one edition to another.

I1. Children's Books Show [(1934-35)]

Participant in an exhibition of children's books, Librairie Fischbacher, Paris, 1934 or 1935, reported in *Gebrauchsgraphik*, see J11.

I2. Kennedy Show [(1939)]

An exhibition at the Kennedy Gallery, New York, ending November 24, 1939, and involving some material from *Madeline*, A24, and *Small Beer*, A39. Bemelmans was interested in a cocktail party at the Waldorf-Astoria prior to the opening (Letter to Sam Golden, August 8, 1939).

Sam Golden wrote to Bemelmans November 29, 1939: "How did the Kennedy show go? I am not so sure that throwing lots of sketches around on the side of the window was such a good thing, because, in a way, it took away whatever precious quality there may be to an original sketch. However, you certainly broke down one of the most straight-laced and dignified fronts, and almost made the Kennedy Gallery look human."

I3. Castleton China Company Show [(1949)]

"Designs on China by Contemporary Artists." Associated American Artists Gallery, New York. [Probably] September, 1949. China transfer from painting (of benches and a little opera stage).

A number of artists were included in the show, many by commission. These included Braque, Picasso, Modigliani, and John Marin. From the A.A.A. the show proceeded to Marshall Fields Department Store in Chicago and thence around the country.

Reviewed: Ralph Pearson, "A Modern Viewpoint," *Art Digest*, vol. 24, Oct. 1, 1949, p. 10. Reproduction included. Bemelmans' contribution to the show is particularly praised and described as "a group of gay semi-abstract picturings of opera."

I4. Ferargil Show [(1950)]

An exhibition of watercolors at Ferargil Gallery, 63 E. 57 Street, New York; Oct. 30 to Nov. 12, 1950.

The catalogue, printed in navy upon cream vellum, is folded twice; it contains a brief essay signed "F.N.P." and a drawing on the cover. The show contained original material from Rosebud, A38.

Announced: *Art Digest*, Vol. 25, Nov. 1, 1950, p. 16.

Announced: *Art News*, Vol. 49, Nov. 1950, p. 47.

I5. Philadelphia Show [(1951)]

An exhibition of forty works at the Art Alliance of Philadelphia; Mar. 6 through Apr. 1, 1951.

The catalogue is four pages and has text by Frederic Newlin Price.

Announced: *Art Alliance Bulletin*, Vol. 29, No. 6, March 1, 1951, pp. 9-12.

I6. Ferargil Show [(1951)]

An exhibition at Ferargil Gallery, 63 E. 57 Street, New York.

Announced: *Art Digest*, Vol. 25, June, 1951, p. 18.

Reviewed: *Time*, Vol. 58, July 2, 1951, p. 48.

I7. Michigan Show [(1951)]

A group of 20 works, mostly watercolors, borrowed from the Ferargil Gallery in New York, at the Hackley Art Gallery, Muskegon, Michigan, ending October 25, 1951. Included "Gypsy Music," 2 illustrations from *Rosebud* (A38), several views of Capri, and a self-portrait of the artist in his Paris studio, a version of which became the endpapers for *Small Beer*, see A39a and later *The Best of Times*, see A3a..

Announced: *Muskegon Chronicle*, October 16, 1951.

I8. Ferargil Show [(1952)]

An exhibition of 25 1951 gouaches and oils at Ferargil Gallery, 63 E. 57 Street, New York. Included work from *How to Travel Incognito*, A20.

Mentioned: *New York Post*, April 25, 1952, Art Exhibition Notes

Announced: *New York Post*, Sunday April 27, 1952.

Announced: *Art Digest*, Vol. 26, May 1, 1952, p. 21.

Announced: *Art News*, Vol. 50, May, 1952, p. 46.

I9. Texas Show [(1952)]

An exhibition of gouaches and watercolors at the Junior League of Houston, c. January-February, 1952.

I10. Ferargil Show [(1952)]

An exhibition of watercolors at Ferargil Gallery, 63 E. 57 Street, New York, December 16 through 31, 1952.

The show included images from the Côte d'Azur, Paris, Nassau, Ischia, Viennes, Morocco, Cordoba, Alceciras and New York.

Announced: *Art Digest*, Vol. 27, Jan. 1, 1953, p. 21.

Announced: *Art News*, Vol. 51, Jan., 1953, p. 48.

I11. Hammer Show [(1955)]

An exhibition of paintings at Hammer Galleries, 51 East 57th Street, N.Y., November 30 through December 31, 1955.

The show included images from *Parsley*, A36; *Madeline*, A24; *Madeline's Rescue*, A30; and pictures of Monaco, Spain, Campobello, Copenhagen, California, Ecuador and Morocco.

The brochure contains a partial list of Bemelmans collectors, including among others Charles Boyer, Joseph Cotton, Gracie Fields, Olivia de Havilland, Helen Hayes, Leland Hayward, William Randolph Hearst Jr., Alfred Hitchcock, Ali Khan, John F. Kennedy, Beatrice Lillie, Joshua Logan, Sir Charles Mendl, Aristoteles Onassis, Comte Armand de la Rochefoucault, Artur Rubinstein, and Orson Welles.

Announced: *Arts*, Vol. 30, Dec. 1955, p. 48.

Announced: *Art News*, Vol. 54, Dec. 1955, p. 54.

I12. Hammer Show [(1956)]

An exhibition of original illustrations from the *Madeline* series at Hammer Galleries, 51 East 57th Street, N.Y., December 1956.

Announced: *Art News*, Vol. 55 No. 8, Dec. 1956, p. 58.

Announced: *Arts*, Vol. 31, Dec. 1956, p. 53.

I13. "First" French Show [(1957)]

An exhibition at Durand-Ruel Gallery, Paris; Oct. 22 through Nov. 6, 1957.

Reviewed: *New York Herald Tribune*, Paris, under headline "Bemelmans' First Show," by Yvonne Hagen, Oct. 23, 1957.

Note: In Leonard Lyons' column in *The New York Post*, August 24, 1949, there is mention of a current show of paintings in Paris by "the late Ludwig Bemelmans," so-called because the painter was convinced canvases by dead artists sold for more than canvases by living ones. No gallery reference is made.

I14. Hammer Show [(1958)]

An exhibition of 50 Paris oils at Hammer Galleries, 51 East 57th Street, N.Y.; December 2-24, 1958.

27 images were from *My Life in Art*, A32.

Announced: *Art News*, Vol. 57, Dec. 1958, p. 60.

Announced: *Arts*, Vol. 33, Jan. 1959, p. 57.

Advertised: *Arts*, Vol. 33, Dec. 1958, p. 7, with a picture of a woman and a rose.

I15. Hammer Show [(1959)]

An exhibition of twenty-four works at Hammer Galleries, 51 East 57th Street, N.Y.; Dec. 1 through 24, 1959.

The show contained the original art from *Madeline and the Gypsies*, A26, recently published; 24 pieces.

Announced: *Arts*, Vol. 34, Dec. 1959, p. 64.

I16. City Museum Show [(1959-1960)]

"Bemelmans' New York," an exhibition of paintings arranged by the Museum of the City of New York, Fifth Avenue at 103rd Street, with the assistance of the Hammer Galleries; Oct. 14, 1959 to January 3, 1960.

The catalog, published between black paper-covered boards, 22.8 x 15.5 cm., contains two full-color and twenty-six black and white illustrations. The title-page verso reads © 1959 by Ludwig Bemelmans. There is a brief essay on the fifth leaf, signed in script, "LB" and dated Ischia, July 13, 1959. The catalog was designed by Ervine Metzl.

Announced: "through Bemelmans' paint box," *New York Herald Tribune Magazine*, October 7, 1959, with six black reproductions.

Advertised: *Art in America*, Vol. 47, No. 4, Winter 1959, p. 118 with a black illustration of the 59th Street Bridge.

I17. Oklahoma Art Center Show [(1960)]

"Bemelmans' New York," an exhibition of paintings arranged by the Museum of the City of New York, Fifth Avenue at 103rd Street, with the assistance of the Hammer Galleries, at the Oklahoma Art Center; March 5 through April 12, 1960.

I18. Phoenix Art Museum Show [(1960)]

"Bemelmans' New York," an exhibition of paintings arranged by the Museum of the City of New York, Fifth Avenue at 103rd Street, with the assistance of the Hammer Galleries, at the Phoenix Art Museum, Phoenix, Arizona; May 1 through May 21, 1960.

I19. Legion of Honor Show [(1960)]

"Bemelmans' New York," an exhibition of paintings arranged by the Museum of the City of New York, Fifth Avenue at 103rd Street, with the assistance of the Hammer Galleries, at the California Palace of the Legion of Honor, San Francisco, California; June 4 through July 4, 1960.

I20. San Diego Show [(1960)]

"Bemelmans' New York," an exhibition of paintings arranged by the Museum of the City of New York, Fifth Avenue at 103rd Street, with the assistance of the Hammer Galleries, at The Fine Arts Gallery of San Diego, San Diego, California; July 22 through Aug. 31, 1960.

I21. Paris Show [(1960)]

"Bemelmans' New York," an exhibition of paintings arranged by the Museum of the City of New York, Fifth Avenue at 103rd Street, with the assistance of the Hammer Galleries, at Bernheim-Jeune Gallerie, Paris; Oct. 1 through Oct. 31, 1960.

L22. Hammer Show [(1960)]

"Bemelmans' New York," an exhibition of forty-eight works arranged by the Museum of the City of New York, Fifth Avenue at 103rd Street, with the assistance of the Hammer Galleries, at Hammer Galleries, 51 East 57th Street, N.Y.; Dec. 1 through Dec. 31, 1960.

Reviewed: *Arts*, Vol. 35, Jan. 1961, p. 54.

L23. Hammer Show [(1961)]

An exhibition of casein paintings at Hammer Galleries, 51 East 57th Street, N.Y., December 5-30, 1961.

The exhibition contained the illustrations from *Madeline in London*, A27. Autographed copies of the book were available for $3.50.

L24. Hammer Show [(1962)]

An exhibition at Hammer Galleries, 51 East 57th Street, N.Y., December 4-29, 1962. (Preview, December 3, 5-7 P.M.)

The exhibition contained 10 recent paintings from *On Board Noah's Ark*, A35, and 16 from *Marina*, A31.

Announced: *Art News*, Vol. 61, Dec. 1962, p. 55.

L25. Düsseldorf Show [(1963)]

An exhibition of 67 oils and gouaches, at the Kunstverein für die Rheinlande und Westfalen, Düsseldorf Kunsthalle Grabbeplatz, Düsseldorf, January 24-February 24, 1963.

Catalogue: *Ludwig Bemelmans*, by Karl-Heinz Hering with a title-page photograph by Vytas Valaitis. The catalogue contains an essay on Bemelmans by Gabriele Henkel, a partial bibliography, and a partial list of Bemelmans collectors from the Hammer Galleries, see I11.

The show contained pictures from the *Madeline* series, as well as of Havana, Capri, Mallorca, Paris, the Côte d'Azur, New York and other locales; with a painting titled "Gypsy Boy (Model for Pepito)—1955." Pepito came to life in *Madeline and the Bad Hat*, 1956/7; see A25a and A25a(bis).

mans and were created in the last ten years of the artist's life. Included was the cover art for *Italian Holiday*, A22.

Reviewed: *Art News*, Vol. 62, Jan. 1964, p. 14.

L26. Guild Hall Show [(1963)]

An exhibition of paintings and drawings at Guild Hall, Main Street, East Hampton, N.Y.; Sept. 7 through Sept. 29, 1963.

The catalog is black and white and contains a reproduction of "Swimming Pool in East Hampton. The show contained material from the *Madeline* series (see A24-A30) and also from *Marina*, A31, *On Board Noah's Ark*, A35, *My Life in Art*, A32, *The High World*, A16, and *Italian Holiday*, A22.

L28. Hammer Show [(1974)]

An exhibition of paintings and drawings at Hammer Galleries, 51 East 57th Street, N.Y.; Feb. 5 through Feb. 23, 1974.

The catalog, 20 x 20 cm., has eight pages and all of the works on show are reproduced, twenty-four in full color and five in black. The show contained work from the *Madeline* series (see A24 through A30) as well as from *Parsley*, A36, and *On Board Noah's Ark*, A35.

Reviewed: *Art News*, Vol. 73, April, 1974, p. 98.

L27. Hammer Show [(1963)]

An exhibition of 134 paintings, watercolors and drawings at Hammer Galleries, 51 East 57th Street, N.Y.; December 3 through 31, 1963. (Preview, December 2, 5-7 P.M.)

The works were selected from the collections of Madeleine Bemelmans and Barbara Bemel-

L29. Ohio Show [(1975)]

An exhibit of original illustrations from the Lee Walp Family Juvenile Collection at The Grover M. Hermann Fine Arts Center, Marietta College, Marietta, Ohio, October 4-27, 1975.

Included were (a) a 9 x 25 cm. pencil rough sketch for *Madeline's Rescue* and (b) a 36 x 26 cm. watercolor, "Madeline in Spring," given by the artist to Mr. and Mrs. L. J. Walp.

I30. Comsky Show [(1975-76)]

An exhibition of watercolors and drawings at Comsky Gallery, 9489 Dayton Way, Beverly Hills, California; Dec. 2, 1975 through Jan. 3, 1976.

Among other works the show contained "Avillons," a watercolor featuring Madeline, Miss Clavel, the eleven other little girls, and Pepito the Bad Hat. There was a special children's opening reception, Tuesday December 2, 1975 from 3:00 to 5:00 p.m.

I3I. Bucks County Show [(1987)]

An exhibition of about 75 sketches and paintings at the Tom Zimmerman Salon, 160 South Main Street, New Hope, Pennsylvania, November 27 through December 21, 1987 (reception Friday December 4 from 5 p.m.).

N O T E: There was a *vernissage* which was held at Lüchows German Restaurant, East 14th Street, New York in November 1956. It was a private showing of one evening only, with a very large buffet. The two-leaf catalogue, in a cover of the Lüchows menu, read "Bemelmans 1956 Vernissage Lüchows." There were gouaches and some oils of France, Spain, Austria, Switzerland, Italy, the Eiffel Tower and magic carpets from *Madeline's Christmas*, and illustrations from *Madeline and the Bad Hat*.

Reviews and Articles
About Bemelmans
and His Work

Reviews and Articles
About Bemelmans
and His Work

LISTED HERE ARE (A) REVIEWS of Bemelmans' work and articles about Bemelmans as they appeared in periodicals or books, listed chronologically; (b) dissertations about Bemelmans; and (c) books in which Bemelmans is discussed, quoted, eulogized. When a publication was dated only by month it is placed as though it appeared on the first. It should be noted that reviews of Bemelmans' exhibitions of drawings and paintings, catalogues of those exhibitions, and announcements of such shows, are all referred to in section "I."

Bemelmans' was an often-printed name not only in the publishing, but also in the social, world of New York. I have *not* made the attempt in this section to include the many references to his escapades which sparkled in regular observers' columns in the major New York papers; or to list the standard mini-

reviews of books that appear as a regular part of publishers'
announcements or editorial speculation in publications such as
Publisher's Weekly or *Bookseller*. The norm in those publications
was for a book to be projected, and often briefly described,
weeks before publication; or evaluated as to impact and sales
shortly afterward, again in only a paragraph or two.

I. PUBLISHED ARTICLES ABOUT BEMELMANS

1. Margaret Vincent Buddy, untitled review of *Hansi*, *Scribner's Magazine*, Vol. 96, p. 33, 1934

2. Anonymous, untitled review of *Hansi*, *The Horn Book Magazine*, Vol. 10, p. 354, November 1934.

3. M. G. Davis, untitled review of *Hansi*, *New York Herald Tribune Books*, November 11, 1934, p. 8.

4. A. T. Eaton, untitled review of *Hansi*, *New York Times Book Review*, November 11, 1934, p. 17.

5. R. C. Benét, untitled review of *Hansi*, *Saturday Review of Literature*, Vol. 11, p. 296, November 17, 1934.

6. J. W. Maury, untitled review of *Hansi*, *Boston Evening Transcript*, November 21, 1934, p. 2.

7. Anonymous, untitled review of *Hansi*, *Booklist*, Vol. 31, p. 134, December 1934.

8. Anonymous, untitled review of *Hansi*, *Catholic World*, Vol. 140, p. 378, December 1934.

9. Anonymous, untitled review of *Hansi*, *Wisconsin Library Bulletin*, Vol. 30, p. 244, December 1934.

10. Irene Brock McElherman, untitled review of *Hansi*, *Canadian Bookman*, Vol. 17, p. 58, 1935.

11. Anonymous [H. K. Frenzel], "Kinderbücher (Children's Books)," review of *Hansi*, *Gebrauchsgraphik*, Vol. 12, pp. 10-11, 24-25, February 1935.

12. Anonymous, "Twin Cities," review of the illustrations by Bemelmans for an article titled, "Twin Cities," *Fortune*, Vol. 14, pp. 86-88, July 1936, including 1 black illustration. See G37.

13. M. L. Becker, untitled review of *The Golden Basket*, *New York Herald Tribune Books*, September 20, 1936, p. 10.

14. A. C. Moore, untitled review of *The Golden Basket*, *The Atlantic Monthly*, October 1936.

15. Anne Eaton, untitled review of *The Golden Basket*, *New York Times Book Review*, October 4, 1936, p. 12.

16. Anonymous, untitled review of *The Golden Basket*, *Boston Evening Transcript*, October 10, 1936, p. 8.

17. Anonymous, untitled review of *The Golden Basket*, *Booklist*, Vol. 33, p. 90, November 1936.

18. Anonymous, untitled review of *The Golden Basket*, *The Horn Book Magazine*, Vol. 12, p. 355, November 1936.

19. A. C. Moore, untitled review of *The Golden Basket*, *The Horn Book Magazine*, Vol. 12, p. 346, November 1936.

20. Edith Rees, untitled review of *The Golden Basket*, *Library Journal*, Vol. 61, p. 809, November 1, 1936.

21. Anonymous, untitled review of *The Golden*

Basket, *New York Herald Tribune Books*, November 15, 1936, p. 12.

22. M. F. Potter, untitled review of *The Golden Basket*, *Library Journal*, Vol. 61, p. 929, December 1, 1936.

23. Anonymous, untitled review of *Hansi*, *World Affairs*, Vol. 100, p. 261, 1937.

24. Josephine Dodge Kimball, "Noodle," review of *Noodle* by Munro Leaf, *Scribner's Magazine*, Vol. 102, p. 62, 1937.

25. John Chamberlain, untitled review of *My War With the United States*, *Scribner's Magazine*, Vol. 102, p. 70, 1937.

26. Tom Squire, untitled review of *My War With the United States*, *The Nation*, Vol. 145, p. 136, 1937.

27. Josephine Dodge Kimball, untitled review of *The Castle Number Nine*, *Scribner's Magazine*, Vol. 102, p. 62, 1937.

28. Anonymous, untitled review of *My War With the United States*, *Springfield Republican*, July 2, 1937, p. 12.

29. "F.B.," untitled review of *My War With the United States*, *Chicago Daily Tribune*, July 3, 1937, p. 6.

30. Anonymous, untitled review of *My War With the United States*, *Time*, Vol. 30, p. 54, July 5, 1937.

31. Anonymous, untitled review of *My War With the United States*, *Saturday Review of Literature*, Vol. 16, p. 21, July 10, 1937.

32. Anonymous, untitled review of *My War*

With the United States*, *New York Times Book Review*, July 10, 1937, p. 13.

33. Anonymous, untitled review of *My War With the United States*, *New York Times Book Review*, July 11, 1937, p. 2.

34. William Soskin, "A German Artist's Picture of America," review of *My War With the United States*, *New York Herald Tribune Books*, July 11, 1937, pp. 1-2.

35. Robert Van Gelder, untitled review of *My War With the United States*, *New York Times Book Review*, July 11, 1937, p. 2.

36. Anonymous, "Handy Guide to Dilettante Archaeological, etc.," sketch, *New York Times*, July 14, 1937, p. 19.

37. "Bemelmans Back Home With Material For Book," portrait, *New York Herald Tribune*, July 14, 1937.

38. Truitt Brookledge, untitled review of *My War With the United States*, *Boston Evening Transcript*, July 17, 1937, p. 4.

39. Anonymous, "Man About Town Tries His Hand at Many Trades," portrait, *Newsweek*, Vol. 10, p. 21, July 24, 1937.

40. Tom Squire, untitled review of *My War With the United States*, *The Nation*, Vol. 145, p. 136, July 31, 1937.

41. Anonymous, untitled review of *My War With the United States*, *Christian Science Monitor*, August 4, 1937, p. 10.

42. Anonymous, untitled review of *My War*

With the United States, Booklist, Vol. 34, p. 3, September 1, 1937.

43. Anonymous, untitled review of *My War With the United States, Cleveland Open Shelf*, September 1937, p. 19.

44. Anonymous, untitled review of *The Castle Number Nine, New York Times Book Review*, November 14, 1937, Section 7, p. 14.

45. Anonymous, untitled review of *My War With the United States, Wisconsin Library Bulletin*, Vol. 33, p. 176, December 1937.

46. Anonymous, untitled review of *My War With the United States, The Horn Book Magazine*, Vol. 14, p. 317, January 1938.

47. C. E. Scott, untitled review of *My War With the United States, Library Journal*, Vol. 63, p. 34, January 1, 1938.

48. Marie Scott-James, "Noodle," review of *Noodle* by Munro Leaf, *London Mercury*, Vol. 39, p. 250, 1938.

49. Anonymous, "The Humor of Ludwig Bemelmans," illustrated portrait, *Publisher's Weekly*, Vol. 134, pp. 1508-1510, October 22, 1938.

50. M. L. Becker, untitled review of *Quito Express, New York Herald Tribune Books*, October 23, 1938, p. 8.

51. A. T. Eaton, untitled review of *Quito Express, New York Times Book Review*, October 30, 1938, p. 12.

52. Anonymous, untitled review of *Quito Express, Cleveland Open Shelf*, November 1938, p. 20.

53. Anonymous, untitled review of *Quito Express, The Horn Book Magazine*, Vol. 14, p. 371, November 1938.

54. R. A. Hill, untitled review of *Quito Express, Library Journal*, Vol. 63, p. 819, November 1, 1938.

55. Anonymous, portrait, *Saturday Review of Literature*, Vol. 19, p. 7, November 12, 1938.

56. Anonymous, untitled review of *Life Class, New York Times Book Review*, November 13, 1938, Section 6, p. 5.

57. Anonymous, untitled review of *Life Class, New York Times Book Review*, November 14, 1938, p. 17.

58. Anonymous, untitled review of *Quito Express, Booklist*, Vol. 35, p. 102, November 15, 1938.

59. L. S. Bechtel, untitled review of *Quito Express, Saturday Review of Literature*, Vol. 19, p. 18, November 19, 1938.

60. A. L. Shea, untitled review of *Quito Express, Library Journal*, Vol. 63, p. 936, December 1, 1938.

61. Irene Weise, untitled review of *Quito Express, Boston Evening Transcript*, December 3, 1938, p. 1.

62. Anonymous, untitled review of *Quito Express, The New Republic*, Vol. 97, p. 149, December 7, 1938.

63. Anonymous, untitled review of *Life Class*, *The Spectator*, Vol. 163, p. 410, 1939.

64. B. Alsterlund, biographical sketch with portrait, *Wilson Bulletin*, Vol. 13, p. 522, April 1939.

65. Ashton Sanborn, untitled review of *Small Beer*, *Boston Evening Transcript*, July 1939, p. 1.

66. Anonymous, untitled review of *Small Beer*, *Cleveland Open Shelf*, August 1939, p. 15.

67. Rose Feld, untitled review of *Small Beer*, *New York Herald Tribune Books*, August 27, 1939, p. 6.

68. Anonymous, untitled review of *Small Beer*, *New York Times Book Review*, August 30, 1939, p. 13.

69. Anonymous, untitled review of *Small Beer*, *The New Yorker*, Vol. 15, p. 62, September 2, 1939.

70. Robert Van Gelder, untitled review of *Small Beer*, *New York Times Book Review*, September 3, 1939, p. 5.

71. Anonymous, untitled review of *Small Beer*, *Time*, Vol. 34, p. 54, September 4, 1939.

72. Anonymous, "Speaking of Pictures: This is the Story of Madeline and Her Appendix," *Life*, Vol. 7 No. 10, September 4, 1939, pp. 6-9. A condensation of *Madeline*, A24, is given along with a photograph of Bemelmans and of his daughter, Barbara. 13 black and yellow and 2 black illustrations are used. A brief biography mentions that *Madeline* will appear September 5, 1939, but the publisher gives the date as September 15. See A24a.

73. Otis Ferguson, untitled review of *Small Beer*, *The New Republic*, Vol. 100, p. 137, September 6, 1939.

74. Anonymous, untitled review of *Madeline*, *New York Times Book Review*, September 24, 1939, Section 6, p. 12.

75. J. V. McAree, "American Was Lucky Who Jeered at Hitler," describing "Bride of Berchtesgaden," *Toronto Globe and Mail*, October 3, 1939.

76. Anonymous, untitled review of *Small Beer*, *Springfield Republican*, October 15, 1939, p. 7e.

77. Marion Strobel, untitled review of *Madeline*, *Poetry*, Vol. 55, p. 221, 1940.

78. Anonymous, "Ludwig Bemelmans Arrives NYC," sketch, *New York Times*, September 24, 1940, p. 3.

79. M. L. Becker, untitled review of *Fifi*, *New York Herald Tribune Books*, November 10, 1940, p. 12.

80. Z. C. Durrell, untitled review of *Fifi*, *Saturday Review of Literature*, Vol. 23, p. 9, November 16, 1940.

81. Anonymous, untitled review of *Fifi*, *Commonweal*, Vol. 33, p. 121, November 22, 1940.

82. Anonymous, untitled review of *Fifi*, *Springfield Republican*, December 1, 1940, p. 7e.

83. Anonymous, untitled review of *Fifi*, *The New Yorker*, Vol. 16, p. 125, December 7, 1940.

84. Anonymous, biographical portrait, *Current Biography, 1941*, 1941.

85. Anonymous, untitled review of *The Donkey Inside*, *College English*, Vol. 2, p. 721, 1941.

86. M. E. Clark, untitled review of *The Donkey Inside*, *Library Journal*, Vol. 66, p. 79, January 15, 1941.

87. Clifton Fadiman, untitled review of *The Donkey Inside*, *The New Yorker*, Vol. 16, p. 77, January 18, 1941.

88. L. J. Halle, Jr., untitled review of *The Donkey Inside*, *Saturday Review of Literature*, Vol. 23, p. 7, January 18, 1941.

89. Anonymous, untitled review of *The Donkey Inside*, *New York Times Book Review*, January 18, 1941, p. 13.

90. F. H. Bullock, untitled review of *The Donkey Inside*, *New York Herald Tribune Books*, January 19, 1941, p. 3.

91. Katherine Woods, untitled review of *The Donkey Inside*, *New York Times Book Review*, January 19, 1941, p. 3.

92. Anonymous, portrait, *Newsweek*, Vol. 17, p. 54, January 20, 1941.

93. Anonymous, portrait, *Time*, Vol. 37, p. 83, January 20, 1941.

94. Anonymous, untitled review of *The Donkey Inside*, *Time*, Vol. 37, p. 80, January 20, 1941.

95. Otis Ferguson, untitled review of *The Donkey Inside*, *The New Republic*, Vol. 104, p. 93, January 20, 1941.

96. Anonymous, untitled review of *The Donkey Inside*, *The Nation*, Vol. 152, p. 108, January 25, 1941.

97. Anonymous, interview, *New York Times*, January 26, 1941, Section VI, p. 2.

98. Anonymous, biographical sketch, *Stage*, Vol. 1 No. 4, pp. 46-47, February 1941.
    Contains 8 black and white photographs.

99. Anonymous, untitled review of *The Donkey Inside*, *Commonweal*, Vol. 33, p. 429, February 14, 1941.

100. Anonymous, untitled review of *The Donkey Inside*, *Booklist*, Vol. 37, p. 269, February 15, 1941.

101. Anonymous, untitled review of *The Donkey Inside*, *Current History and Forum*, Vol. 52, p. 61, April 1941.

102. Graham McInnes, untitled review of *The Donkey Inside*, *Canadian Forum*, Vol. 21, p. 28, April 1941.

103. Robert Littell, untitled review of *The Donkey Inside*, *Yale Review*, Vol. 30, p. vii, Spring 1941.

104. J. I. B. McCulloch, untitled review of *The Donkey Inside*, *Yale Review*, Vol. 30, p. 614, Spring 1941.

105. Graham McInnes, untitled review of *The Donkey Inside*, *Canadian Forum*, Vol. 21, p. 28, 1941-42.

106. Lena Ruppert, untitled review of *Hotel Splendide*, *Library Journal*, Vol. 66, p. 901, October 15, 1941.

107. Anonymous, untitled review of *Hotel Splendide*, *New York Times Book Review*, December 3, 1941, p. 29.

108. Anonymous, untitled review of *Hotel Splendide*, *The New Yorker*, Vol. 17, p. 136, December 6, 1941.

109. Rose Feld, untitled review of *Hotel Splendide*, *New York Herald Tribune Books*, December 7, 1941, p. 4.

110. Anonymous, portrait, *Time*, Vol. 38, p. 114, December 15, 1941.

111. Otis Ferguson, untitled review of *Hotel Splendide*, *The New Republic*, Vol. 105, p. 869, December 22, 1941.

112. S. C. Gross, untitled review of *Hotel Splendide*, *Saturday Review of Literature*, Vol. 24, p. 22, December 27, 1941.

113. Robert Van Gelder, untitled review of *Hotel Splendide*, *New York Times Book Review*, December 28, 1941, p. 4.

114. J. Hampson, untitled review of *Hotel Splendide*, *The Spectator*, Vol. 169, p. 584, 1942.

115. Anonymous, untitled review of *Hotel Splendide*, *Punch*, Vol. 203, p. 561, 1942.

116. Anonymous, untitled review of *Hotel Splendide*, *College English*, Vol. 3, p. 517, 1942.

117. Anonymous, untitled review of *Hotel Splendide*, *Canadian Forum*, Vol. 21, p. 381, 1942.

118. Anonymous, untitled review of *Hotel Splendide*, *Booklist*, Vol. 38, p. 155, January 1, 1942.

119. Anonymous, untitled review of *Hotel Splendide*, *Best Sellers*, Vol. 1, pp. 178-179, January 21, 1942.

120. Anonymous, "Home Splendide: Ludwig Bemelmans Lives in This NY Apartment," portrait, *House and Garden*, Vol. 82, p. 20, August 1, 1942.

121. E. H. Crowell, untitled review of *I Love You, I Love You, I Love You*, *Library Journal*, Vol. 67, p. 738, September 1, 1942.

122. Clifton Fadiman, untitled review of *I Love You, I Love You, I Love You*, *The New Yorker*, Vol. 18, p. 58, September 5, 1942.

123. Virgilia Sapieha, untitled review of *I Love You, I Love You, I Love You*, *New York Herald Tribune Books*, September 6, 1942, p. 4.

124. Beatrice Sherman, untitled review of *I Love You, I Love You, I Love You*, *New York Times Book Review*, September 6, 1942, p. 3.

125. Anonymous, untitled review of *I Love You, I Love You, I Love You*, *New York Times Book Review*, September 7, 1942, p. 17.

126. Anonymous, portrait, *Time*, Vol. 40, p. 101, September 14, 1942.

127. Anonymous, untitled review of *I Love You, I Love You, I Love You*, *Time*, Vol. 40, p. 100, September 14, 1942.

128. Anonymous, untitled review of *I Love You, I*

Love You, I Love You, *The Nation*, Vol. 155, p. 245, September 19, 1942.

129. Anonymous, untitled review of *I Love You, I Love You, I Love You*, *Booklist*, Vol. 39, p. 29, October 1, 1942.

130. E. L. Buell, untitled review of *Rosebud*, *New York Times Book Review*, October 4, 1942, p. 35.

131. C. O. Skinner, untitled review of *I Love You, I Love You, I Love You*, *Saturday Review of Literature*, Vol. 25, p. 14, October 17, 1942.

132. A. M. Jordan, untitled review of *Rosebud*, *The Horn Book Magazine*, Vol. 18, p. 417, November 1942.

133. E. G. Mullan, untitled review of *Rosebud*, *Library Journal*, Vol. 67, p. 954, November 1, 1942.

134. Anonymous, untitled review of *Rosebud*, *Saturday Review of Literature*, Vol. 25, p. 28, November 14, 1942.

135. M. L. Becker, untitled review of *Rosebud*, *New York Herald Tribune Books*, November 22, 1942, p. 12.

136. Anonymous, untitled review of *Rosebud*, *Catholic World*, Vol. 156, p. 372, December 1942.

137. Edward Weeks, untitled review of *I Love You, I Love You, I Love You*, *Atlantic Monthly*, Vol. 170, p. 144, December 1942.

138. Anonymous, untitled review of *Rosebud*, *The New Yorker*, Vol. 18, p. 105, December 12, 1942.

139. F. A. Boyle, untitled review of *Now I Lay Me Down To Sleep*, *Library Journal*, Vol. 68, p. 845, October 15, 1943.

140. Robert Littell, untitled review of *I Love You, I Love You, I Love You*, *Yale Review*, Vol. 32, p. viii, Winter 1943.

141. Anonymous, untitled review of *Now I Lay Me Down To Sleep*, *Kirkus Reviews*, Vol. 12, p. 3, January 1, 1944.

142. Anonymous, untitled review of *Now I Lay Me Down To Sleep*, *Booklist*, Vol. 40, p. 165, January 1, 1944.

143. Barbara Berch, "The Man with the Needle," portrait, *Collier's*, Vol. 113, p. 57, February 19, 1944.

144. Anonymous, untitled review of *Now I Lay Me Down To Sleep*, *Springfield Republican*, February 20, 1944, p. 7e.

145. Russell Maloney, untitled review of *Now I Lay Me Down To Sleep*, *Book Week*, February 20, 1944, p. 1.

146. W. S. Schlamm, untitled review of *Now I Lay Me Down To Sleep*, *New York Times Book Review*, February 20, 1944, p. 5.

147. F. H. Bullock, untitled review of *Now I Lay Me Down To Sleep*, *Weekly Book Review*, February 20, 1944, p. 3.

148. Anonymous, portrait, *Newsweek*, Vol. 23, p. 92, February 21, 1944.

149. Anonymous, "Epileptic Allegory," review of *Now I Lay Me Down To Sleep*, *Time*, Vol. 43,

p. 102, February 21, 1944, beginning p. 102.

150. Anonymous, untitled review of *Now I Lay Me Down To Sleep*, *New York Times Book Review*, February 21, 1944, p. 13.

151. Mark Schorer, untitled review of *Now I Lay Me Down To Sleep*, *The New Republic*, Vol. 110, p. 288, February 28, 1944.

152. Anonymous, untitled review of *Now I Lay Me Down To Sleep*, *The New Yorker*, Vol. 20, p. 82, March 4, 1944.

153. Phil Stong, untitled review of *Now I Lay Me Down To Sleep*, *Saturday Review of Literature*, Vol. 27, p. 8, March 4, 1944.

154. James Stern, untitled review of *Now I Lay Me Down To Sleep*, *The Nation*, Vol. 158, p. 314, March 11, 1944.

155. Anonymous, untitled review of *Now I Lay Me Down To Sleep*, *Best Sellers*, Vol. 3, p. 172, March 15, 1944.

156. C. G. Paulding, untitled review of *Now I Lay Me Down To Sleep*, *Commonweal*, Vol. 39, p. 548, March 17, 1944.

157. Edward Weeks, untitled review of *Now I Lay Me Down To Sleep*, *Atlantic Monthly*, Vol. 173, p. 125, April 1944.

158. Orville Prescott, untitled review of *Now I Lay Me Down To Sleep*, *Yale Review*, Vol. 33, p. xiv, Spring 1944.

159. Anonymous, untitled review of *Now I Lay Me Down To Sleep*, *Extension*, Vol. 38, p. 21, May 1944.

160. K. O'Brien, untitled review of *Now I Lay Me Down To Sleep*, *The Spectator*, Vol. 174, p. 112, 1945.

161. Charles Marriott, untitled review of *Now I Lay Me Down To Sleep*, *Manchester Guardian*, January 5, 1945, p. 3.

162. Anonymous, untitled review of *Now I Lay Me Down To Sleep*, *Times Literary Supplement* (London), January 13, 1945, p. 17.

163. Anonymous, untitled review of *The Blue Danube*, *Kirkus Reviews*, Vol. 13, p. 38, February 1, 1945.

164. Anonymous, "Ludwig Bemelmans Discusses New Book," interview, *New York Times*, February 25, 1945, Section II, p. 3.

165. Anonymous, untitled review of *Yolanda and the Thief* by Ludwig Bemelmans and Jacques Théry, *Life*, Vol. 18, pp. 55-57, March 12, 1945.

166. H. G. Kelley, untitled review of *The Blue Danube*, *Library Journal*, Vol. 70, p. 306, April 1, 1945.

167. Russell Maloney, untitled review of *The Blue Danube*, *New York Times Book Review*, April 8, 1945, p. 3.

168. Rose Feld, untitled review of *The Blue Danube*, *Weekly Book Review*, April 8, 1945, p. 2.

169. Anonymous, untitled review of *The Blue Danube*, *Time*, Vol. 45, p. 99, April 9, 1945.

170. E. A. Laycock, untitled review of *The Blue Danube*, *Boston Globe*, April 11, 1945, p. 17.

171. A. J. Liebling, untitled review of *The Blue Danube*, *The New Yorker*, Vol. 21, p. 83, April 14, 1945.

172. Sterling North, untitled review of *The Blue Danube*, *Book Week*, April 15, 1945, p. 2.

173. C. K. Bausman, untitled review of *The Blue Danube*, *Springfield Republican*, April 15, 1945, p. 4d.

174. Anonymous, untitled review of *The Blue Danube*, *New York Times Book Review*, April 26, 1945, p. 21.

175. Anonymous, untitled review of *The Blue Danube*, *Booklist*, Vol. 41, p. 255, May 1, 1945.

176. Anonymous, untitled review of *The Blue Danube*, *Cleveland Open Shelf*, May 1945, p. 12.

177. Anonymous, untitled review of *The Blue Danube*, *Best Sellers*, Vol. 5, p. 30, May 1, 1945.

178. Harold Fields, untitled review of *The Blue Danube*, *Saturday Review of Literature*, Vol. 28, p. 30, May 19, 1945.

179. Edward Weeks, untitled review of *The Blue Danube*, *Atlantic Monthly*, Vol. 175, p. 123, June 1945.

180. Anonymous, untitled review of *The Blue Danube*, *Extension*, Vol. 40, p. 20, June 1945.

181. Anonymous, untitled review of *The Blue Danube*, *Sign*, Vol. 24, p. 613, June 1945.

182. Anonymous, untitled review of *The Blue Danube*, *Wisconsin Library Bulletin*, Vol. 41, p. 84, July 1945.

183. Anonymous, untitled review of *Yolanda and the Thief* by Ludwig Bemelmans and Jacques Théry, *New York Times*, November 23, 1945.

184. Anonymous, untitled review of *Yolanda and the Thief* by Ludwig Bemelmans and Jacques Théry, *Newsweek*, Vol. 26, p. 100, December 3, 1945.

185. Anonymous, untitled review of *Yolanda and the Thief* by Ludwig Bemelmans and Jacques Théry, *Time*, Vol. 46, p. 97, December 10, 1945.

186. Jasper R. Lewis, untitled review of *Hotel Bemelmans*, *Forum and Century*, Vol. 106, p. 364, 1946.

187. K. O'Brien, untitled review of *The Blue Danube*, *The Spectator*, Vol. 177, p. 374, 1946.

188. R. Mallett, untitled review of *The Blue Danube*, *Punch*, Vol. 211, p. 323, 1946.

189. Anonymous, untitled review of *Hotel Bemelmans*, *Kirkus Reviews*, Vol. 14, p. 305, July 1, 1946.

190. June Johnston, untitled review of *Hotel Bemelmans*, *Book Week*, September 8, 1946, p. 6.

191. Richard Watts, untitled review of *Hotel Bemelmans*, *New York Times Book Review*, September 8, 1946, p. 5.

192. Edward Angly, untitled review of *Hotel*

Bemelmans, Weekly Book Review, September 8, 1946, p. 4.

193. J. H. Jackson, untitled review of *Hotel Bemelmans, San Francisco Chronicle*, September 16, 1946, p. 14.

194. Anonymous, untitled review of *Hotel Bemelmans, New York Times Book Review*, September 19, 1946, p. 29.

195. Jack Iams, untitled review of *Hotel Bemelmans, Saturday Review of Literature*, Vol. 29, p. 17, September 28, 1946.

196. Anonymous, untitled review of *Hotel Bemelmans, Time*, Vol. 48, p. 114, September 30, 1946.

197. Edward Weeks, untitled review of *Hotel Bemelmans, Atlantic Monthly*, Vol. 178, p. 154, November 1946.

198. Robert Warshow, untitled review of *Hotel Bemelmans, The Nation*, Vol. 163, p. 529, November 9, 1946.

199. Jasper R. Lewis, untitled review of *Dirty Eddie, Forum and Century*, Vol. 108, p. 249, 1947.

200. Anonymous, untitled review of *Hotel Bemelmans, Booklist*, Vol. 43, p. 134, January 1,1947.

201. Francis Hackett, "The Good Germans," review of *The Blue Danube*, in *On Judging Books*, New York: J. Day, 1947.

202. Anonymous, untitled review of *Dirty Eddie, Kirkus Reviews*, Vol. 15, p. 294, June 1, 1947.

203. Anonymous, portrait, *Saturday Review of Literature*, Vol. 30, p. 12, August 16, 1947.

204. Harrison Smith, untitled review of *Dirty Eddie, Saturday Review of Literature*, Vol. 30, p. 12, August 16, 1947.

205. J. O. Supple, untitled review of *Dirty Eddie, Chicago Sun Book Week*, August 17, 1947, p. 3.

206. Richard Mealand, untitled review of *Dirty Eddie, New York Herald Tribune Weekly Book Review*, August 17, 1947, p. 4.

207. Frank Nugent, "Bemelmans Bazooka," review of *Dirty Eddie, New York Times Book Review*, August 17, 1947, beginning p. 5.

208. Richard Watts, untitled review of *Dirty Eddie, The New Republic*, Vol. 117, p. 28, August 18, 1947.

209. J. H. Jackson, untitled review of *Dirty Eddie, San Francisco Chronicle*, August 18, 1947, p. 14.

210. Anonymous, untitled review of *Dirty Eddie, The New Yorker*, Vol. 23, p. 77, August 23, 1947.

211. Irving Howe, untitled review of *Dirty Eddie, The Nation*, Vol. 165, p. 205, August 30, 1947.

212. Anonymous, untitled review of *Dirty Eddie, New York Times Book Review*, August 30, 1947, p. 13.

213. Anonymous, untitled review of *Dirty Eddie, Time*, Vol. 50, p. 86, September 1, 1947.

214. Edward Weeks, untitled review of *Dirty Ed-*

die, *Atlantic Monthly*, Vol. 180, p. 120, October 1947.

215. Anonymous, untitled review of *Dirty Eddie*, *Best Sellers*, Vol. 7, p. 132, October 15, 1947.

216. Anonymous, untitled review of *Dirty Eddie*, *Theatre Arts*, Vol. 32, p. 84, 1948.

217. R. Mallett, untitled review of *Dirty Eddie*, *Punch*, Vol. 215, p. 18, 1948.

218. Anonymous, untitled review of *Dirty Eddie*, *Theatre Arts*, Vol. 32 No. 2, p. 84, February 1948.

219. Anonymous, portrait, *New York Post*, February 7, 1948.

220. Anonymous, untitled review of *The Best of Times*, *New York Times Book Review*, November 4, 1948, p. 27.

221. Nona Balakian, untitled review of *The Best of Times*, *New York Times Book Review*, November 7, 1948, p. 6.

222. Anonymous, untitled review of *The Best of Times*, *Time*, Vol. 52, p. 113, November 8, 1948.

223. J. H. Jackson, untitled review of *The Best of Times*, *San Francisco Chronicle*, November 11, 1948, p. 18.

224. Anonymous, untitled review of *The Best of Times*, *The New Yorker*, Vol. 24, p. 149, November 13, 1948.

225. Iris Barry, untitled review of *The Best of Times*, *New York Herald Tribune Book Review*, November 14, 1948, p. 3.

226. Anonymous, untitled review of *The Best of Times*, *Saturday Review of Literature*, Vol. 31, p. 99, November 27, 1948.

227. Anonymous, untitled review of *The Best of Times*, *Booklist*, Vol. 45, p. 135, December 15, 1948.

228. Anonymous, untitled review of *The Best of Times*, *Catholic World*, Vol. 168, p. 336, January 1949.

229. Anonymous, untitled review of *The Best of Times*, *Springfield Republican*, January 16, 1949, p. 18a.

230. Anonymous, "Alarums and Excursions," biography, *Theatre Arts*, Vol. 33 No. 2, p. 9, March 1949.

231. Anonymous, portrait, *Saturday Night*, Vol. 64, p. 26, April 19, 1949.

232. Anonymous, untitled review of *The Eye of God*, *Kirkus Reviews*, Vol. 17, p. 443, August 15, 1949.

233. H. S. Taylor, untitled review of *The Eye of God*, *Library Journal*, Vol. 74, p. 1201, September 1, 1949.

234. Anonymous, untitled review of *The Eye of God*, *Booklist*, Vol. 46, p. 25, September 15, 1949.

235. Anonymous, untitled review of *The Eye of God*, *The New Yorker*, Vol. 25, p. 109, October 29, 1949.

236. J. K. Hutchens, untitled review of *The Eye of God*, *New York Herald Tribune Book Review*, October 30, 1949, p. 4.

237. D. M. Mankiewicz, untitled review of *The Eye of God*, *New York Times Book Review*, October 30, 1949, p. 4.

238. Anonymous, untitled review of *The Eye of God*, *Booklist*, Vol. 46, p. 82, November 1, 1949.

239. Edward Weeks, untitled review of *The Eye of God*, *Atlantic Monthly*, Vol. 184, p. 88, November 1949.

240. Anonymous, untitled review of *The Eye of God*, *Christian Science Monitor*, November 10, 1949, p. 15.

241. J. H. Jackson, untitled review of *The Eye of God*, *San Francisco Chronicle*, November 11, 1949, p. 20.

242. Anonymous, portrait, *Time*, Vol. 54, p. 120, November 14, 1949.

243. Anonymous, untitled review of *The Eye of God*, *Time*, Vol. 54, p. 120, November 14, 1949.

244. Niccolo Tucci, untitled review of *The Eye of God*, *Saturday Review of Literature*, Vol. 32, p. 20, November 19, 1949.

245. Feike Feikema, untitled review of *The Eye of God*, *Chicago Sunday Tribune*, November 29, 1949.

246. L. S. Munn, untitled review of *The Eye of God*, *Springfield Republican*, December 25, 1949, p. 10b.

247. Anonymous, untitled review of *The Eye of God*, *Daughters of the American Revolution Magazine*, Vol. 84, p. 26, 1950.

248. B. Pomer, untitled review of *The Eye of God*, *Canadian Forum*, Vol. 29, p. 239, January 1950.

249. Kathleen Graham, "Wit and Satire," review of *The Eye of God*, *Toronto Globe and Mail*, January 21, 1950.

250. Anonymous, portrait, *Saturday Night*, Vol. 65, p. 28, March 14, 1950.

251. A. L. Shea, untitled review of *Sunshine*, *Chicago Sunday Tribune*, April 27, 1950, p. 10.

252. Anonymous, untitled review of *Sunshine*, *Kirkus Reviews*, Vol. 18, p. 260, May 1, 1950.

253. L. S. Bechtel, untitled review of *Sunshine*, *New York Herald Tribune Book Review*, May 7, 1950, p. 7.

254. "E. L. B.," untitled review of *Sunshine*, *New York Times Book Review*, May 14, 1950, p. 30.

255. "R. F. H.," untitled review of *Sunshine*, *Springfield Republican*, May 28, 1950, p. 5c.

256. Anonymous, untitled review of *Sunshine*, *Booklist*, Vol. 46, p. 321, June 15, 1950.

257. Anonymous, untitled review of *Sunshine*, *Wisconsin Library Bulletin*, Vol. 46, p. 22, July 1950.

258. A. M. Jordan, untitled review of *Sunshine*, *The Horn Book Magazine*, Vol. 26, p. 281, July 1950.

259. Anonymous, untitled description of *Sunshine*, *The Horn Book Magazine*, Vol. 26 No. 4, p. 281, July-August 1950.

260. Alice McQuaid, untitled review of *Sunshine*,

Library Journal, Vol. 75, p. 1305, August 1950.

261. Paul Pickrel, untitled review of *The Eye of God*, *Yale Review*, Vol. 39, p. 282, Winter 1950.

262. Anonymous, "Says Lady Mendl Was Sane," report, *New York Herald Tribune*, April 26, 1951. An account of Bemelmans' evaluation of Lady Mendl's mental condition at the time of her death. See as well A43.

263. Henry C. Pitz, "Ludwig Bemelmans," biographical sketch, illustrated, *American Artist*, Vol. 15 No. 5, pp. 48-49, May 1951.

264. Anonymous, "Resolutely Gay," portrait, *Time*, Vol. 58, p. 78, July 2, 1951.

265. Anonymous, untitled review of *How to Travel Incognito*, *American Mercury*, Vol. 75, p. 113, 1952.

266. Anonymous, "People Watcher," biographical sketch, *Time*, Vol. 59 No. 13, p. 40, March 31, 1952.

267. Anonymous, untitled review of *How to Travel Incognito*, *Booklist*, Vol. 48, p. 257, April 15, 1952.

268. J. H. Jackson, untitled review of *How to Travel Incognito*, *San Francisco Chronicle*, April 30, 1952, p. 20.

269. Anonymous, untitled review of *How to Travel Incognito*, *Booklist*, Vol. 48, p. 278, May 1, 1952.

270. Anonymous, untitled review of *How to Travel Incognito*, *Kirkus Reviews*, Vol. 19, p. 235, May 1, 1952.

271. J. A. Barry, untitled review of *How to Travel Incognito*, *New York Times Book Review*, May 4, 1952, p. 5.

272. Anonymous, untitled review of *How to Travel Incognito*, *The New Yorker*, Vol. 28, p. 137, May 10, 1952.

273. Paul Engle, untitled review of *How to Travel Incognito*, *Chicago Sunday Tribune*, May 18, 1952, p. 7.

274. Anonymous, untitled review of *How to Travel Incognito*, *New York Times Book Review*, May 21, 1952, p. 25.

275. Gouverneur Paulding, "True Bemelmans Gothic," review of *How to Travel Incognito*, *New York Herald Tribune Book Review*, May 25, 1952, p. 5.

276. Anonymous, untitled review of *How to Travel Incognito*, *Manchester Guardian*, June 6, 1952, p. 4.

277. Kathleen McDowell, "Bemelmans Incognito," review of *How to Travel Incognito*, *Toronto Globe and Mail*, June 14, 1952.

278. Anonymous, "Cuckoo!," review of *How to Travel Incognito*, *Time*, June 16, 1952, p. 106. Bemelmans wrote a reply to the editor, June 30, 1952, which was published as "Poodles, Pigs, Love, etc." I give it in full: "Sir: Thank you for the excellent review [June 16] of 'How to Travel Incognito.' May I point out, however, that I wrote other

books: 'The Donkey Inside'—on Ecuador. 'The Blue Danube'—on the misery of Germany. 'The Best of Times'—on postwar Europe. 'Fifi'—about a poodle. 'Madeline'—about a little girl. 'Dirty Eddy'[sic]—about a pig. 'The Eye of God'—about a mountain. I shall, however, heed your advice. My next book is about love. Its title: 'With the Greatest of Pleasures.' Love. [signed] Ludwig Bemelmans. New York City."

279. Frank Hauser, untitled review of *How to Travel Incognito, New Statesman and Nation*, Vol. 43, p. 740, June 21, 1952.

280. Robert Kee, untitled review of *How to Travel Incognito, The Spectator*, Vol. 189, p. 32, July 4, 1952.

281. Anonymous, untitled review of *The Happy Place, Kirkus Reviews*, Vol. 20, p. 499, August 15, 1952.

282. "H. S.," untitled review of *How to Travel Incognito, Saturday Review*, Vol. 35, p. 49, September 13, 1952.

283. "E. L. B.," untitled review of *The Happy Place, New York Times Book Review*, September 21, 1952, p. 32.

284. E. T. Dobbins, untitled review of *The Happy Place, Library Journal*, Vol. 77, p. 1661, October 1, 1952.

285. Anonymous, untitled review of *The Happy Place, Saturday Review*, Vol. 35, p. 66, November 15, 1952.

286. Anonymous, "Poor Bunny,"review of *The Happy Place, Toronto Globe and Mail*, November 15, 1952.

287. Polly Goodwin, untitled review of *The Happy Place, Chicago Sunday Tribune*, November 23, 1952, p. 22.

288. Anonymous, untitled review of *The Happy Place, Time*, Vol. 60, p. 106, December 8, 1952.

289. Anonymous, untitled review of *Madeline's Rescue, Kirkus Reviews*, Vol. 21, p. 109, February 15, 1953.

290. Anonymous, untitled review of *Madeline's Rescue, Bookmark*, Vol. 12, p. 157, April 1953.

291. Phyllis McGinley, untitled review of *Madeline's Rescue, New York Times Book Review*, April 26, 1953, p. 30.

292. Anonymous, untitled review of *Father, Dear Father, The New Yorker*, Vol. 29, p. 79, April 29, 1953.

293. Anonymous, untitled review of *Madeline's Rescue, Wisconsin Library Bulletin*, Vol. 49, p. 130, May 1953.

294. Anonymous, untitled review of *Madeline's Rescue, Time*, Vol. 61, p. 108, May 4, 1953.

295. Anonymous, untitled review of *Madeline's Rescue, Booklist*, Vol. 49, p. 308, May 15, 1953.

296. Anonymous, untitled review of *Madeline's Rescue, Saturday Review*, Vol. 36, p. 48, May 16, 1953.

297. Polly Goodwin, untitled review of *Madeline's*

Rescue, Chicago Sunday Tribune, May 17, 1953, p. 14.

298. L. S. Bechtel, untitled review of *Madeline's Rescue, New York Herald Tribune Book Review*, May 17, 1953, p. 10.

299. "J. D. L.," untitled review of *Madeline's Rescue, The Horn Book Magazine*, Vol. 29, p. 213, June 1953.

300. E. C. Alexander, untitled review of *Madeline's Rescue, Library Journal*, Vol. 78, p. 1002, June 1, 1953.

301. Anonymous, untitled review of *Father, Dear Father, Kirkus Reviews*, Vol. 21, p. 342, June 1, 1953.

302. H. S. Taylor, untitled review of *Father, Dear Father, Library Journal*, Vol. 78, p. 1322, August 1953.

303. Mason Warner, untitled review of *Father, Dear Father, Chicago Sunday Tribune*, August 23, 1953, p. 3.

304. Marion Hargrove, untitled review of *Father, Dear Father, New York Herald Tribune Book Review*, August 23, 1953, p. 4.

305. James Stern, untitled review of *Father, Dear Father, New York Times Book Review*, August 23, 1953, p. 3.

306. Lewis Gannett, untitled review of *Father, Dear Father, New York Herald Tribune*, Paris, August 25, 1953, p. 19.

307. Lee Rogow, "Younger Bemelmaniac," portrait, *Saturday Review*, Vol. 36, pp. 13-14, August 29, 1953.

308. Lee Rogow, untitled review of *Father, Dear Father, Saturday Review*, Vol. 36, p. 13, August 29, 1953.

309. Anonymous, untitled review of *Father, Dear Father, The New Yorker*, Vol. 29, pp. 79-80, August 29, 1953.

310. Anonymous, interview, *New York Times*, August 30, 1953, Section 7, p. 17.

311. Anonymous, "Bemelmania," portrait, *Time*, Vol. 62, p. 84, August 31, 1953.

312. Anonymous, untitled review of *Father, Dear Father, Time*, Vol. 62, p. 84, August 31, 1953.

313. Anonymous, "Bemelmans Abroad," illustrated portrait, *Newsweek*, Vol. 42 No. 9, p. 86, August 31, 1953.

314. Anonymous, untitled review of *Madeline's Rescue, U. S. Quarterly Book Review*, Vol. 9, p. 303, September 1953.

315. Anonymous, untitled review of *Father, Dear Father, Booklist*, Vol. 50, p. 10, September 1, 1953.

316. Anonymous, untitled review of *Father, Dear Father, Catholic World*, Vol. 177, p. 479, September 1953.

317. William du Bois, untitled review of *Father, Dear Father, New York Times Book Review*, September 5, 1953, p. 13.

318. "R. F. H.," untitled review of *Father, Dear Father, Springfield Republican*, September 13, 1953, p. 8c.

319. Anonymous, untitled review of *Father, Dear*

Father, Wisconsin Library Bulletin, Vol. 49, p. 207, October 1953.

320. Edward Weeks, untitled review of *Father, Dear Father, Atlantic Monthly*, Vol. 192, p. 80, October 1953.

321. D. Grumbach, untitled review of *Father, Dear Father, New York Herald Tribune Books*, Vol. 12, p. 16, October 1953.

322. Anonymous, untitled review of *Father, Dear Father, Times Literary Supplement*, London, November 6, 1953, p. 710.

323. Norman Shrapnel, untitled review of *Father, Dear Father, Manchester Guardian*, November 10, 1953, p. 4.

324. John Usborne, untitled review of *Father, Dear Father, The Spectator*, Vol. 190, p. 607, November 20, 1953.

325. Anonymous, untitled review of *Madeline's Rescue, Times Literary Supplement*, London, November 27, 1953, p. 15.

326. K. T. Kinkead, untitled review of *Madeline's Rescue, The New Yorker*, Vol. 29, p. 189, November 28, 1953.

327. Anonymous, untitled review of *Father, Dear Father, Catholic World*, Vol. 177, p. 479, December 1953.

328. "J. A.," untitled review of *Madeline's Rescue, The Spectator*, Vol. 190, p. 682, December 4, 1953.

329. A. Smith, untitled review of *Madeline's Rescue, New Statesman and Nation*, Vol. 46, p. 733, December 5, 1953.

330. Larry Rogers, untitled review of *Father, Dear Father, Canadian Forum*, Vol. 33, p. 263, 1954.

331. Anonymous, "Book Award," sketch, *New York Times*, March 9, 1954, p. 29.

332. May Massee, "Caldecott award to Bemelmans," illustrated portrait, *Library Journal*, Vol. 79, pp. 484-485, March 15, 1954.

333. Anonymous, "Bemelmans' 'Madeline's Rescue' Wins Caldecott Medal for 1953," *Publishers Weekly*, March 20, 1954.

334. Art Buchwald, "Mr. Bemelmans Opens a Bar," *New York Herald Tribune*, April 24, 1954. Reprinted in *New York Herald Tribune*, Paris, same date, p. 5. In the "Letters From the Mailbag" column of May 24, 1954, Ludwig Bemelmans writes to the editor explaining why tourists do *not* find his bistro at No. 4, Rue de la Colombe, which is written about by Buchwald (and which is addressed again in *La Bonne Table*, C1).

335. Anonymous, "Reader's Comments," review of *Father, Dear Father, The Horn Book Magazine*, Vol. 30 No. 3, p. 192, June 1954.

336. May Massee, "Ludwig Bemelmans," biographical sketch with illustration, *The Horn Book Magazine*, Vol. 30 No. 4, pp.263-269, August 1954.

337. Anonymous, untitled review of *The High World, Kirkus Reviews*, Vol. 22, p. 679, October 1, 1954.

338. "E. A. G.," untitled review of *The High*

World, *Saturday Review*, Vol. 37, p. 76, November 13, 1954.

339. L. S. Bechtel, untitled review of *The High World*, *New York Herald Tribune Book Review*, November 14, 1954, Part 2 p. 2.

340. A. S. Morris, untitled review of *The High World*, *New York Times Book Review*, November 14, 1954, Part 2 p. 32.

341. M. F. Kieran, untitled review of *The High World*, *Atlantic Monthly*, Vol. 194, p. 96, December 1954.

342. "J. D. L.," untitled review of *The High World*, *The Horn Book Magazine*, Vol. 30, p. 441, December 1954.

343. Polly Goodwin, untitled review of *The High World*, *Chicago Sunday Tribune*, December 12, 1954, p. 8.

344. Anonymous, untitled review of *To the One I Love the Best*, *Kirkus Reviews*, Vol. 23, p. 27, January 1, 1955.

345. Anonymous, untitled review of *To the One I Love the Best*, *Booklist*, Vol. 51, p. 217, January 15, 1955.

346. K. T. Willis, untitled review of *To the One I Love the Best*, *Library Journal*, Vol. 80, p. 364, February 1, 1955.

347. M. B. Snyder, untitled review of *To the One I Love the Best*, *Chicago Sunday Tribune*, February 27, 1955, p. 3.

348. E. H. Smith, untitled review of *To the One I Love the Best*, *New York Herald Tribune Book Review*, February 27, 1955, p. 6.

349. Elliot Paul, untitled review of *To the One I Love the Best*, *New York Times Book Review*, February 27, 1955, p. 6.

350. Anonymous, untitled review of *To the One I Love the Best*, *Bookmark*, Vol. 14, p. 132, March 1955.

351. Anonymous, untitled review of *To the One I Love the Best*, *Wisconsin Library Bulletin*, Vol. 51, p. 42, March 1955.

352. Anonymous, untitled review of *To the One I Love the Best*, *The New Yorker*, Vol. 31, p. 118, March 5, 1955.

353. Cleveland Amory, untitled review of *To the One I Love the Best*, *Saturday Review*, Vol. 38, p. 22, March 5, 1955.

354. Anonymous, untitled review of *To the One I Love the Best*, *Booklist*, Vol. 51, p. 296, March 15, 1955.

355. Edward Weeks, untitled review of *To the One I Love the Best*, *Atlantic Monthly*, Vol. 195, p. 74, April 1955.

356. R. Reuland, untitled review of *To the One I Love the Best*, *New York Herald Tribune Books*, Vol. 13, p. 307, April 1955.

357. Kathleen McDowell, "Bemelmans," review of *To the One I Love the Best*, *Toronto Globe and Mail*, April 23, 1955.

358. Anonymous, untitled review of *The World of Bemelmans*, *Kirkus Reviews*, Vol. 23, p. 522, July 15, 1955.

359. Anonymous, untitled review of *The Best of*

Times, *Manchester Guardian*, August 23, 1955, p. 4.

360. Anonymous, untitled review of *The Best of Times*, *New Statesman and Nation*, Vol. 50, p. 279, September 3, 1955.

361. Oswell Blakeston, untitled review of *The Best of Times*, *The Spectator*, September 9, 1955, p. 344.

362. "E. L. B.," untitled review of *Parsley*, *New York Times Book Review*, September 25, 1955, p. 34.

363. Anonymous, untitled review of *The Best of Times*, *Kirkus Reviews*, Vol. 23, p. 757, October 1, 1955.

364. William Hogan, untitled review of *The World of Bemelmans*, *San Francisco Chronicle*, October 7, 1955, p. 15.

365. Anonymous, untitled review of *The World of Bemelmans*, *The New Yorker*, Vol. 31, p. 196, October 8, 1955.

366. Russell Lynes, untitled review of *The World of Bemelmans*, *New York Times Book Review*, October 9, 1955, p. 5.

367. Anonymous, untitled review of *The World of Bemelmans*, *New York Herald Tribune Book Review*, October 16, 1955, p. 16.

368. John Haverstick, untitled review of *The World of Bemelmans*, *Saturday Review*, Vol. 38, p. 19, October 22, 1955.

369. Anonymous, untitled review of *Parsley*, *Booklist*, Vol. 52, p. 105, November 1, 1955.

370. Anonymous, untitled review of *Parsley*, *Chi-cago Sunday Tribune*, November 13, 1955, p. 12.

371. Anonymous, untitled review of *Parsley*, *San Francisco Chronicle*, November 13, 1955, p. 2.

372. "L. S. B.," untitled review of *Parsley*, *New York Herald Tribune Book Review*, November 13, 1955, p. 2.

373. Anonymous, untitled review of *The World of Bemelmans*, *Booklist*, Vol. 52, p. 128, November 15, 1955.

374. Margaret Bloy Graham, "Artist's Choice: Parsley," review of *Parsley*, *The Horn Book Magazine*, Vol. 31, pp. 474-475, December 1955.

375. "J. D. L.," untitled review of *Parsley* with 1 black illustration, *The Horn Book Magazine*, Vol. 31, p. 446, December 1955.

376. Kathleen McDowell, "Bemelmans is a Humorist Based Solidly on Reality," review of *The World of Bemelmans*, *Toronto Globe and Mail*, December 3, 1955.

377. "R. H. V.," untitled review of *Parsley*, *Saturday Review*, Vol. 38, p. 35, December 17, 1955.

378. Shelton L. Root, Jr., "Ludwig Bemelmans and His Books for Children," illustrated sketch, *Elementary English*, Vol. 34 No. 1, pp. 3-12, January 1957.

379. Anonymous, untitled review of *Madeline and the Bad Hat*, *Kirkus Reviews*, Vol. 25, p. 138, February 15, 1957.

380. E. L. Buell, untitled review of *Madeline and the Bad Hat*, *New York Times Book Review*, March 10, 1957, p. 36.

381. Anonymous, untitled review of *Madeline and the Bad Hat*, *Booklist*, Vol. 53, p. 410, April 1, 1957.

382. Anonymous, untitled review of *Madeline and the Bad Hat*, *Bookmark*, Vol. 16, p. 162, April 1957.

383. Anonymous, untitled review of *Madeline and the Bad Hat*, *Wisconsin Library Bulletin*, Vol. 53, p. 403, May 1957.

384. E. S. Ross, untitled review of *Madeline and the Bad Hat*, *Saturday Review*, Vol. 40, p. 51, May 11, 1957.

385. Polly Goodwin, untitled review of *Madeline and the Bad Hat*, *Chicago Sunday Tribune*, May 12, 1957, Part 2, p. 3.

386. M. S. Libby, untitled review of *Madeline and the Bad Hat*, *New York Herald Tribune Book Review*, May 12, 1957, p. 6.

387. E. T. Dobbins, untitled review of *Madeline and the Bad Hat*, *Library Journal*, Vol. 82, p. 1353, May 15, 1957.

388. Anonymous, untitled review of *The Woman of My Life*, *Kirkus Reviews*, Vol. 25, p. 554, August 1, 1957.

389. Anonymous, untitled review of *Madeline and the Bad Hat*, *The Horn Book Magazine*, Vol. 33, p. 296, August 1957.

390. Anonymous, untitled review of *Holiday in France*, *Kirkus Reviews*, Vol. 25, p. 614, August 15, 1957.

391. W. K. Harrison, untitled review of *Holiday in France*, *Library Journal*, Vol. 82, p. 2042, September 1, 1957.

392. Art Buchwald, "He's Giving Up the Chi-Chi Life," portrait, *New York Herald Tribune*, Paris, September 2, 1957. Bemelmans "will now devote the rest of his life to serious painting."

393. George Adelman, untitled review of *The Woman of My Life*, *Library Journal*, Vol. 82, p. 2139, September 15, 1957.

394. Anonymous, untitled review of *The Woman of My Life*, *Booklist*, Vol. 54, p. 65, October 1, 1957.

395. Anonymous, untitled review of *The Woman of My Life*, *San Francisco Chronicle*, October 11, 1957, p. 19.

396. Anonymous, untitled review of *The Woman of My Life*, *The New Yorker*, Vol. 33, p. 197, October 12, 1957.

397. B. R. Redman, untitled review of *The Woman of My Life*, *Saturday Review*, Vol. 40, p. 26, October 12, 1957.

398. Anonymous, untitled review of *The Woman of My Life*, *New York Times Book Review*, October 12, 1957, p. 17.

399. Rose Feld, untitled review of *The Woman of My Life*, *New York Herald Tribune Book Review*, October 13, 1957, p. 5.

400. Morris Gilbert, untitled review of *The*

Woman of My Life, New York Times Book Review, October 13, 1957, p. 49.

401. Anonymous, untitled review of *The Woman of My Life, Time*, Vol. 70, p. 132, October 14, 1957.

402. Anonymous, untitled review of *The Woman of My Life, Booklist*, Vol. 54, p. 105, October 15, 1957.

403. Milton Crane, untitled review of *The Woman of My Life, Chicago Sunday Tribune*, October 20, 1957, p. 4.

404. Kathleen McDowell, "The Reality in Bemelmans," review of *The Woman of My Life, Toronto Globe and Mail*, October 26, 1957.

405. Anonymous, untitled review of *The Woman of My Life, Best Sellers*, Vol. 17, p. 253, November 1, 1957.

406. Anonymous, untitled review of *Holiday in France, Booklist*, Vol. 54, p. 165, November 15, 1957.

407. Morris Gilbert, untitled review of *Holiday in France, New York Times Book Review*, November 17, 1957, p. 51.

408. William Hogan, untitled review of *Holiday in France, San Francisco Chronicle*, November 17, 1957, p. 24.

409. Emily Maxwell, untitled review of *Madeline and the Bad Hat, The New Yorker*, Vol. 33, p. 234, November 23, 1957.

410. Anonymous, untitled review of *The Woman of My Life, Times Literary Supplement*, London, November 29, 1957, p. 717.

411. Edward Weeks, untitled review of *The Woman of My Life, Atlantic Monthly*, Vol. 200, p. 164, December 1957.

412. G. W. Stonier, untitled review of *The Woman of My Life, New Statesman*, Vol. 54, p. 789, December 7, 1957.

413. Fanny Butcher, untitled review of *Holiday in France, Chicago Sunday Tribune*, December 8, 1957, p. 4.

414. Anonymous, untitled review of *My Life in Art, Kirkus Reviews*, Vol. 26, p. 634, August 15, 1958.

415. Morris Gilbert, untitled review of *My Life in Art, New York Times Book Review*, November 2, 1958, p. 16.

416. Anonymous, untitled review of *My Life in Art, The New Yorker*, Vol. 34, p. 235, November 22, 1958.

417. A. S. Plaut, untitled review of *My Life in Art, Library Journal*, Vol. 83, p. 3446, December 1, 1958.

418. Anonymous, untitled review of *My Life in Art, Times Literary Supplement*, London, December 12, 1958, p. 714.

419. William Hogan, untitled review of *My Life in Art, San Francisco Chronicle*, December 17, 1958, p. 37.

420. Selden Rodman, "From Inns to Oils," sketch about Bemelmans, *Saturday Review*, Vol. 41, p. 18, December 20, 1958.

421. Selden Rodman, untitled review of *My Life in Art*, *Saturday Review*, Vol. 41, p. 18, December 20, 1958.

422. Anonymous, untitled review of *My Life in Art*, *New Statesman*, Vol. 56, p. 892, December 29, 1958.

423. Anonymous, untitled review of *My Life in Art*, *Booklist*, Vol. 55, p. 254, January 15, 1959.

424. Anonymous, untitled review of *My Life in Art*, *New York Herald Tribune Book Review*, January 18, 1959, p. 9.

425. Anonymous, untitled review of *My Life in Art*, *Apollo*, Vol. 69, p. 97, March 1959.

426. E. L. Buell, untitled review of *Madeline and the Gypsies*, *New York Times Book Review*, September 13, 1959, p. 58.

427. Anonymous, untitled review of *Madeline and the Gypsies*, *Kirkus Reviews*, Vol. 27, p. 700, September 15, 1959.

428. Anonymous, untitled review of *Madeline and the Gypsies*, *Booklist*, Vol. 56, p. 124, October 15, 1959.

429. L. E. Cathon, untitled review of *Madeline and the Gypsies*, *Library Journal*, Vol. 84, p. 3309, October 15, 1959.

430. Polly Goodwin, untitled review of *Madeline and the Gypsies*, *Chicago Sunday Tribune*, November 1, 1959, Section 2 p. 12.

431. M. S. Libby, untitled review of *Madeline and the Gypsies*, *New York Herald Tribune Book Review*, November 1, 1959, Section 12 p. 4.

432. C. H. Bishop, untitled review of *Madeline and the Gypsies*, *Commonweal*, Vol. 71, p. 214, November 13, 1959.

433. Anonymous, "Play Lion," review of *Madeline and the Gypsies*, *Toronto Globe and Mail*, November 18, 1959.

434. Charlotte Jackson, untitled review of *Madeline and the Gypsies*, *Atlantic Monthly*, Vol. 204, p. 173, December 1959.

435. Robert Sage, untitled review of *My Life in Art*, *New York Herald Tribune*, Paris, December 24, 1959.

436. Anonymous, untitled review of *Madeline and the Gypsies*, *Wisconsin Library Bulletin*, Vol. 56, p. 68, January 1960.

437. A. Garvin, "Art and Artists," sketch, *Critic*, Vol. 18, pp. 62-63+, January 1960.

438. Charlotte Jackson, untitled review of *Madeline and the Gypsies*, *San Francisco Chronicle*, January 31, 1960, p. 30.

439. Anonymous, untitled review of *Madeline and the Gypsies*, *The Horn Book Magazine*, Vol. 36, p. 124, April 1960.

440. Anonymous, untitled review of *Are You Hungry Are You Cold*, *Kirkus Reviews*, Vol. 28, p. 527, July 1, 1960.

441. Edward Weeks, untitled review of *Are You Hungry Are You Cold*, *Atlantic Monthly*, Vol. 206, p. 112, September 1960.

442. Fanny Butcher, untitled review of *Are You Hungry Are You Cold*, *Chicago Sunday Tribune*, September 11, 1960, p. 3.

443. Rumer Godden, untitled review of *Are You Hungry Are You Cold*, *New York Herald Tribune Book Review*, September 11, 1960, p. 4.

444. Morris Gilbert, untitled review of *Are You Hungry Are You Cold*, *New York Times Book Review*, September 11, 1960, p. 5.

445. Anonymous, untitled review of *Are You Hungry Are You Cold*, *Time*, Vol. 76, p. 109, September 12, 1960.

446. William Hogan, untitled review of *Are You Hungry Are You Cold*, *San Francisco Chronicle*, September 12, 1960, p. 35.

447. Anonymous, untitled review of *Welcome Home*, *Kirkus Reviews*, Vol. 28, p. 815, September 15, 1960.

448. Anonymous, untitled review of *Are You Hungry Are You Cold*, *Best Sellers*, Vol. 20, p. 205, September 15, 1960.

449. Richard McLaughlin, untitled review of *Are You Hungry Are You Cold*, *Springfield Republican*, September 25, 1960, p. 5d.

450. G. M. Casey, untitled review of *Are You Hungry Are You Cold*, *Library Journal*, Vol. 85, p. 3460, October 1, 1960.

451. Martin Tucker, untitled review of *Are You Hungry Are You Cold*, *Saturday Review*, Vol. 43, p. 20, October 1, 1960.

452. S. M. Black, untitled review of *Are You Hungry Are You Cold*, *The New Republic*, Vol. 143, p. 18, October 3, 1960.

453. Anonymous, untitled review of *Are You Hungry Are You Cold*, *Booklist*, Vol. 57, p. 116, October 15, 1960.

454. Anonymous, untitled review of *Welcome Home*, *Saturday Review*, Vol. 43, p. 101, November 12, 1960.

455. G. A. Woods, untitled review of *Welcome Home*, *New York Times Book Review*, November 13, 1960, Part 2 p. 59.

456. Anonymous, "The Story of Bemelmans' 'Madeline,' " *Publishers Weekly*, Vol. 178 No. 20, November 14, 1960, pp. 16-17.

457. N. F. Elsmo, untitled review of *Welcome Home*, *Library Journal*, Vol. 85, p. 4217, November 15, 1960.

458. Emily Maxwell, untitled review of *Welcome Home*, *The New Yorker*, Vol. 36, p. 228, November 19, 1960.

459. Charlotte Jackson, untitled review of *Welcome Home*, *Atlantic Monthly*, Vol. 206, p. 125, December 1960.

460. "M. W. B.," untitled review of *Welcome Home*, *The Horn Book Magazine*, Vol. 36, p. 506, December 1960.

461. Polly Goodwin, untitled review of *Welcome Home*, *Chicago Sunday Tribune*, December 11, 1960, p. 9.

462. Charlotte Jackson, untitled review of *Welcome Home*, *San Francisco Chronicle*, December 11, 1960, p. 43.

463. M. Bradbury, untitled review of *Are You Hungry Are You Cold*, *Punch*, Vol. 240, p. 134, 1961.

464. Anonymous, untitled review of *Welcome Home, Wisconsin Library Bulletin*, Vol. 57, p. 54, January 1961.

465. Anonymous, untitled review of *Welcome Home, Booklist*, Vol. 57, p. 300, January 15, 1961.

466. M. S. Libby, untitled review of *Welcome Home, New York Herald Tribune Lively Arts*, February 12, 1961, p. 75.

467. Anonymous, untitled review of *Italian Holiday, Kirkus Reviews*, Vol. 29, p. 770, August 15, 1961.

468. Alice Dalgliesh, untitled review of *Madeline in London, Saturday Review*, Vol. 44, p. 40, November 11, 1961.

469. Anne Nicolson, untitled review of *Italian Holiday, Chicago Sunday Tribune*, November 12, 1961, p. 3.

470. Anonymous, untitled review of *Madeline in London, Chicago Sunday Tribune*, November 12, 1961, Section 2 p. 10.

471. J. R. Blanchard, untitled review of *Italian Holiday, Library Journal*, Vol. 86, p. 3955, November 15, 1961.

472. Deirdre Haines, untitled review of *Madeline in London, Toronto Globe and Mail*, November 18, 1961.

473. Herbert Mitgang, untitled review of *Italian Holiday, New York Times Book Review*, November 19, 1961, p. 42.

474. Anonymous, untitled review of *Italian Hol-

iday, Booklist*, Vol. 58, p. 223, December 1, 1961.

475. Anonymous, untitled review of *Italian Holiday, Best Sellers*, Vol. 21, p. 378, December 1, 1961.

476. Anne Ross, untitled review of *Italian Holiday, New York Herald Tribune Books*, December 10, 1961, p. 4.

477. Anonymous, "Art, as Bemelmans Sees It," sketch, *Design*, Vol. 63, pp. 106-108, January 1962.

478. Anonymous, untitled review of *Italian Holiday, Saturday Review*, Vol. 45, p. 68, January 6, 1962.

479. Anonymous, untitled review of *Madeline in London, Booklist*, Vol. 58, p. 314, January 15, 1962.

480. J. H. Dohm, untitled review of *Madeline in London, Library Journal*, Vol. 87, p. 320, January 15, 1962.

481. Book Review Advisory Committee, untitled review of *Madeline in London, Library Journal*, Vol. 87, p. 320, January 15, 1962.

482. Anonymous, untitled review of *Madeline in London, The Horn Book Magazine*, Vol. 38, p. 41, February 1962.

483. Anonymous, untitled review of *On Board Noah's Ark, Kirkus Reviews*, Vol. 30, p. 301, March 15, 1962.

484. F. K. Cylke, untitled review of *On Board Noah's Ark, Library Journal*, Vol. 87, p. 1780, May 1, 1962.

485. Anonymous, untitled review of *Italian Holiday*, *Wisconsin Library Bulletin*, Vol. 58, p. 179, May 1962.

486. William Hogan, untitled review of *On Board Noah's Ark*, *San Francisco Chronicle*, May 16, 1962, p. 41.

487. Anne Nicolson, untitled review of *On Board Noah's Ark*, *Chicago Sunday Tribune*, May 20, 1962, p. 3.

488. Herbert Kupferberg, untitled review of *On Board Noah's Ark*, *New York Herald Tribune Books*, May 20, 1962, p. 9.

489. Anonymous, "Buoyant Return," illustrated portrait, *Newsweek*, Vol. 59, p. 98, May 21, 1962.

490. Anonymous, untitled review of *On Board Noah's Ark*, *Booklist*, Vol. 58, p. 678, June 1, 1962.

491. Anonymous, untitled review of *On Board Noah's Ark*, *New York Times Book Review*, June 2, 1962, p. 17.

492. Paul Showers, untitled review of *On Board Noah's Ark*, *New York Times Book Review*, June 10, 1962, p. 10.

493. William Barrett, untitled review of *On Board Noah's Ark*, *Atlantic Monthly*, Vol. 210, p. 113, July 1962.

494. Anonymous, "Ludwig Bemelmans Dies," obituary, *New York Times*, October 2, 1962, p. 39.

495. Anonymous, "Ludwig Bemelmans Dies," obituary, *New York Herald Tribune*, October 2, 1962.

496. Anonymous, "Author, Painter Satirized War, Movie Colony," obituary, *Toronto Globe and Mail*, October 2, 1962.

497. Anonymous, "The Irresistible Ludwig Bemelmans," portrait, *New York Herald Tribune*, Paris, October 4, 1962.

498. Anonymous, obituary, *Publisher's Weekly*, Vol 182, p. 30, October 8, 1962.

499. Anonymous, obituary, *Time*, October 12, 1962.

500. Anonymous, obituary with portrait, *Illustrated London News*, Vol. 241, p. 569, October 13, 1962.

501. Anonymous, "Madeline's Master," illustrated portrait, *Newsweek*, Vol. 60, p. 115, October 15, 1962.

502. Anonymous, "Bemelmans, 64, Dies; Humorist And Illustrator," obituary, *New York Herald Tribune*, Paris, October 30, 1962.

503. M. S. Libby, untitled review of *Madeline in London*, *New York Herald Tribune Books*, November 12, 1962, Section 12 p. 28.

504. Anonymous, obituary, *Wilson Library Bulletin*, November 1962.

505. G. A. Woods, untitled review of *Madeline in London*, *New York Times Book Review*, November 12, 1962, Part 2 p. 54.

506. Anonymous, obituary, *Current Biography*, December 1962.

507. Dorothy Nyren, untitled review of *The Street Where the Heart Lies*, *Library Journal*, Vol. 87, p. 4453, December 1, 1962.

508. Nicholas Wollaston, untitled review of *On Board Noah's Ark*, *New Statesman*, Vol. 64, p. 835, December 7, 1962.

509. Anonymous, untitled review of *The Street Where the Heart Lies*, *The New Yorker*, Vol. 38, p. 97, January 5, 1963.

510. Stephen McKenna, untitled review of *The Street Where the Heart Lies*, *Best Sellers*, Vol. 22, p. 294, January 15, 1953.

511. William Barrett, untitled review of *The Street Where the Heart Lies*, *Atlantic Monthly*, Vol. 211, p. 133, February 1963.

512. Burling Lowrey, untitled review of *The Street Where the Heart Lies*, *Saturday Review*, Vol. 46, p. 28, February 16, 1963.

513. John K. Hutchens, " 'Street Where the Heart Lies' Held Top-Form Bemelmans," review of *The Street Where the Heart Lies*, *New York Herald Tribune*, Paris, March 12, 1963.

514. Martin Levin, untitled review of *The Street Where the Heart Lies*, *New York Times Book Review*, April 7, 1963, p. 36.

515. Joseph N. Gelmon, untitled review of *The Street Where the Heart Lies*, *Toronto Globe and Mail*, May 4, 1963.

516. K. T. Willis, untitled review of *La Bonne Table*, *Library Journal*, Vol. 89, p. 4335, November 1, 1964.

517. Rex Stout, untitled review of *La Bonne Ta-*ble, *New York Times Book Review*, November 8, 1964, Section 7 p. 58.

518. Anonymous, untitled review of *La Bonne Table*, *Best Sellers*, Vol. 24, p. 333, November 15, 1964.

519. Marilyn Utter, untitled review of *La Bonne Table*, *Christian Science Monitor*, December 3, 1964, p. 4b.

520. Francis Hope, untitled review of *La Bonne Table*, *New Statesman*, Vol. 68, p. 892, December 4, 1964.

521. Horace Sutton, "The Last of Bemelmans," obituary and review, *Saturday Review*, Vol. 48, p. 49+, February 20, 1965.

522. N. E. Paige, untitled review of *Quito Express*, *Library Journal*, Vol. 90, p. 2009, April 15, 1965.

523. Anonymous, untitled review of *Quito Express*, *Booklist*, Vol. 61, p. 873, May 1, 1965.

524. A. Gribbin, untitled review of *Quito Express*, *National Observer*, Vol. 4, p. 20, June 14, 1965.

525. R. H. Viguers, untitled review of *Quito Express*, *The Horn Book Magazine*, Vol. 41, p. 406, August 1965.

526. Patrick Groff, "The Children's World of Ludwig Bemelmans," illustrated sketch, *Elementary English*, Vol. 43 No. 6, pp. 559-568, October 1966.

527. Anonymous, untitled review of *Yolanda and the Thief* by Ludwig Bemelmans and Jacques Théry, *The New Yorker*, 1979.

528. Ann A. Flowers, untitled review of *Madeline's Christmas*, *The Horn Book Magazine*, Vol. 61, p. 718, 1985.

529. Gene Langley, untitled review of *Tell Them It Was Wonderful*, *Christian Science Monitor*, September 12, 1985, p. 24.

530. Anonymous, untitled review of *Madeline's Christmas*, *Bulletin of the Center for Children's Books*, Vol. 39, p. 22, October 1985.

531. Peggy Forehand, untitled review of *Madeline's Christmas*, *School Library Journal*, Vol. 32, p. 189, October 1985.

532. Herman Elstein, untitled review of *Tell Them It Was Wonderful*, *Library Journal*, Vol. 110, p. 88, October 15, 1985.

533. Edward Koren, untitled review of *Madeline's Christmas*, *New York Times Book Review*, November 10, 1985, p. 37.

534. Jonathan Yardley, untitled review of *Tell Them It Was Wonderful*, *Washington Post*, November 27, 1985, Section E p. 2a.

535. Phoebe-Lou Adams, untitled review of *Tell Them It Was Wonderful*, *Atlantic Monthly*, Vol. 256, p. 118, December 1985.

536. Jonathan Yardley, untitled review of *Tell Them It Was Wonderful*, *International Herald Tribune*, December 10, 1985.

537. G. Martin, "The Most Romantic Bar: Martinis . . . and Madeline," a portrait of the Bemelmans Bar at the Carlyle Hotel, *New York*, Vol. 21, December 19-26, 1988.

538. Jacqueline F. Eastman, "Safety in the Structures of Art," a critique of the *Madeline* books, in Susan R. Gannon and Ruth Ann Thompson, eds., *Cross-Culturalism in Children's Literature: Selected Papers from the 1987 International Conference of the Children's Literature Association at Carleton University, Ottawa*, Children's Literature Association, n.d. (c. 1988)

539. Anonymous, "Madeline at 50: Invitation-only Party at Carlyle," sketch, *New York Times*, September 14, 1989, Section 3 p. 19.

540. Anonymous, "Madeline at 50: Invitation-only Party at Carlyle," sketch, *International Herald Tribune*, September 16, 1989.

541. Elizabeth Pearce, "La Cuisine Agité," a portrait of Bemelmans and behind-the-scenes reminiscence of *La Bonne Table*, in *Gastronome*, Vol. XII No. 2, Autumn 1990, pp. 14-21, with illustrations from *La Bonne Table*.

542. Jacqueline F. Eastman, "Aesthetic Distancing in Ludwig Bemelmans' *Madeline*," in Francelia Butler, Barbara Rosen and Jean Marsden, eds., *Children's Literature 19*, New Haven: Yale University Press, 1991.

543. Jody Shields, "A Bemelmans Baedeker," *House & Garden*, Vol. 163 No. 10, October 1991, pp. 90-94. With photographs of, and full-color illustrations by, Bemelmans; an illustration is also reproduced with the contents, p. 18.

II. BOOKS AND DISSERTATIONS ABOUT BEMELMANS

Jacqueline F. Eastman, *Ludwig Bemelmans*, in Twayne's United States Author Series, Children's Literature, forthcoming, 1992.

———. "A Study of the *Madeline* Books of Ludwig Bemelmans," Ph. D. Dissertation, Department of English, University of Alabama, 1989.

Stephen C. Fieser, "Ludwig Bemelmans and Travel Illustration," M.F.A. Dissertation, Department of Visual Communication, Syracuse University, 1986.

III. PUBLICATIONS IN WHICH BEMELMANS IS QUOTED OR REFERRED TO

Americana Annual 1963 [obituary].

Anonymous, "Modern Living: These Are the Ingredients for Five Great Soups," *Life*, Vol. 30 No. 16, April 16, 1951, pp. 112-120; in which there is a full-color photograph of Bemelmans giving his approval to bouillabaisse. (One of the recipes given is that of Louis Diat, chef of the Ritz-Carlton which was the original Hotel Splendide.)

Barbara Bader, *American Picture Books from Noah's Ark to The Beast Within*, Macmillan, 1976.

Britannica Book of the Year 1963 [obituary].

John Cech, ed., *American Writers for Children, 1900-1960* which is Vol. 22 of *Dictionary of Literary Biography*, a Bruccoli Clark Book, Gale Research, 1983.

Anne Commire, *Something About the Author*, Volume 15, Detroit: Gale Research, 1979.

Fairfax M. Cone, *With All Its Faults*, Little, Brown, 1969.

Hume Cronyn, *A Terrible Liar*, William Morrow, 1991.

Current Biography Yearbook 1962 [obituary]. (As well, biographies appeared in earlier editions of *Current Biography*)

Brian Doyle, editor, *Who's Who of Children's Literature*, New York: Schocken Books, 1968.

Editors of *Holiday*, eds., *Holiday Magazine Book of the World's Fine Food*, with an Introduction by Ted Patrick, New York: Simon & Schuster, 1960. Includes an excerpt from E148.

Editors of *Life*, eds., *Picture Cook Book*, New York: Time, Inc., 1958. Includes a photograph of Bemelmans serving Bouillabaisse.

Editors of *The New Yorker*, eds., *The Complete Book of Covers of The New Yorker 1925-1989*, Alfred A. Knopf, 1989.

Muriel Fuller, editor, *More Junior Authors*, H. W. Wilson, 1963.

Miriam Hoffman and Eva Samuels, *Authors and Illustrators of Children's Books*, R. R. Bowker, 1972.

Lee Kingman and others, compilers, *Illustrators of Children's Books, 1957-1966*, Boston: Horn Book, 1968.

D. L. Kirkpatrick, ed., *Twentieth Century Children's Writers*, St. Martin's Press, 1978; Gale Research, 1989.

Stanley J. Kunitz, editor, *Twentieth Century Authors*, first supplement, H. W. Wilson, 1955.

Lyn Ellen Lacy, *Art and Design in Children's Picture Books: An Analysis of Caldecott Award-Winning Illustrations*, Chicago: American Library Association, 1986.

Eden Ross Lipson, *The New York Times Parent's Guide to the Best Books for Children*, revised and updated edition, Random House, 1991.

Frances Carol Locher, ed., *Contemporary Authors*, Vols. 73-76, Gale Research, 1978.

Bertha E. Mahony and others, compilers, *Illustrators of Children's Books, 1744-1945*, Boston: Horn Book, 1947.

————. *Illustrators of Children's Books, 1946-1956*, Boston: Horn Book, 1958.

May Massee, "Ludwig Bemelmans," in *Caldecott Medal Books: 1938-1957*, Boston: Horn Book, 1957.

P. David Pearson, Dale D. Johnson, Theodore Clymer et al., *A New Day*, Boston: Silver Burdett & Ginn Inc., 1991.

Henry C. Pitz, *Two Hundred Years of American Illustration*, New York: Random House, 1977.

Gerard J. Senick, ed., *Children's Literature Review*, Vol. 6, 1983-1984, Gale Research, 1985, pp. 57-76. Includes "Author's Commentary" by Bemelmans, excerpted from an extended quotation in Shelton L. Root, Jr., "Ludwig Bemelmans and His Books for Children," *Elementary English*, Vol. 34, No. 1, pp. 3-12, January 1957; see J377.

Norah Smaridge, *Famous Author-Illustrators for Young People*, Dodd, 1973.

Lee J. Walp, "The Author: Ludwig Bemelmans," in *The Booklover's Answer No. 13*, Webster, N.Y.: R. J. Hussey, March-April, 1965.

Harry R. Warfel, *American Novelists of Today*, American Book Co., 1951.

Who Was Who in America, Vol. 4, 1961-1968, Marquis-Who's Who Inc., 1968.

A Bemelmans Chronology

A Bemelmans Chronology

TITLES OF BOOKS, pamphlets, stories and signed cartoons included in sections A, B, C, D, E and G are chronologized here. Book and pamphlet titles appear in block capitals. Story and cartoon titles appear in quotes. Some adaptations have been included for interest. For fuller descriptions and all adaptations, see section H.

Dates in square brackets denote the beginning of the week in which the publication occurred.

Publication dates marked with an * are not precisely known.

When the publication date for a magazine was given as a month only, it is assumed publication took place on the 1st.

When the publication date for a book is given as a month only, it is assumed the publication took place on the last day of the month.

A. Work During Bemelmans' Lifetime

1926

July 4.	G61.	"The Thrilling Adventures of Count Bric à Brac," comic, in *The World Magazine*, begins.

1932

ADVERTISEMENT ART for General Foods

1933

Apr. 29.	G60a.	"Noodles, the Trained Seal," cartoon, in *The Saturday Evening Post*.
Dec. 16.	G60b.	"Pastry chef cartoon," in *The Saturday Evening Post*.

1934

Oct. 11.	A14a.	HANSI. The Viking Press.
Fall.	A14b.	HANSI. E. M. Hale & Co.

ADVERTISEMENT ART for Borden

EXHIBITION in Paris

1935

Feb. 13.	H14.	"Noah," with Bemelmans sets, opens on Broadway.
Mar. 8.	G62.	"Silly Willy" cartoons in *Young America* begin.

| Mar. | A14c. | HANSI. Lovat Dickson. |
| Dec. | E1. | "The Count and the Cobbler," in *Harper's Bazaar*. |

ADVERTISEMENT ART for Arrow Shirts

EXHIBITION in Paris

1936

| Sept. 11. | A13. | THE GOLDEN BASKET. The Viking Press. |

EDITORIAL ILLUSTRATION for *Story*

ILLUSTRATION for *Fortune*

1937

Mar. 1.	E5.	" 'No Trouble at All'," in *Vogue*.
May 15.	E6.	"Postkarten aus Wien," in *Vogue*.
May.	E2.	"Theodore and 'The Blue Danube'," in *Story*.
June.	E7.	"Sacre du Printemps," in *Story*.
July 2.	A33a.	MY WAR WITH THE UNITED STATES. The Viking Press.
July-Aug.	E3.	"May Massee: As Her Author-Illustrators See Her," in *The Horn Book Magazine*.
Sept. 1.	E8.	"Jungles, Beards, Pythons, Parrots and How to Influence People," in *Vogue*.
Sept.	E9.	"The Elephant Cutlet," in *Town & Country*.
Oct.	E4.	"Inside, Outside," in *Story*.
Oct. 30.	E10.	"Quito," in *The New Yorker*.

Nov. 1.	A6.	THE CASTLE NUMBER NINE. The Viking Press.
Nov.	E11.	"Prison? It's Wonderful," in *Globe*.
Dec.	E12.	"Poor Animal!" in *Globe*.

ILLUSTRATION for Frederick A. Stokes Co.

1938

Apr. 1.	E13.	"Chile con Amore," in *Vogue*.
May.	E14.	"My First Actress," in *Stage*.
June.	E15.	"Garden Spots," in *Stage*.
July.	E16.	"Busboy's Holidays: Dinner at Luchow's and a Trip to the Sea," in *Town & Country*.
July 4.	A33b.	MY WAR WITH THE UNITED STATES. Victor Gollancz.
Sept.	E17.	"The Coming Out Party," in *Town & Country*.
Sept. 30.	A37a.	QUITO EXPRESS. The Viking Press.
Nov. 14.	A23a.	LIFE CLASS. The Viking Press.
Dec. 10.	E18.	"Why Doesn't Somebody . . .," in *The New Yorker*.

COVER ART for *Town & Country*

EDITORIAL ILLUSTRATION for *Story*

ILLUSTRATION for Harper Publishers, *Stage, Town & Country*

1939

Jan.	E19.	"Transgressor in Galapagos," in *Town & Country*.
Feb.	E20.	"Back to Quito," in *House Beautiful*.
Mar.	E21.	"My English Suit in Paris," in *Town & Country*.

June.	E22.	"Speaking of Ashes," in *Stage*.
Aug. 1.	E25.	"He Couldn't Write About the Fair," in *Vogue*.
Aug.	E23.	"Have You a Reservation?" in *Reader's Digest*.
Aug.	E24.	"Dear General, What a Surprise!" in *Town & Country*.
Aug. 5.	E26.	"The Isle of God," in *The New Yorker*.
Aug. 12.	E27.	"Dog Story," in *The New Yorker*.
Aug. 28.	A39a.	SMALL BEER. The Viking Press.
Aug. 28.	A39a(bis).	SMALL BEER (Deluxe edition). The Viking Press.
Sept.	E28.	"True Love Story," in *Town & Country*.
Sept. 15.	A24a.	MADELINE. Simon & Schuster.
Sept. 23.	A29.	"The Bride of Berchtesgaden," in *The New Yorker*.
Sept.	A23b.	LIFE CLASS. John Lane at the Bodley Head.
Oct.	E30.	"Italian Paradise," in *Town & Country*.
Oct. 9.	A33c.	MY WAR WITH THE UNITED STATES. Sun Dial Press.

EDITORIAL ILLUSTRATION for *Stage*

ILLUSTRATION for *Town & Country*, *Stage*

EXHIBITION at Kennedy Gallery

1940

| Feb. | E31. | "I Love America," in *Town & Country*. |
| Mar. | E32. | "Buenas Días, Gran Hotel," in *Town & Country*. |

Mar. 15.	E33.	"La Spécialité de la Maison," in *Vogue*.
May.	E34.	"The Donkey Inside: Escape and Farewell," in *Town & Country*.
May 11.	E35.	"Mespoulets of the Splendide," in *The New Yorker*.
May.	A39b.	SMALL BEER. John Lane at the Bodley Head.
June 1.	E36.	"Art at the Hotel Splendide," in *The New Yorker*.
June 1.	E38.	"I love you—I love you—I love you—," in *Vogue*.
June.	E37.	"S. S. Mesias," in *Town & Country*.
July 6.	E39.	"The Ballet Visits the Splendide's Magician," in *The New Yorker*.
July 27.	E40.	"The Splendide's Magician Does a New Trick," in *The New Yorker*.
Aug.	E38.	"Episode from the Paris of the Past," in British *Vogue*.
Aug.	E41.	"Fifi," in *Town & Country*.
Sept.	E42.	"The Painted Grapes," in *Town & Country*.
Sept. 14.	E43.	"Easy Money at the Splendide," in *The New Yorker*.
Sept. 28.	E44.	"Adolf in Ecuador," in *The New Yorker*.
Nov.	E45.	"The Morale of the Natives," in *Town & Country*.
Nov. 9.	E46.	"The Homesick Bus Boy of the Splendide," in *The New Yorker*.

Nov. 12.	A12	FIFI. Simon & Schuster.
Dec.	E47.	"Peruvian Legend," in *Town & Country*.
Dec. 21.	E48.	"The Splendide's Night in Granada," in *The New Yorker*.
✿	A14d.	HANSI. Cadmus (E. M. Hale).

COVER ART for *Town & Country*

ILLUSTRATION for *Vogue*

1941

Jan.	E49.	"This is Romance," in *Town & Country*.
Jan. 17.	A8a.	THE DONKEY INSIDE. The Viking Press.
Jan. 17.	A8a(bis).	THE DONKEY INSIDE (Deluxe edition). The Viking Press.
Feb. 1.	E51.	" 'Dance for Charity'," in *Vogue*.
Feb.	E50.	"Sweet Land of Liberty," in *Glamour*.
Mar. 22.	E52.	"The Splendide's Hispano," in *The New Yorker*.
Mar. [22].	A2.	AT YOUR SERVICE: THE WAY OF LIFE IN A HOTEL. Row-Peterson.
Apr.	E53.	"The Donkey Inside," in *Reader's Digest*.
Apr.	E54.	"Vacation," in *Town & Country*.
Apr. 12.	E55.	"The Head-Hunters of the Quito Hills," in *The New Yorker*.
May-June.	E56.	"Sacre du Printemps," in *Story*.
June.	E57.	"That's Panama," in *McCall's*.
July.	E58.	"Air Mail to Barbara," in *Town & Country*.

July 12.	E59.	"The Lost Mandolin of the Splendide," in *The New Yorker*.
July 30.	A8b.	EL BURRO POR DENTRO. Editora Moderna.
Sept.	E60.	"The Splendide: The Perfect Behavior of a Crazy Fool," in *Town & Country*.
Sept. 6.	E61.	"Pale Hands Beside the Circular Bar," in *The New Yorker*.
Oct. 1.	A33d.	MY WAR WITH THE UNITED STATES. Modern Library.
Oct. 11.	E62.	"The Valet of the Splendide," in *The New Yorker*.
Oct. 15.	E63.	"Cher Ami," in *Vogue*.
Nov. 29.	E64.	"The Murderer of the Splendide," in *The New Yorker*.
Dec. 1.	A18a.	HOTEL SPLENDIDE. The Viking Press.
Dec. 1.	A18a(bis).	HOTEL SPLENDIDE (Deluxe edition). The Viking Press.
Dec.	E65.	"Le Chagrin d'Amour Est Formidable," in *Town & Country*.

ADVERTISEMENT ART for Saks Fifth Avenue

1942

Jan. 24.	E66.	"The Splendide's Meringue Glâcée," in *The New Yorker*.
Mar. 1.	E67.	"Sweet Death in the Electric Chair," in *Harper's Bazaar*.
Mar.	E68.	"How to Almost Open a Musical," in *Town & Country*.

Apr. 1.	E69.	"Ludwig Bemelmans' Splendide Apartment," in *Vogue*.
June 1.	E70.	"Souvenir," in *Vogue*.
June 6.	E71.	"Watch the Birdie," in *The New Yorker*.
July.	E72.	"Little Girl with a Headache [Camp No Mo Pie]," in *Town & Country*.
Sept. 4.	A21a.	I LOVE YOU I LOVE YOU I LOVE YOU. The Viking Press.
Oct. 1.	A38.	ROSEBUD. Random House.
Oct.	E73.	"Man of the World (First Episode)," in *Town & Country*.
Nov.	E74.	"Man of the World (Second Episode)," in *Town & Country*.
Nov.	A18b.	HOTEL SPLENDIDE. Hamish Hamilton.

COVER ART for *The New Yorker, Town & Country*

1943

Feb.	E75.	"Man of the World (Third Episode)," in *Town & Country*.
May 1.	E77.	"Post Card Home," in *Vogue*.
May.	E76.	"Man of the World (Fourth Episode)," in *Town & Country*.
June.	E78.	"The Royal Kiss, Which is the 5th Episode of Man of the World," in *Town & Country*.
July.	E79.	"Yolanda and the Thief," in *Town & Country*.
Aug.	E80.	"The Panama Canal, Which is the Sixth Episode of Man of the World," in *Town & Country*.

Sept.	E81.	"Now I Lay Me Down to Sleep (Seventh Episode of Man of the World)," in *Town & Country*.
Oct.	E82.	"Now I Lay Me Down to Sleep (Final Episode of Man of the World)," in *Town & Country*.
Oct. 25.	A34a.	NOW I LAY ME DOWN TO SLEEP. The Viking Press.
Nov. 12	A34a(bis).	NOW I LAY ME DOWN TO SLEEP (Deluxe edition). The Viking Press.
Dec.	A21b.	I LOVE YOU I LOVE YOU I LOVE YOU. Hamish Hamilton.
❁	A18c.	HOTEL SPLENDIDE. Hugo Gebers Förlag.

COVER ART for *The New Yorker*

ADVERTISEMENT ART for Dubonnet

1944

Feb. 18.	A34b.	NOW I LAY ME DOWN TO SLEEP. The Viking Press.
Feb. 21.	A18d.	HOTEL SPLENDIDE. Sun Dial Press.
Oct.	E83.	"Joyride," in *Town & Country*.
Oct. 10.	H10a.	"Now I Lay Me Down to Sleep" radio adaptation airs on CBS.
Dec.	E84.	"Through the Eye of the Needle," in *Town & Country*.
Dec. 15.	A34c.	NOW I LAY ME DOWN TO SLEEP. Hamish Hamilton.

COVER ART for *The New Yorker*

1945

Feb.	E85.	"Knife and Fork in Hollywood," in *Town & Country*.
Feb. 13.	A21c.	I LOVE YOU I LOVE YOU I LOVE YOU. Sun Dial Press.
Feb.	A18e.	HOTEL SPLENDIDE. Editions for the Armed Services.
Mar.	E86.	"The Blue Danube," in *Town & Country*.
Apr.	E87.	"The Blue Danube, II," in *Town & Country*.
Apr. 6.	A4a.	THE BLUE DANUBE. The Viking Press.
May	A21d.	I LOVE YOU I LOVE YOU I LOVE YOU. Editions for the Armed Services.
July.	E88.	"Art for Art's Sake," in *Town & Country*.
Aug.	A39c.	SMALL BEER. Pocket Books.
Sept.	E89.	"Irons in the Fire," in *Town & Country*.
Oct. 9.	H13.	"Yolanda and the Thief," film, distributed by MGM.
✿	A18f.	HOTEL SPLENDIDE. Alfred Scherz.
✿	A34d.	NOW I LAY ME DOWN TO SLEEP. Hamish Hamilton.

1946

Jan.	E56.	"It All Depends on How You Want It," in *Circle*.
Mar.	E90.	"Gramercy Nocturne," in *Town & Country*.

Mar. 4.	A34e.	NOW I LAY ME DOWN TO SLEEP. Sun Dial Press.
Spring.	A21e.	ICH LIEBE DICH ICH LIEBE DICH ICH LIEBE DICH. Alfred Scherz.
June.	E91.	"Servant Trouble," in *Town & Country*.
July.	E92.	"The Fat Canary," in *Town & Country*.
July 21.	E93.	"The Reluctant Waiter," in *Boston Herald News Week*.
July 21.	E94.	"The Reluctant Waiter," in *Oregon Journal News Week*.
Aug.	E95.	"The Fat Canary," in *Town & Country*.
Sept.	E96.	"The Fat Canary," in *Town & Country*.
Sept. 6.	A17a.	HOTEL BEMELMANS. The Viking Press.
Sept. 20.	A4b.	THE BLUE DANUBE. Hamish Hamilton.
Oct.	E97.	"The Fat Canary," in *Town & Country*.
Oct. 7.	A4c.	THE BLUE DANUBE. Sun Dial Press.
Nov.	E98.	"The Fat Canary," in *Town & Country*.
Dec.	E99.	"Introducing Ludwig Bemelmans," in *Holiday*.
✿	A21f.	IH, HVOR JEG ELSKER DIG. Thaning & Appel.
✿	B1.	EEN KERST GESCHIEDENIS. C. G. A. Corvey.

COVER ART for *The New Yorker*

1947

Jan.	E100.	"Come, Fly With Me to Paris," in *Holiday*.
Feb.	E101.	"Back Again in Paris," in *Holiday*.
Mar.	E102.	"Switzerland," in *Holiday*.
Apr.	E103.	"Under a Tyrolean Hat," in *Holiday*.
Apr. 12.	A21g.	JE T'AIME JE T'AIME JE T'AIME. Au blé qui lève.
May.	E104.	"Return to Munich," in *Holiday*.
May.	E105.	"No. 13 Rue St. Augustin," in *Town & Country*.
May 24.	E106.	"The Antlers of the Alpenrose," in *The New Yorker*.
June.	E107.	"Story of a Bavarian," in *Holiday*.
July 1.	E108.	"The Story of a Bavarian and His Travels: I," in *The New York Herald Tribune*, Paris.
July 8.	E109.	"The Story of a Bavarian and His Travels: II," in *The New York Herald Tribune*, Paris.
July 15.	E110.	"The Story of a Bavarian and His Travels: III," in *The New York Herald Tribune*, Paris.
July.	A4d.	THE BLUE DANUBE. Hamish Hamilton.
Aug. 18.	A7a.	DIRTY EDDIE. The Viking Press.
Aug.	A18g.	HOTEL SPLENDIDE. Penguin.
Nov. 21.	A8c.	THE DONKEY INSIDE. Hamish Hamilton.
Fall.	A17b.	HOTEL SPLENDID. Alfred Scherz/ Phoenix.
Fall.	A24c.	MADELINE. Alfred Scherz/Phoenix.

✿	A18h.	HOTEL SPLENDIDE. Thaning & Appel.
✿	A24b.	MADELINE. Illustrationsforlaget.
✿	A42.	A TALE OF TWO GLIMPS. Columbia Broadcasting System.

COVER ART for *The New Yorker, Theatre Arts*

ADVERTISEMENT ART for C.B.S.

1948

Jan.	A34f.	E ORA ANDIAMO A LETTO. Longanesi.
Apr.	E111.	"Gypsy Music," in *Holiday*.
May.	E112.	"Folie de Grandeur," in *Holiday*.
May [8].	A23c.	LIFE CLASS. Penguin.
June 11.	A7b.	DIRTY EDDIE. Hamish Hamilton.
Aug.	E113.	"Venice," in *Holiday*.
Sept.	E114.	"Promenade Sur Mer," in *Holiday*.
Oct.	E115.	"Mademoiselle Regrets," in *Holiday*.
Nov. [6].	A3a.	THE BEST OF TIMES. Simon & Schuster.
Nov. [27].	A21h.	I LOVE YOU I LOVE YOU I LOVE YOU. New American Library.
Dec.	A18i.	HOTEL SPLENDIDE. Penguin/Hamish Hamilton.
✿	A4e.	THE BLUE DANUBE. Hamish Hamilton/ Geroge Jaboor.
✿	A7c.	DEN DRAMATISKA GRISEN. Wahlström & Widstrand.
✿	A18j.	HOTEL SPLENDID. Editorial Sud-americana.

| ❀ | A24d. | MADELINE. Beyronds. |
| ❀ | A34g. | SZERTELEN ÉLET. Bibliotheca. |

COVER ART for *The New Yorker*

1949

Mar.	E116.	"The Wicked Ironmonger," in *Theatre Arts*.
May.	E117.	"My First Actress," in *Theatre Arts*.
June.	E118.	"The Master of the Alpenrose," in *Town & Country*.
July.	E119.	"Serpents in Aspen," in *Town & Country*.
July 22.	H10b.	"Now I Lay Me Down to Sleep" opens at Stanford University Memorial Auditorium, staged by Hume Cronyn.
Aug.	E120.	"Vienna Revisited," in *Holiday*.
Aug.	E121.	"Holiday for Heroes," in *Town & Country*.
Sept.	E122.	"Diary With a Blank Page," in *Holiday*.
Sept.	E123.	"The Turn of the Tide," in *Town & Country*.
Sept. [17].	A3b.	THE BEST OF TIMES. Cresset Press.
Oct. 28.	A10a.	THE EYE OF GOD. The Viking Press.
Nov.	E124.	"Isle of Capri," in *Holiday*.
Dec.	E125.	"Sunshine, Sunshine, Go Away," in *Good Housekeeping*.
Dec.	E126.	"Cinderella Isle," in *Holiday*.

✿   A8d.   THE DONKEY INSIDE. Readers Union/ Hamish Hamilton.

COVER ART for *The New Yorker*

EDITORIAL ILLUSTRATION for *Theatre Arts*

ILLUSTRATION for *Theatre Arts, Art Digest*

ADVERTISEMENT ART for radio, *Theatre Arts*

EXHIBITION at Associated American Artists

1950

Mar. 2.	H10c.	"Now I Lay Me Down to Sleep" opens on Broadway.
Mar. 24.	A34h.	NOW I LAY ME DOWN TO SLEEP. New American Library.
May.	E127.	"The Film Test," in *Town & Country*.
May 15.	A41.	SUNSHINE: A STORY ABOUT THE CITY OF NEW YORK. Simon & Schuster.
May 26.	A10b.	THE SNOW MOUNTAIN. Hamish Hamilton.
Aug. 17.	A7d.	COCHON D'EDDIE! Robert Laffont.
Oct.	E128.	"Road to Salerno," in *Holiday*.
Oct.	E129.	"To Elsie With Love," in *Town & Country*.
Dec.	E130.	"Christmas in Tyrol," in *Holiday*.
Dec.	E131.	"Adieu to the Old Ritz," in *Town & Country*.
✿	A10c.	THE SNOW MOUNTAIN. Hamish Hamilton/Star edition.

COVER ART for *The New Yorker*
EDITORIAL ILLUSTRATION for *Theatre Arts*
ILLUSTRATION for *Theatre Arts*
EXHIBITION at Ferargil Gallery

1951

Mar. 28.	A7e.	DIRTY EDDIE. New American Library.
Apr.	E132.	"How to Be a Prince," in *Holiday*.
Apr.	E133.	"The Happy Place," in *Woman's Home Companion*.
May.	E134.	"Madame Takes the Count," in *Holiday*.
June.	E135.	"The Perfect Marriage," in *Holiday*.
July.	E136.	"Mad Masquerade," in *Holiday*.
Sept. 15.	E137.	"Fingerprints, Monsieur?" in *Vogue*.
Dec.	E138.	"Madeline's Rescue," in *Good Housekeeping*.
❋	A10d.	GUDS ØJE. Wangels Forlag.

COVER ART for *Holiday, The New Yorker, Town & Country*
ADVERTISEMENT ART for Strathmore Co.
EXHIBITIONS at Art Alliance of Philadelphia,
Ferargil Gallery, Hackley Art Gallery of Muskegon

1952

Jan.	E139.	"Mighty Vesuvius!" in *Holiday*.
Feb. 15.	A7f.	DIRTY EDDIE. Pan Books.
Apr. 29.	A20a.	HOW TO TRAVEL INCOGNITO. Little, Brown.

May.	E140.	"The Best Way to See France," in *Holiday*.
May 20.	A20b.	HOW TO TRAVEL INCOGNITO. Hamish Hamilton.
June.	E141.	"The Color of Spain," in *Holiday*.
June.	E142.	"Remember Me?" in *Woman's Day*.
Sept. 18.	A15.	THE HAPPY PLACE. Little, Brown.
Oct. 21.	H4a.	"Madeline," animated film, released by Columbia Pictures.
Nov. 21.	A24e.	MADELINE. Derek Verschoyle.
Dec.	E143.	"The Borrowed Christmas," in *Holiday*.
Dec.	E144.	"Fröhliche Weihnachten," in *Town & Country*.

COVER ART for *Holiday*
ILLUSTRATION for Doubleday and Co.
ADVERTISEMENT ART for Harper Publishers
EXHIBITIONS at Ferargil Gallery, Junior League of Texas

1953

Jan. 10.	E145.	"The Dog That Travelled Incognito," in *Collier's*.
Feb.	E146.	"On Innkeeping," in *Holiday*.
Feb.	E147.	"Monsieur Soulé," in *Holiday*.
Feb.	E148.	"To Be a Gourmet," in *Holiday*.
Mar. 4.	A7g.	SILENZIO, NON SI GIRA! Mondadori.
Apr.	E149.	"Paris: City of Rogues," in *Holiday*.
Apr. 3.	A30a.	MADELINE'S RESCUE. The Viking Press.
June.	E150.	"That Old World Flavor Down Where the Würzburger Flows," in *Town & Country*.

June 6.	E151.	"Madeline at the Coronation," in *Collier's*.
Aug. 24.	A11a.	FATHER, DEAR FATHER. The Viking Press.
Aug. 24.	A11a(bis).	FATHER, DEAR FATHER (Deluxe edition). The Viking Press.
Sept.	E152.	"Two-Faced Tangier," in *Holiday*.
Sept. 13.	E153.	"Father, Dear Father," in *New York Herald Tribune This Week*.
Oct.	E154.	"Road to Marrakech," in *Holiday*.
Oct. 11.	E155.	"Ludwig Bemelmans," in *New York Herald Tribune This Week*.
Oct. 22.	A11b.	FATHER, DEAR FATHER. Hamish Hamilton.
Nov. 23.	A30b.	MADELINE'S RESCUE. Derek Verschoyle.
Dec. 10.	A14e.	YAMANO KURISUMAS. Iwanami Shoten.
Dec. 20.	E156.	"Paris in the Snow," in *New York Herald Tribune This Week*.
Dec. 25.	E157.	"A Texan, a Parisian and a Baby," in *New York Herald Tribune*, Paris.
❋	A5.	THE BORROWED CHRISTMAS. American Artists Group.
❋	A20c.	"INCOGNITO" DURCH FRANKREICH UND PARIS. Wolfgang Krüger.
❋	A11c.	MIT KIND UND KRÜMEL NACH EUROPA. Kiepenheuer & Witsch.

COVER ART for *The New Yorker*

ADVERTISEMENT ART for C.B.S., The Viking Press

1954

Jan.	E158.	"Bemelmans' Magic Cities," in *Holiday*.
Jan.	E159.	"My First Visit to Paris," in *Holiday*.
Jan.	E160.	"The Old Stag and the Tree," in *Woman's Day*.
May.	E161.	"In the Heart of Paris," in *Town & Country*.
May 9.	E162.	"Voyage," in *New York Herald Tribune This Week*.
July 31.	A24g.	MADELINE. Simon & Schuster.
Aug.	E163.	"Caldecott Award Acceptance," in *The Horn Book Magazine*.
Sept. 10.	A11d.	PÈRE, CHER PÈRE. Domat-Montchrétien.
Oct. 6.	A16a.	THE HIGH WORLD. Harper.
Oct.	A24h.	MADELEINE. Cocorico.
✿	A24f.	MADELINE. Blüchert Verlag.
✿	A30c.	MADELINES RETTUNG. Blüchert Verlag.

COVER ART for *The New Yorker*

ADVERTISEMENT ART for Harper Publishers, Mars Chocolate

1955

Feb. 13.	E164.	"The Street Where the Heart Lies," in *Boston Sunday Herald This Week*.
Feb. 15.	E165.	"The One I Love the Best," in *Vogue*.
Feb. 24.	A43a.	TO THE ONE I LOVE THE BEST. The Viking Press.
Mar.	E166.	"My Craziest Tour of Paris," in *Coronet*.

May.	E167.	"The Dog of the World," in *Holiday*.
July 28.	A43b.	TO THE ONE I LOVE THE BEST. Hamish Hamilton.
Sept. 21.	A36a.	PARSLEY. Harper.
Oct. 7.	A46.	THE WORLD OF BEMELMANS. The Viking Press.
Dec.	E168.	"Madeline's Christmas," in *Good Housekeeping*.
Dec.	E169.	"Deck the Halls with Boughs of Holly," in *Town & Country*.
✿	A17c.	HOTEL SPLENDID. Kiepenheuer & Witsch.
✿	A29.	MADELINE'S CHRISTMAS IN TEXAS. Nieman-Marcus.

COVER ART for *Holiday*, *The New Yorker*

ADVERTISEMENT ART for Harper Publishers, Italian Line

EXHIBITION at Hammer Galleries

1956

Jan.	E170.	"Midas Tour of Italy," in *Holiday*.
Jan.	A18k.	CLIENTI IN MARSINA. Mondadori.
May 24.	A17d.	HOTEL BEMELMANS. Hamish Hamilton.
Aug.	E171.	"The Texas Legend," in *McCall's*.
Dec. 1.	A25a.	MADELINE AND THE BAD HAT. The Viking Press.
Dec.	E172.	"I Love Paris in the Wintertime," in *Town & Country*.

Dec.	E173.	"The Austrian Emperor's Favorite Dishes," in *Woman's Day*.
Dec.	A28a.	MADELINE'S CHRISTMAS. McCall's.
✿	A43c.	ALTE LIEBE ROSTET NIGHT. Kiepenheuer & Witsch.

COVER ART for *The New Yorker*

ADVERTISEMENT ART for The American Rayon Institute, *The New York Times*

EXHIBITIONS at Hammer Galleries, Lüchows

1957

Mar. 8.	A25a(bis).	MADELINE AND THE BAD HAT. (Deluxe edition). The Viking Press.
May.	H9a.	"Madeline & Genevieve," Dell Comic.
June.	E174.	"Hotel Splendide Revisited," in *Town & Country*.
June.	E175.	" 'No Trouble at All'," in *Town & Country*.
Aug.	E176.	"Love at the Splendide," in *Town & Country*.
Aug.	E177.	"Otto Kahn's Top Hat," in *Town & Country*.
Sept.	E178.	"Moving Day," in *Town & Country*.
Sept. 16.	A24i.	MADELINE. André Deutsch.
Sept. 16.	A30d.	MADELINE'S RESCUE. André Deutsch.
Oct.10.	A45a.	THE WOMAN OF MY LIFE. The Viking Press.
Oct.	A20d.	"INCOGNITO" DURCH FRANKREICH UND PARIS. Rowohlt.

Nov. 7.	A45b.	THE WOMAN OF MY LIFE. Hamish Hamilton.
Nov. 13.	D1a.	HOLIDAY IN FRANCE. Houghton Mifflin.
Dec.	E179.	"The Best Way to See Cuba," in *Holiday*.
Dec.	E180.	"A Gemütliche Christmas," in *Town & Country*.
✿	A18l.	HOTEL SPLENDID. Ullstein-Taschenbucher Verlag.
✿	A20e.	INCOGNITO. Le Club français du livre.
✿	A43d.	TILL DEN JAG ÄLSKER HÖGST. Hugo Gebers Förlag.

COVER ART for *Holiday*

ADVERTISEMENT ART for McIlhenny Co., Owens-Corning, Hiram Walker & Sons, Inc.

EXHIBITION in Paris

1958

June 6.	D1b.	HOLIDAY IN FRANCE. André Deutsch.
July 24.	A16b.	THE HIGH WORLD. Hamish Hamilton.
Aug.	E181.	"Gala in Monte Carlo," in *Town & Country*.
Sept.	E182.	"When You Lunch With the Emperor," in *Vogue*.
Sept. 19.	A25b.	MADELINE AND THE BAD HAT. André Deutsch.
Sept. 30.	A24j.	MADELINE. The Viking Press.
Oct. 29.	A32a.	MY LIFE IN ART. Harper.
Nov. 14.	A32b.	MY LIFE IN ART. André Deutsch.
Dec.	E183.	"The Best Way to See Rio," in *Holiday*.

Dec.	A26a.	MADELINE AND THE GYPSIES. McCall's.
✿	A25c.	MADELINE UND DER BÖSE BUBE. Blüchert Verlag.
✿	A45c.	DIE FRAU MEINES LEBENS. Kiepenheuer & Witsch.

EDITORIAL ILLUSTRATION for *Art in America, Town & Country*

ADVERTISEMENT ART for McIlhenny Co., Owens-Corning, Hiram Walker & Sons, Inc.

EXHIBITION at Hammer Galleries

1959

Jan.	E184.	"A Quick One," in *Town & Country*.
Mar.	E185.	"Brazil's Fantastic New Capital," in *Holiday*.
Apr.	E186.	"But I Like Mexico!" in *Town & Country*.
June.	E187.	"How I Took the Cure," in *Holiday*.
Sept.	E188.	"Sao Paulo: Skyscrapers and Poison Toads," in *Holiday*.
Sept.	E189.	"Invitation to a Castle," in *Town & Country*.
Sept. 11.	A26a(bis).	MADELINE AND THE GYPSIES. The Viking Press.
Oct.	E190.	"Bemelmans Paints New York," in *Holiday*.
Fall.	A20f.	INCOGNITO OF DE VERFIJNDE KUNST DER ZELFVERHEFFING. Ad. Donker.
Dec.	E191.	"Randy," in *Mademoiselle*.
Dec. 13.	H2.	"The Borrowed Christmas" on NBC Television.

✿   A32c.   MEIN LEBEN ALS MALER. Blüchert
                Verlag.

COVER ART for *The New York Herald Tribune Magazine,*
The New Yorker

EXHIBITIONS at Hammer Galleries, City Museum of New York

1960

Sept. 12.   A1a.   ARE YOU HUNGRY ARE YOU COLD. World
                        Publishing Company.

Sept. 28.   A44a.   WELCOME HOME! Harper & Bros.

Oct. 16.   H4e.   "Madeline," adaptation of children's
                        books, appears on NBC Television.

✿   A16c.   ALLE JAHRE WIEDER. Kiepenheuer &
                        Witsch.

✿   A7h.   DIRTY EDDIE. Grosset & Dunlap.

✿   A45d.   DIE FRAU MEINES LEBENS. Deutscher
                        Bücherbund.

✿   A17e.   HOTEL BEMELMANS. Grosset & Dunlap

✿   A19.   HOW TO HAVE EUROPE ALL TO YOURSELF.
                        European Travel Commission.

✿   B2.   THE KIND PEASANT, THE BIG BEAR AND
                        THE LITTLE BIRDIE. n.p.

✿   H4a.   "Madeline," film, released by
                        Rembrandt Films.

✿   H5a.   "Madeline and the Bad Hat," film,
                        released by Rembrandt Films.

✿   H6a.   "Madeline and the Gypsies," film,
                        released by Rembrandt Films.

✿   H9c.   "Madeline's Rescue," film, released
                        by Rembrandt Films.

| ✿ | A30e. | MADELINES REDNING. Illustrationsfor-laget. |
| ✿ | H12. | "Sunshine," film, released by Rembrandt Films. |

COVER ART for *The New Yorker, Town & Country,*
ILLUSTRATION for Golden Press
EXHIBITIONS at Oklahoma Art Center, Phoenix Art Museum, San Francisco, San Diego, Paris, Hammer Galleries

1961

Jan.	E192.	"Caviar: The Noblest Roe of them All," in *Playboy.*
Mar. 16.	A16d.	THE HIGH WORLD. Hamish Hamilton.
Apr. 7.	A1c.	ARE YOU HUNGRY ARE YOU COLD. André Deutsch.
Apr.	A39d.	SMALL BEER. Capricorn.
June.	E193.	"My Riviera Cruise," in *Holiday.*
July 3.	A45e.	THE WOMAN OF MY LIFE. Hutchinson & Co. (Arrow).
Aug.	E194.	"Madeline in London," in *Holiday.*
Aug. 31.	A26b.	MADELINE AND THE GYPSIES. André Deutsch.
Oct. 6.	A27a.	MADELINE IN LONDON. The Viking Press.
Oct. 17.	A22.	[BEMELMANS'] ITALIAN HOLIDAY. Houghton Mifflin.
Oct.	A1b.	ARE YOU HUNGRY ARE YOU COLD. New American Library.
✿	A16e.	ALLE JAHRE WIEDER. Bertelsmann Lesering.

✻   A1d.   ALLONS ENFANTS. . . . Kiepenheuer &
                       Witsch.
✻   A25d.   MADELINE OG DET SORTE FÅR. Illustra-
                       tionsforlaget.

COVER ART for *Holiday*
ADVERTISEMENT ART for T.W.A.
EXHIBITION at Hammer Galleries

1962

May 18.   A35a.   ON BOARD NOAH'S ARK. The Viking
                       Press.
May.   A1e.   LA GUERRA IN CASA. Longanesi.
June.   E195.   "Cinderella Isle," in *Argosy*.
Aug.   E196.   "The Soul of Austria," in *Holiday*.

COVER ART for *Holiday, The New Yorker*

B. Posthumous Works

Nov. 30.	A27b.	MADELINE IN LONDON. André Deutsch.
Nov.	A35b.	ON BOARD NOAH'S ARK. Collins.
Dec.	E197.	"Gala at the Tour d'Argent," in *Playboy*.
Dec. 19.	A31.	MARINA. Harper.
Dec.	A18m.	CLIENTI IN MARSINA. Mondadori.
✿	A26c.	MADELINE OF ZIGOJNERNE. Illustrations-forlaget.

EXHIBITION at Hammer Galleries

1963

Jan.	A1f.	ARE YOU HUNGRY ARE YOU COLD. Readers Union/ André Deutsch
Jan. 7.	A40a.	THE STREET WHERE THE HEART LIES. World Publishing Company.
Apr.	E198.	"Visit to an Irish Castle," in *Holiday*.
May 27.	A18n.	HOTEL SPLENDIDE. The Viking Press.
✿	A24k.	MADELINE. Illustrationsforlaget.
✿	A40b.	DIE STRASSE, IN DER MEIN HERZ WOHNT. Kiepenheuer & Witsch.

COVER ART for *Story*

EXHIBITIONS at Düsseldorf, East Hampton, Hammer Galleries

1964

| Jan. | E199. | "Franz Josef: A Habsburg Marriage," in *Holiday*. |

Feb.	E200.	"The Marvelous Mission to Moscow," in *Holiday*.
Mar. [23].	A40c.	THE STREET WHERE THE HEART LIES. MacFadden-Bartell.
May [18].	A8e.	THE DONKEY INSIDE. E. P. Dutton.
Oct. 28.	C1a.	LA BONNE TABLE. Simon & Schuster.
Nov. 30.	C1b.	LA BONNE TABLE. Hamish Hamilton.

1965

Aug.	A1g.	ARE YOU HUNGRY ARE YOU COLD. Mayflower Books.
✿	A35c.	NOAHS ARCHE. Kiepenheuer & Witsch.

1966

Feb.	A24m.	MADELINE. Scholastic Book Services.
Nov.	A24l.	MADELINE. Otto Maier.
✿	A9.	THE ELEPHANT CUTLET. Audrey Arellanes.

1967

✿	A24n.	MADELINE. The Viking Press/ Scholastic.
✿	A30f.	MADELINE'S RESCUE. Scholastic Book Services.

1968

Feb.	A24o.	MADELINE. Sphere Books.
Sept.	A45f.	THE WOMAN OF MY LIFE. Hutchinson & Co.

| ❋ | A25e. | MADELINE AND THE BAD HAT. Viking Seafarer. |

1969

| ❋ | A24p. | MADELINE. Viking Seafarer. |

1971

| ❋ | A24q. | MADELEINE. Éditions des deux coqs d'or. |

1972

Apr. 15.	H6d.	"Madeline and the Gypsies" opens at Children's Theatre Company of Minneapolis.
Nov. 10	A24r.	GENKINA MADELINE. Fukuinkan Shoten.
Dec.	A30g.	MADELEINE SE REDDING. Human & Rousseau.
❋	A27c.	MADELINE IN LONDON. Viking Seafarer.

1973

May 10.	A25f.	MADELINE TO ITAZURAKKO. Fukuinkan Shoten.
May 10.	A30i.	MADELINE TO INU. Fukuinkan Shoten.
May 10.	A26e.	MADELINE TO JIPUSHII. Fukuinkan Shoten.
June.	A43e.	ALTE LIEBE ROSTET NICHT. Buchgemeinde Alpenland.
Oct.	A26d.	MADELINE AND THE GYPSIES. Viking Seafarer.
❋	A30h.	MADELINE'S RESCUE. Viking Seafarer.

1974

May.   A24s.   MADELEINE. Human & Rousseau.

EXHIBITION at Hammer Galleries

1975

On demand.   A32a(bis).   MY LIFE IN ART. Harper/Ann Arbor
                             Microfilms.

Apr.   A45g.   DIE FRAU MEINES LEBENS. Bastei Verlag-
                             Gustav H. Lübbe.

EXHIBITIONS at Marietta, Ohio; Beverly Hills, California

1977

✿   A24t.   MADELINE. Puffin.

✿   A25g.   MADELINE AND THE BAD HAT. Puffin.

✿   A26f.   MADELINE AND THE GYPSIES. Puffin.

1978

post-Dec.   A24u.   MADELINE. Carlsen/if.
15.

post-Dec.   A24v.   MADELINE. Carlsen Verlag GmbH.
15.

post-Dec.   A24w.   MADELINE. Carlsen/if.
15.

✿   A27d.   MADELINE IN LONDON. Puffin.

✿   A30j.   MADELINE'S RESCUE. Puffin.

1980

Feb.	A24x.	MADELINE. Diogenes.
July.	A36b.	DIE BOK EN DIE BOOM. Qualitas.
July.	A36c.	I-PARSLEY. Qualitas.

1982

*	A30k.	MADELINE'S RESCUE. Scholastic Children's Choice.

1984

Oct. 19.	H6f.	"Madeline and the Gypsies" opens at Children's Theatre Company of Minneapolis.

1985

Sept.	A24y.	MADELEINE. L'École des loisirs.
Oct. 1.	A28a(bis).	MADELINE'S CHRISTMAS. Viking Kestrel.
Oct. 10.	A28b.	MADELINE'S CHRISTMAS. André Deutsch.
Nov.	C2a.	TELL THEM IT WAS WONDERFUL. The Viking Press.
Dec.	E201.	"Madeline's Christmas," in *McCall's*.

1986

Mar.	A30l.	LE SAUVETAGE DE MADELEINE. L'École des loisirs.
Nov.	A24z.	MADELINE. Penguin.

1987

Mar.	A24aa.	MADELINE. Mondadori España.
Spring.	A24bb.	MADELINE. Dainippon Kaiga.

June.	C2b.	TELL THEM IT WAS WONDERFUL. McGraw-Hill.
Sept. 11	A24cc.	MADELINE. Viking Kestrel.
❋	A28c.	LE NOEL DE MADELEINE. L'École des loisirs.

EXHIBITION in Pennsylvania

1988

Feb.	A24dd.	MADELEINE. Qualitas.
❋	H4g.	"Madeline," videotape, released by DIC.
❋	A28d.	MADELINE'S CHRISTMAS. Puffin.

1989

Sept. 15.	C1c.	LA BONNE TABLE. David R. Godine.
Sept.	A24ee.	MADELINE/MADELINE'S RESCUE/MADELINE AND THE BAD HAT. Puffin.
Dec. 15.	A28e.	MADOLENU NO KURISUMASU. Yugaku-sha Ltd.

1990

Sept. 2.	H9g.	"Madeline's Rescue" opens at Children's Theatre Company of Minneapolis.
Sept.	A8f.	THE DONKEY INSIDE. Paragon House.
Nov. 23.	H4l.	"Madeline," opens at Emmy Gifford Children's Theater of Omaha.
Dec.	A36d.	DIE BOK EN DIE BOOM. Anansi-Uitgewers.

✿	H4i.	"Madeline Dolls" released by Eden Toys.
✿	H8a.	"Madeline's Christmas," videotape, released by CINAR.

COVER ART for *Gastronome*.

1991

Oct.	E202.	"Shirt Tale of Paris," in *Travel Holiday*.
✿	H5b.	"Madeline and the Bad Hat," videotape, released by CINAR.
✿	H6h.	"Madeline and the Gypsies," videotape, released by CINAR.
✿	H7a.	"Madeline in London," videotape, released by CINAR.
✿	H9h.	"Madeline's Rescue," videotape, released by CINAR.
✿	H9l.	"Madeline's Rescue and Other Stories about Madeline," videotape, released by Children's Circle Home Video Library.

1992

Sept.	A11e.	FATHER, DEAR FATHER. James H. Heineman.
Sept.	A20g.	HOW TO TRAVEL INCOGNITO. James H. Heineman.
Sept.	A21j.	I LOVE YOU I LOVE YOU I LOVE YOU. James H. Heineman.
Fall	H4i (bis).	"Madeline Toys and Accessories" released by Eden Toys.

An Index of Foreign Language Titles

An Index of
Foreign Language
Titles

FOREIGN TITLES OF BOOKS, films and published or anthologized stories are included here. However, many of Bemelmans' *chapter titles* in volumes from section A are not in English and have not been published separately or anthologized; they are not included. Book titles appear in boldface, other works are set off by quotation marks.

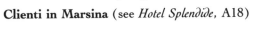

Alle Jahre Wieder (see *The High World*, A16)

Allons Enfants . . . (see *Are You Hungry Are You Cold*, A1)

Alte Liebe Rostet Nicht (see *To the One I Love the Best*, A43)

"Buenas [sic] Días, Gran Hotel" (Original title; see E32)

"Cher Ami" (Original title; see E63)

"Chile Con Amore" (Original title; see E13)

Clienti in Marsina (see *Hotel Splendide*, A18)

"La Spécialité de la Maison" (Original title; see E33)

"Le Chagrin d'Amour Est Formidable" (Original title; see E65)

Le Nöel de Madeleine (see *Madeline's Christmas*, A28 and H8)

Le Sauvetage de Madeleine (see *Madeline's Rescue*, A30)

Madeleine (see *Madeline*, A24 and H4)

Madeleine à Londres (see *Madeline in London*, H7)

Madeleine et le petit barbare (see *Madeline and the Bad Hat*, H5)

Madeleine et les tziganes (see *Madeline and the Gypsies*, H6)

Madeleine sauvée des eaux (see *Madeline's Rescue*, H9)

Madeleine Se Redding (see *Madeline's Rescue*, A30)

Madeline Og Det Sorte Får (see *Madeline and the Bad Hat*, A25)

Madeline Og Zigojnerne (see *Madeline and the Gypsies*, A26)

Madeline To Inu (see *Madeline's Rescue*, A30)

Madeline To Itazurakko (see *Madeline and the Bad Hat*, A25)

Madeline To Jipushii (see *Madeline and the Gypsies*, A26)

Madeline und der Böse Bube (see *Madeline and the Bad Hat*, A25)

Madelines Redning (see *Madeline's Rescue*, A30)

Madelines Rettung (see *Madeline's Rescue*, A30)

Madolenu No Kurisumasu (see *Madeline's Christmas*, A28)

Mein Leben Als Maler (see *My Life in Art*, A32)

Mit Kind und Krümel Nach Europa (see *Father, Dear Father*, A11)

"Monsieur Soulé" (Original title; see E147)

"No. 13 Rue St. Augustin" (Original title; see E105)

Noahs Arche (see *On Board Noah's Ark*, A35)

Père, cher père (see *Father, Dear Father*, A11)

"Postkarten aus Wien" (Original title; see E6)

"Promenade Sur Mer" (Original title; see E114)

"Putzi" (see as well "Inside, Outside," E4)

"Sacre du Printemps" (Original title; see E7 and E56)

Silenzio, Non Si Gira! (see *Dirty Eddie*, A7)

Snuff (see *Noodle*, G31)

Szertelen Élet (see *Now I Lay Me Down to Sleep*, A34)

"Theodore en De Blauwe Donau" (see F16b; originally "Theodore and 'The Blue Danube' ", E2)

Till Den Jag Älsker Högst (see *To the One I Love the Best*, A43)

Yamano Kurisumas (see *Hansi*, A14)

THIS INDEX INCLUDES entries for books, stories, and other creative works by Ludwig Bemelmans; authors and titles of works about Bemelmans; foreign-language titles and names of translators of Bemelmans' works. No attempt has been made to index by title the illustrations noted in Section G; Bemelmans' illustrations appearing in advertisements are indexed under the name of the advertiser. Items listed in Section H are indexed by type of material (e.g., dolls, motion pictures, toys). Art exhibits noted in Section I are indexed under name of the exhibiting gallery. Index references to reviews cited in Section J are grouped under the title of the book reviewed; entries have been made for authors (but not for titles) of the reviews. Personal names occurring in the annotations and bibliographic descriptions have been indexed selectively. References are to item numbers in the bibliography, with page numbers given for a few unnumbered items. The following stylistic conventions have been observed: (1) titles of books appear in italics, titles of stories and parts of books in roman type (when a story title also serves as the title of a book an entry is made for each form); (2) initial articles (a, the, die, der, etc.) have been omitted from titles, regardless of language; (3) variations in British and American spellings are entered under the American form only.

This book was composed in
Cochin and Nicholas Cochin Black
by American–Stratford Graphic Services, Inc.
Brattleboro, Vermont.

It was printed and bound in the United States
on 60# Booktext Natural paper.

The typography and binding were designed by
Beth Tondreau Design, New York.